THE SUPERHERO ANOMALY

A Comical look at Balancing Life & Business

BY AARON RYAN

TRUE STRENGTH ONLY COMES FROM VULNERABILITY & BALANCE. AND ALSO REALLY GOOD COFFEE.

THE SUPERHERO ANOMALY

A Comical look at Balancing Life & Business

by Aaron Ryan

© 2024 Aaron Ryan and CM LLC.
Published in 2024, Edition 1.

ISBN # 9798990878938

Copyright © 2024 (Library of Congress number forthcoming.) All Rights reserved. Unauthorized duplication or copying prohibited by law. The scanning, uploading, and distribution of this book via the Internet or via any other means without the express written permission of the publisher or copyright holder is illegal and punishable by law. Please purchase only authorized print or electronic versions and do not participate in or encourage electronic piracy of copyrighted materials.

Edited by Denouement Editing. Published independently.

Photos by Mike Wilson of *NowhereMan Photos*.

CHAPTERS

Contents

Preface 11

No: Your Favorite Word 17

Why I Threw Away $460,000 21

How Voiceovers Saved Me 27

There Can Be Only One 33

The Intrepid Tale Of An iPhone-Addict Guy 37

A Moment Of Silence For Bibbidi-Bobbidi-Boo 41

Clean Spaces And Parallel Lines 45

Stars, Listens & Likes Oh My 53

Expenses Vs. Investments 59

Your Life Is A Ministry 65

Running A Successful Business Of...Anything 69

Fake It Till You Make It 105

A Beautiful Craziness 109

When My Voice Meant Nothing 115

The $1000 I Will Never See Again 123

The Big Versus 137

Thank Goodness I Only Do Jobs For Exposure 147

Pardon Me, Your Butt Is Showing 153

Invoicing & Patience 159

The Thrill Of The Hunt 165

That Glorious Disconnect 171

Hobbies = Good AND Bad 177

Your Key To Success 183

No Thanks. I Already Know Everything 189

Drop That Beer And Get Off The Couch 195

It's Not You, It's Me... 201

A Most Unconventional Me 207

Father Forgive Me, For I Have Spammed 213

Accursed Red Badges And Pavlov's Dog 219

May I Speak With The Person In Charge Of Purchasing?......... 225

How Not To Fly A Drone Into A Tree... 229

Take Five 235

You Deserve A Break Today 239

Please, Can You Please Say Thank You? Thank You 243

Tell The Truth 249

Battle Scars... 255

Every Day An Easter Egg Hunt... 259

Pinocchios 265

There Can Be Miracles... When You Believe 271

A Long, Long Time Ago, Thinking Was Invented 277

When Life Gives You Murder Hornets 283

The 10 Commandments Of A Successful Businessperson 287

Politics, Politics, Politics 295

Organization: Your BFF 303

I Hate Burpees.. 307

The Biggest Myth In The Universe 311

Maybe Depeche Mode Had It Right All Along 319

Psssst! Hey, Sellout! Yeah, You! Over Here! 325

I'll Give *You* Free Work! 335

Mentorship: Just Do It.. 339

In Search Of	345
Quitcher Whinin'	349
You'll Never Get A 100% Job From A 50% Attempt	353
Focusing While Working At Home	357
Your Makeup	359
Living The Dream	363
Goonies Never Say Die	367
Oh What A Rat You Are	373
Listen To Oscar	379
More Cheese With Your Whine?	383
You Can't Do Everything	389
Integrity: It's All You've Got	393
Weddings Suck	397
Don't Be A Jackass	401
With Great Power Comes Great Responsibility	405
I Simply Can't Not Fly	411
From Darkness To Dawn	421
About The Author	429
Recommended Reading	431
Bibliography	433

Preface

ROOTS

No, not the movie series. I'm talking about beginnings.

I'm Aaron Ryan, and I'm a do-everything-guy. No, seriously. In my lifetime I've been an author, voiceover artist, wedding videographer, stage performer, musician, producer, rock/pop artist, executive assistant, service manager, paperboy, CSR, poet, tech support, worship leader, and more. The diversity of his life experiences gives him a unique approach to business, life, ministry, faith, and entertainment.

Let's go back a while. No, not that far. You don't need to know my birthdate, because that would tell you how old I am, and I'd have to slap you silly for asking this old girl for her birthdate.

Suffice it to say that I'm somewhere between 40 and dead. As I'm not dead yet, and as I'm closer to the 40-mark….AND…as I am still fairly lucid with a decent memory, let's take a stroll back through the annals of time. But just long enough to where the word "annals" was invented.

I was born in '73 (darnit, cat's outta the bag and my editor didn't catch it!) and grew up in the Valley, which is North Bend, Snoqualmie, and Riverbend, Washington. I loved it there…it was woodsy, it was spacious, and it was full of air, which I've heard is essential for survival and also helped fill my lungs at an early age so that I might use them in voiceovers. See? It was fate from the start.

I can also remember way back, singing "Ben" to my family members from around the corner in the kitchen while they all sat on the couch in the living room, so that they wouldn't "watch" me while singing and I wouldn't get stage fright. This performance has all the hallmarks of an entrepreneur in the making: I didn't feel truly in my own skin performing in front of people yet; but if I could do it with some measure of protective invisibility (hint: studio, hint: voiceovers) so much the better.

Jumping forward to 1993, at the ripe age of 20, I joined a firm in Seattle that specialized in selling PSAs (Public Service Announcements) to local businesses, and airing said PSAs on local radio, sponsored by said businesses. Telemarketing was not necessarily a new thing for me since I had worked at another organization prior to this one: raising funds for the right to keep and bear arms, which I of course cared nothing about at the time; I simply needed money to put more Top Ramen, Saltine crackers and Coke on my college-age table.

I never knew how formative this job would be to my "here and now" of voiceovers.

THE JOY OF COLD-CALLING

When I was telemarketing, I had no clue how much I'd really enjoy it. Now, no one likes to be disturbed during dinner, and those Disturbers truly don't like disturbing the Not-to-be-Disturbed. But I had a job to do, doggone it, and I was going to see it through. I really, really wanted to succeed at this job, not just because the pay and the bonuses were good, but because I really, really enjoyed it.

The name of the game was: cold call the potential client. Inform them about our current campaign to encourage parents to talk with their kids about drinking and driving…or about a kid-code to prevent abduction…or about encouraging youth sports and activities. Sell client on the value of sponsoring these good reputation-building PSA's. And then – dah-d-d-dah….I present to you, Aaron Ryan at his finest! I got to read the actual script to the client, with their name in it, and allow them to hear what the PSA would sound like.

I loved it! They loved it! So much that that beautiful dial tone greeted me emphatically after several of those script readings! YAY! *"Well, Jack, I never said I was Dan Rather…ah-ha-ha-ha-ha…. [pause] …. hello, Jack? Jack, are you there?"*

Jack was not there. Jack didn't like Aaron's presentation, or had better things to do, or Jeopardy was on, so Jack had to go. But Aaron learned a thing or two, and perfected his presentation, and improved his performance, his outreach, his marketing skills, his communication prowess, and *hey presto!* He eventually earned several awards at that company, including Rookie of the Year and Sales Rep of the Month. It was a fantastic time of growth, succeeding, and lots of Top Ramen and Coke.

What that job gave me, more than anything else, was a huge love for performing voiceovers. I had no idea these even existed! What was a voiceover anyway? I mean, you don't really think about things like, "Hey, that guy has a fantastic voice in that commercial" or "Wow, he really communicated that message to me, it hit me like a pound of bacon right in my heart." I had never heard of Don LeFontaine and just assumed that Mel Blanc was just.... some.... guy. I never knew that voiceovers could be a full-salary career profession that could actually pay for cars... food... bills... and mortgages. It just didn't occur to me.

I had tasted greatness, and I liked the taste. It was at this time that I began authoring as well, although that took a back burner for a few decades.

ACTING...BRILLIANCE!

Granted, I was always a bit of a performer, and more than a bit of a ham. Credit our family's moving multiple times when I was a kid to giving me the ability to adapt to a new situation and laugh my way through it...and to help others laugh their way through it too. So, performing came naturally. So much so that I had a natural love for it. And wanted to continue to perfect it.

I did jingles. I did singing. I did speaking. I produced musical CDs. But nothing, save singing, quite touched voiceovers as far as the fun of it: to use my voice to so communicate something in such a unique way...to move people...to compel...to motivate...to inspire. I did them off and on over the years, at various voiceover jobs, in tandem with jingles, some radio theatre, and then in my own media production company that I unofficially started in 1997: I would perform them in tandem with whatever video I produced.

When I wasn't doing voiceovers, I was doing singing. Singing and performing had been a natural fit for me since high school, much more than acting even. In fact, I became a Christian performer on the coattails of having produced a musical CD in 1994 (released in 1997), and I loved it. I toured it around, and it was a wonderful experience. But there was just one problem.

It went straight to my head.

BEING VULNERABLE

Being vulnerable is difficult. Arms-lengthing is easy. I chose the latter. I was struggling with some growing pains as it were, and had started to medicate with smoking. I couldn't really handle the fame that came to me, and I began to immerse myself in image management. I couldn't (wouldn't?) tell anyone about my issues, and it was easier to perform them away anyway, so that's what I did.

I chose to go the route of no transparency, and it ended up costing me my budding career. Did I enjoy it? Did I miss it? Did I want more? Yes to all three. But it wasn't time. I wasn't ready for the limelight, and I certainly couldn't handle the fame that went to my head, because my heart was aching for some real connection, and I denied it that connection in the name of The Almighty Ego.

So I hung up my hat, left my cape on the doorstep and bade farewell to the stage. That was 2000.

I think, if I look back in the rearview mirror of my life, I made a sound decision to walk away from that stage. I was not maintaining transparency with people, I was fully immersed in cover-ups, and I wasn't really being me. And if there's one thing I learned at VO Atlanta, the conference I first attended in 2019, Kay Bess said "Be Yourself." This is absolutely critical to your success as a businessperson. I need to be me, not some poser.

Voiceovers allowed me to be myself, but from the comfort of a dark studio with no one watching.

I crept back into the shadows, as it were, behind the camera, and began to serve my multimedia customers through my burgeoning multimedia production company that I started in 2003 with an official business license. It was much more comfortable for me to serve them from the other side of the lens, and when they needed a voice to narrate their promo script, their instructional narration, whatever, I was there.

And I loved it. It hearkened back to the days of telemarketing, which reminded me of that which I fell in love with in the first place: voiceovers.

MOVING RIGHT ALONG

So, onward I went, in full swing with my media company, performing video transfer, videography, video production, and, naturally, because it began with 'v', voiceovers.

And all along, voiceovers and authoring were there with me. But in the great scheme of things, the seeds of discontent began to take root, and some areas of my multimedia profession, namely, wedding videography, began to sour. Simultaneously, we were giving birth to our first child and moving into a new home. I was now our sole breadwinner, and I needed to make more money for some breathing room. I didn't know exactly what I was going to do, nor did I know what I could or should do. I just knew that I needed to make some money.

I've also made a concerted return to authoring, and I've penned fictional sci-fi quadrilogy entitled "Dissonance" that has *really* taken off. Check it out at www.dissonancetheseries.com. It has brought me immeasurable fulfillment: this process of creation. That's what we were born to do: *create*. Whether that's artistic works, or the end result, creating money…we were born to create. And I love what I do.

Right under my nose, all along, were my vocal cords: ready to bring a sea change, and my fingers, ready to type wonders.

On that note, please know that I am a full time voice actor and author. However, my income primarily comes from voiceovers. But the issues and concerns I'm going to lightheartedly address in this book pertain not only to voiceover artists, but businessmen and businesswomen in *any* field, and any industry.

In this book, 'voice actor', 'voiceover artist,' 'voice talent' and 'author' are synonymous with entrepreneur, whatever field of specialty you practice in. I'm a voice actor and author, so I look at things through those contexts and lenses, but many of the same rules will indefatigably apply to you as an entrepreneur, regardless of your craft.

All of these observations have helped me stay sane, stay focused, stay driven, stay healthy and stay happy. I *love* what I get to do every day: create. I hope you can too.

This book is about seeking balance while preserving sanity in work and life. After all, it's all about balance, or you tip over. And if you tip over, you capsize. And if you capsize, well, it's not long before you drown. And there'll be no drowning on my watch, *thankyouverymuch.*

No: Your Favorite Word

THE VERY OPPOSITE OF YES

We live in such a negative society. People pull each other down in new and creative ways that would make Jesus want to shake His head and remove them from His book of life. Politicians do this so well. To quote Brian Regan's parody of a political commercial, said in the most negative gritty political voice he could muster:

"Apparently he wanted more money to provide for his family!"

What a shame. Get that politician out of there; he has no moral compass! But in reality, we're very quick to be negative, and it's far easier to remember the negative than it is the positive.

One word associated with negativity is, of course, the word "no." It means the very opposite of Yes. We want "Yes Men" in our society because yes is such a strong force for good. It's an agreeable word, and it promotes unity. Now it *is* true that even if cats could speak, they wouldn't use the word "yes" when asked if they'd like to be tied together.

My former pastor once said, "You can tie two cats together by their tail, and you'll have union… but you won't have unity!" Heartily agreed. Yes makes sense only when it makes sense. The good thing is that "yes" can also make sense when you're saying "no."

Even "no" can be a positive word. In fact, it can be the *most* positive word that you adopt…ever.

NO MEANS YES.

No means yes, I care about my time. No means yes, I value myself enough not to sell out. No means it is completely ok that I do things for myself once in a while.

Ryan Holiday, author and marketer, said "Don't say maybe if you want to say no."[1] And to quote my audiobook client and good friend *Thibaut Meurisse*, here's a great chunk of wisdom for you:

"First, to say no effectively, you must know your values and goals. Otherwise, you risk saying yes to every opportunity or request. For any request, see whether it aligns with your priorities. Remember, your values and goals should dictate most of your decisions....remember...giving up a chunk of your time is giving away a part of your life. Therefore, instead of saying 'yes' all the time, make 'no' your default answer. Accept requests only when you have a valid reason to do so. Thus, realize that valuing your time is a sign of self-respect. Standing up for your values and goals is giving them respect. Finally, understand that to have the biggest impact possible on the world, you must be ruthless with the way you use your time. People pleasers seldom reach their true potential because they fail to set their priorities and fight to protect them. Instead, they disrespect their time (and themselves) by saying yes to everything. Don't be a doormat. Set your priorities. Value yourself enough to value your time. Then, use your time to achieve your biggest goals and make a positive impact on the world. Note that I'm not saying you should never spend time helping other people. I'm saying you should learn to say no more often so that you can focus more effectively on your priorities. This way, you'll be more likely to achieve your goals."[2]

Unfortunately, in life there are those that I like to call "human umbilical cords." They plug into you and drain you dry. They are *incredibly* needy, and some of them are downright unteachable. If you spend yourself to destitution giving, or trying hard to teach them, your well of reserves can dry up.

Don't do that to yourself. Anne Lamont said "No is a complete sentence." No means no. And an anonymous author once said "Lack of boundaries invites a lack of respect."

Make "no" your favorite word. Saying "no" to others protects your own interests and ensures that you won't fall behind. Saying "no" to others is saying "yes" to yourself. It's why you put your own oxygen mask on in a failing airplane before you secure the mask of those around you.

Do I feel like a jerk for saying no? No. Especially when I say it to a telemarketer. Or to junk food. Or even to my 4-year-old, who frequently wanders into my office during the day to ask if he can play with one of my Transformers. It doesn't really matter to him that they are up on that high shelf for Dada's inspiration; the only thing that matters to him is that I say "yes", and allow him to play with them. But Dada's gotta work. Dada's gotta turn his "yes" into a "no", with zero guilt. Happens multiple times a day. If Dada doesn't say "no", then there will be no jobs...and then no money for Transformers. Eventually he'll get it and stop hating me. *fingers crossed*

The word "no" is very, very empowering. It's equipping. It's enabling you to fulfill your own destiny and accomplish your goals. You have to focus on them *today*, not "someday." As Rodney Saulsberry puts it, "I hear you – 'I'll get to it someday.' Well, someday is not on the calendar. You have Monday, Tuesday, Wednesday, Thursday, Friday, Saturday and Sunday – but *someday* is not an option."[3]

Saying no to others is saying yes to yourself, and that's not only OK, it's critical.

Warren Buffett, the guru of investors, has this to say for what separates the doers from the dreamers:

Pick your friends wisely – you are who you hang around with!
Go to bed a little smarter each day – read a lot. Read a TON. Buffett spends sometimes 80% of his day reading.
Improve your communication skills – honing your communication skills daily, both written and verbal, is key to his being propelled forward in life and business
Say "no." It's no mistake that he put this last one in there. He says "The difference between successful people and really successful people is that really successful people say no to almost everything."[4]

Shall we continue with this book? (Hint: your answer here should be the opposite of "no.")

TAKEAWAY & ACTION STEP

"Saying 'no' can be the ultimate self-care." – Claudia Black

Are you a "Yes Man"? When was the last time you said no to someone and didn't feel a pang of guilt? What do you need to say 'no' to in order to say 'yes' to yourself? Write down 5 people in your life that you need to say 'no' to more – without feeling guilty – in order to say 'yes' to you and your own dreams.

Why I Threw Away $460,000

HUMBLE SUPERHERO BEGINNINGS

Jason didn't have a wedding videographer. I had a simple 8mm analog tape video camera and apparently had an "S" on my chest. That's truly how it began.

I had met Jason in 2001 at my old church, and we had become good friends. He'd been a friend to me during a bit of a dark time, and now he was getting hitched. Tying the knot. Renouncing singledom. Entering lifelong enslavement and bondage. I added that last one because at the time I had sworn off the idea of marriage as a fool's errand, and committed myself to business alone. I was married to business, so why would I want to be unfaithful and cheat with, you know, a human?

At the time I was doing multimedia services like video production, video transfer, and corporate videography. I had never really given wedding videography a thought, and not because of the potential *bridezilla*[5] factor. It just hadn't occurred to me. Jason and I talked, and I thought, what the heck. At the very least, it should be documented. And I was just the guy to do it. So, I strapped on my cape, laced up my rubber boots and curly-cue'd my gelled-down hair, and flew off to Oregon, faster than a wedding videographer bullet, to save the day. Little did I know that it would be the start of a very lucrative career, several hundred clients, lots of good, stable income, and, on many occasions, the biggest headache of my life.

453 weddings later, after $460,000 earned, I said *peace out*.

PARTING IS SUCH SWEET SORROW...OR NOT

Why a headache? Well, let's look at a headache for a moment. A headache has a slow evolution where you first realize everything isn't what it's cracked up to be. Then, you start feeling discomfort. Ultimately, you despair even of life, and want to harm small animals. Your cat senses this and runs away to dial 911 on his cat phone. The end result is you wind up wishing you had never purchased videography equipment and develop a lifelong contempt for matrimony itself, at which point you join a local monastery and renounce all pop culture and cheeseburgers for good.

There has been a massive sea-change in the wedding industry. Overly emotional and immature, narcissistic wedding clients whittle down your $1500 package to $800 and then still expect all of the $1500 package trimmings.

And once you state politely that you're unable to give those to them because they only belong in the $1500 package as is clearly stated in the wedding contract you silly freak, they run right to Yelp[6]. I've since learned to stop calling wedding clients silly freaks: it's about as effective as smearing yourself with butter and swimming naked with elephant seals.

So I decided to give up headaches and weddings at the same time, since they are scientifically and empirically the same thing. I gave them up for good, and as of 2018 had stopped collecting wedding clients for the following year. I used to collect them and store them in the freezer until they decided to behave; some are still in there, pleading with me and promising positive Yelp reviews.

On Friday November 22nd, 2019 - doubtless in commemoration of Lee Harvey Oswald's[7] infamous assassination – I took up position in my book depository and took out my wedding business. Poor taste in analogies? Perhaps. But ultimately, it's now a matter of history. I left it behind, and drove away in tears of gladness. I threw off the yoke of slavery and indentured servitude to brides (bleccchhhh1) and grooms (hurrrrllll!!) and weddings (Raaalllppphhh!!!!) and drove off into the sunset.

I sighed contentedly, looked back on all of that wedding bliss and happy nonsense behind me, and plowed into a parked car. Once I was outfitted with a rental and had filed the proper insurance paperwork, I was on my merry way home once again, resolving to not look in the rearview mirror at brides, grooms and weddings. It was over.

No more campaigning. No more voting contests trying to solicit votes to win "best wedding videographer." No more frantic refreshing of standings.

No more merciless clients. No more walking on eggshells due to clients deciding to go berserk because you wouldn't throw in an extra add-on for free.

No more Saturdays busy doing something other than being with my family.

No more wedding expos and manning of booths and slapping on a fake smile just to try to get work.

No more maintenance of expensive equipment.

No more laborious production of narcissistic projects for clients with backwards priorities who are obsessed with a wedding day and not with a marriage life.

No more time-consuming rendering of videos.

No more ridiculously unabating stress over potentially receiving negative Yelp reviews from bridezillas, destroying my business' reputation due to a misunderstanding on their part.

No more client pre-wedding meetings and buying them coffee.

No more. No more. No more.

It was done. The Ring had gone into Mount Doom.

THE EDGE OF EVOLUTION

As an artist, you may try your hand at multiple arts. For me, I've always been a right-brain. So much so that they're still staring at case studies of my head X-rays when I was born, wondering why the left cranial hemisphere just isn't there. I've been an artist, a poet, a singer, a dancer, a writer, a voice talent, a jingle singer, etc.. I've made Top Ramen in ways that would defy logic and win prizes. I have a profound, innate need to create sentences such as "I have a profound, innate need to create sentences." It comes from a place deep within, where exists only my heart, Papa Smurf, and a profound, innate love for Gandalf and all things Lord of the Rings. I must create: profoundly and innately.

Curiously, as I was driving away that night, *Edge of Evolution* by Alanis Morissette was playing. Here are some of the lyrics:

Here I leave my story, I leave it in the dust
Although this psychology's been entertaining enough
Herein lies the witness objective with my stuff
But we're ready to push envelopes into full-blown consciousness
So here we go out here on the edge of evolution
Numbers growing out here on the edge of evolution

Apropós, no? To hear that song just made me weep, similar to how one would weep when they see a rainbow, or a unicorn, or a rainbow riding a unicorn. The vision of my past receding into the distance, and my future becoming brighter and brighter was beautiful, epic, fantastical, and rich with color.

To further underscore that this was the right decision, and that I wasn't under the influence of another monastery-guided headache, on my way home I received a contract approval email from a voiceover client. What a sign from the heavens! Or, at least, from a computer server somewhere, perhaps located in the heavens.

Sure, I could go on serving wedding clients aka wallowing in freakish misery forever. I could subject myself to abhorrent mistreatment and whiny pleas of "I'm dying the day after my wedding, so please won't you give us the Platinum package for the price of the Bronze package [cough cough cough] can't you see I'm dying…" I could spend time away from my wife and kiddos and sacrifice every Saturday to be with the wonderful narcissists. But I've chosen a better path, and that's one of *drum roll, if you please* *Author and Voiceover Artist Extraordinaire*.

I'm in *LOVE* with what I do now.

I intentionally shuttered a company I had sunk thousands of dollars into for advertising, equipment, marketing, training, upgrades, insurance, more equipment, and other extraneous expenses like psychological counseling and therapy to deal with the clients.

Sure, I'll miss the free reception meals and the placement at the kids table, but I experience far less headache producing voiceovers for clients, and I can order into the local restaurant which I hear serves great butter-smeared elephant seal.

TAKEAWAY & ACTION STEP

Find what you love to do, and you'll never work a day in your life. There is no labor in love.

What are you drowning in? What can you take steps to leave behind so that you're fulfilling your dreams? Write them down and keep track of them.

How Voiceovers Saved Me

RESCUED

The solution was with me all along. I knew it, I just didn't realize it at any point until just a few years ago.

For many years I had been tooling around in the singing realm: forgetting my first love, not fully understanding where I needed to be all along. What I *did* know was that I loved being in the studio far more than I loved being on stage. I really, *really* loved being behind that mic. Admittedly, there's a little bit of narcissism in hearing oneself in real time. When you're good at something, there's nothing wrong with being grateful for your craft, but in line with that there's a deep-seated, profound appreciation of being able to make beautiful sounds that, well, sound beautiful. I loved singing because I knew I had a gift and it sounded good. I love voiceovers for the same reasons.

But there was a difference between singing and performing in front of people, and performing voiceovers without an eye on you. Some people can handle fame. I'm not one of those people. It's like pouring gasoline on a flame. It's too much for me. I detonate with ego and it feeds the beast that I need to stay asleep. *There, there, that's a good beast. You sleep now. Good boy.* With singing, I was from-the-stage untouchable, and I was singing at them. I was disconnected.

I wish I had the foresight of Gandalf. He was offered the Ring by Frodo. His response says everything that we need to know about Gandalf, and speaks to the power of pride being inflamed, and his humility:

No!' cried Gandalf, springing to his feet. 'With that power I should have power too great and terrible. And over me the Ring would gain a power still greater and more deadly.' His eyes flashed and his face was lit as by a fire within. 'Do not tempt me! For I do not wish to become like the Dark Lord himself. Yet the way of the Ring to my heart is by pity, pity for weakness and the desire of strength to do good. Do not tempt me! I dare not take it, not even to keep it safe, unused. The wish to wield it would be too great for my strength. I shall have such need of it. Great perils lie before me."[8]

For me, voiceovers hold very little in similar peril. Yes, I'm very active on social media and so I do have random people coming up to me and saying "Aaron Ryan???" And I must confess that it's caught me unawares at times, because in this era of social media, if you're active, and you have a following – and I do, across multiple channels that I need to be respectful of – you're kind of a celebrity. I'm no Peter Cullen, Don LeFontaine, Stephen King or Suzanne Collins, but I do have a following, and so there are definitely dangers of ego.

What voiceovers and authoring bring to me are two things I never had in the singing and performing realm: humility, and the ability to give back. Humility because of what I just shared in regard to my pride. Giving back, because the door is wide open to support and affirm in this industry.

GIVING BACK

Community. What does that word mean to you? Potlucks? Pen pals? Bingo night? Or does it mean something deeper, richer, more connective? I think Alanis Morissette said it best. She often says it best:

There are so many parts that I have hidden and that I yet lost
There are so many ways that I have cut off my nose despite my face
There are so many colors that I still try to hide while I paint
And there are so many tunes that I secretly sing away
But come along
Yeah, invite these part-time writers
Hello, this invitation
Is one that I've stopped fighting oh oh
Thank you for seeing me
I feel so less lonely
Thank you for guiding me
I hear your bide, your empathy
Ha-a this intimacy ha-a-a-a
There were so many times I thought I have died,
not the usually known
There were so many moments, forever lonely in my location

You come along
To celebrate each feeling
Come, there you are
How long have I been fighting?
Thank you for seeing me
I feel so less lonely
Thank you...[9]

I'm an Alanis fan. She's expressive, she writes poignant lyrics and incredible pieces of musical genius, and this is one of my favorites. It speaks to community: to deep connectedness. And that's something that all of us need, even the most committed cave dwellers.

With a few exceptions, I've never known such community as I've known in voiceovers, except for maybe in my church. Overall, it is a super strong, empowering, affirming community. Have I taken some hits from this community as well? Of course. Nothing is perfect. No ecosystem is immune from frustration or issues from time to time. Granted, as with anything and anywhere, there are cliques, and there are what might be perceived or labeled as the "untouchables."

But the overwhelming majority is uber-supportive and involved with each other. I was genuinely surprised by it, because after all, where else do you affirm your competitor? Where else do you train your competition? Where else do you raise up threats to your own income? Where else do you find people ready and willing to counsel you into stealing what could have been their income?

The voiceover community – with rare exception, because I have had a few run-ins with members of "the old guard": the toxic few who like to attack and label and stir up all kinds of incendiary nonsense – is incredibly supportive. There are countless Facebook groups and other online communities, as well as hosted conferences, to attest to that.

LOSING THE WILL TO LIVE

I must say that at first I was grateful. Wedding videography, from the start, was exciting. I was able to marry (pun intended) my skills in video editing with my business acumen, and create a competitive business providing a high level wedding videography product to commemorate their special day. It was beautiful, it was enjoyable, it provided great income, and I loved it.

Now, I hate it with every fiber of my being and the fire of a thousand suns. I want *nothing* to do with the wedding industry ever again, and I'm committed to harming small animals if I'm forced to be a part of it.

Over the past few years, I've noticed a cruel shift in the mentality of brides and grooms. There is an undercurrent of entitlement, of overbearing indentured servitude for the vendors, and a resounding refrain wherein clients whittle your $1500 wedding videography package down to $800 - but they still feel entitled to all the bells and whistles from the $1500 package, and if you don't give it to them they run straight to Yelp. I've had it happen, I resent it, and I hate the very nature of the business. I strove to provide a classy product and service since I started – but the change in mentality has gutted my desire to serve in this industry, and left me hollow. I've been broken after giving my all. I've been betrayed after going above and beyond. And it's stung. And it's hurt. I recently received a negative Yelp review from a wedding client of *six years ago*. That's an awful long time to nurse a grudge, and I pity them for that. We had a negative exchange, and while I've moved on, they apparently couldn't. Many of the wedding clients I've talked to or obtained are a downright vindictive bunch, and I'm done. A voiceover pro is quoted as saying that you don't want to attract "clients that expect a gourmet meal at a fast food price and at drive-through speed."[10]

And so….bub-bye. On November 22nd of 2019 we filmed our last wedding and we're all done. I no longer need the income to sustain our family.

Since moving into our new home in Lynnwood in the fall of 2015, I sought and sought for a new line of work to bring in extra income. I never once thought of dropping wedding videography, as it brought in a decent income chunk per year as part of our overall multimedia income picture. But the more the industry changed, the more I craved something new. Something rewarding. Something *else*.

But in late 2019, as I gratefully sat back and watched my remaining wedding clientele list shrink, with great relish I witnessed the passage of my original dream. It was with a contented sigh and a smile that splits my face at the ears that I watched my wedding videography business diminish and recede into the past, to be forgotten. In fact, at one point way back when I started penning this book, an upcoming wedding client of mine cancelled, because they couldn't fit wedding videography into their budget. It truly broke me emotionally to see them go. *insert uproarious laughter here.*

Now, let me clarify something. I am *deeply* grateful for the resources and income that wedding videography has brought to my family and me. I truly am. It's been a vehicle, truly, a vehicle to get me from there to here, to provide rich experiences and wonderful income possibilities. It's allowed me to fulfill some dreams. So please do believe me when I say that I *am* grateful.

I just upgraded from a Volkswagen bus to a Ferrari, that's all.

Voiceovers have literally saved my sanity. They've rescued me and provided something with a tenth the stress, a tenth the frustration and uncertainty, and a million times the fun. They have taken over our income spectrum and provided us an incredible amount of wealth and connections, through far less work and virtually zero overhead, than wedding videography ever could. For that, I'm also deeply grateful. They've been my Moses through the Red Sea of wedding videography. Just picture Moses with an impressive Sennheiser MKH416 and headphones on, and floating wedding clients, and you've got the picture crystal clear.

Being an entrepreneur has never ever been a hobby for me. Since I've been in business, it has always been a part of my arsenal of services that I can offer to clients. I've had training, I've had networking, and I've had hands-on experience that has equipped me to subtract the one and add the other. And so again, I'm enormously grateful for what they're doing for our bottom line, because I've always treated it like a business, and I've always intended to succeed at it. I never went into voiceovers *hoping*. It was always intending.

During my day, I'm always working with music. It inspires me, moves me, and keeps me thinking creatively. As I wrote this chapter I was listening to "Eyes Wide Open" by Tony Anderson from *The Heart of Man* soundtrack. It's beautiful, it's stirring, it's rich, it's sweeping. And, call me a sap, but it moved me to tears as I think back how far I've come, and what I've been *removed* from in order to enjoy the privilege of voiceovers. For it is just that: it truly is a rich privilege. *Who am I*, I ask myself, *to be so fortunate as to be gifted in this category of vocation, that I might be able to share in its treasures?*

Have you ever heard the phrase, "Good is the worst enemy of best"? It's totally and indefatigably and categorically true. We often choose good, which is the worst enemy of best. I am so grateful that I've chosen the latter, and am enjoying rich blessing because of that choice.

It's not a career. It's a dream. And I'm living it. And I'm grateful beyond words. I get to wake up laughing each day, knowing that I get to head out to my shop and create. That the dream I'm living is *mine*, and not some boss's dream. No: it's all mine, and I rise or fall on my own merits, and whether or not I give my all. That, to me, is something you can't put a price tag on.

There Can Be Only One

HACKINGS AND BEHEADINGS: O WHAT FUN!

Once upon a time there comes along a movie that blows you away with its incredible ideologies. No, I'm not talking about Bill & Ted's Excellent Adventure. I'm talking about Terminator. The Matrix. Inception. Movies with concepts that are beyond the scope of mortal thinking.

Highlander is such a movie! Ohhhhh, it had everything: Immortals slashing their way to win The Prize, which, if you remember, included omniscience, sweeping 80's music video camera shots, cheap monster graphic effects, and 80's arm-candy women with feathered hair and lots of rouge. For me, I would be content with just an endless supply of cheeseburgers. But I'm sure you feel the same.

On the one side you have Connor McLeod of the clan McLeod (played by Christopher Lambert, who starred in this movie and, well, really only this movie), hailing from the Highlands, which is another way of saying he lives so far up there that he's nearly in outer space, so he has to wear a kilt so that he can flash all of us mortals down here. There's no air up there, but he's an immortal, remember.

And on the other side, you have The Kurgan, played by Clancy Brown: a man who has an effeminate name who got to play a man who does not have an effeminate name. The Kurgan was a barbarian of a man hellbent on world domination accomplished through performing the worst Christian Bale Batman-voice-impression possible. Someone give that man a lozenge, and an even more masculine name. I think Agamemnon will do nicely.

When *Highlander* came out on Showtime in 1986, I was hooked. Mostly because I was a zit-faced angst-ridden teenage boy who loved seeing people hack at each other with swords, set to furious guitar riffs by Queen. It was a time of questioning, so Queen and swords was just the right recipe. *I see a little silhouetto of a man…*

Scaramouche, Scaramouche, will you do the fandango? See? There was a question mark right there. Questioning.

My favorite element was Sean Connery, a Scottish man who hails from Spain (because, ya know, casting reasons) who played Juan Sánchez Villa-Lobos Ramírez, a name which in ancient Latin means "My Name is Much Too Long." Unfortunately, Mr. SVLR gets dispatched much too quickly, so you never, in fact, get to see an immortal ask for a martini: shaken, not stirred. This is disappointing of course, but not enough to make me hit stop and switch to *Purple Rain*, another musical movie hit for the angst in teenagers everywhere, featuring music by the artist formerly known in life as the artist who was formerly known as *Unpronounceable Symbol*, who is the artist formerly known as Prince. But you do have to hand it to the makeup artists for making Sean Connery look like he was still 35, when in fact in 1986 he was 328.

Ultimately, *Highlander's* plot centers around lots of people cutting each other's heads off, because beheadings were en vogue, it was a Friday night and there was nothing better to do. But then the scriptwriters said, "no, that sucks...let's have them be freaking *immortals* with freaking swords...yeah!!!" And then everyone agreed and went out and drank much beer. Thus, *Highlander* was born, and zit-faced angst-ridden Queen-loving teenage boys everywhere were pleased.

How does this relate to voiceovers, you ask? Hold on to your neck, and I'll tell you. It's a cut-throat affair, and you've got to keep your kilt about you, aye, lad.

A CUT-THROAT AFFAIR

Voiceovers – and business - can be competitive. There is really only one voice out there that's going to win a role, and one person who's going to win that job - unless of course there's more than one, in which case I need to curse loudly, tear this up and start writing an entirely different chapter. Ultimately, we're all vying for the same thing: to win the Prize. Thank goodness we use microphones and not Dragonhead Katana swords.

When you and I are going up for the same role, we're dead-set (see what I did there?) on winning The Prize, and looking down upon our vanquished foes lying in a heap at the bottom of the hill. The hill, of course, being that little step up from the bottom floor leading into our isolation booth, littered with dead voiceover bodies who tried to get in our way.

Did you know that way, way, waaaaaaaaaay back in the olden days, when Barack Obama was president, there were still "killing contests"[11] happening in such far-off, distant and undeveloped places of the world? I'm talking about Arizona. I am not kidding. In these savage contests, hunters would bait and kill as many wild animals as possible. Participants competed for prizes like belt buckles, cash, trophies, a free Grand Canyon souvenir snake-belt, and Joe Arpaio's pink underwear. They would boast about how much fun it is to kill innocent animals with "like-minded" people. Horrifyingly, youth clubs also held competitions, sending a message to young children that killing animals is a game.

I'm telling the truth. And it's an evil truth that won't go away, exactly like Milli Vanilli music.

Thankfully, progress has been made on this front, but it just serves to continually reveal how savage our society still can be. I think we're getting better though. We've downgraded to body-slamming 55-year-old ladies outside Chick Fil-A now.[12] BUT! Witnesses report NO animals were savagely hunted. Phew. I feel better, because that could have been an awful scene.

It's this kind of savageness that is represented in *Highlander*. There truly can be only one Prize winner. Were there two winners, then they would just be constantly striving, and it would be a bad pairing, much like peanut butter and bratwurst, and much like Anthony Wiener and texting.

But as voiceover artists, we've just *got* to land that role. And we'd do anything to get it. Heck, we may even body-slam our 55-year-old cohorts if they get in our way. But thankfully, as we voiceover artists have evolved, our measure of self-control has evolved as well, and it's not quite as cut-throat as it could be. There's nothing enjoyable or funny about a voiceover artist beheading, and so we practice civility in the highest sense.

Still…should another businessperson get in our way… *cue scary music and maniacal laugh here*

THERE CAN BE ONLY ONE

At one point in *Highlander*, Sean Juan Sánchez Villa-Lobos Ramírez Gonzalez Vasquez-Hildebrandt Smith-Conchita Anderson McGillicuddy McGurk Connery says to Connor McLeod, "My name is much too long." McLeod is confused, so SJSVLRGVHSCAMMC clarifies: "If your head comes away from your neck, it's over." I'd venture to say that during Juan's introduction of his name to Connor, Connor's head should have in fact fallen clean off from the weight of Juan's name…but, ah! Thank goodness. There it stayed, in all its Michael Bolton-esque glory.

(Disclaimer: I hate Michael Bolton).

As business people, thank goodness the battlefield exists only in our minds. And truly, if our *head* comes away from our audition, it is indeed over. We need to focus. We need to get into our roles with passion. Unbridled and unassailable passion. Passion unmatched since the dawn of time. Passion that rivals THE Passion. You know what I'm talking about. There's only one kind of passion like this. I'm talking about Nancy Pelosi let's-impeach-him-right-this-very-minute-okay-how-about-in-a-few-months-from-now Passion! It's that kind of unrelenting passion that gets things done! Oh yeah and also gives us great TV drama.

Speaking of TV, here comes a great audition that I better get to before you do. After all, there can be only one.

But in order to get into the zone, in order to *really* inhabit the role so that I'll be awarded the job, I'll need something. Something to equip me. Something to fire me up with a fury and bring out the best drama I can muster.

Press play on that Queen cassette, baby. *grabs sword*

Sincerely,
Clancy Agamemnon Ryan

The Intrepid Tale Of An iPhone-Addict Guy

SHUT UP AND TAKE MY MONEY

So, it's iPhone season again. I simply must have the new iPhone every year. I'm an Apple-Loving Creative Guy. I crave the new iPhone like crack Cocaine, which is a statement that should make you curious about my proclivities.

I want the new iPhone. And I don't mean any cheap second-gen prior-to-this-one version. No, no. No, I must have the latest and greatest. I don't know what this says about me, but when I ask Siri what she's wearing, and she says, "Silicon, memory, and the courage of my convictions", then say no more. Shut up and take my money, because baby, you had me at silicon.

Ah, Silicon Valley. You who continue to provide me rectangular electronic enslavement each year around the beginning of fall, and then you have that British guy produce those videos where everything is Just So Shiny; he could soothingly whisper "Aaron, eat mangled animal carcass", and I would do it.

And so? Each fall I become a drunken swooner, allured by the Apple iPhone's glimmering siren call. It's your fault, Fruit Company, that we have no money for food or heat in October, and you know it. Each year I tell my wife this will be the last upgrade, and each year she gets to burst out in wild laughter, which I take to mean that she utterly believes me.

But in truth, aside from being able to manage my business on the go, the iPhone has saved me from many a danger. Here are a few examples, and I would not be alive today were it not for a little-known company's little-known invention straight out of Cupertino:

I've oft times needed a level in order to install something, and my iPhone has an app with a Level in it! So, I was able to install something completely level by using my iPhone, calling a skilled contractor, and paying them to install it correctly since I am incapable of installing things and using levels.

I've needed a compass, and had my iPhone all along, so I was able to text Santa and see which direction I was pointing.

I've experienced actual, real-life emergencies (my child's head cracked open and gushing blood, the dog impaled on a weathervane; someone drank all the beer, the Seahawks game started late) where I took care of handling it on-the-go with my trusty iPhone.

I've lost my socks and been able to call Information: they graciously informed me that they were behind the couch.
And best of all, if I can't find that Apple TV remote which is intentionally designed to be the size of an atom, I can control my TV with my iPhone rather than get up and search for it. Sidebar: I am lazy.

Surely, Jesus Himself would have owned an iPhone when he was here, had Steve Jobs been around then. I cannot confirm or deny if Steve Jobs went to Heaven, but I know all of my previous iPhones are there.

SELFIE? IS THAT A NEW FRENCH POODLE?

Yes, I could use my iPhone for selfies (I do). I could use it for maintaining my calendar (I do). I could actually use it for making phone calls even. *insert incredulous laughter here* Ultimately, however, I'm all about the data. It's about checking my business accounts at all times, making sure I keep my finger on the pulse of my business on-the-go, which is of paramount consequence to me, to the point where I use words like "paramount" and "consequence" together in a single sentence for maximum impact.

So what can a business owner do with their iPhone? No, no... *besides* Angry Birds I mean, which is essential for business. What makes the iPhone so helpful for running a business? I'm honestly glad you've asked. Here's a list that is in no way meant to be conclusive, absolute, definitive or helpful in any way:

Creating voice memos on the go to remind you of things to do, such as when you are forty miles away from your home and you realize that you forgot to close the garage door after you left. Also for reminding yourself to buy more beer.

Responding to clients right away when they need something urgently, which is almost never. Hang on, a zillion emails just came in and all my phones are ringing.

Playing loud music to drown out the constant din of your small children.

Turning the loud music down in order to respond to your wife who asks you if you remember that you have small children. Asking Siri to confirm that you do.

Programming geofence-based reminders to take care of business once I return home through the garage door. Which is still open.

Checking calendar when my agent calls and asks me if I'm available, which allows me to pull a Peter Dickson[13], say "one moment", and then flick slowly through my calendar, pretending I'm in demand. "Pathetic, I know, but I can't help myself."

It's a phone, but it's so much more. It's your life in your hands. And it's meant to enable productivity. When I see people using their smartphone and touting that "it takes great selfies", I have to laugh at the narcissism and pity the naiveté. It's so much more, and it's critical for your business so that you can play Fortnite during meetings in which you wish the speaker's head would explode so that they could adjourn until janitorial services arrive.

GIVE ME LIBERTY, OR GIVE ME UPGRADES! (BUT MAY I HAVE BOTH PLEASE?)

So, here we go again. I bought my iPhone 15 Pro Max, and I bought my wife the 15 Pro. So if you email me anytime around iPhone release time on any given year, please note that my email or text replies may be laden with over-ecstatic gibberish and hyperactive drivel, because there will be nothing else that I'm focused on at the moment. I ask you to bear with me, and then I ask that you please explain how you got my number.

I will always buy the new iPhone. Not because our family doesn't require shelter or groceries – we do – but I think a good hard lesson of the hard knocks of life, and going without, is indispensable. I am capable of monitoring my children's sunken cheeks for signs of malnourishment, and at the point where we'll need to take shelter at the onset of a thunderstorm, I'll simply call ahead on my BEAUTIFUL EXPENSIVE SHINY NEW MUST-HAVE IPHONE to determine that there are enough bunks: five for the emaciated four of us; one for my iPhone. There's plenty of space on the floor next to it for tardy homeless folk.

Will you be more successful in voiceovers if you have an iPhone instead of an Android? Perhaps. (The real answer is 'yes' if you want to be cool like a celebrity). Will you prosper more if you have a smartphone as opposed to *not* having a smartphone? Most definitely. It's hard for me to promise anything anymore, really, except for the fact that at the end of this chapter, you are now much older.

In truth, I *love* my iPhone. Romantic love. It's shiny. It takes great selfies, yes. But it's for so much more than that. Buying it for selfies implies that I find my appearance becoming enough to grace a camera screen, which is of course not true, which is of course why I'm in the vocation I'm in. It spares you the horror of seeing that rectangular thing with the Apple logo glued to my face, its mechanical tail wrapped around my neck and its spiny legs gripping my face in its warm addictive embrace. Someone call Ripley, because I think an iPhone is going to burst out of my chest soon.

Tell her she can come in through the garage.

Sincerely,
Alva

TAKEAWAY & ACTION STEP

iPhones rule, and you know it.

Buy an iPhone and nothing else. (Well, maybe some food and drink here and there. Especially coffee.)

A Moment Of Silence For Bibbidi-Bobbidi-Boo

GONE IS THE FANTASY

You got into voiceovers because you wanted to do something fun. You thought it would be easy. You thought if you just put yourself behind a mic, and made magical sounds, you'd be an instant hit and receive worldwide acclaim. Basically, you fell for the uber-demonstrative in-your-face solve-all-your-problems infomercial and ordered that mic/interface/headphones bundle from Tonka for four easy payments of $39.95.

But wait! There's more! You "acted now", so you get a second Tonka mic… completely free! Nothing can stop you now.

I've got news for you. There simply is no Bibbidi-Bobbidi-Boo.

As with all things, there's no fairy godmother to make your dreams come true, no magic carpet ride to whisk you away to success, and no potion you can drink – unless it's Strawberry Gatorade Vodka – to enable you to carve out your indelible mark in the annals of voiceover history. There is only one thing…ever…that can enable you to be successful. It's looking ridiculously sexy, like me.

I'm kidding. It's more along the lines of Tony Robbins motivational stuff. In truth, I'm talking about tenacity:

- Tenacity is repetition.
- Tenacity is consistency.
- Tenacity is being in it for the long haul.
- This is a fourth bullet point for added emphasis.

As my good friend and repeat audiobook client Thibaut Meurisse says, "Success is a process and not an event."[14] These things take time. There are those out there that are perfectly (read: appallingly) content with microwaved Hungry Man meals. You know those meals: the kind that make you want to puke coat hangers in the end, whose flavor dimly reminds you of the succulent tang of automobile tire. And then…there are those that get rich, thick beef stew through crock pots. How will you choose to fill your belly? The thick broth aisle is this way; Discount Tire is over there. As Yuri Lowenthal and Tara Platt say, "As with any art or creative industry, the path to success is not a straight one in this business. Nor does it come with a map. You can be phenomenally talented and still have to work hard. You may work hard for a year or for ten years before you feel you've *made it*. In fact, you may work for twenty years, be wildly successful, and *still* feel like you haven't made it. So make sure you're having fun. The only thing you can truly do (besides having fun) to create the best odds of succeeding is to get prepared and stay prepared, so that when the opportunities that you create pop up, you can take full advantage of them."[15] I'll have the crock pot, thanks, and I'll continue to ladle out the goodness over the long haul.

The road to success is no respecter of persons, and will demand and exact much from you, if you let it. If you truly want to be successful someday, you're going to have to pay your dues. No magic wands will be waived. No VIP lists get you inside. No secret passwords grant you unfettered access to the riches that lie therein. There's simply no fast track, and there are no fairy godmothers.

Sorry, Cinderella. Don't quit your day job.

Rather, just like in every other industry, vocation, endeavor or passion-based pursuit, it requires *Cubitum Crisco*. In other words, elbow grease. You've got to market hard, audition hard, network hard, push hard, pray hard, work hard, commit hard, think hard, plan hard, organize hard, hope hard, intend hard, focus hard, and do all of that over and over again, 24/7/365. Basically, whatever you're already doing, do it a *lot* harder.

In other words, it's still so easy, *embryos* can do it! Act now for only four easy payments of $39.95 and get a SECOND embryo for FREE!

Voiceovers, like many pursuits, are entrepreneurial in nature. What that requires of you is not just putting a mic in front of your face and headphones on your ears. It's about looking sexy, like me. It's also about structure... ecosystem... branding... goal-setting... treating it like a business. Rinse and repeat.

Any coach who promises you the moon and sells you on the idea that in exchange for your purchase of a $2500 coaching package you'll be booking jobs right and left within a week...is out of their freaking mind, and needs to swap "coach" for "predator." Because that's really who they are, and that's really *all* they are. It's predatory predation of prey, plain and pimple. I'm pelling you the pruth, and not pying to you.

Plan on a marathon, not a sprint. Anyone in their right mind will tell you that.

HOW OLD ARE YOU, AARON?

Where am I at in all this? Oh, I've definitely paid my dues. I've faced rejection, rigor, duress, politics, deflated ego, hurt feelings, and people speaking the truth. One of my favorite truths ever spoken to me was by a coach during a coaching session. He said: "There were moments where I didn't believe you." Ouch!
I've been talked to by lots of Simon Cowells. Sometimes it's politics, politics, politics. *sigh* I served my time. What helped me is that I looked sexy through all of it. No seriously, as Saulsberry says, "The combination of acknowledging your blessings and the passage of time is a powerful antidote to whatever ails you emotionally."[16] But I also think looking sexy doesn't hurt.

I feel like an old soul, because I watched voiceovers on the periphery for many, many years. I would stick my toe in the water, and it wasn't the right time. Or I got distracted with other creative pursuits that paid the bills but weren't my heart's delight. Or I got roped into doing one wedding... which turned into fifty weddings... which turned into four-hundred-and-fifty-three weddings and a funeral.

I cannot begin to even express to you how overjoyed I am to be out of the wedding videography business, because weddings suck and happiness is stupid.

A MOMENT OF SILENCE FOR BIBBIDI-BOBBIDI-BOO

"All good things happen to those who wait." It's a time-honored adage, and one worthy of great respect. Wait for it. *Work towards it*, by all means! But don't rush things, and don't expect a miracle. Jesus does those primarily for people in *pain*. Your third-rate mic isn't causing you pain; your lack of acoustically-treated space isn't causing you pain; your sadness over not booking work isn't *causing* you pain; you're just **being a pain.**

So please stop it at once, and start looking sexy. Like me.

I've been doing multimedia, voiceovers included, for a long, long time, and I've paid my dues on a number of fronts. What I've learned is that while there are many ways to skin a cat, cats never taste good raw. You need to gather wood. Crumple paper. Start a fire. Watch it grow. Feed it. Give it time.

The best tasting cat is a cooked one, where the skin just falls right off the bone and the juices are so sweet.

Please stop dialing the ASPCA. I am not advocating skinning or cooking cats. Unless of course it's my wife's: you can have that one.

I'll be over here looking sexy.

TAKEAWAY & ACTION STEP

"A dream does not become reality through magic; it takes sweat, determination, and hard work."
– Colin Powell, former U.S. Defense Secretary

Are you chasing fantasies that this will be easy? They call it "clawing your way to the top" for a reason. Renounce the magic carpet fantasy. Write down your goals, and don't stop there. Write down your comprehensive 3-month, 6-month, and 1-year plans for how you'll hit those goals.

Clean Spaces And Parallel Lines

BEFORE YOU DO ANYTHING ELSE

Before you do anything else, get organized. If that entails buying a planner, buying a voice memo app, buying "reminder" software, whatever it might be, find a way to:

Record your goals
Monitor your progress toward your goals
Jot down your thoughts
Make your plans
Record your achievements
Organize your life

If you want to be successful in business – *any* business, you need to 1) be organized. Disorganization will absolutely kill your forward momentum, and it will rob you of progress. And 2) you *must* learn the art of repetition. Bill DeWees says in his book, "I've worked very, very hard, but it's not complicated work. I basically just do the same thing every day, over and over again."[17] Repetition is absolutely critical. Don't do just do it once. *Live* by it.

You know those people. The ones that you text your address to, or your contact information. You know you've done it before: you see it right there in the text thread. Yet here they are, for the third time, asking for your address…or your website. They are too lazy to flick their finger just that little bit to scroll up and find your contact information, because they were already too lazy to grab it the first time you sent it to them. It's far, far easier for them to simply place the onus back on you to *resend*, rather than for them to actively seek to find it. I don't cater to that.

Give a man a fish, feed him for a day. Teach a man to fish, feed him for a lifetime. Buddy, you can search for that information, and in so doing, realize that you're disorganized, and in so doing, start getting organized, and in so doing, stop making me do your work for you.

People like this are walking umbilical cords that plug into you and drain you, drain *your* time, drain *your* energy, because they're just not motivated to plug into organization, to stay plugged into success. They bleed your patience dry, and they're a giant time suck. And last I checked, nature abhors a vacuum.

When such family or friends – yea, even potential customers – ask yet again for my website or contact info or something I've already told them, I'll redirect them to scroll through the messages…or better yet, I simply won't respond. Ha!

Ultimately, if they want to contact me, they'll look for it and find it, and thus be empowered in their detective work. It's right there; they just don't want to look it up. I won't do it for them, especially if they're responding to a message of mine that contains my signature….which contains my contact information.

And then there's the other people. Those idiots who are driving in the lane to your left, and with ten spare feet before you, they think they can merge right in front of you to take a right turn at the next street.

Or the maniacs in the fast lane who veer across four lanes with a hundred feet to spare just so they can take that exit. It's selfish, it's disorganized, it's failure to plan, which is the same as planning to fail. Such people are dangerous, and don't deserve a driver's license. They put your very life in danger.

Don't be a maniac. Get organized, and you'll beat other professionals to the clients that are waiting for someone organized.

I'll cite Paul Strikwerda again, when he says "Just think of a few people who 'have made it.' Do they seem distracted or dedicated? Are they bad planners or are they well organized? Do they focus on futilities or do they lead their lives 'on purpose'? More importantly, do they zoom in on what they want, or on what they don't want?"[18] You must be organized and focused.

I'd highly recommend Thibaut Meurisse's books. He's an audiobook client of mine, and, as of this writing, I've narrated seven self-help books of his, including his entire "Master Yourself" series. He is an incredible and insightful writer, and Master Your Focus is a worthy book on this subject.

Additionally, you need to have goals. S.M.A.R.T. Goals. Specific, Measurable, Attainable, Realistic/Relevant and Time Bound. Goals that you can't see are no goals at all. You must know where you're heading and track your progress there. Every single day I work off of a Goals Worksheet, tracking things like sending 50 advertising emails, connecting with at least 20 people on LinkedIn, following at least 10 video producers or businessperson on Twitter, sending at least 20 Instagram emails, contacting 20 E-Learning developers, 20 realtors, 20 casinos, 10 Vimeo producers, posting a new ad or meme, doing searches on Craigslist, etc.. Every. Single. Day. Rinse and repeat. Over and over. These are my daily goals which ensure that I'm feeding the pipeline. They're how I stay organized and focused. Without goals, you're wandering adrift aimlessly on the Spaceship of Frail Hope.

OLDER BROTHERS SUCK

I'm a bit OCD. OK, I'm a lot OCD. I'm certifiably OCD about cleanliness and organization. While I'm no Tony Shaloub *Monk,* I'm definitely on the want-to, *nay,* need-to-keep-things-organized side. As a businessman, I've always run a tight ship. It's been essential for me to maintain a smooth operation, find my files quickly, get to where I need to go, take care of tasks that require me to, and keep my finger on the pulse of my operation. Without the ability to be organized, I would lose sight and sink.

My older brother was not the most ideal older brother. He still isn't. If there was a trade-in program, I would have taken it. Right after I made my bed when I was a kid, he would be lurking outside my door and would throw it open, come flying across the room, and jump on my bed and wriggle around, messing it all up. And I would be disassembled with rage.

My brother would intentionally disrupt my bed, my heart, my life, in that one act, and I'd have to do it all over again. And then there would be the horrible PTSD and anxiety from not knowing when he'd strike again, entering my room, my *sanctum,* without my blessing, and defiling my most holy place. OK that was a bit dramatic, but still: *Grrrr.*

I'm past it. I'm not bitter. Don't judge me. *runs and makes bed with military cadence just in case*

MY OUTLOOK ON LIFE

I live and die by Outlook. Email, Calendar, Contacts, Reminders, Notes. Sure, there are comparable programs such as OpenOffice, FreeOffice, LibreOffice, etc. I have been with Outlook when it was Schedule+ way back when Grover Cleveland was present, and I ain't leavin' now. It's enabled me to stay organized with calendars, contacts, reminders, and most importantly, email. But that's just software. My preference for something to keep me organized stems from a desire to be organized.

Do you use email signatures? I do. In fact, I have *entire* emails created as "email signatures" in Outlook. Rather than having to type up the same email over and over again, i.e., a marketing message, I use a premade email signature as *the entire body text of my email*. It's great for contract emails, invoice emails, marketing emails, and more. Why copy and paste? Why retype? Create entire emails based out of the signatures. This is very easily done in Microsoft Outlook and elsewhere.

My making my bed and wanting to keep things at parallel angles since a young age is part of my makeup. I would have made a great drill sergeant if I wasn't such a white-bread tenor. The lengths that the military goes to in order to keep hair trimmed, beds made, closets neat, shoes lined up, and uniforms impeccable is, well, impeccable. That's what I've wanted.

Granted, here and there my pages are angled on my desk. But they do sit crisscrossed with other papers, if they're in the same stacked pile, so I keep them distinct and separate.

I *love* Outlook. I think it's wonderful. All of my contacts in one place. All of my emails in one place, organized – *mais oui!* – by folder according to client or subject. All of my calendar appointments, popping up helpful reminders for me to handle tasks. It's wonderful. It's fast. It's robust. I live and die by it because it's saved me so much time hunting for contact information. It's eliminated the uncertainty of what's happening with my day. It's all right there.

That organization also helps me to respond to emails with lightning quickness, whether I'm at my desk or mobile. I've actually had clients joke "I got your response to my email before I even sent my email."

I don't know about you, but I *loathe* waiting for a reply to my inquiry emails. Oftentimes when I send out an inquiry for a handyman to fix something at our home (you know, because I'm generally inept) I fire off seven or eight emails to contractors on Craigslist. The one who replies right away is always the one who gets my attention. The one who replies weeks later, asking me "do you still need the work done?" is deplorable. Why would I be waiting that long for their quote? I've moved on.

How do you expect to get or keep work with such infrequent and tardy communication? People want answers *now*. My customers are no different. I can't tell you how many times I'm emailed, "Wow, that was quick!" Or "Thanks for the speedy reply!" It is my pride and delight to reply quickly and give them the answers that they need and deserve, in order to give myself work that I need and deserve.

Look, you don't have to run out and buy Microsoft Office 365. But at least find similar software like OpenOffice, or if you're just looking for an Outlook clone, you can use something like emClient. Great software + great organization = great success. A winning formula. Don't rely on notes and scattered documents in different places. Don't do it. Get organized.

GET 'EM RECORDED

Another indispensable tool in my life is my voice memo app. I'll probably develop senility or dementia because I commit all of my important reminders to a smartphone program: the invaluable, indispensable Voice Memo app. It's something I've used in one form or another for several years now, whether it be a microcassette recorder, a digital recorder, or now, an app. I've committed literally a few *days* of my life across 46 years into the memory banks of these little devices, because what I'm thinking of right then and right there is too important to forget. I can try to commit it to memory, but what's going to happen when I get home? Heck, with my preschooler-brain, which remembers only Pixar characters, what's going to happen when I get home? I'll be inundated by little people, and will forget to take care of…hmm…what was it again?

It's literally been my best friend in business. It's saved me in times of crises…it's helped me stay on top of what I've needed to take care of in order to function at my highest capacity.

Voice Memos allow me to offload my important thoughts into temporary storage so I can stay untethered as best as I can, go on with my day, and then upon returning home, take care of all of the memos I've recorded, or make a note to act on them later. They're that critical to my optimum functionality.

As a business owner, you have to find and implement tools all the time that will help you improve productivity. If it's a productivity tool, check into it – it just might shave valuable hours off of your week. Like this next one.

A SHORTCUT TO QUICKNESS

Keyboard Shortcuts. This is a highly productive tool that helps me stay organized, and something I discovered entirely on my own. They are "text replacement" on iPhone. (Hint: They're in the settings menu, under Settings > General > Keyboard > Text Replacement.) They are a massive time saver. MacOS has the same thing as iOS and generally completes phrases with a two-, three-, four- or more-letter phrase that autocompletes and types up something so you don't repeatedly need to.

Mac does this by default in most cases. And there are PC programs that do the same thing, that you can download, i.e., PhraseExpress. Same thing. Other programs include TextExpander, AutoHotKey, Breevy, and the like. They're all *such* timesavers!!! I don't want to waste time. The point being, why continue to type the same @#&*(#$% thing over and over and over…and over again – such as a marketing message in a cold email to a prospective client – when you can simply type "vm" (voiceover marketing message, that's just the acronym I gave it to make it manageably short) and have it automatically convert to your marketing message. Case in point, when I just typed that into this manuscript, it pasted my marketing message right here. So, I type "vm", and it gets converted automatically to:

Hi there! I saw your page and was just wondering if you keep a roster of reliable voice actors for your projects? Could you use one that delivers fast & right the first time? I've been doing voiceovers since 1993, and I'm an established name. Many clients have trusted me to tell their story, including 4Ocean, Nutrisystem, Cadillac, Wrangler, Deloitte, John Deere, Unicef, Microsoft, Enterprise Rent-a-Car, and more. You can hear my demos at asupervoice.com. Thanks for considering me! I look forward to hearing back.

Neat, huh?

BRING IN THE HOOVER

I'm one of those people that panic when my phone battery drops below 99%. *Where's a charger?!?! I need a charger!* I can be a bit OCD with that. I also have to clear out all the little red badges on the apps on my phone because a red badge signifies to me that there is something still outstanding, and I want to make sure everything is taken care of in a timely fashion.

But what about you? What else needs to be vacuumed up, cleaned and organized? How are your file folders, meaning both hard copies in a file cabinet, as well as file folders on your computer desktop? How are files named? Are they named with a naming convention prefix of "year-month-day" (i.e., 2019-07-01) so that they always appear in chronological order? How are your documents organized? Can you find them easily? Are they labeled with generic filenames, or with keyword descriptors so you can search for them and actually know where they are?

How's not only your desktop, but your *desktop*? Is it clean and tidy, or is piled up with content innumerable?

How are your Internet browser tabs? Are they scattered? Is one of them playing music and you can't find which one? Are you still using Internet Explorer? MacOS Leopard? Windows XP?

How's your backup system? Do you go to a redundant hard drive? A separate server? The cloud? All of the above? What would happen on the day a meteor hits your house (just yours)? What would you do? That is the million dollar question – would it cost a million dollars to replace everything you lost? Would even a million dollars be able to replace such precious content?

In your moment of need, where you're trying hard to find that one demo to send to an interested party that only wants a Dutch-middle-aged-female-Klingon-impression, would you be able to find it? Or would they move on from you to simply throw casting out there on the online marketplaces, because you can't find it and could only assure them with a "Trust me; I can do it"?

Bring in the Hoover. Put on the apron. Pull out the Endust. Let's start cleaning and get you more organized. It's the key to being a smooth operator.

Stars, Listens & Likes Oh My

ALWAYS REMEMBER: Someone's endorsement of you...or lack thereof...has very little to do with your trajectory.

You know that funny feeling you got in your tummy when you fell in love as a lanky, scrawny teenager? Or that feeling you get when you walk into a room and everyone was there in the dark, and they jump out and yell *SURPRISE!!* Or that sensation you get when you do that voiceover and you catch yourself out in the wild on the radio, in a commercial, or before a movie? And even when you get a trophy after a race, or you win first prize?

It's rewarding. It's affirming. It's a celebration of living life and of accomplishment. Of something happening that's monumental. In short, it's being accepted. In short, it's being chosen.

In Voiceovers – and in business - that's what our careers are all about: being chosen. When I was awarded my first Nutrisystem national TV spot[19] in 2017, I was chosen out of 103 other competitors. I was elated! I was so grateful and walking on Cloud Nine.

When we're chosen to voice a particular project, the die has been cast, and our name comes up, it's fantastic and wonderful. But what about all those other races-in-the-running, where we're striving neck and neck with other just-as-talented colleagues, our friends, our voiceover family, and we're running at breakneck speed toward that Finish Line called "Chosen"? What happens until that point? Do we get hung up on wanting to be heard, liked, listened to, thumbs-upped, loved, affirmed, celebrated, accepted, chosen? Do we enter a state of suspended animation while we wait patiently for the results? In that breathless hum of still silence, what happens?

EYES ON THE PRIZE

I'm gonna go all Biblical on y'all. 1 Corinthians 9:24 says *"Do you not know that in a race all the runners run, but only one gets the prize? Run in such a way as to get the prize."* Wow! There's no mention of standing still and waiting to see if we're accepted and chosen? Nothing about sitting there twiddling our thumbs and hinging our confidence and sense of self-worth on whether or not a thumbs-up icon appears? Not a single reference to pacing, waiting to see if we've even been listened to? Nothing about star ratings?

Nope. It's eyes on the prize, baby. It says "run". It doesn't say stop, or even pause. It's a constant marathon, not a sprint...it's a never-ending race, not a quick jaunt. The race of voiceovers began when you first decided to lend your voice to people's ears and stepped out in faith in trusting that you'd one day be chosen...and it doesn't ever end. And when you "finish" the race, another race opens up anew before you. A race of yet another contest. A race of continued focus on being chosen, and neither hanging your hat on, nor holding your breath for, results that signify to you that you *might* finish first in the previous race.

But really? Who even cares? It's a race, stupid. (Sorry.) *Run.*

KEEP GOING

In voice acting, as with actual acting, it's a numbers game, and it always will be. You reap what you sow. You *must* be willing to get back up and hop back into your studio – even if you *just* sat down to process auditions you just did. The numbers are always against you. And as Morpheus said to Neo in *The Matrix*, "Time is always against us." There are hundreds of others throwing their hat in the ring too. What have you got to lose by throwing your hat in the ring and auditioning? More to the point, what do you have to lose by *persisting* in throwing your hat, even when it seems like that particular voiceover job is out of your caliber or comfort zone? You do stretch before a race, don't you? Why wouldn't you stretch yourself for this one?

My point is this: keep going. Don't sit and wonder. Don't wait for the results of a previous audition and let them hold you back and impact your confidence level and sense of readiness to run a new race. You're better than that. *Keep going.*

Audition, audition, audition. And when you're done, audition some more. Then, in your spare time, audition. And if you can't find something to do, audition. *Run that race and don't look back.* There are plenty of opportunities out there. And if you're not on any of the pay-to-play sites or suffering a lack of actual audition material, then do some practice reads and send them to mentors...or family...or friends...and allow them to critique you and help you grow in your running ability. I've auditioned for jobs in March and been awarded them in July. I've auditioned for them in September and been awarded them in February. You never know when that award will come back around, so stop waiting for it and checking on the results. Leave the Stars, Listens & Likes (Oh my!) behind you.

And one more thing? Always do auditions before you go to record your booked jobs. The booked jobs are booked, so relax. Invest into the future and continue to work towards new clients. Have something coming down the pipeline at all times. Additionally, when you're done with that salad of an audition, you're then warmed up for the actual meat and potatoes of the actual paid job.

Regardless of whether or not you actually "get the prize" from a previous audition, don't look backward. Runners look forward. It's how they avoid obstacles – like worry. Like concern over previous performance. Don't look back.

You can't steer your life by the rearview mirror. My good friend Paul Strikwerda says, "Treat your audition like a balloon. Let it go! The end result is up in the air anyway."[20] Outstanding way to put it.

RATINGS CAN BE DECEIVING

Just like the movies and all the critics and panners, looks can be deceiving. Did you know *Avengers* received poor reviews?[21] Did you know that *Psycho*, *The Shining* and *Fight Club* all got negative reviews when they first premiered? Critics are often wrong![22] Plenty of evidence to support that they are.

Here's a good example. In one coaching session with my coach and dear friend Scott Burns[23], we were approaching our own finish line of sorts: 4pm. (Our coaching sessions ran from 3pm to 4pm.) When 4pm rolled around, Scott asked me, generously (because that's who he is), "This is great stuff! You wanna keep going?!?!" He wasn't asking so that he could charge me overtime by the way – he was genuinely interested because we were on a roll. But unbeknownst to him, I had been eyeing my email and seeing audition opportunities come through. I saw one in particular and just *knew* I could do it well. I told Scott, "Actually, buddy, I would *love* to – but you've lit a fire under my butt, and I have some auditions waiting, and I really feel like I can do them well." So, we parted, I did the audition, and I seriously knocked it out of the park. It was SO good. I mean, cherry pie good. Summer BBQ good. Wizard of Oz good. Living in Heaven good. *Running in such a way as to win the prize good.* I seriously hit a home run. (It may have actually landed in another zip code).

For the next few days, I anxiously awaited. I think it was a decent-paying job, if I remember...but I don't remember the content. I just remember that I nailed it. That's all I needed. I was *going* to get that job, or my name isn't *Aaron Ryan, Voiceover Talent Supreme*. I was so deliriously giddy and staring at my inbox, just *waiting* for that Voice123 job to approve me. I eagerly checked back on the audition results over the next day. Waiting, waiting, waiting. At one point, I checked back in, and finally saw the result there, waiting for me, in all its glory, pronouncing my utter victory and being chosen at last, hahaha!! Oh glory be!!!!!

One star.

Wait, what?

Out of four stars.

Actually, I didn't say "Wait, what?" I screamed *"WHAT?!?!?!?!"*

25% goodness, out of 100%.

You have got be kidding me!!!

Last place.

I. Was. Incredulous. I simply couldn't believe it! *But* ... *but* .... *But* ... I stammered. I knocked that audition outta the park! I was floored. And thus, subsequent diminishing ensued, such as "they don't know talent from a hole in the wall." "They're crazy." "Their loss, not mine." And the inevitable, *"Whatever."* I must say, it really wrecked my day, and I became a sulk-fest.

I hung my hat on four stars...or c'mon, gimme at least three! But only *one???* Ridiculous.

That taught me a very hard lesson NOT to rely on the star system of Voice123[24] (which thankfully has been done away with) ...or the thumbs up/listened system of Voices...or the rating system of VoiceRealm (which I've since left; they're appalling and juvenile). I could have been rated one out of four stars for any one of a number of reasons! Try these:

- I was their fourth choice out of four.
- Their ex-husband was named Aaron
- They were bloated from lunch
- Jupiter wasn't aligned with Pluto
- Their baby girl accidentally clicked the one star (and then submit) when she was watching ABC Kid TV (PSA: now *CocoMelon!*) on their phone
- It was a Thursday

I prefer Reason Number One. But who knows?!?! And honestly, who cares. Really? *Who... freaking... cares. Run that race.* I had to keep going and chalk it up to experience, and just know that it's ok. It doesn't matter one bit. Regardless of whether or not they interpreted it as a home run, *I still hit a home run.*

Go. Just go. I mean it. Go. Hey, are you still here?

Go run that race and don't look back. We all like affirmation, sure. Just don't stand still, looking back and waiting anxiously because you're captive to the results of the previous race. Don't let everyone else hurtle past you toward the finish line and you haven't left the gate just because you need to know whether... [insert whatever you've been waiting on here.]

I'm an author as well. Every time one of my books hits the bestseller list, or reaches #1, it's AWESOME. It's an affirmation of sorts. But I know that in a few days, it will start its lonely abysmal slide, and I'll have to work the marketing ropes again to get it back up there. Rinse and repeat. It never ends. What helps me is that I know I wrote something good, and that's all that matters. Not people's acceptance of it.

Expenses Vs. Investments

SO MUCH TO SPEND, SO LITTLE TIME

So what's to do? What's to be done? You want to be successful in voiceovers and you have equipment to purchase. Do you get your equipment on eBay, Craigslist, Amazon, elsewhere? Do you spend a little bit more money and go through Sweetwater? B&H? Do you buy ProTools? Or do you drop all the way back down to Audacity simply because it's free? There are so many choices to make in order to run a successful voiceover business and have what you need to be able to produce good quality voiceovers as a professional voiceover artist. There are so many choices to make if you want to become a successful entrepreneur.

HARDWARE

Let's talk about hardware first. From my own personal experience, I like to spend a *decent* amount of money and get a huge bang for my buck. I don't like to spend a *massive* amount for high-end software that I may ultimately be disappointed with. The same is true for hardware purchases. At the time, I didn't want to pull the trigger on a venerable $1000 Sennheiser MKH 416 mic because I can do pretty much just as much with a microphone that is $400-$500 less and still get tremendous broadcast quality. So personally, I decided (notice I didn't say "settled") on the Neumann TLM 102 mic. A fantastic mic which performed fantastically! And then I ultimately upgraded to the 416. How do I determine if that's a necessity? We'll get to that later, I promise.

And then as far as a preamp, I got the Grace M101, since it was recommended to me by my coach, the wonderful Scott Burns. For my interface, I got a Scarlet FocusRite 2x2. For my reference monitors, I really wanted to have good reference monitors and I didn't mind buying a little bit more higher end monitors, so I got Yamaha HS5's.

Beyond that, I did need a good quality shock mount for my Neumann mic, and I needed good cabling, and I needed a good studio.

All told, the studio was the most expensive thing at $1800 for a custom build. That in itself is where I start, and that's where my audio dies if it's not good. You really do need to have a tremendous environment for recording your professional voiceover audio, or it could be all for naught. So, after you factor that in, my mic was 600-ish dollars, my reference monitors were about $400, the peripheral equipment like the preamp and my Scarlet for another $400. Cables and sundry and all of that were maybe another $100. Not too shabby. I already had a good decent working computer that could handle processing not just raw audio but audio that was laden with all kinds of EQ and plug-ins in order to have it sound broadcast-ready. For that, I recommend Reaper, which leads us into software.

The point is, I spent thousands and thousands of dollars on hardware, because I needed the best, because I wanted to *be* the best.

SOFTWARE

On the software side, I started out in video editing - so I was very familiar with Sony Vegas Pro (which I already had), and I knew that it came with a decent audio interface for editing audio as well, so I decided to just use that. It has its pros and its cons, and of late, it has had more cons then pros. So, I moved on to iZotope RX6 Advanced, but found that it was a little slow at real-time editing, and I needed to do processing after all of my material has been recorded. All of that takes time.

Finally, after a little bit more searching, I landed on Reaper. As a PC user probably until I die - just simply due to the fact that that's where I started and that's what is most familiar - I absolutely *love* Reaper. Though just $60 in price, it's worth $60,000 to me. The capabilities are tremendous: it is very robust software with tremendous functionality potential, and it is incredibly fast. FX and plug-ins render in real time and I'm not sitting around processing a bunch of audio after I've recorded it, which just takes forever. It is fantastic. For the price, you would do very well to get Reaper if you're on a PC. Reaper also works on a Mac!

Many people swear by ProTools, although it is expensive. You can use something as simple as TwistedWave, Logic Pro X, or of course Adobe Audition. Then of course there is Audacity, which is free…but it's free for a reason. It's not a comprehensive piece of software, has no plug-in stack, and rendering to .wav or .mp3 is fine but time-consuming as it doesn't natively allow you to use those raw files unless you render them.

With so many choices, I would highly suggest downloading free demos of each, so that you can get familiar with what the software operates and feels like. Of course, on both platforms, you have the ability to make a monthly purchase to use software like Adobe Audition, which is an industry standard, and it should be: it's super good and robust software. Audition works for both PC and Mac. But Reaper is my personal favorite.

I did not want to make a monthly payment *ad nauseum* for my software, so I elected to simply buy it outright in the case of iZotope, Reaper, and Sony Vegas. But that's just my choice. If you are comfortable working on a subscription basis, feel free to make a monthly payment for Adobe Audition which runs around $30 a month.

SOURCECONNECT

Beyond that, there's additional functionality-based software that you can purchase such as SourceConnect which is another $30/month subscription, or you can buy the Standard version for $650. SourceConnect allows you to be slightly more competitive in the field because you have the ability to record and provide the files immediately to the client with them on the line…they receive it in nearly real time. And oftentimes you don't have to do any sort of processing on the audio in the end, because they just take the raw .wav files and do everything with them on their own end. Very little work for not a huge investment.

That's the keyword here: *Investment.*

The point, yet again, is, I spent thousands and thousands of dollars on software now as well, because I needed the best, because I wanted to *be* the best.

PLANNING FOR SUCCESS

If you really want to be a successful professional voiceover artist – or in any entrepreneurial pursuit for that matter, you need to look at expenses as *investments*, not as expenses. An expense is something that gets you from A to B. An investment is something that has the potential to get you from A-to-Z eventually. It's buying the higher priced item because it's more powerful and will last longer than the lower priced item. It's paying that little bit extra because you know that this will last you a long time.

Investments also have a psychological effect in that you are looking far more long-term than an expense looks into the future. An expense is *reactive*; whereas investment is *proactive*. It's looking to the long term. Anytime I make money from a voiceover job, I'm thinking, "how can I invest that back into my business and graduate to the next level of competitiveness or the next level of functionality, or the next level of proficiency?" Ultimately, I want to be one of the key players in the professional voiceover artist industry, and I can only do that by treating my business as such: a *business*. Not a hobby.

Once you switch from the expense mindset to the *investment* mindset, you'll be propelling yourself into the future. Seriously! And believe me, it goes without saying that I know *all too well* that so many entrepreneurs start and stop at the very beginning because of all the startup costs. But once you make that mental switch from expense to investment, you'll begin to see the long term, and you'll begin to see long-term goals and shoot for them rather than simply handling short term needs. If startup expenses scare you, then you need to perhaps refine your focus of what an entrepreneurial pursuit consists of. Every single one of them requires startup costs. And the startup costs for voiceovers are minimal by comparison. Take getting into cosmetology: it could be anywhere from $5000 to $20,000![25] A career in voiceovers doesn't require as much of you.

I believe in you! I've said it before, I'll say it again: You can do this. Treat your expenses as investments into your business and you'll grow.

Eventually, in the long run, you can afford some of the higher end stuff. The 416. The StudioBricks. The custom builds. Pro Tools. Whatever. Work with what you have now, do the very best you can with it, make your money, and then put some of that money back into upgrading your existing setup.

To quote my good friend and audiobook client Thibaut Meurisse, "Upgrade yourself."[26]

Time to reframe your focus.

Time to invest into, and thus rev up, your voiceover business.

On December 9, 2008, negotiators revealed the terms of an emerging deal between the White House and Congress under which a short-term $15 billion bailout for the Big Three would be overseen by a federal "car czar" or trustee. This was known as the "government bailout." Why was this done? To *stimulate the economy*. To *increase* business. It was done because of a diehard belief in investing into something worth growing.

If by now you're still reluctant to invest into the economy of your own voiceover business, then perhaps you deserve to go bankrupt. Just sayin'.

Your Life Is A Ministry

YEAH. IT'S A MINISTRY.

Let's talk about ministry for a moment. There are all kinds of ministries out there. And sometimes, the very word "ministry" can be a term that just makes you cringe. *Ugh, not those Christians again.* Or maybe you've had a bad experience with a ministry. *There's no way I'll donate to that ministry again – they're a bunch of crooks!* Or perhaps you've served and just gotten burnt out on ministry and lost love for it, and have nothing left to give. To quote Buttercup: *I will never love again.*

As a businessperson, how does ministry even pertain to voiceovers in the slightest? What do they have to do with each other in any way shape or form?

Let's explore it together.

WHAT IS MINISTRY?

First of all, what is ministry? Isn't it an outreach of some kind, an attempt to connect with others, to serve them, for their benefit, so that they are edified, affirmed, helped, or loved? To explain further, ministry and Christianity are mutually exclusive; they don't have to belong in the same sentence. Ministry is not a term coined by the Christians nor the Red Cross. It's not owned by either, and there's no claim made to it. Ministry is simply, according to Merriam Webster:

ministry
 noun
min·is·try | \ ˈmi-nə-strē \
plural **ministries**
Definition of *ministry*
1: MINISTRATION the ingenuity of destruction … had outrun the *ministry* of healing— Dixon Wecter
2: the office, duties, or functions of a <u>minister</u> was well prepared for the *ministry*

3: the body of ministers of religion : CLERGY joined the Presbyterian *ministry*
4: a person or thing through which something is accomplished : AGENCY, INSTRUMENTALITY heroic believers become such by the *ministry* of heroic pain— Austin Phelps
5: the period of service or office of a minister or ministry. Many reforms were enacted during his *ministry*.
6 *often capitalized*
a: the body of ministers governing a nation or state from which a smaller cabinet (see CABINET entry 1 sense 3b) is sometimes selected
b: the group of ministers constituting a cabinet
7a: a government department presided over by a minister the *Ministry* of Foreign Affairs
b: the building in which the business of a ministry is transacted

I like definition number four. A person or thing through which something is accomplished. So, what is *something* then? It's the opposite of nothing. When I do nothing for anyone, no one benefits. (Except maybe me when I need one of those movie nights with my feet up and I don't need to serve anyone). But when I do something for someone, both of us benefit. Both the server and the servee (I just coined that) benefit. We both receive some kind of joy and fulfillment through the service.

Ministry is, to me at least, an outreach of giving, whether that's through finances, service, or other resources.

HOW ARE VOICEOVERS A MINISTRY?

I once did a voiceover for a church video. I had no idea what I would be seeing. I was simply given a script. I couldn't see the end product, and no clue what they were producing. It was up to ME to breathe life into that script. It was spellbinding in every way, and I got to minister that message to people.

Another example. I was recently tasked with narrating an audiobook on tithing. I'm a Christian, so this is an easy fit for me, because it's Biblical, and I believe it. So, I narrated it. I wasn't prepared for a story of giving (cited in the book) to hit me so emotionally at one point while voicing it. It was absolutely *moving*, and I had to choke back tears as I was reading it. That narration actually ministered to *me,* the voice talent. I was nearly crying!

Ultimately, however, this project and the one before it were opportunities for ministry. I wasn't hired to simply read words. I was hired to lift them off of the page, to float them through my microphone, down the XLR cable, into the computer, into my DAW, into the mp3 file, into WeTransfer, into the client's computer, into their video editing program, into their video, into the finished product, into whatever medium they were broadcasting it in, and then into the listener's or viewer's ears. But it didn't stop there. It went into their heart too. At least, that's always the goal. The goal is to *minister* to your listener. The goal is be a person or thing through which something is accomplished.

The ministry of giving is the ministry I employ here. When I narrate, I give. It is our job, our pleasure, our *ministry,* to *give* through narration.

WHAT'S THE "SOMETHING"?

As a voiceover artist, it's always my goal to bring words to life. To transport the listener. When I was hired by *Discover Long Island* to bring their words to life, I had to envision all of the places that they were describing, as I am neither from there nor have I ever been there. But when I saw the finished video, it ministered to me, much like the church video I mentioned above.

The "something", whatever it is: only you can figure out what you're supposed to do with any given script. But for me, the "something" that I'm supposed to accomplish is:

Not sound like I'm reading
Whisk the listener away to a different time or place
Make them feel emotion
Try to give them goosebumps
Compel
Urge
Inspire
Motivate
Call to action

I can only accomplish that something when I *earnestly believe* what it is that I'm reading. That's the only way that something can be accomplished through what I do. That's the only way real ministry can happen.

Now, when the Red Cross serves, or the Union Gospel Mission doles out soup or soap, or World Vision brings support to communities, or Habitat for Humanity builds houses, they're all performing a ministry, a "something" that is being accomplished through them. Why should voiceovers be any less of a ministry? I am hired to help accomplish something through what I do. That, my friends, is a ministry. Whether you're being asked to tug at heartstrings or appeal to pocketbooks, the goal is the same. Whether you're being asked to promote a car or a homeless shelter, to plead the case for that new truck or saving those feral cats and dogs, the goal is *always* the same.

The something I'm trying to accomplish is every bit the something that the video producer wants to accomplish…or at least it sure needs to sound like that.

Do I always hit my mark? Not always. Some are goofy reads…some are less emotional. Some don't make you weep, they make you smirk. Are those any less of a ministry? Nope. A child can be inspired through a goofy cartoon. A family can dream about that new minivan. A businessman who works too hard can dream about getting away for a vacation in Long Island. It's my job to make that as real as possible. To minister to them.

The only area of voiceovers that is prohibited from being any kind of a ministry for me is with my son. My toddler is emphatically against me reading Storytime to him in any accent whatsoever. If I slip into my British accent to read the book that way, the immediate response I get…and I do mean immediate…is "NORMAL!" He wants me to read it normal. Aside from that little sidebar, voiceovers are still a ministry. My son will eventually learn that his Dada has the greatest British Storytime accent. His eyes will be opened in time.

What's your ministry?

Running A Successful Business Of...Anything

CAN YOU RUN A BUSINESS?

Lest this book be entirely comprised of levity or emotion, let me offer you a bulk of substance right here and now.

So here it is. The chapter you've been waiting for.

Let's make one thing clear. I'm a businessman first, and one that happens to do voiceovers. It should always be your identity first, and then your craft. If you put your craft before your identity, you're limiting yourself in terms of income, goals, scope, forecast, abilities, reproducibility, and long-term projections. Your identity is the basis for all you do. I am a businessman. I'm intent on running a business, and that business involves voiceovers. As my friend Paul says, "If we believe that what we do professionally defines who we are as a person, any blow to our business is personal. The truth is, what we do professionally is only a small aspect of who we are and how we contribute to the world."[27]

You can do voiceovers as a hobby, or you can do voiceovers as a business. The choice, and the subsequent income tier, is entirely yours. Is business scary? Indeed it is. It's fraught with all kinds of risks. "Successful entrepreneurs don't start a business to explore options or to enjoy a hobby. They don't 'give things a try.' Opening up shop is not an experiment. It's a calculated risk."[28] That's from Paul again. He chose to treat his business as a *business* and not a hobby. Do you want to *try* voiceovers, or run a *business* of voiceovers? They're not one and the same.

But believe it baby. It is entirely possible. The Great Prophet George Lucas once said, *"Your focus determines your reality."* Qui-Gon Jinn imparted that wisdom to a young Anakin Skywalker, and my life was never the same once that phrase clicked with me. I love that mantra! It's central to everything I do in voiceovers. I saw a meme of it in 2016 and it rocked my world. Think of it! Your *focus* determines your *reality*. Wow! What you intensely concentrate on and aim for dictates how your life will turn out, what you will receive, where you will be, etc. A truly amazing notion.

This is perhaps what this entire book is all about, and you're going to find a ton of gold nuggets in this chapter that you perhaps had never known to dig for. It all boils down to this question, and only you can answer this for yourself: Would you like to do voiceovers as a hobby, and make a bit of money, or would you like to do it as a business and make a *lot* of money?

In business, I've learned from another great phrase, and that's "It's not enough to stare up the steps; you have to step up the stairs." How incredibly true. You must move forward. You must develop unstoppable forward momentum. And to do that, you must take the first step toward your goals rather than looking longingly, wistfully upon them. The former takes you *there*. The latter keeps you *here*.

This book isn't just about voiceovers. It's about business. It's about running a business well. To do that, there is a lot to digest, a lot to assimilate, a lot to incorporate, and a lot to master. But with a few key details locked in, you can make sure that you're not a hobbyist. You can ensure your future as a successful voiceover *businessperson* as opposed to relegating voiceovers to the realm of hobby only. As I've said many times before to many a soul, I'll say again to you: YOU CAN DO THIS. Predating any major odyssey or trek, there's always that little thing called fear. Will I make enough? Will this work? Will I succeed? Will I regret it in the end? I love what Bill DeWees says about this: "The reality of success is only reached by passing through the barren wasteland of fear; however, anxiety and apprehension are natural to this process. Everybody experiences them. The question is not, 'Do you have fear?' because fear is inevitable. You cannot completely escape fear. The question is this – 'Do you have enough desire to carry you through the fear to reach genuine confidence?' That is the real question."[29] Amen, Pastor Bill.

RECIPE FOR SUCCESS

Here are more than a few tips to impart to you before you go launching into the great unknown of cyberspace intent on world domination with your fantastic voiceover skills. Remember that the entire world can see you. You can't get far in business these days without being on social media. They're so intertwined anymore, it's like having to throw the socks away after you've spent an hour peeling off the sap that your kid tracked in. The socks and the sap are now inseparable. What I mean is, Google and many search engines will index you higher if they keep seeing you here and there, especially, very active on the social media networks such as Facebook, LinkedIn, Reddit, Quora, Instagram, Twitter, Tumblr, Pinterest, forum boards, etc. The more active you are, the more Google will see you, and the more your SEO index will climb based on how many links there are floating around out there linking back to your site.

The point in all of that is that you must remember that the entire world can see you. Make sure that what you're throwing out there into cyberspace is the best representation of you. Make sure that it accurately portrays you in a non-incendiary light. In other words, don't burn your business reputation to the ground by consistently posting inflammatory political rants in the single Facebook profile that you have that you use for both business and personal posts. Your business message gets diluted – and in fact cheapened to the point of undesirability – the more you weaken it with neighboring political rants. I know of one businessperson who is a fierce Democrat who wildly posts anti-Trump messages all the time, and I wonder how much more successful he'd be if he were posting about his business all the time, and as fiercely. So please. Make a separate Facebook *page* for your business, and keep that page innocuous and antiseptic, full of palatable messages promoting your business, and not polluted by crazy rants.

Another thing. When you approach clients, they're not your best buddy you're sitting down to a beer with. Determine that you're going to communicate professionally. Don't use incorrect words in your proposals, i.e., "myriad." It means "many"; it's not a noun. For example, use it correctly when you say "There are myriad ways in which I can serve you" not, "There is a myriad of ways I can serve you." (This one gets my goat). Don't use crazy memes or emojis or GIF's in messages. Don't use crazy stationery or background patterns in your emails. Don't use lazy words like "prolly." It's *probably.* And don't use the shortened abbreviations for "You' such as "u." Don't say "cul8r." That's how you talk to your friends, or your BFF. Don't be lazy. Spell it out. Speak professionally, because you're speaking to professionals.

I highly advise getting your hands on a book called *The E-Myth* by Michael Gerber. In it he breaks down three critical roles played by a small business owner. They are:

- Technician – the person that actually gets the work done. This would be you recording, rendering and sending your auditions and recorded jobs.
- Manager – the person that manages the company. That would be you sending contracts and invoices, and doing marketing and accounting and taxes.
- Entrepreneur – the person that has the *vision*. This is the most critical role. You must have a forward- and upward-looking agenda driving you to succeed, to improve, to grow and blossom as a business. Yes, a business. Not just a person; a business. One of the goals that I try to check off my list every day is to spend 10 minutes brainstorming how I can A) benefit my business financially, and B) benefit the voiceover community as a whole through some new, unique offering.

You're going to have to be a technician, a manager, and an entrepreneur if you're going to go anywhere.

There are hordes of opportunities out there for you to grow. You can attend webinars put on all the time.

Several businesspersons have a side business of training and business coaching on the subjects of marketing and advertising. There are Facebook groups galore. There are Reddit groups galore. There are countless books on starting out in voiceovers. You will never want for resources in this industry. But the onus is on you to take advantage of them.

You don't want to just *reach* a bar. You want to *set* a bar.

Tip for you. Get a smartphone. It's your best friend in business. It helps you keep your finger on the pulse of your business. It enables you to reply to potential jobs when you're away from the office. You can use the Voice Memo app to record your thoughts when you're out and make sure you stay on top of things. It's called a smartphone for a reason. I use the latest iPhone, and it's a lifesaver. I mean it. I've been able to edit my website pages when I've noticed an error when I'm out. When I've been sick in bed, at least I can respond to potential customers that way (after I've woken up of course). When I've needed to catch up on industry blogs or webinars on the go, I can do that too. If you're living with a dumbphone still, you're living in the Stone Age and hindering your own progress. Might as well shoot yourself in the foot and get it over with. No really, shoot yourself. I'll hold.

So, what do you need to start a business, other than the dream of starting a business? Well, you'll need:

Business license. No brainer.

Stage name. Do you want to use one? Will you want privacy? Does anonymity serve you in your performance?

Resume. You use one to get work in the regular world, right? Why wouldn't you use one here, listing your voiceover experience and the clients you've served? Some websites and agencies will actually require this of you.

Branding & Logo. An image goes before you. A logo precedes you and equates your name with a visual reminder for clients to remember. Get something that is real, stylish and memorable. Get something that is you. Seen a black swish lately and thought "Hey, that's Nike!"? Same thing applies here. You want recognition. You want a stamp you can put on things to say "this is me and this is who I am." And beyond that, you need to figure out who you are, and what your story is. Celia Siegel has an excellent book called *"Voiceover Achiever: Brand Your VO Career. Change Your Life."* In it she declares "Branding has the uncanny ability to transform not only your voiceover career but your life – to give you the swagger and confidence to be who you truly are and pulverize the competition (while, of course, maintaining your good standing in the voiceover community). When you put branding at the heart of everything you do, you know where you're heading and you can sail through even the choppiest waters."[30] After reading Celia's book, I rebranded, and thus you see the "Superman"-inspired logo permeating this book, from the cover to the last page. My branding is "Super human being. Superhuman voice." I give back greatly to the VO community, as my love language is giving, and it brings me great pleasure to see others succeed. That's the first part. The second part deals with my diversity as a voice actor, being able to perform all kinds of genres and vocal styles that I've learned over the years, and been hired for. It fits me, and it's unique to me. Win, win.

Website. What kind of website will you develop? Will you do it yourself for free on Wix or Weebly? Or will you pay someone who is a pro at developing websites? (I highly recommend Chris Cummings with Integrity Web Design: chris@iwdonline.com). But please – for the love of Pete, whatever you do, do NOT get a forwarding domain and point it to your Voices.com or Voice123 profile pages. This is an instant disqualifier for many in the industry, especially agents. And why would you want to send a potential client to a site with thousands of your competitors anyway? Strikes me as a bit foolhardy. Don't do that. Get your own website, and it's best to have it designed by someone else who knows what they're doing, who can give you your money's worth and come up with something that is branded, that is an accurate reflection of you, and that really shows off your vocal flair. I purchase my domain names through GoDaddy, and I host my site at SiteGround – both for reasons of cost. I have a *lot* of domain names through GoDaddy, so I like to pay as little for them as possible. And I want fast hosting that loads my site quickly – so I host it at SiteGround. The choice is yours, but you want a website that is slick, easy to navigate, features your demos front and center, loads quickly, and is desktop- and mobile-friendly for purposes of SEO (which we'll discuss later).

Disposable Phone Number. Consider getting a disposable phone number from apps like Burner or Hushed. Protect your personal phone number *and* know when a call comes in that is specifically for business so you don't answer the phone as just "Hello?"

Computer. What type of workstation do you have? Will you use a cheapo donated computer, something handed down to you? Or will you seek to get something top-of-the-line that will last you years and years to come, with competitive specs? Don't shaft yourself here. You need a powerful tower to compete and produce. Will you go Mac? PC?

Internet Service. We use Frontier where I'm at, and that gives us 100 mbps down / 100 mbps up speeds. Those are amazing. There are Gigabit services you can use now as well. Sometimes, particularly for longform narration or unedited raw files, you'll need to upload massive .wav or AIFF files to the end user. You can use free services like Dropbox, OneDrive, Google Cloud, Amazon Cloud, iCloud, WeTransfer or HighTail...but whichever you choose, make sure you have the bandwidth to make use of sending your files to the cloud and not making your customer wait. Internet transfer speeds are getting exponentially better. And always use a LAN line instead of WIFI, by the way, as it for the foreseeable future it will always be faster and more stable.

Software. I talk about this more in depth in my book, "How do I get started in Voiceovers?", but ultimately, the choice is yours. Don't use Audacity, that's all I ask. There's a *reason* it's free. Many people use Adobe Audition. Or Reaper. I use Reaper. Or they use Logic Pro X or Twisted Wave. Or Pro-Tools, which is overkill. Don't use free software like Audacity or Garage Band. You need something that has a built-in and running-in-real-time plugin chain to make your files broadcast-ready while reviewing. You need something that will save you time and streamline your workflow. I love Reaper for its live plugin chain, simplistic interface, ease of use, punch-and-roll, custom programmable action sequences like macros, quick rendering, and customizable keyboard shortcuts. There are tons of videos online to help you make your choice and provide demo walkthroughs of your software.

Computer backups. This is so crucial in this day and age. At home, we have several computers, and they all dump their data from specific folders via AllWay Sync, a backup program, onto our "server." Those backups are automatic, pulling new files every 15 minutes. That server data is then backed up to the cloud using BackBlaze. I can also use the BackBlaze app and then be able to access my files on the go. I cannot tell you how many times this has saved me when I overwrote or deleted a file, or needed to access something on the go.

Taxes and accounting software. Quicken? Quickbooks? Peachtree? Something else? Make sure you treat your business like a business, and track your income and expenses so that you'll have everything you need for your Schedule C at the end of the year.

Contract and invoice templates. For goodness sake, do not go into *any* business dealings with *any* client without the protective cover of a contract. An agreement done over email with a text proposal and a "sure, go ahead" reply is *not* a contract. You need something fool proof, with legalese to cover your back. You need something ironclad that ensures that both you and your customer know full well the terms and conditions of your working arrangement, with particular emphasis on how, and more importantly, *when* (not if; *when*) you'll get paid. You must have a contract document in place with your logo, contact information and legal clauses on there in order to protect yourself. Anything less is inviting trouble and a dinner bell for predatory clients with nefarious motives.

Price list. We've discussed the GVAA rate guide. You can modify it and personalize it to suit you. Clients will ask you for your "rate card." Don't be stuck up a creek without a paddle and just say "uh…uh….". Have something ready to give them. Many times you'll be asked for a quote on a project. If you don't know what to quote, the client doesn't know what to decide as far having you do their voiceover.

Coaching. The very best expense (investment!) you can have before any hardware, software, resources, conferences, networking expenses, advertising expenses, or anything else. A coach can tell you A) if you have it, B) if you don't have it, and C) if you don't have it, how you get it. Coaching is <u>essential</u> in this business. I'll cover this more in depth in a later chapter.

Preferred Genre(s). What will your preferred voiceover genre(s) be? Do you like commercial or corporate voiceovers? Narration? IVR? Characters & animation? E-Learning? Audiobooks? It takes a big man to narrate audiobooks. I am not a big man. You must decide what your preferred genre(s) are and really lock and load on those genres. Give your clients your niche…make sure you have one. It's ok to specialize in multiple genres, but you should always have your niche voice and know what that is, in terms of branding and in terms of appeal.

Demo Reel. Unless you are an experienced audiophile with a great home studio and a knack for mixing and production, please don't do this yourself. Be sure to use someone that is heavily vetted, who can produce something impacting, professional, and hard-hitting. This is your calling card. This is what your clients will ask for before anything else. No demo reel (or crappy demo reel) = Nothing to go on = No clients interested in you. Additionally, you are not impartial or objective. Someone else, a professional, producing your demo will be impartial and will be able to provide you the very best scripts that highlight what makes you..._you_. There are people who produce demos for a living, and they do it well. The list goes on. As Chris Agos says, "without a demo, your career will be dead before it begins."[31] As far as what to put on your demo, listen to Elaine Clark. "The first cut on each demo is the most important. Lead with your 'money voice.' It should showcase your personality and signature way of interpreting copy. The last spot should be a callback, a reminder of who you are and what niche you fill. No matter how outrageous or diversified the spots are in the middle of the demo, the listener should never lose focus of who you are and what you have to offer."[32]

Payment Platforms. Decide if you want to use Paypal, Square, Venmo, Zenefits, ACH, ChasePay, Zelle, TransferWise, Bill.com, etc., or all of them. Checks and money orders work too, but ultimately it's the Digital Age – make sure you have at least two methods of digital currency exchange.

Taxes. Make sure you have good accounting software, or a good accountant, to help you stay up on paying your taxes. Voiceovers is a business, and as such, you need to responsibly pay taxes on your income.

Business cards. Planning to go to mixers, Meetups, Chambers of Commerce? You'd be a fool to go unequipped! Bring business cards, period. Have them professionally designed or go through an online service like VistaPrint or Zazzle to have them designed for you at an affordable cost so you have something you can pass out to prospective clients.

Voice Memos. These will save your business, and they might literally save your life. When you're out and about, and you have so much going through your head, you _must_ remember to stay on top of what you need to stay on top of. Offload your important thoughts and notes-to-self while you're out, so that you remember to take care of them when you get home.

Apparel. You'd be amazed at how many people look at your clothes when you're out, and how many people read what's written on your shirt. I *love* to go out to a public festival where there are lots of people around, wearing a shirt that says "ask me about voiceovers." How can I lose when doing so? Well, only if I forget to bring business cards too.

Advertising costs. Be willing to invest in putting yourself out there with Google ads, Facebook ads, Instagram ads, LinkedIn ads, etc. Try them! What harm can come of it?

Networking. Can you head out to a Chamber of commerce meeting? Can you connect with local business people who are looking for IVR? E-Learning? Promotional videos? Voices for their commercials? Yes, you can.

Marketing. It's been said that a career in Voiceovers is 85% marketing and 15% voiceovers. I would go so far as to say that's wrong. It's actually 95% marketing and 5% voiceovers. The smarter you market, the smarter you are. Always be on the hunt. The leads are out there. Don't put all of your eggs in the one basket of the pay-to-play's (P2P's) or with your agents. Be willing to track down potential leads and find your own business. I love what Thomas Edison said: "Genius is 1 percent inspiration and 99 percent perspiration." And I find what Bill DeWees has to say about it really insightful: "It seems to me most people approach a voice over business like winning the lottery, as if they think maybe voice over will provide a good retirement plan. This is just like people who think the lottery is a good retirement plan. They go out and buy a couple of lottery tickets every week, hoping they will hit the jackpot. Most voice over talents approach marketing as if they're playing the lottery. They get an agent, or more than one agent. They fill a few auditions and keep relying on their agents, hoping that something will eventually hit big. They hit for home runs only, and they wait around a lot." [33] Voiceovers is a *business*, not a hobby. Not a "try it out", "dip-my-toe-in-the-water" affair. It's an enterprise, and a career. It's not a get rich quick scheme. It's not even a get rich *slow* scheme. It's a methodical turning over of rocks every single day, looking for clients to market to. I will say it again: it's a *business*, not a hobby.

Blogging. This is so critical for the search engine optimization (SEO) of your website, and for engagement with clients, with fellow VO colleagues, and more. You can hold contests to drive up your subscriber base. You can write blogs and share them on social media, encouraging people to subscribe. You can comment on *other* people's blogs and link back to yours. Blogging shows Google that you're an authority on a subject, and it's a great way to keep your site fresh in the search engines, with fresh content.

Social Media. It's called that for a reason. In my old sales job there were people with "Commission breath." Don't be those guys. Start *real* conversations with people. Inquire into their lives. Sow into their lives. As Theodore Roosevelt said, "People don't care what you know until they know that you care." Show that you care by stopping trying to sell, and starting trying to develop relationships with potential clients. They'll appreciate you for your humanity and be more inclined to reward you with business. You've heard the saying. You never get a second chance to make a first impression. Paul Strikwerda talks about covert vs. overt marketing: "Overt Marketing is about you. Covert marketing is about the customer."[34] He also says "effective marketing is a compelling, engaging conversation. It's about building profitable relationships and creating an amazing experience around your brand, product or service."[35] That all starts with relationship first.

When you get clients, add them to a client list. Grow that sucker. Harvest every email from everyone who positively inquires in response to your marketing messages – these inquiries are called "buy signals" – and grow your own list of clientele, of cold leads, warm leads, and existing/repeat clients. That list is *gold* to you. Also remember, you should have two lists:

Your "featured" client list: those clients who have name recognition. For example, I wouldn't list the studio that got me the Nutrisystem job, I would list Nutrisystem itself as my client. They are the name that people will remember.
Your "actual" client list: Those production studios and audiobook authors and casting directors who you directly work with, who have hired you to voice for a product or a name brand or an audiobook.

Any responsible businessowner is going to conduct regular follow-ups and check-ins with previous clients. When they come to mind, contact them. Follow-up with them. Thank them for past work! *Compliment them* on their videos that they've produced using your voice. Be sincere! They want to know that they did a good job too. But make sure you stay top of mind with them. Check in with them at regular intervals and let them know that you're still here. Ask how the previous project turned out with your voice attached to it. See if they'll let you use it in your portfolio.

When you're done with a client on an online VO marketplace, ask for their contact information so you can convert them to a regular client and follow up with them. (Keep in mind that this is not possible on undesirable sites like The Voice Realm, which I'll cover later.) Clients aren't going to automatically remember you. They're bombarded with requests from voice talent to join their roster all the time. It's up to *you* to ensure that they remember you.

You can ask for ratings and reviews from clients as well. Facebook reviews, Yelp reviews, Google Local reviews, LinkedIn recommendations and endorsements, etc. This helps with your SEO and your online reputation as well. Offer a discount for doing so. This helps you establish your presence online, and by leaving you a review or endorsing you, they're doing you a favor. Do one for them in return by extending them a thank you discount.

Call them at Christmastime! Send them a follow-up postcard! Send them a customized mug with your info on it! Why not? Keep in touch with them and let them know that you appreciate them. Sure, they may throw the card in the trash. Or – they may say "Oh yeah!" and pin your card up on the wall for later recall and voiceover jobs. You can also friend them on Facebook if you're comfortable with that – but remember to, as I cautioned earlier, keep an eye on what you post.

Remember this: You don't want to lose a client because of incendiary political posts or annoying rants and tirades against whatever you feel frustrated with at any given moment.

Jobs are everywhere. You can get jobs from:

- Repeat customers
- Online marketplaces
- Direct emails out
- Direct Emails In
- Website inquiries
- LinkedIn
- Twitter

- Instagram
- Facebook
- Google ads
- YouTube
- Free forums
- Craigslist
- UpWork
- Alignable
- Phone calls
- Reddit
- Quora
- Blogging
- iTunes App Store
- Google Play Store
- Agents
- Vimeo
- Advertising on your car
- Wearing custom apparel
- Business networking meetings
- And more!

With YouTube in particular, you can go to a channel, click on the producer's name, and find their "about" information, if it's listed – contact them to offer compliments on their videos and channel, and to offer your services. YouTube has around one *billion* visitors per month!

Protect your auditions, especially if they're with a direct client with whom you've never done business before, or they're overseas. Watermark them. Swap a word. Fade them out at the end. Instead of reading their actual phone number in the spot, say "phone number". Instead of reading their actual website, say "website.com." Protect your product so that the client can't just run off with it and use it. At best, it would just result in a grudge. At worst, it could motivate you to get into a nasty court battle that might not end in your favor, and will undoubtedly cost more in the end than what you would have been paid just to record the job. Protect your interests with your auditions and also your recorded jobs. Your product is an intangible one: it's digital. Make sure you have strings attached to it until your services have been secured.

When you're done with a job, request release of payment and a positive review, and all of that. But – always make sure that you go into that process with the understanding that just because you recorded and sent the deliverables, that doesn't mean the job is automatically done. Expect changes. Go in knowing that there very likely will be punch-ins (not billable) and/or pickups (billable). Proceeding with that understanding puts you in a great space to be okay with whatever additions or changes come that may stall final payment. A job isn't final until it's final.

Speaking of jobs, remember this: A job is never a job until it's a job. Don't get your hopes up! When a client tells you "Oh yeah! We're *totally* gonna use you!", take that with a grain of salt. In your conversation with them, say "I look forward to partnering with you!" And in your mind say "Sure thing, pal. Moving on." And move on! Plant those seeds, water them, but don't throw all of your emotion and expectation into the bucket of waiting. There are more definite and confirmed clients out there just waiting for your call or email. Some clients may be in all good faith earnest about using you, but have no sense of timeline. They may express interest in you in February, and you'll get the job in November. They may tell you "you're the man" in 2019 and then cast you in 2021. It will be an unexpected blessing when it comes back. Let it be so. Don't hang your hat on that job and forego everything while you're waiting in the wings.

One thing I learned while telemarketing PSA's is to not be afraid to bid high. Often you never have the slightest clue of a client's budget. And just because they tell you they are a nonprofit, or that they "only have so much" doesn't mean that that statement is wholeheartedly honest. They are in business to make a profit too, and if they can keep overhead (you) down, then they make more in the end. Don't be afraid to push for what you need. Sure, they may push back, but sometimes they'll see reason, and cave. When that happens, you stood your ground effectively and secured for yourself what you A) wanted, and B) deserved. A well-respected professional says, "Stop making excuses for those who don't respect you enough to pay you a decent fee. Unless you've seen their balance sheet, you don't know what they can or cannot afford."[36]

The reverse is also true: be willing to quote lesser fees and bulk discounts and earn yourself a client who will *shower* you with work. The GVAA rate guide at globalvoiceacademy.com/gvaa-rate-guide-2/ is an indispensable tool you should have in your arsenal that will show you what you should earn for any type of job.

Make sure to have a script revision policy for when a client delivers you a script to record, you record it, and then they come back with changes. Those changes are billable. Have a minimum session fee in place for when such changes occur.

Do you really want to be taken seriously as a business? Then get your own website and custom domain. Furthermore, get your personal branded email. Don't rely on a free service like Gmail or Hotmail or Yahoo. Mikesvoiceovers@yahoo.com. Really? How about Mike@mikesvoiceovers.com? Or Mike@mikethemic.com or something unique like that? What makes more of an impression on you? The one who has actually invested into their own branding is the one I'm going to go with.

If you're using Gmail or another provider's email address for your business, you're building their brand, not yours."

I understand that many people really, really like Gmail's advanced email capabilities and the tie in with Google calendar. It's Microsoft Exchange for free, is what it is. And so, if you must, you can get your domain-affiliated email address and make it forward to the email system of your choosing. But do consider investing into your image with a custom domain name and domain-based email. It shows you believe in yourself enough to spend a little on yourself.

Think of it this way. The aspiring voiceover guy who hosts his free site on Wix, uses free software like Audacity, records in a closet that has not been acoustically-treated, uses a USB mic he already has – or worse, is on loan from a friend – or *worse*, records his auditions on his *iPhone*, eek! Oh yeah, and he has a free Yahoo email. *sigh*

I don't know about you, but using a free email address at a domain unaffiliated with your voiceover pursuits screams uninvested fly-by-night newbie to me.

SEO AND YOUR WEBSITE

Search engine optimization is the process of affecting the online visibility of a website or a web page in a web search engine's unpaid result, referred to as *natural*, *organic*, or *earned* results.

According to visual report by seotribunal.com in ecommerce:

- The 70-80% of search engine users are ignoring the paid ads and are only focusing on the organic results
- Get a keyword rich URL (domain name) – you can get them for cheap through GoDaddy. A website like seattlevoiceactor.com is better than "supervoiceover.com" because people in Seattle around me will be searching for a Seattle voice actor. If you can get something keyword-rich, so much the better. Then you can give customers the fancier-looking and more memorable supervoiceover.com domain to forward to. But wherever you list your website online, since that's where Google sees it, make sure to use the keyword-rich domain name. In print, you can use the fancy one.
- Get security on it! Get an SSL https:// certificate on it! Google likes SSL based websites a *lot*. It's a great way to tell Google that you believed in your site enough to protect it and all visitors who exchange data with it.
- Wordpress sites – Wordpress is a CMS (Content Management System) website. Why they're good: "WordPress is used by **60.3%** of **all** the **websites** whose content management system we know. This is **30.2%** of all websites."
- Websites need to be SEO rich[37], meaning they need to have a ton of content that matches the backend tags of the website. Meta tags, alt tags, CSS coding, page attributes all must match the focus keywords and key phrases, or Google will get confused.

According to NetmarketShare, in 2017, Google accounted for over 79% of all global desktop search traffic, followed by Bing at 7.27%, Baidu at 6.55% and Yahoo at 5.06%. According to Internet Live Stats, Google receives over 63,000 searches per second on any given day.

Websites need to be mobile compliant - 52% of online users are less likely to engage with a company if they had a bad mobile experience. 90% of users switch devices while completing an online task.[38]

You need to have meta-tags on your website. Yoast SEO is a common plugin used for Wordpress websites and really helps you in a user-friendly interface to optimize your website. It tells you if you're red, yellow, or green in terms of the optimized nature of each page. It's a great tool to make sure the individual pages on your website are optimized and in good SEO standing.

Alt-tags – you need to have these behind every picture on your website. Each time you load a picture into your page on your site, you need to program it with alt tags, or "alternative text". The text is what Google sees...Google doesn't see the picture; it sees the code behind the picture. You can get a free Wordpress plugin tool called *Smush* which helps you optimize photos for your website. Also, your website photos need to load fast. Plugins like Smush help "crunch" the photos to a streaming size. Remember in the old days of a 44.1kbps modem, when you'd hear the dit-dit-d-d-dit-d-d-dit-d-d-dit desperately trying to load a distant website, and the photos would buffer so slowly, loading in a slow row crawl down the page? You'd pull up a website, go catch a movie, and come back: with any luck, the picture will now be 33% loaded! Blazing! Don't do that to your customers. No need for massive-resolution images on your website: make sure they stream. Smush can tell you if your pictures are too big.

You should program each and every website you create into Google Search Console. It's the new version of Google Webmaster Tools. This tells you up-to-date metrics on how your website is performing, what pages need attention, how quickly they load, who is visiting, what's missing, what page they're leaving from, and how long they spent there, etc. It's excellent. It also tells Google to be aware of your site, and to properly index it. If you have a website, then you must use Google Search Console. You must have your site properly indexed and crawled for Google to see it. Your webmaster can help you with this. If you've done your own website, there are usually tools built into the website that help you gain a commanding grasp over your website to see where it needs improvement.

Can't afford hosting? Wix or Weebly have free, Google-friendly options. Wix is the best as far as tools & layout. Each one works on WYSIWYG, or "What you see is what you get", more or less a drag-and-drop style of website creation. But do see what I wrote previously about using free websites. Free websites usually have *other* branding on them, ownership insignias, banner ads, etc. All annoying distractions that cheapen your overall brand quality and image. Reference what I talked about earlier with having someone develop your website who knows what they're doing.

Ultimately, I would encourage you to have your website designed. Have it designed by someone experienced with visuals and branding. They will be impartial much more than you will be. If you design your own website, much like producing your own demo, you're more inclined to punch yourself in the arm with a validating "atta boy" since you did it and now you can take the credit. Let someone else do it who does it for a living. Let them brand you and give you the website of your dreams: something that will be incredibly fun to visit, that speaks highly of who you are, and sells you in an instant. Celia Siegel is excellent at branding. She asks "Do you like it? Your brand should inspire you. It should be something that makes you happy to show up for work every day and to put yourself out there. It should help give you the confidence you need to share your voice with people."[39] She's a pro. Go with Celia.

Here's something you always need to remember. As far as it depends on you, and as far as it is possible without being uber shameless, *every* time you post something somewhere, put your signature and links to your pages. Use free posting sites like Doodeeo, Soundcloud, Reddit, Quora, Jam-Pan, even Craigslist. You better believe Google tracks that! Put them in your email signatures too. It's creepy, but Google sees that too, crossing in cyberspace. I don't know how, but it does. Some sites have "nofollow" tags in their website which restrict Google from detecting and indexing outbound links back to your site, so that's a bummer there. But get yourself listed where you can, for free, in as many different places, and always list your actual organic hosted site - not your forwarding domain – in your posting, as I mentioned previously.

Do you like to write? Then you're a shoo-in for blogging. Blogging is huge. It tells Google that you're an authority on a subject. Google likes sites that are authorities on subjects. Sites that have people coming to them in droves and contain lots of content which references other content. It sees you as kind of an encyclopedia of sorts, or perhaps a "Wikipedia of voiceovers." That helps you climb up the search engines because you're promoting content that people want to read. And it's a great outlet! And get this: it does *not* actually have to be about voiceovers! Write about your life: that's connective content that people will be naturally interested in. One of my favorite chapters in this book came from one of my favorite blog articles. It has to do with the birth of my second son. It's amazingly personal and vulnerable. But if it's about voiceovers and how that ties into and affects your life, so much the better for you and your ranking. Remember: *content is king*. Always. Google loves content. A good blog post should have 500-1000 words on it. Blogging only works if you can do it at least about once a month at 500+ words, and it be really good original content. Google lives and dies by finding sites that are authorities on what people are searching for. Content tells them if you are an authority. It must be original, well written, etc. Even if no human ever reads it, Google will.

You might be a fellow voiceover artist. If so, you should by now have a demo reel. Why not make videos out of them? Why not post them in your YouTube channel so that Google sees them? You better believe they'll get crawled and indexed in Google's search engine, and sometimes, they'll even play at the top of the search results. That's pretty good territory to have your videos showing up in. It's also a visual connection point, which is far more effective for potential customers and colleagues. You can also make a playlist of both your own video (audio demo) creations as well as other videos that you may find in YouTube that feature your voice! And then embed that playlist in your website so they have a video playlist as well as your audio playlist.

Another thing that you should have on your website is a press kit. A complete, zipped press kit containing all of your current demos, your photo, and your resume. This is something that an agent or a promotions director, producer or potential customer might want, if they don't have time to download your demos at that very moment. Alternatively, their role may just be that of "gatherer", taking your info and passing it on to the party that does make the casting decision. If you have a complete press kit containing everything a potential client needs to know about you, and they can download it and take it with them, so much the better…especially since they might not remember your name or website.

Make sure you're collecting reviews for your business! As much as I loathe Yelp (because of filtering out positive reviews, oh and because they're quite frankly a "billion-dollar bully"[40]), they're in there too.

Recruit reviews in this order: Google Local Reviews, Yelp Reviews, and Facebook reviews. All of these tell other customers that you're legitimate – but they also tell Google (see why I listed Google first?) that your customers (aka *other accounts beside yourself*) are speaking up for you and validating you as a business. Offer discounts and other incentives for clients that leave you a positive review.

Get quality backlinks for your website. Sign up for sites like FatJoe.co that can build local citations and link back to your site. That way, Google is seeing your website listed on *other* sites, which establishes presence and networking and authority. Write comments on other bloggers' blogs that allow you to post your website. Google will see that link back to you!

These sites can't just be any sites though; they have to be quality, established sites. I like to comment on Paul Strikwerda's and others' blogs because they are excellent writers…but also because Google will see me…because it sees them!

Get a good domain monitor like Uptime Robot. This is a free service you can sign up for that will alert you if your website is down for any reason. And it will alert you if the website is back up. This is great if – God forbid – you've been hacked.

That way you can log in and see what might have been affected, and get yourself back up and running again. I believe the free plan includes up to 5 websites. I've used it for years and it's been very helpful in moments of unexplained website downtime.

Sitechecker.pro is a great website tool to use to check the SEO compliance of your website. It will give you an SEO score and make recommended improvements. Kind of the same thing that Yoast will do, which I mentioned earlier.

I cannot recommend highly enough that you obtain the VoiceZam player. It's available at voicezam.com and it's amazing...and it's only $13 per month. This demo player is embeddable into your website, and it will give you statistics and metrics of your audio demos: who is listening to them, what demos are being listened to the most, how long are they being listened to, what internet provider is providing that bandwidth, etc. Additionally, you can create individual "Zamlinks" and send those to people so they can go directly to a specific audio file or demo group, and that way you can track how many listens you're getting from your marketing emails. It's very effective, and at a great price. VoiceZam is very important to me - I use it to help keep my finger on the pulse of my business, and it's tremendously effective in helping me do that. VoiceZam is another element on your website that potential clients can download if they don't have the time that very minute to listen to all of your demos. Like your press kit, mentioned earlier, they can download your demos from the VoiceZam player and take them with them for later reviewing.

Finally, one bit of advice for the Interwebs. As far as you're able, say, if you have two different monitors connected to your computer, use one browser for business and one for personal. So, for example, Chrome for business and Opera for personal. Or Internet Explorer. Or Safari. Whatever. That way, you maintain better segregation between what you're doing in your personal life on Facebook, and what you're doing in your business life on Facebook. Between LinkedIn and LinkedIn. Twitter and Twitter. Instagram and Instagram. Don't lose clients because of your personal life.

MARKETING & SOCIAL MEDIA

Social Media is about cultivating relationships! Engage with people! It's not all about "pay attention to this new thing I'm doing, and you really should buy from me." It doesn't work that way. You have to engage with people. In his book "How to Win Friends and Influence People", Dale Carnegie said "a person's name is to that person the sweetest and most important sound in any language."[41] It's so true. You really can't charge right in, using your best announcer voice, and hope to compel the masses to buy your product. They scatter like roaches. (Free tip: don't call your customers roaches). Instead, *engage* with them. Talk about them. Don't go blaring how awesome you are; rather, highlight *advantages* to them casting you, after getting to know them. Don't tout you; tout them. Do you want to be known as "the guy who does voiceovers?" Or "the voiceover guy, and look! there's a glimpse into his personal life"? The touch of humanity can't be overstated here. People don't like mannequins with sandwich boards. They like humans. Be a real human. I confess I'm not an expert here…there are voiceover colleagues that are far better at this online, such as Tracy Lindley. But one of the greatest types of conversation you can have with a potential client is almost entirely one-sided: *theirs*. Listen! God gave you two ears and only one mouth for a reason.

LinkedIn totally creeped me out at first. I was receiving connection suggestions for people I'd only ever interacted with *once* years ago. I was sure they were scouring my contacts and accessing emails behind my back. I'm convinced that the NRA owns LinkedIn. *smile* But truth be told, it's made up of Six. Hundred. Million. Members. In. Twenty. Four. Different. Countries. That's, uh, a handful of people. A really big handful. That's a lot of people for you to connect with! 138 Million members are in the U.S alone. You have a gold mine of potential connections you can make there that can bring you business. For LinkedIn, you should post at least 3x a week. Don't post personal content. Post business content. Post advertisements or infographics, sure, but try to come up with original content and questions that engage people. No one likes the "look at me, look at me, look at what I can do, look at what I can do" approach. I'm no expert with that, as I mentioned above. But the right thing to do is, again, to connect on a human level.

I was told early on by a marketing professional that for every one post I create that is a "selling" post, I should create six posts that are more interactive and connective. Again, people don't care what you know until they know that you care.

Don't have time to do all these postings all the time? You can use tools like Hootsuite that schedule posts at regular intervals for you instead. I don't like these programs, however, as I am more spontaneous than they would be. What they post and when they post it might be different than what I'm feeling then. I may have felt it before, but I may not feel it now, nor may it be relevant. And an ad that you've scheduled on Monday morning to post on

Wednesday afternoon might not reverberate Wednesday afternoon if it's automatically posted once news of yet another school shooting is trending. It will be completely unwelcome, cold, and very inhumane. I try to stay of the moment and spontaneous.

As far as marketing goes, here's the kicker, and this is what has always been most comfortable for me. I don't like to barge into people's lives and harass them for business. I don't bombard people and constantly push too much of a good thing. It's like when New Kids on the Block came and went…they were everywhere and people loved it. Then they were *still* everywhere…and people hated it. Michael Jordan has done it. Bo Jackson did it. People flame out when their audience tires of them. Take it from a pro: "Overexposure kills. Underexposure doesn't create any traction."[42]

I like to "gentle" my way in. Before my wife and I started dating, she once told me that I'm "a gentler." I responded, "I have antlers???" She reiterated, "Uh, NO….you're a gentler." She explained that I use gentleness and humility to connect with people. I think she's right! The system I use is the "ASK" approach:

- Allowing
- Sensitive
- Kind

This process Allows them to make the decision whether or not to welcome me into their life. It's Sensitive to their schedules and they can respond when they want to. It's Kind, and polite. We need that in the world today. We need manners. Why not approach them with gentility and respect? This is one of the reasons I hate cold calls. The phone ringing says answer me NOW. Drop what you're doing and answer me NOW. An email or a text allows me to respond when it's convenient for ME. That's why I love the ASK approach.

Some people say that based on marketing statistics and metrics, your marketing message should be 50 to 125 words only. And your best subject line length should be 28-51 characters. What would you say on an elevator? How quickly could you make your pitch? How do you start? I usually ask a question. My question is "Need a Voiceover Artist with <1 Hour turnaround?" That opens the door to a conversation. JimBob might say, "Golly, *do* I need a voiceover artist with under one-hour turnaround? Dad-gum, I never thunk it before. Huh! Hey Matilda! Do we need a voiceover artist back in that there shop, hunny? Well shoot. I'm plumb out of idears on that one." Your goal isn't to make a sale to JimBob; it's to start a conversation with JimBob.

Did you know YouTube is owned by Google? You can post content on YouTube that will readily be indexed by Google. Make sure you have video of your audio demos! Turn them into videos! If you don't have a video editor, get one for free like Windows Movie Maker or iMovie. Drop in your audio and incorporate simple graphics, your logo, and some text, for example your contact information and website. Post those suckers! Put 'em up online. Google will index them and then when people search for a voiceover talent in your area, provided you have the right keywords in there, they may find you that way!

Alignable: Hmmm. It's like the poor-man's LinkedIn. I don't really like Alignable too much, but it is yet another networking platform where you can develop contacts. It is a place where you can receive recommendations, post events or advertisements, connect with people, etc. But what I don't really like about it is that there is very little logic to who you can and cannot connect with, even if they're local to you. Each month you're awarded 30 free connection credits to use within your area. You can try, but even if someone is 3 blocks away - ahem, my area – I am for whatever reason told that I can only connect with people in, ahem, my area. Hmmmmm. Additionally, their app is simply deplorable.

Got a Reddit account? Neither did I up until 6 months ago. Now, I really enjoy Reddit! And not because I'm increasing in Karma! Although it's always nice to increase in Karma, sure. What I like about Reddit is that it's a community forum where you can connect with other potential clients as well as colleagues, offer your demos, request feedback, contribute to the community, ask questions, answer questions, and more. It's really a great place to connect with potential clients and just engage with them.

Speaking of answering and asking questions, Quora is great for that as well. Quora is festooned with all kinds of voice acting questions – you can really connect with lots of people on there who are seeking answers to questions like "Is it really possible to make a full-time income in voiceovers?" And "What do I need to get started?" and questions of that nature. Quora really is also a great community to connect with voiceover colleagues and become a mentor to them. In turn, you may have something to offer them in the way of coaching, if you do that.

Did ya forget about Craigslist? Don't! It's still alive and well, and Google loves it! If you remember, many years ago Google had a "PageRank" browser plugin, and you could see which sites had a high "Google PageRank." Those were the sites that you wanted to try to get on. Craigslist was one of those. I think its score was 8/10, if I recall. Craigslist is replete with forums to connect on a non-X-rated level with those who would like your services! And if you're flush with a little extra cash here and there, try posting an ad in multiple cities advertising your services! You might just be surprised what $5 a month per city can get you in terms of business. Additionally, you can use the tool SearchTempest[43] to scour *all* major metropolitan cities on Craigslist in the jobs or gigs category for voiceover jobs and gigs. I've scoured them. I've found listings. I've been awarded jobs through finding the clients on Craigslist. It's possible. You can do it, and hey, you don't even have to hook up with anyone weird!

Facebook – maybe you've heard of the little-known Menlo Park startup that came from a Harvard student. No? Didn't think so. The truth is that Facebook is a behemoth, a juggernaut, an unstoppable brute in the online world. The more you can develop an online presence, the better you are at people knowing who you are and wanting a piece of your voiceover goods. Facebook, though, has groups designed for showcasing what you've done. You have only to look. They are frankly too numerous to list here. But you can look up E-learning groups. Explainer video groups. Commercial production groups. Others. You can – and would be wise to – spend some time researching groups that work for you and allow you to connect with potential clients in such a broad community. Facebook is indeed broad, and the contacts you can make there are equally as broad, because they work by referrals, and the communication you have is (mostly) public.

Some agents will even ask if you're active on social media, and they want to make sure that you are. Possibly (and I daresay unfortunately) because some of them want not only a 10% cut of any jobs they themselves get you, but also 10% of anything that you book for yourself. Eeek. I say, if you see an agreement like that, *run*. If you're working hard to solicit and obtain your own business, why share your spoils with someone who had no stake in it? I do completely get that they deserve their share for any work they scour up for you. But not any work you scare up for yourself, through your own efforts. "Not gonna do it," as George Bush Sr. would say.

However you slice it, stay active on social media. Connect with people. Be mindful about what you post and what you're putting out there as far as your brand goes. Celia Siegel elaborates: "Whatever platform (or platforms) you choose, pay attention to your written voice. As with every other aspect of your brand, your writing needs to be consistent and distinctively on brand. Do you have a wicked sense of humor? An air of almost-overconfident grandeur? A casual way about you? Then be sure to write your posts that way."[44]

One of the single most important things that you need to do as an entrepreneur – nay, as a *business* – is to register yourself on Google Local. Create a business site under Google Local for your voiceover business *yesterday*. You'll enter all of your information in the business, and then Google will mail you out a postcard to verify that you truly are at the local address that you say you are. When that's confirmed, you'll have a local business location live on Google Local! A bit redundant-sounding to be sure, but ultimately, you'll have a place that people can see pop up in search results and see that you're a local business. People like to support local businesses! And, once again, this is excellent for SEO since you're telling Google that you're here, you're located right here, and you're ready to do business. And if you're not willing to list your home address online as your place of business, I don't blame you. Get a Post Office Box or a UPS Store box that allows you to use the physical representation of the address, and use that address as your business location.

Comment on client videos on YouTube. Make sure to do this! If you have a YouTube account – and you darn well better, because Google owns YouTube – then you can use that Google account to comment on client videos that have been posted that make use of your voice. Thank them for choosing you! Compliment them on a video well done! This is a great way to show them that you went to see their video and admire their handiwork (and also to hear sweet beautiful you!), but it's also a great way to increase visibility and let others see your comment and instantly know that YOU were the voice behind such a great video. It's a wonderful and free way to increase exposure.

Here are some tidbits:

- Contact 20-50 leads per day. Expect a 10% return rate. 3-5% of those turn into paying clients. I actually contact closer to 150 people a day.
- 80% of sales come between the 5th & 12th contact. We're bombarded by notifications! Make sure that you are keeping in touch with potential clients at regular intervals, reminding them that you still exist, and by interacting with them.
- Market *benefits*, not features. Make sure that in your marketing you're not touting all these great and wonderful, life-saving messianic abilities of yours. Make sure that you are touting what they will get. Touting benefits that they would like, not who you are. Your marketing is not about you; it's about how you solve a problem.
- Diversify: Do direct marketing. Get agents. Attend local networking events. Whatever. Don't put all your eggs in one basket.
- Social media was designed to *create community*…not to advertise. I'm guilty of this because I don't nearly use social media for its utmost potential of "sociality", and I need to. But rather than wearing your sandwich board and ringing your bell all the time, a much more attractive approach is by interacting and engaging. Don't make people unfollow and mute you, or worse, disconnect and unfriend you. Give them a chance to hear you by hearing them.
- You need to constantly fill your pipeline. Make sure you're hunting down clients, and reminding existing clients that you're here. They will neither hunt *you* down nor remember that *you* exist.
- Instagram Ads – Instagram is fairly targeted, and moreover, it's very simplistic to create a running ad on there. I *really* like Instagram. I like it for its visual appeal, and its ability to reach a lot of people. And the ad cost isn't bad.

- Same with Facebook Ads, although they have never really brought me any business.
- With any postings that are outside of your existing Facebook or LinkedIn groups where the members already know what the group is about, for all of your posts make sure to use hashtags. Hashtags can include the following types if you're trying to attract business to yourself: #Voiceover #VoiceTalent #VoiceoverArtist #VoiceActor #VoiceActing #NeedVoiceover #videoproductioncompany #CorporateVideo #Filmmaker #VideoProducer #VideoProduction #MediaProduction #productioncompany #creativedirector #brandagency #videoagency #Videography #ProductionStudio #ExplainerVideo #Elearning #marketingagency #thatvoiceoverguy #videoproductionagency #instructionaldesigner #contentagency #videoadvertising #adagency #brandvideo #videocreator #mediacompany, etc.
- Conversely, if you're trying to attract other voice talent to yourself, use hashtags such as #Voiceoveractor #voiceactor #voiceacting #voiceovers #voiceover etc. I have to do the same thing for authoring: #readers #bookreaders #yabooks #scifibooks #selfhelpbook #booklovers etc.

In all of your marketing, remember this great mantra: *People love to buy; and they hate to be sold.* It's true. Penny Abshire said "Tell me, don't sell me." *Wow!* How many times have you walked into a store and been immediately accosted by Mr. Commission Breath? Ick. They make me want to hide in a corner and rock to and fro whilst chanting "Find a happy place…find a happy place!" They don't attract me to themselves; they repel me. Allow ME to make the move and to state what I need. Listen to me. Listen to me. Listen to me. Don't sing me a song about why you know I need to buy what you're selling. The same is true for you as a marketer. Make sure you listen to your potential customers. Remember, it's not about making a sale; you're trying to solve a problem. To solve a problem, you have to first understand what the problem is. Remember, you have to build a reputation before you can close the sale. After all, they're not buying your product, they're buying *you*.

Are you a cold-caller? Don't tick off the gatekeepers! And certainly, don't try to go around them. These people should be your best friends. These are the people that decide if you gain admission into the Holy of Holies. They're the ones that introduce you respectfully and excitedly...or annoyedly. Think "Yeah, this guy wants to talk with you, he sounds fun!" vs. "I don't know, some guy..." Don't try to be "that voice guy" when you first call. Don't try to impress. Be real. Be connective. Be genuine. Always think of marketing from the client's perspective. Their "what's in it for me?" question shouldn't offend you. It should motivate you to refine your presentation. After all, if you can't answer why they should hire you, why should they even ask that question?

On that note, when you're calling business owners, be respectful of their time. Thank them profusely for taking the time. It's no small feat to run a successful business. When you call them, also make sure that you know who you are. What do I mean by that? Be confident. It worked for Atreju passing through the Sphinxes in *The Neverending Story*. *Know* that you are someone important. I'm not talking cocky or cavalier – but go in with an attitude that they genuinely want to hear from you and you genuinely have something valuable to offer. Convey that to them in the most confident sense. Additionally, you can use a mirror when you're cold-calling. Watch yourself when you converse with these potential clients. Would you want to talk to you?

Are you a member of LinkedIn? LinkedIn is huge, which we've talked about before. You can successfully navigate the huge pool that is LinkedIn...and really connect with a LOT of potential clients there. But you have to connect personally. Remember, "A person's name is to that person the sweetest sound in the whole world" as Dale Carnegie says.[45] Talk to them about *them*. See where they're at. Don't be a kiss-up of course, but primarily don't just scream "I can do this and you should hire me." You want to talk to people about their stuff. Then, when they tire of that, wait for the "So what's up? What can I do for you?" That comes after rapport is established.

Ever had the Birthday song sung to you? Of course you have. Wish people on LinkedIn happy birthday! It's a reminder that you're still here. The customer says to themselves, "Oh that was nice! Oh, wait! That's so and so! I forgot about them!" It's very connective. You can also congratulate people on LinkedIn for their job accomplishments! You do receive these notifications from LinkedIn when your connections have birthdays, anniversaries, and accomplishments. When you reach out to them and in effect *say their name*, as Dale Carnegie talks about, you're making them feel good about themselves – and about you.

If you receive random connections on LinkedIn, by all means accept them! Will you follow their every move in your newsfeed? Probably not. You have no idea who these people are, but they could be a future client. They may be trying to connect with you for the express purpose of establishing a business relationship that needs voiceovers. Why *wouldn't* you connect? LinkedIn is not the place to be suspicious and to avoid people because of being wary. It's a business network; it's not Craigslist personals.

As an experiment, you could even try purchasing a trial membership of *LinkedIn Sales Navigator* to build your business – you can cancel in 30 days but you'd still have *tons* of refined connections that are super warm and super targeted. This is the same type of connective ability that is offered by services such as *UpLead*. People who are in your exact, precise demographics of the target audience you're wishing to connect with.

Have you ever tried LinkedIn groups? Try searching for video producers on LinkedIn. Then look under the "More" dropdown and click on "Groups." What?!?! Didn't see that before, did ya? There are lots of groups at your disposal for connection to clients and colleagues on LinkedIn. Join up, connect, post, interact. Groups are great!

Is any single networking site or social media platform working better for you than another? Then by all means focus all your efforts on that one site. Don't scattershot across three sites giving 33.3%. If you have more of a comfort level / success rate / familiarity with one, then lock and load 100% on that site. Kill it. Annihilate it. Go to town on utter domination until the police come. Find what works best for you and stick with it with all your might. Remember, the key is to work *smarter*, not *harder*. (Although personally I like to work *harder, smarter*.)

As a business, get into a routine of putting reminders on your calendar. Make sure you know what you need to do. Operate by a goal sheet. Create reminders on your calendar to check with clients and see if you can use their video on your platform. Create reminders to send follow-ups and specials. Create reminders to write a blog. Create reminders to do live stream videos on your Instagram. Create reminders to post particular elements on your social media feed. Live and die by those lists. You'll never get anywhere by cruising through on a hope and prayer that you'll actually remember all that you need to get done. You need to make sure you remember to make all of it happen, and stay on top of it. Get into that routine now.

If anyone ever posts something about having joined an agency, or you see that someone is repped by a particular agent, *write that down*. Piggyback on them! There's no harm and no foul in it. What hurt can it do to contact the agency yourself, and ask to be considered as well? Don't expect an answer right away, but do contact them! Send them your A) Demo Reel, B) Resume, C) Short introduction, and D) List of previous big-name clients. Keep the email brief and to the point of course - succinctness is always key when you're sending a similar email to hundreds of other people and you want to stand out – but do contact them and ask to be considered for their roster. Why not? Don't expect a windfall of jobs to come your way, because that's just simply not how it works anymore. *But* – what if that agent landed you a big job, just one big mortgage-paying job? Why wouldn't you reach out with an email that costs you nothing but two minutes of your time?

Instagram. It's where I love to do most of my marketing, with videos and infographics and amusing posts. I really do enjoy Instagram. I love it for its visual appeal, its modern-day interface, its connectivity, but mostly, for its ease of obtaining email addresses to contact. Post on Instagram regularly. Use hashtags to attract business to yourself and to connect with others who perform the target function you're looking to connect with. "But I don't understand Instagram!" you cry feebly! I get it. Believe me. I feel the same way about Twitter. Nonetheless – get on there and start using it. Make a point to schedule Instagram into your day. Have I obtained new clients through Instagram? An emphatic *yes*.

I mentioned SearchTempest earlier: it's an amazing site that will crawl *all* of Craigslist. Make use of this tool every day, because every day, I see voiceover jobs on Craigslist. Scour all of it with SearchTempest. Go to the site and tell it to look for "voice" or "voiceover" jobs in the "gigs" and "jobs" categories of Craigslist. You'll be surprised at the results that you'll find, and I don't mean sultry 1-900 phone voice jobs!

Make sure to *follow* your clients on Instagram, Twitter, Pinterest, LinkedIn, etc. Follow them...and they'll follow you. Like their posts...and they'll like yours. You have to give in order to receive in networking and social activity. You're attracting goodwill to yourself by giving; it's not just always about posting something and saying "pay attention to me." It's about paying attention to *them*. It's a scratch-my-back-and-I'll-scratch-yours society anymore. Get in that ring. Give...and receive. You can see what they're up to in your news feed. They can see yours. Check this out from Paul Strikwerda: "If you want information, you need to give information. If you want people to contact you, you need to contact people. If you want people to refer you, you need to refer people."[46] The door swings both ways.

The only caution I would make on this is be mindful of how many people you're following. Don't just go nuts and follow the whole world. Instagram imposes a 7500 account follow limitation. Twitter is 5000.

Don't friend everyone on Facebook either: I've discussed already why you need to keep your Facebook feed clean, but ultimately you want to see what actually *is* important to you, like your friends and family. But following potential and existing clients is a way to show that you are interested in them for their lives and personality, not just for a meal ticket. Alternatively, you can "like" their posts which also shows interaction with them.

Remember – look for clients online from their perspective. For example, you can search for "I need an explainer video". That should pull up a number of website entries indexed by Google that produce Explainer videos. And *voila*. Now you can contact those companies directly.

What about advertising? Spend a little on Craigslist. It's not a whole lot of dough to spring for an ad on Craigslist in multiple cities: it's $5 per city per month. For 30 days, someone searching in the "Services" category in their city will see your ad stating that you perform voiceovers. Not a bad investment!

Come up with a text heavy ad so that Google will find it as well, throw in some attractive professional pictures of you behind the mic (note: *not* Selfies! I said *professional* photos!) and you've got yourself a month-long ad that will potentially gather some clients for you. People still search their local Craigslist for jobs, voiceover jobs included.

Got a CRM? I highly recommend FirstVoiceData: check it out at firstvoicedatacrm.com. It's Microsoft Access-based, and if you use the MS Office 365 suite with Access, you're golden. It's a flat one-time fee as opposed to an ongoing monthly fee with other online CRM's. I have used this for years and years, and it's greatly benefited my business operations.

Alternatively you can check out VoiceOverview, MailChimp, Zoho or Nimble for keeping in touch with clients – when you're away, when you've won awards, when you have updated demos, when you've signed with an agent, when you've booked a big campaign, to let them know you work with other male/female talent, etc. These are fantastic online advertising solutions to connect with people through a bulk email.

OFFLINE MARKETING & CONNECTION

Offline suggestions, you can do any one of a number of things to establish and keep up a local presence:

- Pick up a local business directory – look through for businesses in your area
- Meetups. These are *so* good! Connect with local business owners by going to free networking meetings of like-minded individuals, or groups composed of your target audience!
- Chambers of Commerce – sometimes there is a limit of 2 times attending before you have to become a member, but sometimes there are free COC groups you can join as well
- BNI – a limit of 2 times attending before you have to become a member
- LeTip – a limit of 2 times attending before you have to become a member
- BizBuilders

- Local videographers who do commercial work. Connect with them through Craigslist
- Real Estate agents – professional narration for their videos

BUDGETING

Let's talk about something that you should have learned when you were five. When you had an allowance. It's called "Budgeting."

One week in voiceovers, I made $800. Another week, I made $1900. Another week, I made $7200. And yet another week, I made $10594. There is no set week or set income in voiceovers. There just isn't.

Clients pay when they pay, you land jobs when you land jobs, and you are constantly faced with an erratic income flow. How do you mitigate that? By budgeting. When I get a $7200 week, I'll usually pay two mortgage payments out of there. I'll still have some leftover, which is great.

But what is even greater is that I won't have to worry about mortgage payments for the next two months! It's amazing! I've just taken that chunk off of my brain, offloaded it and freed up valuable cranial resources to think about what matters more: marketing. As the proud owner of a brain, this makes sense to me.

It used to be where I would receive a set amount every two weeks from my employer. This made it super easy to know exactly what I was going to receive on my paycheck (unless I was hourly with varying hours). The amount was set. I could allocate *these* bills to my first paycheck, and *those* bills to my second one. Easy-peasy.

Not so with voiceovers. As that great philosopher Forrest Gump said, "You never know what you gonna get." You truly don't! So, pay ahead on your bills, and budget the remainder on groceries and all of that. Tackle the big rocks first[47], and then you'll have room for the little rocks.

You'll definitely want to get in this habit early on: paying ahead on your bills will save you the headache of having spent your money, arriving to the point of a bill being due, and then realizing you're the Prodigal Son who splurged and lived in raucous, wild living, and now has none left to pay your mortgage payment to Wells Fargo.

Pay it when you *have* it.

FINALLY: A LITTLE SECRET

I'm going to share something with you that will be a little controversial. I know. *What?!?!?* Yes. Indeed. I am. Brace thyself.

I use something that really helps me in business. I don't have to pay for marketing leads or advertising contacts or subscriptions to lead-based companies. I hate subscriptions. So, what I splurged on, instead, for a one-time purchase, is an e-mail spider program.

Eeek! Spiders!

No. Not that kind of spider. Let me explain. This one has lots of legs to reach out, but isn't furry and won't wrap you up and suck your blood.

An email spider is an incredibly effective little critter that comes in a program. You run the program, find a directory online that you want to "crawl" and then input that directory into the email spider program. I use Email Extractor 6. Once I plug in that domain, I run the search. EE6 will then return to me all valid emails from that page/site/directory that I could potentially contact. If they're in a directory, they're already exceptionally pre-qualified to be warm leads, because they *are* your target.

EE6 returns to me ALL email addresses on that page. Basically, anything with the convention of identifier + @ + domain name + dot + URL extension. Anything that looks like an "@" is returned. They might be old, some of them. They might have left the company, some of them. But ultimately, the overwhelming majority of them are exactly who I need them to be.

Now, don't go all fanatical and try to search all of Craigslist or LinkedIn for email addresses. You'll get your IP address blocked from replying or posting, and your account may be banned or revoked. Email Extractor 6, and other spider programs like it, are bots. There are such things as "Anti-Bots", sentries, and "nocrawl" code embedded into websites that disallow you to crawl them. So, a program like this wouldn't work. Don't attempt to use this on huge networks like Facebook, Twitter, Instagram, etc., either. But directory-based sites that are not massive search-engine based social media sites, you'll find some good luck.

Now, why is it controversial? Because some think you're stealing. It's rightfully called "harvesting", or "data mining." Ultimately, there's nothing illegal about it, it's just frowned upon in some circles, so you need to exercise caution on which circles you decide to use it in. You're obtaining information off the web in a much more efficient way than you would by simply googling, visiting a site, and emailing those people one at a time by clicking all of their email addresses, and then perchance forgetting where you found all of those email addresses in the first place.

By using an email spider such as EE6, you can return to yourself thousands of results that include not only the desired email addresses, but also the source from which they came. In light of that, you can say to them in your marketing email, "I found you on such and such a site…" Many times, a cold email will reply to me, "May I ask where you got my email from?" It's just common courtesy to reply to them where you did, in fact, find them, because if that person is trying to maintain a little contact privacy, you're helping them to remove themselves from one more place on the worldwide web. And you just might get a little thank you business out of helping them, who knows?

That's about all I have to offer in terms of lots of various business tips. I know this chapter was loaded with a ton of info. Read it again, soak it in, and go git 'em.

#youcandothis

Fake It Till You Make It

...THAT YOU KNOW OF

This is a special chapter devoted to all those who make their living from voiceovers, and not from other reputable vocations such as slaughtering four-legged things for general consumption, or Amway.

It's a dog-eat-dog world out there, and yet we maintain a community that promotes encouragement and support, affirmation, coaching, mentoring, and all things non-beef-related. Is beef bad? Well, that's kind of a subjective question because the cattle rancher makes his living off of beef; whereas entrepreneurs may or may not benefit from said beef. I have no beef with this beef, unless the chief with which I have no beef develops a belief in beef with a thief named Lief, who likes beef, which would cause me brief beef grief.

However you slice it (see what I did there?) beef is an invaluable part of our society, because it permeates every level of our food chain, including beef-flavored Top Ramen, which is one of the main food groups for bachelors and latch-key junior-highers everywhere.

In many fake industries such as dentistry, people pretend to know what they're doing and yet we still leave their office cursing their future generations, swinging by Hobby Lobby on the way home to pick up enough crafts to mail a crudely assembled harassment letter. (They sell witch hair at Hobby Lobby, right?) Anyway, these fake industry people eat beef too, which is known for actually pulling out teeth if the meat is tough enough. In some third world countries, they don't actually use dental tools: they simply serve Beef Jerky to their patients with dental extraction needs, and all teeth are effectively ground to powder in a matter of minutes. This also assists with the ability to whistle, which most third world dentists offer in an extraction-whistling lesson bundle conveniently priced at thirty oxen, fifteen sheaves of grain, seventy-two sheep, one red heifer, five packs of JuJubes (which you should *never* eat anyway if you're *ever* planning to see a dentist), and a firstborn child. I know a good deal when I see one. That's a good deal.

However, in many actual industries such as ranching, livestock are murdered (read: assassinated). Those promising heifers full of hope, who stand proud and represent the best of bovine values and ethics, elected by their cow peers, are shot down in the prime of life, before they could even become a cow senator. Now, I'm no tree hugger; I like to gnaw on a good slab of steak like the next cowboy. But ultimately, when you think about it – or perhaps when you watch Faces of Death and then need a cleansing shower afterwards – you can't shake the imagery of a cow getting its throat cut during the butchering process. It's awful. Excuse me for a moment. *takes shower*.

So, Aaron, get to the point. What does this all mean for entrepreneurs?

Pull up a hot slab of beef and a cool glass of milk, and I'll explain.

MUST…HAVE…PROTEIN

It all comes down to this. We're either the cows, or we're the butchers. Now, in voiceovers, we don't want to butcher other voiceover artists. In most societies today, there are generally strict rules in place to forbid people from things like murder, streaking and of course planking, which in India is punishable by a $15,000 fine, house arrest, acid splash, public gossip, and then, just to be safe, murder. Once murdered, India figures, the perpetrator tends not to be able to repeat the offense. But in the United States, you'll want to choose wisely as well.

If you elect to go the way of the cow (which is different from the way of the dog…which in turn is different from the way of the dragon), you'll need to be wary. Around every corner lies a voiceover artist (the butcher) waiting to trap you up and milk you for all you're worth, and feast on some good meat. At this point I'd like to channel my best David Attenborough, complete with stirring symphonic accompaniment:

Voiceover Artists are a hungry species! Always on the prowl, they do enjoy a savory meal, and so they have perfected the cunning craft of the hunt to the point where they'll slay you shamelessly with no reservations, whipping out their salt packets and their dinner bib and diving into the succulent meal that is you. The only way you can possibly get them back at that point is with a good solid dose of mad cow disease, or possibly give them a heart attack. If, however you elect to go the way of the butcher, you are probably going to be safe. Except of course that all eyes will be upon you to see if in the process of providing voiceovers, you're going to harm a cow. You must therefore conduct such predations under the cover of darkness, which is perfect because you're used to being in a small dark cell anyway. And you must be careful not to let anyone else hear the muffled screams of the cow as you're going for the kill, which is perfect because you're used to using noise gates and downward expanders and Waves DeBreath to screen out unwanted noises. Additionally, you must take great care to eat your prey quickly, while it is room temperature and before another Voiceover Artist gets to it, which is perfect because you're used to processing auditions and sending them right away, so you've perfected the art of expediency.

EAT OR BE EATEN

So, that's the way of things. Voiceover artists have evolved as one of nature's finest testaments to predatory instinct and the thrill of the hunt. We know where the cows graze, and we circle their fields with shameless abandon, flexing our claws, dripping with saliva, and savoring the meal to come. That, and it's nice it's nice for you to get out of your studio, which you've been farting in. Don't deny it.

Ultimately, when you look at the businessperson or entrepreneur as a species, the cow and the butcher always come to mind. In fact, psychological studies have been conducted on various focus groups over the years, and when asked whether they identify voiceovers artists with butchers or cows, 98% of them replied "I said no focus groups, dangit!" The other 2% had since lost the will to live and had drifted off to an ethereal oblivion called Tracy Chapman music, murmuring something about saying no to focus groups in the future.

But truthfully speaking…it's a dog-eat-dog, er, butcher-eat-cow world. And a businessperson's gotta eat. So, what is one to do when one is desperate to put food on the table and at the same time not be ridiculed and lambasted by environmentalists everywhere?

I think I have the answer.

Visit your local dentist in India today and ask for the Beef Jerky special. No cows were harmed in the making of said Beef Jerky. The dentists offer great whistling lessons afterward too, during which you'll be able to say, "I thavor the tathte of thucculent beef therved with a thide of theriouthly thatithfying voithover proweth."

Thank you for reading thith.
Thintherely,
The Butcher

A Beautiful Craziness

MAGNIFICENT MAYHEM

If you're a voice talent, you'll know what I say when I say that voiceovers are an extraordinary career that is rife with craziness. Sometimes I wake up laughing knowing that I get to do what I get to do that day. Sometimes I burst out laughing because of what I just got paid. And sometimes I go to bed with a headache, because I can't believe I went through what I went through that day.

It's as unpredictable as the weather in Seattle.

I've received ridiculous sums of money. I've bailed on directed sessions. I've auditioned horribly and been awarded that job. I've auditioned powerfully and not been cast. I've had to take people to collections. I've enjoyed crazy highs and scary lows. I've been consistently inconsistent. I've entered my office with claps and shouts of joy and exited with angry fists batting the air…and I've entered my office with angry fists batting the air and exited with claps and shouts of joy.

It's a beautiful craziness, all of it, and I wouldn't trade it for the world. Here are some observations for you to consider – not that this is going to be your life, or that you'll follow the same patterns. But they are there nonetheless, because this is the life of a hardworking voice talent:

- I wake up at 4:45 am and head downstairs to warm up and hit my morning auditions which usually number in the teens, before they start trickling in throughout the day. And I *must* have coffee. Where coffee is, life goes on.
- I end each day promptly at 5pm because I want to spend time with my family.
- Sometimes I have to deal with clients who don't know what they want, who approve my audition, I provide a few reads based off of my audition, then they change direction, so I give a few more reads based on that, and then they tell

> me it's too much and why couldn't I just stick with my audition tone? !?!?!

I've been in directed sessions where it's a massive script that we get locked in with two reads in under 15 minutes, and I've been in directed sessions where it's only a few lines and we take 2 hours to get them just the way they like them.

The rule of thumb in business is a rule of thirty-seven fingers. There is no single rule. Everything can change, and end up completely opposite from what you expect. I have been awarded jobs where it's a single :15 script. I record ten different alt takes for them, plus about twenty safeties or wilds of the CTA, and send it along. They'll come back and ask for *even more*. It never fails.

It's a business of feast or famine. Monday can suck. Tuesday can blow. Wednesday can stink. Thursday can drag on. And then Friday morning happens and it's if all the clients in the world have turned their guns on you, locked and loaded, and you are bombarded with work quantities the likes of which you've never seen. You can go into the last day of a slow week praying for the week to be over, and by 5pm that day, you'll wish it never ended. A week can turn on a dime.

All this to say that this business certainly keeps me on my toes. I never know what to expect, and that's the beauty of it. Whatever preconceived notions I have about that week in voiceovers, I am always, *always* proven wrong by 5pm Friday. And then I'm proven wrong again on Saturday. The clock resets, the bean counters go back to zero, and I'm back to the rat race again on Monday…and *I freaking love every freaking minute of it*.

Sometimes it's a mess. There are collection issues with some customers. One of my contract clauses specifies that I am to be paid from the net terms date stated on the contract *beginning from the point of deliverables*. All that to say that if they are Net 30, they need to have their payment in to me by thirty days from the date I delivered their files. They don't *issue* it by that date; I need to have it *in hand* by that date. The majority of customers don't seem to understand this, even though it's in black and white. Thankfully, one of my weekly routines is to send courtesy billing reminders out ahead of time. I *hate* collections, but it's a necessary evil, and a pleasurable torment. Torment because of the reasons just stated. Pleasurable because when I get them to pay up, that's one less thing on my mind, and there's more money in the bank.

I have absolutely no clue at the beginning of the week whether I'm going to be successful in generating jobs. Well, that's not entirely true. I could definitely go on record stating that I'm 100% determined. Nonetheless, the cards are dealt as the week goes along, and it's a crazy poker game of ridiculous odds. Here are some examples of what has transpired here and there:

- A repeat customer tells me that a national customer has another project for me. They've booked me several times before to the tune of thousands of dollars each time. So my embers are stoked, and I'm excited. Then a week later he tells me sorry, this time they want a female voice.
- A client could book me through Voice123, and once I send them my contract which reflects the price – which is in and of itself reflective of the stated usage from their listing – they come back and state that they need a full buyout, which was *not* stated in their listing. So I had the project for a few minutes, and then I didn't have it.
- I get a string of casting notices at 5:05pm, right after I've officially signed off for the day, and I head right back into the studio and tackle all of them
- A client sends me an email out of the blue stating that they've picked up my option on a spot for another year, and so *boom!* Send them an invoice for $3000 in residuals. And oh by the way they want to do their other spot too, so be sure to send an invoice for that one for $3300 as well.
- Lo and behold, I've scored a job off of Craigslist – Craigslist, of all places! Turns out it's not just for creepy personals.
- I've joined great VO networking groups and been highly encouraged by the new camaraderie, and then later that same day had to block a voice talent for being toxic.
- I've finished a Monday with 8 jobs. I've finished a Monday with 0 jobs.
- I've finished a week with 4 jobs. I've finished a week with 26 jobs.

- I've sworn that I have no time to write a blog for that week, and yet I put my best foot forward and write a blog that turns out to be one of my best.
- I'll sell no books at all one week. I'll sell five the next.
- I've done massive marketing one week and come away with very few listens on my website VoiceZam player. I've done *zero* marketing another week and booked 23 jobs.
- I was asked to judge an audiobook awards contest, even though I told them I don't do audiobooks.
- As an author, I've had bestsellers and no-sellers. I've written winners and not so much winners. I've done excellent interviews and some that I would like to forget.

There simply is no consistency. The only thing that is consistent, is the inconsistency of it. The only thing predictable about it, is its very unpredictability.

In addition, as far as weekly workflow, I've tweaked and re-tweaked – and re-tweaked – and tweaked yet again, my Reaper recording template to upgrade how my audio sounds upon export, so that my clients can have the best possible quality. It's a constant striving for perfection.

Being in business for oneself is an amazing pursuit. They require one to go with the flow, to roll with the punches, and to take the hits. Like Sylvester Stallone's character Rocky Balboa says in the movie of the same name:

Let me tell you something you already know. The world ain't all sunshine and rainbows. It's a very mean and nasty place and I don't care how tough you are it will beat you to your knees and keep you there permanently if you let it. You, me, or nobody is gonna hit as hard as life. But it ain't about how hard ya hit. It's about how hard you can get hit and keep moving forward. How much you can take and keep moving forward. That's how winning is done!

Keep. Moving. Forward.

Doing voiceovers isn't a symphony. It's the frenetic dissonance heard just *before* the symphony, where everyone is warming up together, there is no melody, and there is no harmony. It's a clash of notes, a collision of volatility, and a fickle overlap of wins and losses, high-stakes gambits and narrow escapes. Sometimes it's bursting forth in victorious flame, sword held high. Other times it's scraping through by the hair of your chinny-chin-chin.

And I wouldn't have it any other way.

Ever since I set out to be an entrepreneur in 2003 – nearly two decades ago – I knew there would be unpredictability, and that I would rise and fall on my own merits…my own efforts. I took the plunge then, and I take the plunge now. What I love about voiceovers is that, like any sales position or career, it's how hungry you are that determines how your week ends. The numbers don't have to reflect massive amounts of booked jobs; they just have to reflect massive amounts of effort: marketing, auditioning, and connecting. It's not the seeds you reap; it's the ones you *sow* each week.

That is what provides you consistency in the midst of uncertainty.

C'mon now, say it with me: "I love beautiful craziness." There. That's Step 1 (of 4,293). Good job. Welcome to our group of successfully healing misfits.

Now go git 'em.

TAKEAWAY & ACTION STEP

Are you pinning your hopes on actually booking work each week? Why? Perhaps refocus on actually marketing your services to as many people as possible.

Results don't have to reflect wins. Results just have to reflect tries. Keep a log of how many auditions you do per week. Record how many marketing outreaches you do. Track those, and look back on a track record of success.

When My Voice Meant Nothing

POWERLESS

I'm going to bare my soul, more or less, and share about one of the most painful events I've ever experienced, and I wasn't even the one experiencing the pain. This might be a messy chapter. So be it. But if you've ever been party to childbirth – and by that, I don't mean you *yourself* were given birth to, because then everyone would qualify – you'll know what I'm talking about.

It all came down to one moment. 270 days led up to this, days filled with joy and excitement, wonder, anticipation, hopes, and fears. 6480 hours during which anything could have gone wrong. 388,800 minutes for a catastrophic failure to happen.

It didn't. But it sort of did.

BUN IN THE OVEN

It was the morning of October 25th, 2018. My son Brennan and I were in the living room, playing. Nothing too out of the ordinary, except I had neglected to check the toaster setting for my English Muffins, which would soon be blackened bricks.

I knew my wife was upstairs in the shower, and I also knew that today was a great day. She and I had both just come back from a marriage retreat two weeks prior that was *much needed*. Holy cow did we need that. It was a very difficult year, with lots of stress and some fighting. OK actually it was a little bit of stress, and lots of fighting. OK it was a lot of stress and a lot of fighting. Don't need to pinpoint the reasons why at this stage, just suffice it to say that we desperately needed the retreat. Two weeks prior, we had left our only son at the time with MeeMaw and Pop-Pop, and headed off to a hotel in Tacoma, where we stayed for the whole weekend. We were anxious to pick him up and see him again on our way home, but we really enjoyed the retreat and were able to patch up some wounds and hit a reset button of sorts.

That was two weeks prior.

This morning, I happened to be lounging on the loveseat wearing only my boxers, because yeah. It was just a loungy morning. I was scrolling through something on my phone, when my wife emerged from the stairs in a towel, and her hair was bedraggled. I looked up and said "Hi, honey!"

Without a word, she approached me, towel wrapped up to her neck and one of her hands on the inside of it, and the other on the outside. It didn't occur to me that she was holding something.

In her eloquent way, she began, "Listen, I just wanted to tell you that I know you've been working hard." *I had been.* "And I know you've been depressed about your weight lately." *Lately? More like my whole life, but OK.* "And I just wanted to tell you that I love you, and I'm proud of you, and let's gain weight together."

She pulled it out, and I saw that glorious wand of pink and blue, with two distinct blue lines through the readout screen at the end. I instantly jumped up and shouted "NO WAY!!" and burst into tears as I grabbed and hugged her. Brennan looked over and noticed something happening that didn't remotely equal the wonder that is *Incredibles 2*, so he dismissed it and returned to his movie.

We jumped, we laughed, we cried. We couldn't believe that we were pregnant again. We thought it would never happen. We're a bit older and we started a bit later. When Brennan came along, he was a surprise in his own right. To know that we would now be on our way to becoming a family of four was just downright beautiful and majestic.

I remember picking him up and twirling him around over and over and over and exclaiming "You're gonna be a big brother you're gonna be a big brother you're gonna be a big brother!!!" He didn't know what brother meant yet – at least I don't think, but he knew what big was. Either way, *please put me back down so I can watch the Incredibles 2, which you're interrupting, thank you very much.*

We couldn't believe it. We sat and talked for a while and just giggled. It was amazing. That was October 25th, 2018.

IT'S GAME TIME

Remember *Aliens*, directed by James Cameron in 1986? Yeah. My favorite movie of all time. The character *Hicks* says to Ripley, "It's Game Time." And he means it, because it is. It's quite literally game time. And it's applicable, because he's a warrior, and so is my wife.

We knew the day was close, but we also knew it could be today. Over the past few months my beautiful wife had been diagnosed with gestational diabetes, and so she really had to watch her sugar intake, and actually had to puncture her beautiful fingers four times a day and test her levels. She had to drink her weight in water each day.

She'd had a checkup on Monday, June 10th, 2019 at Evergreen Women's Clinic in Kirkland, and they said that her fluid was a bit low. Moreover, if she didn't get her levels up by that coming Wednesday – two short days later – they would have to induce.

Janine had heard horror stories of induction. Being induced is basically – from my sheep-brained man's perspective, telling the body to be ready for pregnancy when it actually isn't ready, and turning everything into a locomotive for delivery. A chemical called Pitocin takes care of that.[48] She did not want that. I don't blame her. My cousin and best friend just had his second son, and his wife had to be induced, and she went from 5cm dilation to 10cm dilation in 45 minutes. She had relayed that it was excruciating. I'd rather puke coat hangers based on the horror story I heard of it. Yikes.

Janine obeyed. She drank even more water, she walked regularly, she ate well, and her levels were always good. But be that as it may, when we went into the ultrasound room on Wednesday June 12th and the technician said her fluid was looking kinda low, we knew what that meant. Janine's mouth creased into a frown and her eyes closed. She wanted so badly to have this baby naturally. Brennan was born naturally, but she wanted our second son to be born naturally, and on time, too. Not early. Not by someone else's medicine, but by her own body saying it was time.

We verified it with the doctor, and she said that yes, Janine would have to be induced today. We were prepared, sure enough, as we had brought the diaper bag, Brennan's little bag of clothes and food and snacks and toys, and Janine's hospital bag. We had sent out warning texts to friends and family who were going to take care of our dog and who might need to be called upon, but still, it was begrudgingly so. That baby was coming today, and not by our own will.

I dropped Janine off at Evergreen Women's Clinic and then brought Brennan home to be watched by a longtime family friend who dearly loves him. She was elated to watch him until relief arrived in the form of my brother-in-law who would stay the night, and I would pick him back up from school the following morning. I scatterbrainedly (it's a word) explained everything in detail about dog food, cat food, Brennan food, her food, the pool rules, changing, where diapers are, where the remote is, where the phone numbers are, where the toys are, where we'll be, where we *wanted* to be, etc. Then, yours truly was screaming back down the highway in the "Good to Go" lane. I didn't care about the fee; I needed to be with my wife.

When I found her in room 2141, she was doing well and in good spirits. She was fine. It was a bummer, but it would be fine. She had already been administered some penicillin and Pitocin, and so we were underway. A little unprepared and incredulous, but willing and ready.

A VERITABLE NIGHTMARE

What I'm about to describe can only be described as indescribable. I still shake my head how anyone – *anyone* – can go through what I witnessed my wife go through. Even as I write this, the PTSD in me is kicking in, and I am tearing up remembering the utter pain and trauma we both experienced.

Janine began the slow labor climb at 3:30pm, and things were fine, she walked, she stretched, she talked with our doula, she rested, she ate. At 8:41pm, after some stretching by the doula's boss (she was more experienced, and it was wonderful having her there!) I was behind Janine steadying her standing legs when I saw some droplets hit the floor. I was just reaching for a rag to mop them up, when I heard a splash, and then there was, um, more water. Lots more. Janine's water broke. No turning back now. Here we go.

Her contractions had slowly escalated, as that's what Pitocin does: it tells the body that it's in labor and essentially *forces* it into labor. The contractions were 2-4 minutes apart, then 2-3, then 2, and they were getting stronger. By 9pm, she was starting to hurt, and was moaning. I was behind her, praying for her, thinking in my sheep-brain that it would be just like last time.

It was nothing like last time.

By 9:45 she was in the tub, and she was hurting. Really hurting. The last time we were in this room (the very room, as it turns out, that Brennan was born in), it was a slow climb, but it was manageable, and she moaned very little, and her pushing was controlled, and she owned it. Now, her body was taking off without her, and it was like she had a coat stuck in the door of a train hurtling down the tracks.

#WARRIOR

I use that hashtag because that's what I use in social media when I talk about her. She is a warrior, a freaking warrior made out of stern stuff. She's been through a lot in her life, as we all have, but ultimately, she's been through some *other* things that lots of people have not, and she's weathered them. I love my wife. She is made of untearable fibers, and unbeatable metal that has been forged in the fiery lava of volcanos. If the One Ring was in fact unbreakable, then she was what it was made out of. She is unbreakable, unbeatable, unmeltable. (Just please don't throw her in a volcano to test my theory.) I'll say it again: she is a freaking warrior. I'm so proud of her. I had the highest level of respect for her *anyway*; then when she went through Asher's birth, my respect level reached *stratospheric*.

By 10pm, she was in unbearable pain. As a husband of a wife in labor, there was absolutely nothing I could do. There are in fact things I should *not* do under any circumstances. I knew what those were. My job was to hold her hand, let her clutch me, cry against me, pull me, bite me. She needed someone of equally stern material to weather this storm with her, and up until that time, I was that person.

Have you ever been disassembled? I have. It happened on June 12th, 2019.

Janine started screaming and convulsing. She was being ripped apart from the inside. Was an Alien in there? Her body was forcing her to relinquish control, and she had to simply tag along and weather the pain. She screamed. She screamed more. And then she kept screaming. We got her out of the tub, and put her in bed, and I asked, confusedly, in hope of helping her, "Where's the epidural? When can she get that? The doula boss looked at me and said, "You don't understand; she's having a baby in the next five minutes."

What happened in the next five minutes I'll never really concretely be able to grasp. I heard my wife yell screams I didn't even know were possible. I heard terror and sorrow and uncontrollable blaring. She grabbed me and bit me and pulled my hair and my clothes. I desperately tried to console her, voicing words into her ears and reminding her that I'm here.

Me, the voiceover artist. I, who get hired and paid to encourage and motivate people, was stripped of all my power and ability, as I could simply do nothing except absorb her anguish. And when I say anguish, I mean absolute utter unbearable pain.

My second son, Asher Justus, was born at 10:21pm on June 12th, 2019, at Evergreen Hospital, and for the first minute of his life I didn't even know he was there. All I could hear, reverberating in my ears and my heart and my soul, was the pain of my wife, and for the first time ever in my 46 years of existence, I thought I was going to lose someone right through my fingers. I couldn't understand why it was *that* painful – I mean painful? Sure. But *that* painful, like *it-sounded-like-she-was-being-sawn-in-two* painful? I had no idea my son was even there.

My son had come out, and my wife was still screaming for a bit, but I genuinely thought that I was going to leave the hospital with two sons and no wife. Images of a memorial service cascaded through my head, and it wasn't fair. It wasn't her time to go. It wasn't right. How could my new son do this to her? She needed to be here! I needed her desperately. For the first time in my life, I was mortally afraid – but not for my own life: for the life of another. For the love of my life. My beautiful bride, who chose me and decided to make a home with me and raise a family with me. And I was the one who got her pregnant! I did this to her! How could I have done this to her?

I nearly killed my wife.

The screams died down, and the baby was born, and we all celebrated. And it was joyful and exuberant and wonderful. But somehow, in the midst of all of that, it was devoid of the same rejoicing we had had the first time around. Whereas for the first birth my focus was 50% on my wife and 50% on my son, the second birth was 100% on my wife. I had an unshakeable feeling that she was going to suffer cardiac arrest, and I can still picture her lying on that bed, screams dying down, getting quieter now, and her fast, rapid breaths becoming white noise, blending into the steady beeeeeeeeeeeeeeeeeeeeeeeeeeeep of the flatline. I have never been more afraid, and I hurt still at this typing.

IT'S OVER – I LOVE YOU

My wife is ok. She made an excellent recovery, because, again, she's made of hardened lava. And I finally connected with my son. I took him into my arms and kissed him, but he was far behind in the race of kiss receiving. I had kissed my wife and bawled into her hair through sobbing and tear-filled gratitude that she was still alive. It never occurred to me that the hospital was monitoring her too, and that for any sign of cardiac arrest they would have acted swiftly and accordingly. But she made it. And the hashtag warrior belongs to no other.

What I breathed into her ear. The things I said. I need you. Brennan needs you. Asher needs you. Stay with me. Honey look at me. Honey listen to me. I was absolutely powerless to take any of her fear and pain away. When Asher came out, he actually ripped my wife, and they had to suture her up. I hear this is somewhat common in inductions, but whatever. I don't care about the statistics, I cared about saving my wife, and for the first time in my life I felt utterly powerless to do anything about anything but trust that in the dim reckoning of her mind, in the screaming pounding of her ears, she could hear the voiceover out there somewhere, dim, quietly urging her on and telling her she could do it. That voice was colored through blood and pain and anguish on June 12th, 2019, and it will never be the same.

WHERE DO I GO FROM HERE

I guess if you think about it, I can use what happened and try to channel some of the emotional energy into my performances. I guess I can try to make sense out of it. I feel an awful lot like Frodo in the end of the movie *The Return of the King* where he says: *"How do you pick up the threads of an old life? How do you go on, when in your heart, you begin to understand, there is no going back? There are some things that time cannot mend. Some hurts that go too deep... that have taken hold."*

My old life is gone. A new one has begun, and we're a family of four, and it's good. But there are some things that time cannot mend. Some hurts that go too deep, that have taken hold. I'm actually struggling with *paternal post-partem depression*[49] and PTSD because of what happened. I don't ever want to hear those screams again. I don't ever want to not be able to help my wife. I want to, need to, owe it to be by her side forever, and to love her back to health, and to allow myself to be loved to health as well. You see, I love my wife, and I can't imagine losing her.

It's just that unfortunately I can now actually imagine it.

Thank you, Janine Marie, for loving me enough to start a family, to carry my sons, and to bring them to childbirth and beyond. I love you, I honor you, I salute you, and I am SO grateful for you, beyond words, immeasurable, *forever*.

For the rest of you, I'm sorry, but this one was *not* about voiceovers. It's about life. Isn't it, Asher?

Oh, he's sleeping. *Shhhhhhhhhh...*

The point in all of this? Your voice means something. Your voice means everything. You have a unique voice. *Use it.*

The $1000 I Will Never See Again

THE COPYRIGHT TROLLS ARE ALIVE AND WELL

The Voices In My Head was a satirical blog that I maintained. My books are also satirical in nature, although also educational. They are all intended to be amusing and encouraging edutainment. However, on occasion an issue comes to light that necessitates that I stow the satirical and the funny, and address something somberly, because it has bearings on bloggers, and you need to be protected, especially if you are a blogger or are conducting digital marketing. So, hold on to your butts: this chapter is a long, somewhat chagrinned one. It is not an airing of grievances; it is a play-by-play for you to pay attention to and hopefully avoid. Consider it a very lengthy PSA.

The word of the day is not funny. The word of the day, boys and girls, is *despicable*.

It began in innocence, as many things do. A harmless post, something to encourage and bring joy. It was something that came, intentionally, in the middle of a dark time, to lighten the load and help us all breathe some fresh air in a time where breathing fresh air was a bit scary.

On March 23rd 2020 I published a blog entitled *"We have your Toilet Paper. And if you ever want to see it again..."*[50] This blog contained observations on the times we were living in, including panic-buying and hoarding of things like toilet paper.[51] It also included a "Top Ten" list of amusing activities you can do in order to creatively outlast the pandemic. In this blog, I happened to do a Google search, and then find and use a picture of a man wearing a box over his head: a makeshift mask, comical in its appearance, silly, and underscoring the extents we would all, as a society, go to in order to avoid contracting COVID-19. I would write several subsequent blogs on the subject, as would many of my contemporaries.

Throughout 2020, countless memes have been employed of people in masks, Darth Vader not the least. Masks unfortunately were not going away anytime soon, and unfortunately, they were the new normal.

However, unbeknownst to me, another new normal has been creeping up for years in the slums of the Internet. It is the new normal of cyberbullying, shaming, harassment, and extortion – all born of cowardice, greed, and/or malice.

What I intended to be a humorous and satirical look at the state of our pandemic would later become one of my biggest regrets, and would eat away at my pride.

There are people out there that exist solely to make others miserable. I was about to meet one of them up close and personal…again.

NOT MY FIRST RODEO

I may have mentioned before that my wife and I have been victims of cyberbullying. Ergo, what I was about to encounter was no undiscovered territory or foreign terrain. When I received the first communications, it immediately reeked of extortion and cyberbullying. Perhaps my defenses were already up, and I had unfortunately, through experience, been trained to sniff out jerks on the prowl; be that as it may, here came another one.

On Monday August 3rd 2020, I received a notification from PicRights International, on behalf of Agence France-Presse, stating that they *"noticed that imagery represented by Agence France-Presse has been displayed on your website. However, Agence France-Presse has been unable to find a license for this usage of the imagery by your organisation. Therefore, we are acting on behalf of Agence France-Presse to obtain compensation for your unauthorized past use of their imagery."*

Now, I receive plenty of emails from Nigerian princes, phishing attempts and fake alerts designed to see me surrender any one of a number of payments, but this one seemed more "official." I immediately removed the image from my website and wrote these people back, stating that I had no idea the image was copyright-protected, and that I had removed it.

Nonetheless, they had already invoiced me.

Wait. Invoiced me? Was a transaction ever conducted? Did I purposefully misuse something? Did I seek to defraud? Was there intent? Let us review. No. No. Aaaaaaand no. Nonetheless, I now apparently owed $534 for compensation for *"the past unauthorized usage of the imagery."* Without providing so much as any kind of official copyright registration number, PicRights was now the police, and I was the perp. I scratched my head. Uh....how did it come to this again, can anyone remind me?

Once I read that payment was being demanded, I knew this was legalized extortion: the very same place I had been at before, back in 2013. To test out the lack of officialness of this alleged complaint, I wrote back:

"I had no idea the image was copyright-protected. I assumed it was public domain. I cannot pay more than $300. And I cannot pay until after the 20th. Please advise."

They agreed. $300 was fine, and after the 20th was fine. And that right there confirmed my suspicions of extortion. They were willing to mark down my apparent damages by 56%. FIFTY-SIX PERCENT!!! What negotiating leverage they held on behalf of their complainant. But wait - if there is no set-in-stone global infringement statute that specifically states that $X + Y = Z$, and if they are now *bargaining* with me, then that is discretionary, desperate, capitalist greed-grabbing, plain and simple. Extortionists use threats to exact payments. They can be flexible, because they know that their little trick is working, and they will even pretend to be reasonable and gracious. Which is exactly what PicRights then did, because of the pandemic:

"We fully appreciate that this is a very difficult time. With that in mind, we would welcome the opportunity to discuss this matter with you, in the hope that we can achieve a resolution."

Classic extortionist talk. Absent a global statute delineating clear and tiered financial penalties dependent on the level of the alleged offense, this whole "we'll work with you" policy smacked of a "let's take them for whatever we can get" approach.

I wrote back and requested proof that the image copyright was registered, and on what date. PicRights replied using, I am sure, the same form-letter response they have always used:

"As you probably know, since you are an artist yourself, copyright exists automatically from the moment a photograph is taken or an illustration is rendered. Copyright in original works of authorship is automatic, and registration – while it does carry significant benefits to the copyright owner – is not required for a work to be protected by copyright. Protection attaches immediately when the work is completed which, in the case of a photograph, happens the moment the shutter is clicked. In order for a copyright owner to sue an infringer in the USA, the copyright must be registered but that can be done online by the copyright owner prior to issuing a lawsuit."

Essentially, now there apparently was retroactive protection even absent a formal copyright registration. *Mmm-hmmmmm.* At any rate, sure, they are right: I am an artist myself. However, I would think the formal approach would be having the copyright holder *themselves* come to me and say *"Hey, you, darn you! You used my image, you just better take that down right this minute, do you hear me?"* This is precisely the purpose of using effective cease-and-desist letters, which would be the expected first step. Not arbitrary monetary demands.

Again, my original reply was "I had no idea." I was more than willing to comply, and I *did* comply, removing it right away. Apparently, however, honoring requests is not enough anymore, and the *modus operandi* is to make people miserable through demands for monetary compensation, and threats of legal action through who I would come to find out was their *de facto* copyright troll attorney, Higbee & Associates.

At any rate, after doing my due diligence with some heavy research, here was my reply:

*"Your explanation aside, you and Alfred Hoefinger seem to be proceeding with a **formal** complaint with a **formal** request for payment alleging a **formal** copyright infringement. Therefore, please provide proof that the image copyright was indeed **formally** registered, and on what date. If there is no registration, there is no infringement. In the United States, copyright is filed*

with the Library of Congress, or at the very least, as a "poor man's copyright" mailed certified from oneself to oneself. In this case, I will need proof that either was done. As an artist myself, as you say, I provide mp3s all the time, but none of them are registered with any kind of copyright, and if they were, I would need to go through proper channels to register them for them to indeed be protected legally.

*So, again, please provide proof that the image copyright was indeed **formally** registered, and on what date.*

Also, for your sentence "copyright exists automatically from the moment a photograph is taken"...all the way through "copyright owner prior to issuing a lawsuit", please cite your legal reference where you're deriving such language from.

Also, please provide how you arrived at the arbitrary amount of $534 originally, and how you are authorized to negotiate the price down to $300 on behalf of Agence France-Presse.

Also, per your original email, you stated that the notice to me was sent via hard mail. I have received no such copy. Please fulfill your due diligence by forwarding me the copy of your complaint via hard mail.

*As **you** may know, under digital media law, citing from Title 17 of the US Code:*

the fair use of a copyrighted work, including such use by reproduction in copies or phonorecords or by any other means specified by that section, for purposes such as criticism, comment, news reporting, teaching (including multiple copies for classroom use), scholarship, or research, is not an infringement of copyright. In determining whether the use made of a work in any particular case is a fair use the factors to be considered shall include:

the purpose and character of the use, including whether such use is of a commercial nature or is for nonprofit educational purposes;
the nature of the copyrighted work;
the amount and substantiality of the portion used in relation to the copyrighted work as a whole;
and the effect of the use upon the potential market for or value of the copyrighted work.

In my case, mine was used merely for teaching and commenting, as from my blog, to illustrate a point. Not for profit, and not for recirculation. It was found in a simple Google search and was used for demonstration purposes only, for a limited subscriber base of readership. Therefore, limitations on exclusive rights applies here. In any event, you ought to be sending a formal cease and desist letter from an attorney, not bargaining down a supposed "licensing rights" price and requesting that I pay you outright, whereas any supposed copyright infringement licensing payment should be going to the original copyright holder, not an intermediary.

I'm consulting with an attorney to look into this matter and will be in touch."

Aren't I good? Well, they wrote back and stated that they have *"provided sufficient documents to confirm our partnership with AFP, and the image ownership of AFP."*

I replied:

"You are threatening legal action. Pursuant to discovery and information gathering, I will once again request the following, since it does not appear that the image was even registered with a formal copyright. Once I have this information I too will proceed. Thanks. I'm sure you understand that threatening legal action must be accompanied by substantiated evidence as opposed to a random request for an alleged license infraction payment.

*Again, please provide proof that the image copyright was indeed **formally** registered, and on what date.*
Also, for your sentence "copyright exists automatically from the moment a photograph is taken"...all the way through "copyright owner prior to issuing a lawsuit", please cite your legal reference where you're deriving such language from.
Also, please provide how you arrived at the arbitrary amount of $534 originally, and how you are authorized to negotiate the price down to $300 on behalf of Agence France-Presse.
Also, per your original email, you stated that the notice to me was sent via hard mail. I have received no such copy. Please fulfill your due diligence by forwarding me the copy of your complaint via hard mail"

You can see I am once again asking for proof of the formal registration of the copyright. And you can see that they would not provide it.

I received no response. And then there came the inevitable lull. Nothing, no word. Until of course June 24th 2021, when I received the threat letter from Higbee & Associates.

SUE IS NOT MY FAVORITE WOMAN'S NAME

The letter is too long to be included here, and it would just bore and irritate you. Must be a sad life for Higbee, with everyone they write to mad at them. My customers all seem to like me. Oh well....anyway....

It was multi-paged, as all formal extortion notices tend to be, laden with threats veiled in sympathy, understanding that we are certainly in difficult times, but if you kindly pay us what you owe, we will not take you to the cleaners and demand your firstborn. Amidst all of the heavy-handed "evidence" they presented, there was the threat that a court judgment could be rendered against me, awarding them up to $150,000 in damages.

I more or less knew this day was coming, in the back of my mind. One thing that many Reddit forums[52] and other well-informed articles stated was "they will not go away." Attorneys advised me not to ignore it. I was naïve to think that it might be, that I had somehow proven myself to be a worthy contender through my well-written emails, and that I was not some average Aaron. Indeed, I was above average, and I would not be sued, and I would not pay up, and you are wrong, *thankyouverymuch*.

All of that went out the window. The long story short is that I consulted with an attorney, Darren Heitner of Heitner Legal, after finding and reading one of his articles.[53] Darren's retainer would be reasonable, but ultimately, there was still the chance that I could lose. And then I would be out:

court costs
plus Darren's retainer
plus Agence France-Presse's legal fees

plus Higbee's legal fees
plus the judgment, whatever that might be.

All for harmlessly posting an innocent picture on a blog that was designed to encourage people during a dark time. Sorry for caring, world. Thanks for the karma.

The Internet is a revolutionary and awesome tool that has allowed some truly despicable predators to come out of the woodwork and abuse it. Through the anonymity it affords, through the distancing it provides, people all the way across the world can exact payment from us for whatever way they feel slighted. They can take it to the court system, and they can win. I have seen it happen, and I was not going to be a further victim: not only of the harassment and extortion, but of the courts perhaps deciding (erroneously and unjustly) in their favor.

I decided I had had enough, and I swallowed my pride. I engaged suspension of disbelief. I paid the $1335 and signed their release. Good riddance. I could have taken it to court and argued Fair Use.[54] I could have pleaded my case to a hopefully rational and caring judge. I may have won. I may have lost. Who knows. I was not going to roll the dice.

In August of 2011, I could have just paid $300. Now I was paying $1300. That is a $1000 difference I will never see again, all because of principle. All because of a failed system. All because of legalized extortion and cyberbullying. And I am not alone. Check out these articles and exposés on other victims...

https://gritdaily.com/higbee-and-associates-the-latest-legal-trolling-scam/

https://pubcit.typepad.com/clpblog/2019/02/consumer-warning-copyright-trolling-by-higbee-and-associates.html

https://matthewsag.com/so-you-got-a-copyright-infringement-demand-letter-from-higbee-associates/

https://faceless.marketing/higbee-associates-copyright-trolls/

https://www.techdirt.com/articles/20191124/00071243444/copyright-troll-mathew-higbee-demands-1000-image-only-his-team-viewed.shtml

https://www.avvo.com/legal-answers/i-ve-received-a-letter-from-the-law-offices-of-hig-5063809.html

https://anneofcarversville.com/fashion/2020/4/19/surviving-continued-trolling-by-higbee-associates

https://copyright-demand-letter.com/category/higbee-associates/

https://law.ku.edu/sites/law.ku.edu/files/docs/media_law/2019/Panel-5-Trolls-CLE-042519-2nd.pdf

https://www.extortionletterinfo.com/forum/higbee-letter-lawsuits-forum/recent-articke-investigating-the-higbee-associates-copyright-trolling-operati/

https://www.quora.com/What-should-I-do-when-I-am-being-sued-by-Higbee-Associates-for-using-an-image-I-got-from-Google-without-a-licence-I-got-mail-saying-that-I-used-an-image-without-having-the-licence-and-now-I-m-being-sued-for-5200

https://www.fastcompany.com/40494777/here-come-the-copyright-robots-for-hire-with-lawyers-in-tow

https://www.ballardspahr.com/-/jssmedia/Files/Articles/2019-08-01-unfinished-ballad-of-gunslinger-leibowitz.pdf?rev=54ceea5e6461415e90b5819f498f264e&hash=31F7A46C05C9445FAD15EB2D2DDBB13F

https://jasholdingsltd.com/wp-letter.php?pg=sitelink_search/higbee-copyright-troll/

https://ilr.law.uiowa.edu/print/volume-100-issue-3/copyright-trolling-an-empirical-study/

https://twitter.com/extortionletter?lang=en

https://www.themodernfirm.com/blog/qotw/when-is-a-picture-worth-1000-or-more/

https://culture-fx.com/picrights-higbee-and-associates-extortion-scam-reviews/

https://www.justanswer.com/canada-law/eii6z-debra-received-similar-email-picrights.html

The list goes on. And on. And on.

Paul Strikwerda also has an excellent blog on this.[55] Conversations about Higbee and PicRights: Reddit is rife.[56] Quora is at quota with queries.[57] Communities are counting the complaints.[58] Matthew Higbee, PicRights, CopyTrack, Masterfile, Pixsy, etc.: they're all the same lump of bad coal in your stocking.

AARON, WRAP THIS UP, WILL YOU?

Speaking of stockings, I would wrap it up and put a bow on it, but this is a present I would not wish on anyone. I warned my fellow bloggers about this when I first heard from PicRights in 2020, and it came to light that many of them were using great sites for their free images, such as the following reputable sources:

- Unsplash
- Pixabay
- Creative Commons
- Envato Elements
- Twenty20
- Sites with free images that you can use with or without attribution.

Hindsight is 20/20: if I knew then what I know now. Information truly *is* power. What I wrote in complete innocence out of a desire to encourage and provide a little levity in the midst of a pandemic that affects ALL of us, was met with a pounce for money, in pure capitalist greed.

Look, I did not do this intentionally. Had they asked nicely with a simple warning, or simply sent a cease-and-desist letter, I would have gladly removed the image (I did) and apologized (I did). My eyes would have been opened. The fact that these companies *lurk in waiting* to pounce upon people who do this, seeing only dollar signs...is despicable. Do people not ask anymore, they just assume you are corrupt and malicious? Is that what we have come to as a society? Sickening.

I earn an honest living as a voiceover artist, and paying $1300 does not put my family in the gutter in the slightest. However, there *are* some people out there that that kind of money *would* decimate. Aside from that, there is the whole issue of having to swallow my pride...and forget. Emerge the wiser, and employ discretion, intelligence and strategy going forward. Indeed, I wiped all images from that blog prior, and going forward only use free images with attribution, paid images with a transferred license, or my own created images.

That is my counsel to fellow bloggers, because *bloggers* seem to be the chosen prey of these animals. You must *always* use images that are free. Never just grab them from a Google search. Use images that are absolutely *clear* that they are free. Or use images that are free to use with attribution (crediting the original author with a link). Or use paid images wherein the usage license is transferred to you upon purchase. And - if you are ever pursued by these creatures, do yourself a favor and just pay up early. They will not go away, and the cost will continue to climb. You will lose sleep and peace, and could potentially have a judgment entered against you. Is it worth it? Probably not. Pay up while it's low, learn your lesson, and move on.

I am an author, a blogger, a voice talent, and an encourager. I am no crusader. This fight was not one I wished to take on. I preferred to have lower blood pressure. I have more important things to do, and a more important life to live. I fly and I soar. I do not lurk under bridges. I create, I dream, and I enable, and encourage people with my voice. My climb upward is not over the backs of others. I have no such lofty aspirations to get-rich-quick. My aim is living in integrity; not literally banking on misery.

So, in short, it is actually $1300 I will never see again. But as long as I never see Higbee and Associates or PicRights or Agence France-Presse again, that is a small price to pay. Had I paid it right away, it would have been $300. At this writing and after paying their $1300, I just got a $1000 VO job. So, I believe God just made it even, and I am glad He is in my corner. I could have completely ignored them, but they could have continued to try to notify me, find me, serve me, etc., and eventually, it is all up to a judge, who could have entered a default judgment against me of up to $150,000. Did I cave to avoid that? Maybe. But I did it for my own sanity and peace of mind, and I emerged as the better person, rising above it all.

The reality, however, is that I should never have had to pay *anything*. But thank you, Internet, for allowing mold to grow in the dark corners of your web, and springing up bounty hunters.

I am an entrepreneur. I understand copyright protection and needing to protect the usage of my audio. My contracts all enforce it. If a client of mine violated that contract, would I take them to court? Maybe. I would probably send a cease-and-desist letter first however, as that is just common decency. There would not be any formal demands for remuneration accompanied by legal threats. Even if there were, again: there was a *contract* in place beforehand stipulating that usage, so the end client knows full well what the usage parameters are. In the wild west of the Internet, there are no such contracts or usage parameters. Unfortunately, anything goes – until you are threatened and sued. And such despicable people choose to make that their livelihood. Unconscionable.

Make no mistake: it was not Agence France-Press who cared about the image being used. Do you really think there was some disgruntled photographer in an office in France grumbling as he landed on my site? No. Companies like PicRights employ software that do reverse-searches on imagery, and then *report* it to companies like Agence France-Press, in order to secure them as a client so they can harvest victims for extortion payments. That, quite simply, is what this is. On the flip side, I have photographer friends who I *utterly* respect, and their productions deserve protections, as mine do. There is just a genuine disconnect between the artists who produce, and the henchmen who collect.

That is the difference between copyright trolls and me: I do not have selfish, greedy ambition that comes at the expense of another. I will sleep in peace tonight. Sure, PicRights and Higbee may too, lying on their satin sheets in their gilded beachfront property, rolling amongst gems while the sea breeze blows in hundred-dollar bills. Good for them.

I will opt for the honest, decent life seven days of the week and twice on Sunday instead of soulless vampirism. I end this chapter on a sour note. Again, I desire to encourage and bring laughter, rather than to be mired in frustration and sadness. But the blood of my humor was sucked right out of me in a $1300 gut-punch because of an honest mistake.

My real hope is that if you are a fellow blogger, author, marketer or artist, I hope to have turned this unfortunate experience on its head so that you can benefit from it and be unafflicted by such lowlife leeches from the underbelly of the web. Please do not make the same mistake I did.

$1300 goes a long way. It could have been more, and for that, I am grateful. In my humble opinion, it just should have been zero. But the copyright trolls are alive and well, unfortunately.

HERE'S ONE TO GROW ON:

"Life can only be understood backwards; but it must be lived forwards."

Soren Kierkegaard

The Big Versus

KERNELS OF WISDOM AND NUGGETS OF TRUTH

This will be a challenging chapter. Buckle up. There are things that are of foundational importance to you as an entrepreneur that I highly encourage you to adopt if you want to be a successful business owner. This chapter is dedicated to those things.

I make no bones about that fact that I have never once approached voiceovers as a hobby. Not once. I didn't look at it and say to myself:

- "Hmm. I think I might like to try that."
- "Maybe I'll be successful."
- "Let's give it a whirl and see what happens."

No. For me, *this was it.* If you've read anything I've put out, you'll know how much they mean to me. They're a saving grace, and in fact a ministry. I don't hide the fact that I'm a Christian who loves Jesus – woe to me if I don't preach the gospel – but in this business there are strains of actual *ministry*, both to me and to others. To be chosen to voice someone's script is an incredible extension of trust. To be able to bring their script to life and minister to them through the spoken word is an exquisite privilege the likes of which I had never been exposed to. Oh what an honor it is to be chosen, even if it's about cat food!

But therein lies the nugget. The truth is that the clients are trusting you. They're bestowing upon you a massive amount of hope that you'll be able to produce, and in so doing, represent them well. Now, true, they chose you because your audition compelled them to choose you. But what you and I have to remember is that they didn't have to. They could have chosen *anyone*. The fact that they chose *me?* I don't take that lightly. That's something I resound gratitude over, and I am very "overthanky" in my responses. I want them to know how truly much it means to me to have been chosen.

So now that the weight of the world for the successful delivery of their script is upon your shoulders, what do you do?

It's time to produce.

Yes, this business is a fun pursuit. But it's still a pursuit, and it's still a business.

HOBBYISTS VS. BUSINESSPEOPLE

If you're going to be entrusted to produce quality audio and compelling messages for people, it's time to evaluate where you sit in terms of professionalism. Is Audacity good enough? Is a Blue Yeti mic really going to cut the mustard? Is a handshake deal going to protect you? Or is there something here so worth fighting for that you *must* envelop it in structure... branding... logo... reputation... contracts... clauses... professional audio... investing in yourself... coaching... networking, and more? I love what Tara Platt and Yuri Lowenthal say here: "In all the excitement of a voice-over career, professionalism can be the first trait to go. We cannot stress this fact enough: you will stand out from others by being a consummate professional. And you don't have to know anything about voice acting to act like a professional. Do you think the most talented actors always get the job? Not if they're difficult to work with. You'd be surprised at how often actors will get the job just by showing up, doing the work, being decent to interact with, and then going on their merry way. Be one of these people. It doesn't take a lot of extra effort. Be someone who is reliable, humble, polite, talented, and available."[59]

Do you want to be a hobbyist and do it well? Or do you want to be a businessperson and do it *best*?

Remember, good is always the worst enemy of best.

I recently had a discussion with someone on Facebook where they said that they're just in voiceovers for the enjoyment. While I understand where they're coming from, that statement presumes, incorrectly so, that I am not. I am in this both for enjoyment AND profit. I want a career that pays me...but that I also enjoy, no? Is it an unreasonable expectation to do what I love *and* be able to get paid for it?

Where many of the "do-it-for-love" crowd come from is a place that I never want to be at with voiceovers. My brain just isn't capable of wrapping itself around that. *Yes,* an emphatic *yes* I love what I do, and I want to continue to love it. But it's because I love it so much, that I want to *protect* it within the confines of a business structure that can promote growth, evolution, mastery, and, ultimately, a nice full 401K in the end. Those that proceed in voiceovers purely out of love and don't have the ambition or see the need to charge market rates, will never attain a career that pays their mortgage or funds their dreams. They are missing an inherent sense of self-worth.

In short, they're hobbyists.

So with that, this chapter is hellbent on one mission: to reveal for you The Big Versus…to reveal to you the huge colossal chasm of difference between hobbyists and business owners. Here we go. I suggest disengaging your defenses so that you're not offended, because the next few minutes may just rub you the wrong way. We'll be friends when I return…or will we?

MONEY

Hobbyists make hobby money. Maybe a bit of coffee money here and there. Business owners create revenue. Hobbyists are thinking it might be nice to have a bit of short-term chump change. That name is not a coincidence. Business owners on the other hand are focused on building something that lasts; constructing something that has foundations for the long term.

This industry is far too good to think you can subsist on Fiverr or Just Say Spots or GigNewton or Casting Call Club or The Voice Realm and think you're "making it."

You are missing out on the bigger picture by settling for. There is far too much revenue to be generated in voiceovers, and each time you settle for less, you hurt us all because you're setting improper precedents in the minds of clients that they can get you on the cheap.

I'll quote Paul Strikwerda again: you don't want to attract "clients that expect a gourmet meal at a fast food price and at drive-through speed."[60]

You deserve more.

Lose the hobbyist and earn what you're worth.

PASTIMES

Hobbyists have a pastime. It's an occasional fling. Business owners create an ecosystem. The former jump in every once in a while, subject to their emotions and whims; the latter erect a foundation that weathers time, economy, and more. It's building your home out of straw vs. bricks. There are only a few wise little pigs. Don't let the big bad wolf come blow down your hobbyist house of straw. This is not a leisurely activity that you pop in and out of. My voiceovers are 8am to 5pm Monday through Friday, just like a normal job. They're in an office, just like a normal career. They are growing and I'm moving up, just like a normal vocation. Hobbyists dance around success; business owners *are* the success.

REPUTATIONS

Hobbyists are a dime a dozen. They're the sheep. Business owners are one in a thousand. They're the shepherds. They're the pace-makers, the trendsetters, the goal-hitters.

Hobbyists follow along and aren't convinced that they need to take notes. "Give me a break, I'll remember this for sure." Meanwhile, business owners are scribbling detailed notes to refer back to.

Business owners take everything they've learned and assimilate it into a focused, tailored approach that is unique to their gifting and styles, enabling them to do what they know, and live how they can best grow in skill. They don't stagnate; they start producing, and people take notice. In the end, even chimpanzees have leaders that all the others follow.

ETHICS

Hobbyists have fly-by-night morality that depends entirely on what it will cost them. They don't see the need to obtain a business license because that means that they'll have to pay taxes on their hobby money. They see no need to get an LLC that will cover them in the event of a legal disagreement because of the one-time cost of $150, which seems insurmountable to them.

Business owners, on the other hand, happily register their business with local, state, and federal authorities because they want to be established, and they firmly believe that paying taxes is the right and ethical thing to do.

Hobbyists hope no one notices and seek to stay under the radar. Business people take great pride in knowing how much they've made and knowing that paying taxes is what is required of responsible citizens.

Hobbyists think that what they do is good enough; business owners, on the other hand, are never satisfied. It's never enough! They go the extra step…from marketing, to recording…to auditions. As Yuri and Tara say in *Voice-Over Voice Actor,* "You don't want to give them any excuses not to fall in love with you."[61] Hobbyists use excuses like "It was good enough." Business owners would never say that.

BRANDING

Hobbyists see no need for a logo, branding, or any symbol of who they are. Their identity isn't wrapped up in their craft yet; so there is no need to adopt a symbol of their greatness or their skill. It's futile to pursue any kind of epitome of their offerings; they haven't arrived yet at a place where they see their vocation of monumental importance yet.

Business owners, on the other hand, see a logo and branding as utterly definitive of who they are, and what sets them apart. They are self-aware, and know that providing great service doesn't make them unique; providing great service that is absolutely a cut above the rest is what they strive toward, and *that* is what makes them unique. Concordantly it's easy for them to look at symbols and choose something that demonstrates the qualities that they already, or want to, showcase. Lao-Tzu said, "When you are content to be simply yourself and don't compare or compete, everybody will respect you." Be utterly yourself. Be utterly even *more* than yourself.

It's what Christian Bale said in *Batman Begins:*

As a man, I'm flesh and blood, I can be ignored, I can be destroyed; but as a symbol... as a symbol I can be incorruptible, I can be everlasting.[62]

INVESTMENT

Hobbyists look sadly at every cost, and wish that life didn't exact so much from them. Business owners on the other hand look at expenses as investments. The problem hobbyists have with expenses is that they lack patience: they don't grasp that it first requires a willingness to plant a seed before you can watch it grow and enjoy its fruit. They want the fruit, not the growth.

And sometimes, like Queen, they want it all, and they want it now.

Any good thing worth pursuing takes investment. Business owners who have skin in the game know that their investment can pay back dividends. The pride a business owner feels when they own something outright and bought it with their hard-earned dollars far outweighs the joy the hobbyist feels when they've been given a handout.

The business owner feels gratification. The hobbyist feels relief. That relief, once put into words, would sound like "Phew! Dodged a bullet there. Almost had to spend some money!"

The business owner can successfully say "*I* did this. No one else. Me."

The hobbyist uses everything free and hopes that a producer will like the substandard product they churn out with all their free goods: Wix/Weebly, Audacity, $39 mics on Amazon, cheap headphones, USB mics, and discounted computer speakers. Then they get mad and jealous of all those around them who are succeeding. They wonder why it's not fair and they shake their fist at the world.

I know of one such aspiring voice guy who I gave a *free* consult to that got everything for free and was expecting to succeed. The next post I saw from him he was asking his Facebook friends to give Christmas gifts to his son because he couldn't afford it.

Skin in the game.

CUSTOMER RELATIONSHIPS

Hobbyists have simple email agreements and handshake deals. Business owners seal their deals in blood, with contracts that contain clauses that protect their interests.

Hobbyists throw their finished audio out there and hope to be paid in a timely fashion, with no recourse if they're not. Business owners' contracts contain net terms with defined grace periods and 1% daily late fees.

Hobbyists go for the one-and-done approach with their "clients." They're grateful for that one payoff and then goodness knows if they'll ever see that client again. Business owners develop long-lasting relationships intent on future work.

Hobbyists hope their clients come back. Business owners *intend* for their clients to come back.

Hobbyists don't feel the necessity to create structure or anything that guarantees them a real shot at success. It's not a system for them; it's a random happenstance occurrence of maybe's and hopes and what-ifs.

Business owners don't work that way: they don't wait for their dreams to come true; they *make* their dreams come true through concrete and comprehensive goal tracking and intention.

Remember, intention trounces hope every single time.

PAYMENTS

Hobbyists have fragile and limited payment avenues. They'll take PayPal and maybe Venmo. Even better, they'll just take straight under-the-table cash. Why report that to the IRS?

Business owners provide their clients ease of payment, with multiple possibilities. PayPal. Zelle. Square. Authorize.net. Venmo. Check. ACH. Bill.com. ChasePay. TransferWise. And others.

Business owners know that big clients who pay big bucks work on net terms and issue checks or pay via ACH or direct deposit: all trackable income that hobbyists don't like.

STUDIO

A hobbyist rents studio time. A business demands a home studio. If you're relying on a studio's availability for your every audition and your every recorded job, it's going to cost you, as Yuri Lowenthal and Tara Platt say: "Now, obviously, this comes at a cost, and won't be as flexible as having your own recording equipment."[63]

Hobbyists will unwisely, repeatedly shell out bucks to rent studio time in the short term; business owners will purchase or construct a home studio for the long term.

SELF-WORTH

Here's the most important one. Hobbyists undervalue themselves. They'll allow themselves to be taken advantage of because they don't know the immeasurable value of their own service.

Business owners charge what they're worth. They have a firmly ingrained sense of deserving market rates, and charging rates commensurate with not their identity or length of experience, but rather commensurate with what the service simply costs. It's not based on how long they've been in business, if the economy is on a downturn, do they need something on their resume, or feeling they somehow don't deserve it.

Business owners know the worth of their service, and they charge accordingly.

Hobbyists will charge well under market value out of desperation and wanting badly just to list some "big name" client on their resumé. They have no idea that many clients on the paying end are well aware of what a voiceover artist should make, and when they see the paltry rates that the "voice talent" is charging, they know instantly that they're a novice. That they're not a team player. That they're desperate. That they can be taken advantage of.

These are not the clients you or I want, so why on earth would you be the voice talent that such clients want?

A business owner knows that the service costs what the service costs...period, end of story.

There. Are we still friends? You mad, bro?

The bottom line for myself and for many vetted, tried and true entrepreneurs for whom our careers are not vocations we dip in and out of, this is serious. It's not just a career or some vocation, but rather an honorable calling, a service, and a ministry that has immeasurable value to our clients.

We are carrying someone's messages to the masses. We are their brand ambassador. We are the ones chosen to speak for them. They know that if their clients don't believe us, then they won't believe them either. It's our job to make our clients' clients believe our clients. If they don't believe us, they won't believe them.

We therefore have an enormous responsibility (read: privilege) of being a storyteller. That is a calling and career that every business owner knows is highly sustainable; they just need to approach it the right way.

Perhaps that great prophet Yoda said it best when he told a budding Jedi Master, "No. Try not. *Do* or do *not*. There is no *try*."

A hobbyist tries. A business owner *does*, because there is no *try*.

TAKEAWAY & ACTION STEP

Intention trounces hope every time.

How long have you been hoping to succeed, without a concrete intention to do so? In what ways are you clinging to an unrealistic dream that you're going to attain it? What can you do today to start intending to attain and fulfill your dreams? Write down 3 false or unrealistic hopes you've clung to, and then see how you can turn them into intentions.

Thank Goodness I Only Do Jobs For Exposure

IT'S ALL ABOUT PUBLICITY AND GOODWILL, RIGHT?

There once was a voice talent named Jack
who loved to promote his knack
To clients that we'd love to smack
due to expectations that are whack.

This poem has been brought to you as a courtesy by the Universal Collective Of Voiceover Artists Saddened And In Fact Maddened By Clients Promising Great Exposure And Wonderful Goodwill Resulting From Free Services, otherwise known as The UCOVASAIFMBCPGEAWGRFFS. We've had enough, and we're letting the world know. That's our blimp you may have seen overhead, with various non-profit representatives dangling precariously from it by dental floss, screaming their heads off.

They're out there. Those wonderful clients who promise us that they have somehow managed to arrange, with only the flick of their magic wand and some delightfully Harry Potter-esque incantations (*Expecto petronum*, anyone?), for the entire universe to bend to our will once we agree to sign on the dotted line. The dotted line of course following legalese that reads as follows:

I, The Voice Artist stated herein, hereby acknowledge that Client stated herein does not actually possess the art of sorcery stated herein and is in no way able to guarantee a massive onslaught of business stated herein resulting from my participation in project stated herein, performed at my goodwill because I'm generous as stated herein and Client appealed to my better nature as stated herein and I liked the smell of their perfume and was also drunk off my rocker and hey did you spike my drink and *giggle* I love unicorns, as stated herein.

Whenever I'm approached by a client who is asking if I can participate in a project at zero or minimal cost, my *modus operandus* is to reply with a chortle and snort and ask them:

- "What happened with giving this year?"
- "Don't you still pay your CEO?"
- "What are you smoking, and may I have some?"

Seriously though. Did their donor base evaporate? Did someone spread the malicious rumor that I've stopped eating and have chosen to live itinerantly in a forest somewhere, subsisting on a solid diet of nuts and berries, so I don't need any of your silly money? Did that Christian ministry's donor base disappear because The Rapture happened, and I missed it because I was watching *Deal or No Deal?* Curse you, Howie.

THANK GOODNESS I ONLY NEED 3000 "EXPOSURES" EACH MONTH TO PAY MY MORTGAGE

We've all seen the cartoon where someone is promised lots of *exposure* in exchange for their unbilled participation. The proposer makes his proposal - which unfortunately does not include an expensive engagement ring which the businessperson could then sell to pay for the money that she will most certainly *not* be making from her participation – and the businessperson replies, "Thank goodness I only need 3000 'Exposures' each month to pay my mortgage!"

It's that simple. 'Exposure' doesn't pay bills. And like Paul Strikwerda outlines in his wonderful book *"Making Money in Your PJ's"*[64], those promises of massive exposure and an endless stream of resulting work are never fulfilled. They are about as reliable as Kanye West refraining from interrupting a Taylor Swift acceptance speech.

Unfortunately, I need to foolishly squander money on food and heat *now*, good sir.

Oh those "Save the Children" ads. They tug at our heartstrings. They evoke sympathy and compassion the world over. And they're using our voice to do it! So basically, since it's my voice that's making your viewers cry (#sorrynotsorry), then isn't it just and right that I have a right to just demand a good solid wage for my tear-inducing performance? Or is it the expectation that because you are 501(c)-3 status, that my participation must therefore be a goodwill donation or you'll employ a guilt trip the size of Texas? People with such expectations make me want to harm small animals. They are the type that believe biweekly means twice a week, spell it "your" when it's "you're", and refuse to go swimming in their backyard pool after dusk because, you know, *sharks*.

Let's zoom out on this one and go with a practical example. A company approaches you and requests you to voice their script for a "good cause." Assuming that putting food on your table for your starving and emaciated children is *not* a good cause in its own right, they suggest that you do the project for free, making several reward-based promises to you, examples of which include:

- Free admission to Heaven
- Near-celebrity status
- A sense of reinforced nobility
- Endless esteem
- A bounty of future work just waiting to roll towards you like that great big boulder chasing Indiana Jones out of the cave.

What they fail to tell you is that with #5, you'll face blow-darts whizzing past your head, yawning caverns opening at your feet for a precipitous fall towards deadly stalagmites, and adorable tarantulas to take home as pets. *But you'll still do it for us, won't you? Have you no heart???*

What about the chhhiiiiillllldddddreennnnn?????

Unfortunately, charity jobs won't feed my (emaciated) chhhiiiiillllldddddreennnnn, you silly twit.

Like those good infomercials say, "there's gotta be a better way!" And there is.

HERE'S HOW WE GET 'EM BACK

While giving to charity is a noble pursuit, the art of crazymaking is equally noble. And I'm going to help you with some payback, so good luck! Here we go.

Since the dawn of time:

- cavemen have always intentionally left the toilet seat up to harass their cavewomen.
- Neanderthals of each gender have purposefully left the cover off of the toothpaste, forcing their mate to cry out *"Grunt grunt grrrrrrrrrunt!!!!!!!! Gr-grunt-gr-grunt! Now GRUNT!! And don't come back until you've learned English!"*
- Husbands stay out late and offer weak work-based reasons like "I'm sleeping over at my secretary's house to get some work done" because they're brilliant, highly intellectual and skilled at crafting convincing, innocuous excuses.
- Wives hide the remotes so that husbands go certifiably insane
- Husbands in turn hide the knowledge that they have in fact gone insane
- Teenage kids hide their parents when their friends come over

And you better believe that children have a sinister grasp of crazymaking instinctively from the start. I am not making this up. My 4-year-old takes wee tiny bites out of his Chicken McNuggets to pacify my unreasonable requirement that he eat. (Thus, the emaciation mentioned earlier). Such lackluster commitment! So I go crazy and yell. *I paid for those so you better eat them. Why can't you be a carnivore like Mommy and Daddy? You kids these days. Why when I was your age, I was 9.* Then the tears come, and I get to roll my eyes and go play Call of Duty and do things to people.

In voiceovers, it's no different. So, I will offer you some solutions. Anytime a client approaches you for a free contribution to their paid project – and they will, because A) it's for a good cause, and B) guilt trips are fun – I recommend one of these two highly effective solutions:

If in the presence of said client, slowly take two paces back, and one pace to the left. Cock the head in a slow circle, and bend your knees. Arching your back in true rooster-form, simply yell out at the top of your lungs, "Stroganoff is uplifting with calculus and makes me free like a beaver on the slopes!" The client, having no insight as to why you would exhibit such behavior or declare such nonsense, will back away perplexed as you hold your pose and gaze heavenward, fist upheld in solidarity with your fellow entrepreneur who are also being stiffed by charity people. This, my friend, is the surest and most guaranteed way to make freeloaders leave you alone. They'll make like Fleetwood Mac and go their own way. Their no-pay-for-your-skills request made no sense; thus, deservedly so, an equally senseless reply from you is fitting. And you will be the better for it.

If communication takes place over the Internet only, simply hit the "My time is valuable, block this nincompoop" button, and hit enter to confirm.

There now is a voice talent named Jack
who grew smart about promoting his knack
To clients who have his back
and send lots of money in a stack.

Good luck! (As stated herein.)

TAKEAWAY & ACTION STEP

Know your worth. Don't let yourself get taken advantage of.

Do you value yourself enough to charge what you're worth? Market rates aren't only for the veterans. Newbies aren't disqualified. Market rates are determined by value. The cost of the service is determined by its value, not by your tenure in voiceovers or the client's stated budget. Research the GVAA rate guide at https://globalvoiceacademy.com/gvaa-rate-guide-2/ and know your worth.

Pardon Me, Your Butt Is Showing

A LONG TIME AGO, I DECIDED TO GROW UP

There came a time in my life where I had to make a choice. Either continue in my immature ways, or do the unthinkable and subscribe to AARP.

Faced with these two choices, I chose a cheeseburger and fries to go.

I jest. I did ultimately grow up. And ultimately, I count it a privilege to not be carded for cigarettes. Note: I do not buy cigarettes, although I did used to smoke. I am merely stating how nice it is to *not* be carded for cigarettes. Not to be carded because I do *not* buy them I mean. Because I do *not* buy cigarettes. Stop judging me.

I also count it a privilege to be able to vote, to watch certain videos on YouTube that require age verification, and to purchase alcohol, though the liquor that I tend to purchase are spirits the names of which are only ever mentioned in movies. For example, I was out on a date once, and to impress my date, I requested of the bartender a "Sweet Vermouth on the rocks with a twist please" because:

- I had recently watched Groundhog Day
- I am unquenchably lame

The bartender called security, my date ran off with the bartender, and I called my Pastor for emotional support, who asked me why I was at a bar and then married my date. I am not responsible for the bizarre things that happen around me. A gnome may have even been involved.

Being unquenchably lame comes with its share of challenges. Concordantly, it comes with its advantages as well. One of those advantages is that because I utterly suck, I am not familiar with things that are "cool", save perhaps tap water that is not turned to the side that has a red dot. And because I do not ever care what trends are "cool", I am able to grow up. And because I am able to grow up, I have decided to NOT wear my pants hanging off my ass, and I have decided to say "ass" because I feel it makes a stronger point than donkey, which helps me to avoid dragging the animal kingdom into this fierce melee. #chalkoneupfornature

In short, at some point I decided to grow up.

CONCEAL THY DERRIERE POST-HASTE

I am the type of human who was blessed with hair that continues to remain dark black, despite the fact that some days I feel like I am older than sin, and parts of my body decide to suddenly stop performing their assigned duties. So, I look younger, but I actually am older. The truth of the matter is that I would *prefer* to be older: to be able to confidently use impressive words like "antidisestablishmentarianism" and not live under any pretense; but rather be *fully* rooted in *all* assurance that I can *privately* ask my wife what does that silly word even mean.

Sure, I used to be a strapping buck, a spring chicken, a little wet behind the ears. I used to be a tenderfoot. Green. Fresh off the assembly line. Do I miss it? My body does; but not my mind. Ultimately, I think we would all like to have the mind of God and the body of a juvenile cheetah, because people enjoy fusing unrelated things, and an omniscient miracle-working adolescent *Acinonyx jubatus* would also guarantee movie-deals, book deals, and lots of other deals that feature Almighty Quadripeds.

Where was I.

Ah yes. Just the other day, I was driving. I do this from time to time when I am not recording and I must have Taco Bell or I will perish. On the side of the road, I noticed a man who had to be at least in his thirties, whose bulbous butt-cheeks were outlined clearly through his Perry Ellis briefs, which were on full display as his pants sagged completely below them, ready to fall off as he tried to flee the police for indecent exposure.

All I could do was shake my head, which is all I can ever do when I see phenomena that I simply do not understand, such as Caitlyn Jenner or the DMV. Or the following:

- why God created mosquitos
- what is the deal behind anyone saying the word "yawn", and I must involuntarily obey them
- why my wife scoffs at watching another episode of Whale Wars
- that tiny little pocket *inside* my jeans pocket
- why I simply must win every fake internal argument with a supposed foe
- scratch that last one; I get it

But sagging. *Oi vei.* Is this some sort of new visual mating call? I ask this because I did not witness any large harem of females following after this man and oogling his bum. Cue a comical narration from David Attenborough:

Ahhh, the American male, with his denim sagging below his supple butt cheeks, exposing, for all the world to see, far too much boxer briefs for Planet Earth to sustain, causing a massive exodus of the populace into sanctuaries that were previously the domain of wildlife. A phenomenon truly frightening to behold, as wildlife now replaces wildlife, and now all my viewers have fallen asleep at my narrational wooing. Yawn.

See? I got you! Close your mouth now please.

It is not that I despise this young man for his apparel selection. It is more a case of wanting to screech to a halt, get out, slam my door, saunter across traffic whilst gesticulating and screaming with a high-tenor angst, "What the bleep is bleeping wrong with you pull your bleeping pants up you bleeping bleep!"

So, yes, I despise him.

THOU SHALT NOT SAG

I am a Voice Actor. And yes, I do all my own stunts. But the wagon I am draggin' is never saggin'.

Just the other day, I received a blog article from a voiceover colleague who mentors others. Among many other colorful words in this article which I did not read in its entirety due to Overwhelming Irritating Annoyance Syndrome, I note the following descriptors were used by her:

- Da bomb
- Bomb AH
- Hella bomb
- Beyond bomb

The writer of this blog is apparently a terrorist, and if you will please excuse me while I make a quick phone call.

*Oh! "Bomb" is a word used to describe something that is **cool**???* Well now...see? I did not know that, because if you recall, I am old and unquenchably lame. Had I known that we are now employing detonating similes in our everyday lingo, I would have taken a class on explosives.

I kid. This colleague of mine is respected, and is simply articulating what she likes through comparing said likes to concussion blasts. The truth however is that I found myself distracted by the use of so many explosions in her email that I could not focus on where my dentures were, and my Depends are now soiled.

There are certain laws of decorum for how we should operate as voiceover freelancers if we are going to be taken seriously. We are entrepreneurs. We are businesspeople. We want people to *listen* to us. In my humble opinion, professional conversation with clients or colleagues that we instruct does not include "bomb AH". If we are sending out a marketing email, we should not use "Hella bomb." In all of my test emails I sent out that said "Yo, I'm Aaron Ryan, and I'm da hella beyond bomb AH bomb. Hella. Beyond. AH. Bomb bomb bomb bomb bomb" I am currently 1 for 3,979,286 in replies received. My mom was the only one to ever respond. If I recall, her exact words were "How did you get my email address?"

So, NO, thank you, my ass is NOT showing. Unless I am in the shower of course. I am assured by my wife that it is ok then, as long as I keep the explosive similes to a minimum in there.

from shower "Honey??? What does simile mean? Is that a metaphor for antidisestablishmentarianism???"

HERE'S ONE TO GROW ON:

"Maturity comes when you stop making excuses and start making changes."

PowerPlug

Invoicing & Patience

THE ONE WITH THE EMBRYOS

You remember. The One With the Embryos. Or, better known as the one with the contest between Chandler & Joey vs. Monica & Rachel. Chandler and Joey eventually win the trivia contest, and Monica and Rachel are forced to trade apartments with them, and be relegated to the guys' apartment instead of their expansive suite (how they can afford that suite anyway we'll never know...). But the absolute best part is what Chandler says even before that big contest even begins.

Chandler bets the girls that he and Joey can name every item in the girls' shopping bag. Chandler and Joey win the contest, and Chandler triumphantly demands their winnings[65].

It's hilarious. And oh so true. When we are owed money, how often and heavy-handedly do we relentlessly pursue our debtor? When grace goes out the window, and we slam down the gavel and insist that we be paid right this very minute, what does that do to relationships?

BILLING CYCLES OF DEATH

Many, many years ago, I used to be relentless. I used to be unwavering. I used to put my foot down and demand payment of at least a third up-front (but come on, preferably 50%) on all my projects – both voiceover and video. I used to insist, before I could step into production, that I be paid what I was owed prior to release of unwatermarked files. I put my foot down and staked my hope on this.

I usually didn't get my way.

Now, to be fair, I just wanted to be paid. But, to be honest, I was short-sighted. And, complicating matters further, I was doubtless putting a damper on what could be a long-term relationship with that client. Was it the client's fault that their company has certain accounts payable policies, and that said policymaker is probably someone I'll never even get to appeal to? Even if I could, should I brazenly attempt to change anything?

Let's be super honest for a second. 90-day accounts receivables, ahem, *suck*. They're frankly a bit ridiculous. No one needs that long to pay someone. So do 45-day AR's. And even 30-day AR's are a bitter pill to swallow. Isn't it wonderful when, in this glorious world of idealism and perfection, the stars glitter, rainbows swirl around us, twinkly lights sparkle, there is peace and harmony and love, John Lennon music plays everywhere, unicorns dance, Elvis is alive again, and we're paid the very nanosecond our audio files are transferred? It's like the Glienicke Bridge of Spies[66], and a prisoner exchange; only nicer and sweeter in tone.

Yes, it would be the golden era of voiceover payments. But, unfortunately, the grim reality is that our clients need their clients to pay them too, usually. And even though the threat of being stiffed looms large over everything we do, when there's no escrow account in place to protect us, can we still move to a position of trust?

The answer is yes. It's called "investing into our future."

A HEARTY SIGH OF RELIEF

Man nothing gets us bent out of shape more than money owed to us.

One of my clients is Zillow. They took a long time to pay me. It was a $600 payment that I'd love to have. They're Zillow, after all[67]! What's taking them so long?

My other client, Kathryn, who is a senior producer at a content agency, *always* pays me multiple thousands of dollars on her projects right away. So, what's the deal? Why do they have money and Zillow doesn't? What's the meaning of all of this anyway! You rotten crooks, you have my files, now give me my money!! *insert sound of loud wailing and tantrum-infused fists and feet slamming on the floor here*

But when I go to the post office and find that $600 Zillow check waiting for me that I had forgotten about from 45 days ago, it's like Christmas. It is! It's a "What? Oh yeah!" moment that resonates deeply and puts a skip in my step. It's the intake of breath. It's here! *Yay*! It gives me such a renewed sense of joy knowing that people came through, they proved faithful, they met my need in return for my meeting theirs.

Another instance is actually a bit more painful: a client didn't read the contract, wherein I stipulate that any pickups or script changes necessitate a new session fee. He didn't like that, and our relationship ended. He paid what he owed…eventually. But it was tooth and nail waiting for *that* check to arrive, because of the soured exchanges. I was fair and polite with him, in my estimation: he just didn't like that he hadn't read the contract closely enough.

It gives me a hearty sigh of relief to find that check…to know that trust has been restored, that I made a deposit into the Universal Bank of Patience, and it paid back dividends from the Restored Faith in Humanity Fund. After all, is Zillow really that nefarious? Would they have intentionally stiffed me?

Sometimes, we don't see our payments until the time the ad that we voiced is already running. That can also be a bitter pill to swallow. We hear it on the radio or see it on the web and say "Oh hey, what a nice spot. Sure would be nice to be paid for that, since that's **MY VOICE!!!!**" But there's trust that gets to be built up in the waiting. There is fortitude and hope, and it's all good in the end.

EVER BEEN STIFFED?

Have you been stiffed? I haven't yet. I've been stiffed in video production over the years – I think three times since 2003. But never with voiceovers, *knock on wood*. Overall, it's been a wildly successful venture, and though I was hard-nosed to begin with, now, if a client has net terms that I need to accept, I come to that crossroads of decision with a bit more poise and tolerance.

Am I going to reject this job because they are paying on 45 days and not 30? In 45 days, will I be the happier, or will I be the sadder, because of this choice here and now? My choice *now* affects my mood 45 days from now. I can sow into the future and plant seeds that will take root and grow and produce a money tree (wouldn't that be nice!) that will blossom and bud and produce fruit that I will *need* then. Sure, I'd *like* it now. But who knows if I will *need* it more then? Shouldn't I be investing into my future and receiving returns on investment down the road?

Net terms payments are like gems hidden along a highway. You sometimes don't even know they're there. I just got one today that I had forgotten about. Yes, I keep track of who owes what, but I sometimes forget the little ones, and this was a smaller one. Did $275 bless me today? Yes. Did I know 30 days ago that it would bless me this much? No.

The other caveat is that in the 45 days it takes for me to be paid, they may have another job. They may have two. They may refer me out to another client who has five. The goodwill factor knows no bounds and is no respecter of accounts payable schedules.

The voiceover businessman (or hobbyist) demands payment up front due to either A) an ungrounded faith in humanity, or B) a lack of foresight and vision. I love what the character Mitch Leary says in *In the Line of Fire*:

"Your average American businessman... looks at a product, a marketing scheme, what have you...and he sees the length and width of it. The Japanese see the depth, the long-term effect. We look at the next fiscal quarter. The Japanese look at the next quarter of a century."[68]

Look ahead. Don't listen to Chandler. Is it funny? Yes. Does it appeal to our desire for justice as humans? Yes. Is it long-term-relationship-depriving? Possibly. Let your clients make the calls. Don't be so hard-nosed as to forego relationship in favor of shortsightedness. You'll be blessed with both immediate payments *and* net terms payments on this journey called voiceovers.

No two clients are the same, after all. One will pay now and one will pay then, and both are wonderful, because they're putting money into your pocketbook. It's the mark of an amateur to demand payment *or else*. Consider it a *gift* when a client pays right away and the burden of following up on receivables is one you no longer have to shoulder.

Let the net terms happen. Don't be a Veruca Salt who pouts and demands her Oompa Loompa now. As Violet says to her in the end, "Can it, you nit!"

Net terms are not the end of the world. They're the beginnings of unexpected yet expected blessings. They're seeds waiting to germinate into paying fruit.

The Thrill Of The Hunt

"A hunt based only on the trophies taken falls far short of what the ultimate goal should be." - Fred Bear

HOW CAN I SEEK OUT AND AMASS CLIENTS

The thrill of the hunt.

Amassing marketing contacts. Finding leads. Finding. Scoring. Connecting. That's what it's all about, right? Are you a marketer that thrives on finding leads? If so, read on!

ENTREPENEURS STALKING THEIR PREY

The lioness stalks its prey with stealth. Slowly creeping through the tall reeds, it eyes its wildebeest prize, that great mound of juicy flesh...that succulent payoff. But ultimately, the lioness has something far greater in mind than the final meal. It's not the payoff, really. Rather, it's the moment the wildebeest becomes aware of her, muscles flex, joints spring into action, and the wildebeest blows out of there like a tornado, desperate to evade the predator. *That* is when life happens for the lioness...for the jaguar...for the cheetah...eyes widen as their prey takes off...*and the chase is on*. (I wrote that in my best movie trailer voiceover voice.)

After all, for you and I as entrepreneur marketers, it's not really about the end result, is it? Is it about the securing of a job, really? Or is it about something much deeper?

Marketing is not about the finish line.

Every day, I'm planting seeds. I'm tilling the soil. Every day I'm reaching out to multiple people across Instagram, LinkedIn, Twitter, Craigslist, YouTube, Vimeo, direct email, etc. Every month I'm reaching *back* out to those people. I have a checklist I go off of. All the time, every day - and I do mean *all* day, even into the evening time when I'm just lying around after an exhausting day of reaching out - I reach out. I continue to slink through that grass. You see, my "prey" will never come straight to me. That's not the type of business I'm in. I'm always on the hunt. And just like the lioness, I do it to survive.

I run and hunt my prey on a continuous 24/7 cycle because I need to bring back food to my den. I need to make sure that my wife and sons are provided for, and that I can pay the mortgage on my den. If I don't, well, we're just all aimlessly roaming the Savannah. So, it behooves me to develop an attitude of really *craving* the race...the hunt...the chase. Each morning, I sit down to my computer, and, like the lioness cracks her tendons and flexes her muscles, I crack my fingers and get ready to get my marketing game on.

Sure, I want to track down and get prey like the next lioness. I want to provide for my family. But there's something about scanning the horizon, on sentry, looking for your next target, and then barreling towards that goal, as opposed to hitting it, that keeps me alive.

Reinhold Eissner, who ascended Mount Everest without supplemental oxygen in 1980, was asked "why did you go up there to die?" He said, *"I didn't go up there to die. I went up there to **live**."*

I feel the same way. It's the thrill of the hunt that keeps me alive, that keeps me fit, that keeps me moving. It's the motivation to go out there and do it again...and again...and again, knowing that eventually, because the numbers are in my favor, and I'm perfecting my craft with each hunt, I'm going to score.

Many people don't like marketing. I get it. You have to learn to toot your own horn. Paul Strikwerda says "Being outstanding doesn't make you stand out. If people don't know you exist, don't expect them to hire you. If you really want to play the trumpet professionally, you better learn how to toot your own horn."[69]

He's absolutely right. You have to be shameless about the fact that you *are* worthy, that you *do* have something worthy to offer, and make no apologies for landing in people's lives and their inboxes.

Have you got your tooter ready?

HOW AND WHERE TO HUNT – THAT IS THE QUESTION

How and where to hunt?

- Do you go door to door?
- Do you brave the phones?
- Is it direct email for you?
- Does Twitter turn your crank?
- Is Instagram the way to go?
- Do you need to really hit YouTube and Vimeo hard?
- Is Craigslist the solution?
- Should LinkedIn be the end all be all?

There is no single hunting terrain. Hunting for prospects takes all shapes and can be done across multiple plateaus. Like one social media venue better than another? Lock and load on that one then and ignore the others. It's totally fine. Don't feel like you have to canvas the entire planet. There are ways to simply promote your business broadly and gain traction[70], and there are ways to really connect with people directly and effectively through social media. However you do it, the key point is to be like Nike and *just do it*. Celia Siegel says the same thing: "Rather than spread yourself too thin, choose one or two social media networks and do them well. Once you have one off the ground you can always expand and add another."[71]

According to Quicksprout.com[72], right now:

- 86% of businesses use Facebook for marketing
- 48% use Instagram
- 46% use YouTube
- 44% use Twitter
- 31% use LinkedIn
- 25% use Snapchat (!)

Where will you hunt? The ground is teeming with life. You can continue to subsist on the P2P's if you want...but what if they dried up? What if new legislation outlawed such sites? What would you do then? Where would your food come from?

HUNTERS HUNT, AND GATHERERS GATHER – IT'S DNA

Ultimately, the takeaway is this: a lioness never rests. Sure, she lies down and pants in the hot shade from time to time, in between kills. But what's on her mind during that segue? What is she thinking about in the lull between the chase? If a young rogue elephant traipsed onto her turf, wandering away from the herd, would she let it pass by unmolested? No. She's always ready for the hunt. Always.

That's the mindset that you and I need to have as marketers. What was that? What did you call me, Aaron? Yeah, you read it right. You're not a voiceover artist. You're a marketer who just *happens* to do whatever craft you do. You're an *enthusiast*. Just like I'm a businessman who happens to do voiceovers and authoring. It needs to be in our DNA to hunt and gather. It needs to be second nature, a deep intrinsic compulsion to reach out and see who's looking for us. To find new opportunities wherever and whenever they arise. To look for, or, at least be ready to look.

When I'm out and about with my wife - sometimes even on date night, to her chagrin - I wear one of my "Ask me about voiceovers" T-Shirts. I have several, also to her chagrin, ha! She knows that I'm going to, and she doesn't stop me - because she knows that what I kill, she gets to eat too. She's a hunter gatherer right alongside me, through enabling and support. Plus, I think she's a really pretty hunter gatherer.

ENTREPENEURS SEEK CLIENTS 24-7

If you're a potential client reading this, please pardon all the macabre references. I'm no Jeffrey Dahmer. I'm not about to slay you or harm you or sink my teeth into you, though I do at least reserve the right to size you up for a meal.

Ultimately, I'm thinking about where I can find voiceover clients all the time. It is the greatest thrill to find a potential client who responds favorably. A warm lead who responds with "Nice demo reel! I'll add you to my roster." Or "Thanks for reaching out, what's your cost for _____?" It is *wonderful* to be chosen. It makes the hunt all worthwhile.

The great thing about seeking out clients is that the sources will always replenish. There will always be new listings. New advertising agencies. Directors of Video will be hired from fresh talent. Senior Producers will phase out and replacements will fill their shoes. New postings will go up from content creators. Ad agencies will cycle through clients. Ultimately, the harvest is plentiful...and the lionesses are few. There's enough work to go around. And if you look hard enough, and are bold enough to ask, you'll find potential clients out there who are willing to provide you with an email address to follow up with. It's your job - and no one else's - to keep those, and keep them organized well, so that you can follow up with them at regular intervals, to wish them well and remind them of your presence. Just like a lioness in the grass, hiding out of sight, they won't remember that you're there - until you spring into action and remind them. So ask for email addresses - ask away! Grab them and keep them. Each "potential" client that responds favorably to you, you *must* ask for their email address and program that into your CRM software for follow up. Examples of good CRM software:

- Voiceoverview: www.voiceoverview.com
- Zoho: www.zoho.com/crm
- Nimble: www.nimble.com
- MailChimp: www.mailchimp.com

Again, they won't remember that you're there. It's up to *you* to go seek them out again. That's what marketers do...they go and seek. They hunt. Rinse in the mud, and repeat.

Being in the voiceover industry, much like being an actor, takes a lot of tenacity. It's a very reactive business. You can receive several audition opportunities per day depending on your profile schematics and the notifications you elect to receive from the sources that send you auditions or leads. You have to assume more or less of a sentry role, always on the lookout for opportunities. The same is true with direct marketing. Your radar is always up. I have received audition notifications, run to my studio, recorded and come back to my control room to process and send.

And before I'm finished processing my auditions, another one comes in that I like. And it's right back to the studio. And I do mean running.

You have to be willing to get back in there and record over and over and over again. You have to develop a love for receiving and auditioning and producing. Marketing is no different. The *business* of voiceovers is no different. You must be tenacious. Do you look at voiceovers as passion, or drudgery? Will you continue in your passion even when it *seems* like drudgery?

IT'LL ALWAYS BE ABOUT THE THRILL OF THE HUNT

Re-read the Fred Bear quote at the top of this chapter. Is that you? Do you thrive on the hunt? I do. I'm in a constant state of scanning the horizon, looking for someone to connect with, not to bite their jugular, but to sink my teeth into a great opportunity of partnership for us to devour together. I really, really, *really* love the hunt...and I love being engaged with it. It's a massive payoff to connect with a pre-client and have them convert into an actual client.

But even more than that, it's an even more massive payoff to flex my muscles, to arch my back, to let out a low growl, to vent that steam, and to take off running out across the plains and track down my next meal. Because ultimately, I may *look* like a human male...but I'm really a lioness in the grass...I just have less fur.

That Glorious Disconnect

UNTETHER FOR CRYING OUT LOUD

I didn't know what he meant. We had just unpacked, and I had slung this giant backpack on my back that contained my sleeping bag, pillow, cooking gear, roasting sticks, kindling, canteen, snacks, change of clothes, first aid kit, hatchet, and lots of other things that cumulatively weighed the same as a small asteroid. My best friend (also named Aaron) has always been an avid camper, and I was impressed – and admittedly a little angry – that he was always able to fit everything he needed into practically a Ziploc bag whenever we went camping, and on that little bag he could survive for a fortnight. Me, the snail with everything on my back, would last a few hours and then would be undoubtedly mauled by a large bear.

As we were closing up my car and approaching the trailhead, I did one last check of my phone, which already had dwindling signal and had dropped precariously from "LTE" to "3G" to the dreaded "E", which stands for "EveryHopeYouOnceHadIsNowDead."

There were no new notifications, because life is unfair, and with that, we trudged off. The sun was already setting, and my friend Aaron wanted to get us to the campsite before dark. Little did he know that I wanted that too, as I see approaching predators much better in the full light of day, and planned to place my E phone upright directly in front of him so that he would trip as we both fled. No offense, Aaron.

Aaron took one glance over at me desperately refreshing my mail to see if there any new notifications stuck in pending mode, scoffed, and threw two words my way that would forever be embedded in my psyche and reveal to me just how much of an addict I truly was:

"Dude, untether."

INTERACTION? P'SHAW

It never ceases to amaze – and sadden me – how many people are crowded together on a bus, or a plane, or in the elevator, and we all look like scoliosis victims. I'm including myself in that demographic. Our collective noses are buried in our collective phones, faintly resembling John Hurt in Alien with the Facehugger commanding a death grip over him. We're immersed in the tractor-beam of what we're doing, with a tunnel-vision that would rival a pair of Bushnell binoculars.

You and I have both surely seen those videos on the news where someone is in pain or hurting somehow, and it's amazing how many people just simply walk over them; around them; don't even look at them. It's disgusting, it's sad, and it's not the way it should be.

I think we're deathly afraid of making connections with people for too fleeting of a moment; it demands something from us that we're not prepared to give: after all, we don't know these people, and we aren't sure yet that we *want* to know them. Therefore, we give details sparingly, and we interact sparingly, with that subtle head-bob-eyebrow-raise or that pathetic half-smile creased lip thing that we've learned to master. We're just not sure of people.

Why should we interact with unpredictable humans when there is so much predictable goodness right there in our hands? What can they possibly offer that would be even remotely comparable to news, games, and texting? What's the point?

TAKE THE BLUE PILL

"Take the blue pill, the story ends, you wake up in your bed and believe whatever you want to believe." Those were the words of Morpheus in the acclaimed sci-fi blockbuster *The Matrix*. Morpheus is offering Neo a choice: to take one of two pills that would take him in diametrically-opposed directions, and he has only to choose.

Too often we take the red pill: we want to "stay in Wonderland, and see how deep the rabbit-hole goes." Our iPhones and Androids are rabbit holes to the nth degree.

As entrepreneurs deeply committed to our craft, and intent on running a successful business facilitating them, we sit a lot. We're constantly marketing. We're constantly auditioning and performing outreaches to prospective clients. It gives us great pleasure to pursue this great craft, as it's nothing short of taking the red pill, and going down that rabbit-hole. It's deep, it's alluring, and there are great treasures therein that promise provision, accomplishment, reward, notoriety, acclaim, and gratification.

It's human nature to take the red pill.

But that's why there's a choice. My challenge is for you to take the blue pill. The very existence of the blue pill is what makes the red pill so alluring. We can take that red pill for a while, but without the blue pill, it's meaningless. The endless pursuit of rewards is thrilling…but also exhausting. And even if it's incredibly rewarding and endlessly thrilling, it's sheer imbalance if we're to pursue that non-stop. We need balance.

I urge you to take the blue pill once in a while in your voiceover life. Unplug. Go for a walk. Sit back and stretch out. Meditate. Pray. Play with your kids. Talk to your spouse. Breathe. Unwind.

Untether.

A life of imbalance is how we:

- become overweight
- become addicted
- withdraw socially
- distance
- become narcissistic and self-absorbed
- disconnect from our loved ones

It's really sad how cellular we've become as a society. Gone are the days where we're all singing a song on a Greyhound bus, strangers bound for distant ports, yet bound in heart until then. It's tragic what loss of community we experience when we subtract the "a" from "teach" and are left only with tech. We can all learn something from each other. The question is, are we willing?

CHEEKS & GEMS

Every time I see my infant son, Asher, peering through the baby gate outside my office door, wanting desperately to come in, there are two things that I notice straightaway. Asher has beautiful greenish-brown eyes that leap out at me through the gate, and they're often glistening with emotion as he wants one of two things: either to be let in, or for his Dada to come out. Because either way, he and I are together. In his little 15-month-old mind, that's all he wants: togetherness. He doesn't want to borrow money; he doesn't want food or candy or a sippy-cup; he doesn't want to be tickled. He just wants for me to pick him up and hold him and be together with me.

The second thing are his cheeks. They're incredibly flush with color, and exceptionally squeezable. He's standing there, just outside my door, and he wants me. Have you ever known deep down that you're wanted? When he (and Brennan before him) see me, they walk up to me, and they raise their arms out over their head, and they pine. They want their Dada.

It's the most fulfilling sensation in the world, to be wanted. To know that these little guys want me to pick them up, to hold them, for them to feel loved and wanted back, is an amazing exchange.

Those cheeks and gems are sometimes irresistible. There are times where I truly do need to peel myself away and take that red pill. I need to dive in and get things done. But when you think about it, Aaron was right.

"Dude, untether."

Asher is my blue pill. Brennan is my blue pill. My wife is my blue pill. Running is my blue pill. Hanging out with my family is my blue pill. Spending quality time with those I love is my blue pill. Reading to my kids is my blue pill. Getting away from the office for some balance, for this workaholic, that *is* my blue pill.

In the end, you'll get there. I'll get there. It'll happen. The hustle is real, and it never dies. But we *will* die, unless we take that blue pill once in a while. The rabbit hole isn't always what it's cracked up to be, and the cheeks and gems are still waiting for us out there.

TAKEAWAY & ACTION STEP

Break away and unplug, for health's sake.

Nature abhors a vacuum. Are you allowing one or more areas of your life to suffer because of your drive? Is there an imbalance in your life due to your ambition? What can you do to restore balance? Ask others around you what they really think of your drive and your commitment to it.

Take the little blue pill. No, the other *little blue pill.*

Hobbies = Good AND Bad

ARE YOU ONLY A HOBBYIST?

When you think of a hobby, what comes to mind?

- Playing the drums?
- Sculpting clay?
- Writing poetry?
- Calligraphy?
- Painting?
- Building suspension bridges in your backyard?[73]
- Collecting baseball cards?

What is a hobby, after all, but a pastime? Just that. Something to pass the time. It holds no significant value other than personal fulfillment – which I'm not knocking by the way; we need that! But a hobby brings nothing to your budget; rather it brings *expense* for materials, or training, or other supplies needed to enjoy said hobby. Nothing is added to your career forecast other than a carved-out piece of your schedule dedicated to enjoyment.

Voiceovers, as a hobby, can bring a lot of fulfillment.

They can also *deprive* of fulfillment. You can settle on the nickel and miss the dollar. They can bring you some measure of satisfaction, and rob you of utter contentment. They can pass the time, and in the same stretch, steal your time, never to return it in the long run.

So, enjoy your voiceover hobby! I pray you have fun with it! I hope that it's fulfilling for three weeks, or six months, or perhaps two years. I expect that you'll thoroughly enjoy it and that it fulfills you.

And I pray that you drop it as a hobby like a hot potato.

THE BUSINESS OF VOICEOVERS

If you choose to pursue voiceovers as a hobby, God bless you. No one could blame you: after all, it certainly is an enjoyable one! Hey, you might even make $20 from a project! *(Which, by the way, is what some of the clients on Fiverr are counting on you to say...)*

Or...you could make $5000. Plus residuals. Plus name recognition. Plus connections to future clients and other voiceover jobs in abundance. Plus plus plus.

A hobby brings you temporary fulfillment; a business brings you increasing provision.

Hobbies and crafts are essential for our contentment. Forest Hill Retirement says that they lower the heart rate.[74] They bring us balance and health. They give us the ability to unplug. For me, I sing, I blog, I swim, I run, and I build Lego spaceships with my son. OK, the honest truth is that he's asleep and I've commandeered them to add another sick Lego spaceship to my sick fleet.

But...

What if you could unplug from your 9 to 5, and you could instead make a living off of your "hobby?" What if you could convert it into a business?

- What if instead of buying craft materials, you could buy a business license?
- What if instead of purchasing a cheap tool, you purchased something expensive, because it's the best?
- What if instead of taking the shortcut and getting what's cheap, you could take the long way around and get what you *need?*

I've said before that if you truly treat expenses (short term) as investments (long term), you'll go far. Everything that you expend with voiceovers, divesting yourself of finances for something that is an investment into your future, is a decision that moves you forward into the future of your progress. You're saying, essentially, "I believe in myself and my abilities to produce this money back, and to in fact grow a money tree that will continue to bear fruit for myself, because of this one [insert purchase here]." Some of your investments are veritable time machines, taking you from here to there in the timeline of quality.

Expenses take care of a short-term need; investments produce returns and dividends.

Sure, voiceovers as a hobby might be nice. You might make $5 on Fiverr (aka the F-Word in the Voiceover industry) or $20 on Justsayspots or $100 on The VoiceRealm. These base sites are horrible and corrosive to the voiceover industry. On that note, if you're wanting to succeed in the voiceover industry, you'll avoid these three sites in particular like the Bubonic plague. But with voiceovers as a business, you could gain direct clients for yourself through marketing, and secure a client that will bring you multiple thousands of dollars worth of work per year…or half-year…or quarter.

Let me tell you what I see when someone on Fiverr states that they will do your 1000-word voiceover for $20. I see desperation. I see inexperience. I see lack of knowledge of the industry pay scale. I see sheepishness. I see lack of self-respect. I see "not a team player." But there's no way to police such activity, and it's truly a free country.

However – the main point I'm making here is just to not worry about such offerings. It's not my job to police these people. In this vast universe of the internet, with so many players playing the game, all I can focus on is me, and I want to offer quality offerings at quality pricing, not quality offerings at bargain basement pricing. As Elaine Clark says, "If a talent gives away their services or undermines industry standard rates, they are sending a message that their services have little or no value. It may bring in jobs initially, but those buyers, once they have a budget, will go elsewhere for a higher-level performer."[75] I recently had a disagreement with a lowballer in a voiceover group on Facebook who insisted that the price offering should be what the client can afford. Short of crying out "B___ S___!" I reminded them that the price is the price is the price, and referred them back to the GVAA Rate Guide. What you pay me for voiceovers does not depend on how much you make nor what your balance sheet is. A voiceover service has a universal rate to everyone (based mostly on usage), and I choose to charge that universal rate.

What will your choice be?

TREAT IT LIKE A BUSINESS

Again, I'm a businessman who happens to do voiceovers. I *love* voiceovers, and they are my business, and they are my passion, because they not only bring me joy and fulfillment, they bring me great amounts of resource to provide for my family.

Let me list for you a few things that distinguish me as a voiceover businessman, as opposed to a voiceover hobbyist:

- I've created three voiceover websites to support my business
- I've invested thousands of dollars into a Studiobricks studio (and a custom built studio prior to that one), Sennheiser microphone, Neumann microphone, iZotope software, branded clothing, advertising expenses, and more
- I've attended local Meetups and Chambers of Commerce meetings to promote my business
- I obtained business licensing for myself
- I've labeled my car with vinyl lettering to attract business to myself
- I paid for a custom phone number
- I pay taxes on my voiceovers
- I am constantly seeking to expand my horizons
- Every day, I establish new relationships with potential clients
- I do this 9 to 5 every weekday, and beyond
- I wake up every day excited to go to work
- I've submitted nearly 20,000 auditions
- When I'm out and about, I make voice memos the instant a new idea comes to me for a blog…a live Instagram video…a workshop…a follow-up note for a client…or a broadcast.
- I keep my finger on the pulse of my business by watching my VoiceZam player[76] to see who is listening to my demo reels.
- Every single expense I make into voiceovers is not that. It is *not* an expense. It is an *investment*.

- I set and hit or exceed goals every week
- I invest time into blogging
- I help colleagues and provide free 30-minute voiceover video consults
- I invest a massive amount of time into marketing
- I've written this and several other books

I am a voiceover businessman because I choose to make this my business, not my hobby. Again, I never went into voiceovers with hope...I went in with *intention*. My first step was getting a business license. After that, I could say "It's official." It's no longer a hobby. Yes, I thoroughly enjoy it as one would enjoy a hobby, but I will not relegate voiceovers to the category of hobby, because there is a huge well there that I can tap in order to bring massive provision to my family.

To treat voiceovers as a hobby would be to ricochet off of, to momentarily touch and then leave, and no more, the wonder of a truly satisfying and lucrative career.

BEATING A DEAD HORSE

I'm just another voice (get it?) in this great choir when I share on this. There are many voiceover businessmen just like myself who just happen to do voiceovers, but they are first and foremost entrepreneurs. They understand that in order to succeed, you need structure, planning, goal-setting.

You need drive, determination, and resilience. You need focus, clarity of vision, and aptitude. You must find what works best for you as a business, and then run with it. I don't mean to beat a dead horse, so I'll just chime in and say "What they said."

[pause for effect]

OK, I'll say even more.

Treat voiceovers like a business, make it official, and see yourself reap invaluable rewards heaped upon invaluable rewards.

I'll never forget the first time I was paid for a voiceover job. I thought to myself, "Holy smokes, it actually works!" I expected it to, but that feeling opened up Pandora's box within me. Simultaneously, I thought "It's possible." "This is it." "This is where my income will come from."

This system does work. It's not Amway, it's not a Ponzi scheme, and it's not a Kool-Aid stand. This is an official business that brings in billions of dollars a year in advertising and other forms of revenue for corporate videos, E-Learning, animation, Explainer videos, audiobooks, and more. You can share in those dollars. This system can pay your bills, your car payment, your mortgage, and then some. I'm living proof.

At the time of this writing, I have made more in just this half year in voiceovers than I did in all of the previous year combined. And it is enough each month to pay our mortgage three times over.

It *is* possible.

Go forth and conquer…with a business license.

Your Key To Success

"THANK YOU" IS UNDERRATED

What comes around goes around. Heard that phrase? What do you think it means?

It's usually used in the context of vengeance. It's the story of the cruel manager in Matthew 18:

"Therefore, the kingdom of heaven is like a king who wanted to settle accounts with his servants. As he began the settlement, a man who owed him ten thousand talents was brought to him. Since he was not able to pay, the master ordered that he and his wife and his children and all that he had be sold to repay the debt. "The servant fell on his knees before him. `Be patient with me,' he begged, `and I will pay back everything.' The servant's master took pity on him, cancelled the debt and let him go. Mt. 18:28 "But when that servant went out, he found one of his fellow servants who owed him a hundred denarii. He grabbed him and began to choke him. `Pay back what you owe me!' he demanded. "His fellow-servant fell to his knees and begged him, `Be patient with me, and I will pay you back.' "But he refused. Instead, he went off and had the man thrown into prison until he could pay the debt. When the other servants saw what had happened, they were greatly distressed and went and told their master everything that had happened. "Then the master called the servant in. `You wicked servant,' he said, `I cancelled all that debt of yours because you begged me to. Shouldn't you have had mercy on your fellow servant just as I had on you?' In anger his master turned him over to the jailers to be tortured, until he should pay back all he owed. "This is how my heavenly Father will treat each of you unless you forgive your brother from your heart."[77]

In a *Waltons* sort of ending, the servant would have gone out and said thank you to everyone he met while the sun was going down…he would have been filled with such gratitude because he had been given so much. Instead, he acted vindictively.

To whom much is given, much is required.

THE FIG BAR

I had just given him a fig bar. It was yet another fig bar for this three-year-old, who loved them and didn't want anything else. But as always, it came at a cost. It required something of him, and it wouldn't be given as readily in the future without that requirement being fulfilled. What was the requirement?

"Thank you, Dada."

Please and *thank you*. Two phrases that are building blocks of relationships, that make the world go around, and that are *so* underrated and underused.

My son *loves* fig bars. He has always been a very picky eater, and whereas a lot of kids his age are eating peas and carrots and corn, sometimes it's like pulling teeth with him. He is doing better, now he's eating chicken noodle soup and apples and baked beans and pizza and vegetables and actually trying new things so that we don't have to resort to an IV drip. Phew. *wipes sweat from brow* It's encouraging and awesome and beautiful…and relieving. After all, we don't want him to still be three feet tall when he's fifteen. We need that little finicky guy to eat.

But why is it so important for him to acknowledge that he has been given a gift? Why the exhortation to thank you?

Nature abhors a vacuum, that's why. Nature abhors when something isn't there that should be (gratitude), and when something is there that shouldn't be (taking something for granted).

When something's missing, fill it with gratitude.

THE MODUS OPERANDUS

I have always been the kind of person who operates on gratitude. Sure, there are times where I'm bummed out or flustered or irritated by something, but when I choose to see the light again, I recognize that there are a thousand things for me to be grateful for. Take, for example:

- Nick Vucijik of "Life Without Limbs" Ministry. He doesn't have any limbs. I do. I can be grateful. I saw a meme once that said "I opened two gifts this morning. They were my eyes." Just having eyes that can see is a major gift, and it needs to be acknowledged.
- The Middle east. There is war and strife. I live here.
- We are well-provided-for here.
- Those who have lost relatives to murder. All of my loved ones are alive and safe.
- People with lifelong afflictions. The worst thing plaguing me is persistent IBS. OK, and that bunion on my left foot. And the back pain from being overweight. Oh yeah, and the stress I carry in my neck. But beyond that… oh yeah, and my wrist still hasn't recovered from that fall…and my right index finger aches for whatever reason…and my vision is blurred without my glasses…and I have a hangnail…but again, beyond that…
- 9 to 5 jobs. I am SO grateful for self-employment and working for my own dreams.
- Those who feel they have nothing to offer. God has graciously blessed me with giftings and abilities.
- Families who for whatever reason cannot conceive. We have been graciously given two sons.
- Those who can't get away from work. I am blessed with the ability to go on vacation with my wife when I want to.

I have so immeasurably much to be grateful for. *So much!* There is no end to what I have to be grateful for. And this is a list of just nine things!

Perhaps Alanis Morissette said it best in her song "Thank U"[78]:

Thank you India
Thank you terror
Thank you disillusionment
Thank you frailty
Thank you consequence
Thank you thank you silence

Thank you India
Thank you terror
Thank you disillusionment
Thank you frailty
Thank you consequence
Thank you thank you silence
Thank you India
Thank you providence
Thank you disillusionment
Thank you nothingness
Thank you clarity
Thank you thank you silence

I do tend to quote a lot of Alanis Morissette. She's very quotable with poignant lyrics.

Operating in an "attitude of gratitude"[79] as they say, is such a pillar in my life. Making sure I resonate gratitude back to God for the many gifts and blessings I've received helps me to keep things in perspective. When I get bent out of shape on something, I need to reframe that something into "how does this compare to the list of nine, above?" Is it really that important, in the big scheme of eternity? Is it really?

THE PAYING IT FORWARD

At random times, out of sheer gratitude, following a payout on a large voiceover job I've booked and completed, I'll send a random gift to someone. On occasion I've sent unexpected financial blessings to my good friend Paul Racey, who gave me the kick in the pants I needed to get started in voiceovers. I've sent gifts to my coach and friend (not in that order) Scott Burns, who has enabled me beyond belief with his planet-eating generosity of time, insight, and equipment knowledge.

How else have I paid it forward?

- I've set up other entrepreneur's software and plugins for them at no charge.
- I've reviewed other voice talents' demos and auditions at no charge.

- I answered voice talents' questions all the time during my work day, knowing they're effectively my "competition" (even though they're actually not – the client always has a voice already inside their head of what they want the voiceover to sound like).
- I provided countless free 30-minute video consults for those starting out, or in need of some recharging, to get back on track.
- I did Instagram video updates and encouraging posts to inspire, amuse, delight, and encourage other entrepreneurs (voice talent AND authors) on their journey.
- I maintained a blog designed to encourage and bring laughter and joy
- In our North Seattle Voiceover Meetup, I've tossed money into the raffle to bless someone's day.

Is any of this boasting? Maybe, if you look at things with a pessimistic perspective. But if you look at life through the lens of positive optimism, you'll instantly recognize that I'm simply a conduit for gratitude to continue to flow through me and into others, encouraging and enabling them to do the same.

Pay it forward.

When I used to work for my ex-step-brother-in-law (I know; we have a weird family tree) I was a bit, hmm, *income-challenged*. I would leave for the day, heading home to relax, and reach into my pocket (or satchel, or wallet, or elsewhere; he'd find new and creative places to hide it) and find a mysterious $20 bill that wasn't there before. Or $50. Or even $100. Brent is an incredibly generous soul who loves to bless others, and giving is his bag.

You can bet your bottom dollar that I've taken my own $20's and $50's and $100's and silently slid them into others' wallets for them to find them at unawares. Are there times where I never heard a "thank you" back from them? Absolutely. Is my gratitude contingent upon their gratitude? No. They'll still get another fig bar from me.

Part of the beauty of giving is your right hand not knowing what your left hand is doing.

THE PROVERBIAL RUBBER MEETING THE PROVERBIAL ROAD

You have been blessed with resources: great or small. How do you either clutch them or redistribute them? How do you decide what stays and goes, and who is blessed by what you've received?

Giving is an incredible way of saying thank you for what you've received. I don't know what they're called, but I love the illustration of the old water conveyors…a rigging system of buckets on a pulley system that draw from a well. They continue to draw, they continue to give. They continue to draw, they continue to give. They continue to draw, they continue to give. What they receive, they give away…right away. It's amazing. There have been times in my life where I've taken a gift and passed it right on to someone else, because I already had one, or because someone was in need, or because it just gave me great pleasure to bless someone else. Whatever the reason, the gift allowed me to be the giver, and multiple people were grateful as a result.

Giving and receiving are hugely symptomatic components of gratitude. Giving because it's an outflow of gratitude. Receiving because we need to recharge. There is much to be gained indeed.

Stop. Look around you. What do you see? Anything that you've taken too much for granted for too long? How do you stay grateful and pay it forward? How do *you* stop and say thank you?

I am so immeasurably grateful for what voiceovers have brought into my life. I cannot begin to express my gratitude.

Nature abhors a vacuum. Fill it with gratitude and see what happens.

Having an attitude of gratitude is absolutely critical in *life*. Applying it to the voiceover industry is simply an extension of that. Everything that comes to me is a gift. All opportunities are a sacred blessing that I am immeasurably thankful for. Proceeding in such a mindset, you'll experience a tremendous reassurance that Someone is looking out for you and seeking to provide.

Now go enjoy a fig bar on me.

No Thanks. I Already Know Everything

THE KNOW-IT-ALL

He is known only as "Know-It-All." Dressed in yellow pajamas, with short-cropped hair and bullet-proof glasses that magnify his nearly-crossed eyeballs into the size of small moons, Eddie Deezen's character in *The Polar Express* is simultaneously obnoxious, cute and annoying.

Obnoxious: because he knows everything and insists on talking through a shrill, nasally, clarinet-like tone that just makes you want to squeeze things until they ooze.

Cute: because he is a kid and is therefore worthy of looking at and saying "Awww."

Annoying: because he is a know-it-all who blabs on and on about the most finite details of everything, and is therefore worthy of looking at him and saying "Awww. I would like to squeeze you until you ooze."

Cinema and society are replete with characters like this:

- Peter Griffin of *Family Guy*
- Autor from *Princess Tutu*
- Jack Chick
- Scuttle from *The Little Mermaid*
- Cliff Clavin of *Cheers*
- Timon in *The Lion King*
- Sheldon Cooper of *The Big Bang Theory*
- Starscream from the original *Transformers*
- President Stable Genius[80]
- My Mom
- Your Mom
- Every Mom everywhere ever

- And one of my personal favorites: Otto, the bombastic Nietzsche-quoting hitman in *A Fish Called Wanda*. To quote Otto, "Apes don't read philosophy." And Wanda's response: "Yes, they *do,* Otto… they just don't understand it."

Individuals that think they know it all, that are apparently beyond education, or think they have amassed all the answers already, are almost universally reviled…they are characters that are *lacking* character. Like those who think they can beat the system by dressing up as grannies[81] so they can get the coronavirus vaccine early. It bothers me that I did not come up with this idea first. I would make a wonderful Granny.

In voiceovers, it is the brazen effrontery posed by newcomers who have been in voiceovers for less than a year - and are convinced that they already have all the answers. This same effrontery is readily apparent in those who insist that Michael Bolton falls under "good music" column, which it does not. It falls under the "I will kill you with a hammer if you play Michael Bolton" column.

This same effrontery starts with those who are told *"Hey, you've got a great voice; you should do voiceovers!"* So, they run and do voiceovers, because *"how hard can it be?"* They skip coaching, and buy their $39.99 *Zingyou* (It's in the name! It *zings* you in the end!) microphone bundle and Tonka headphones on Amazon. They slap up a few foam squares. They go hog-wild on promoting their Voices.com page. Or they endorse Fiverr, and are entirely unreceptive to correction by those who have gone before. And then, they do the unthinkable…they start *coaching.* Again, because, *"how hard can it be? I already know everything."*

In my best David Attenborough voice:

Ahh, the revolting hubris of the spring chicken. They are the serial purveyors of misinformation, and should be killed with a hammer.

Such people…need teachability.

Such people…need to recognize that they have two ears and one mouth for a reason.

Such people…are dangerous.

A HAPPY MEAL OF A MESSAGE ON LEARNING

It is a big yellow sign. There are two arches. It represents food all over the world. And the food is not the greatest, although my sons primarily want the toy anyway, not the food. Also, they can lick up all the ketchup from the container before they even touch the French fries. Do not ask me why they do this; I do not know.

McDonald's. It is Americana…and it can be found all over the world. Ray Kroc's restaurant chain roots go back to 1955. By 1958, McDonald's had sold its 100 millionth hamburger.

I am not overly fond of McDonald's food. If you have read my previous blogs and books – *go on, I will wait…*

Welcome back.

…you will note that I am fond of promoting my affinity for Taco Bell and that succulent grade-Q meat and "authentic" Mexican food. I remember when I was 23. It was a very long time ago; I think it was the same year that fire was invented. I suggested to my Mexican *abuela* that we go out to Taco Bell: a place she had never visited since she stopped driving her car in 1735. We ordered our food, sat down, she opened her soft taco, and said, "Aaron, this is *not* Mexican food."

Quite right, Gramma. It is not genuine. Neither is McDonald's, really.

But one genuine thing Ray Kroc said remains as food for the wise. It is an axiom that is timelessly exemplary in its analogy of a growing, living organism. He said, *"When you're green, you're growing; when you're ripe, you rot."*

So, I ask you now, in the name of all that is sacred, are you green? Am I?

TEACHABILITY IS EVERYTHING

I strive to practice teachability. Even so, I do have a few Y-chromosomes floating around somewhere in me, and therefore have a great propensity for my pride to get in the way. This is why I am currently stranded in Tristan da Cunha because I do not ask for directions. If someone could please send a chopper I would appreciate it.

I spent a long time on the sidelines of voiceovers before taking the plunge. Watching. Studying. Waiting. I have learned from the best. Scott Burns, a voiceover coach, is one of those. And Paul Strikwerda. Pat Fraley. Bill DeWees. I have taken great pains to ingest, study, and better myself. That involves really holding myself up to the light so that I can see any impurities floating around in there. I am not talking about my Y-chromosomes or chicken bits.

Let me tell you a story.

It was going to be easy. There were instructions. It surely would not take that long. It would be a challenge, sure, but I enjoy challenges.

I had this big gazebo to put together over our hot tub. I pulled all the parts out and laid them meticulously across my workbench in the garage. All of the parts had their own spaces to reside until I called for them. The first thing I needed to do was to assemble the roof. I needed to attach the center hub to eight long spines that branch out from the center and attach to the supporting rails and the four corner pillars that held everything up.

Roof = done!

Now it was time to connect the four corner pillars to it. I had assembled one of these before, so, even though the instruction manual was back in the garage, and I was out in the yard in the rain, I figured I knew what to do next in order to finish it.

I was having a bit of a struggle connecting the four pillars to the longest spines stemming out from the roof structure. There was some bowing, and the roof pinnacle had sunken below the pillars I had managed to erect thus far. They were splayed out in odd directions across the grass, reminiscent of what happens when one is launched from a cannon into a wall of granite. "Oh, well…" I thought. I was getting it connected as fast as I could so as to minimize the bowing as soon as possible. When the pillars were up, and all four roof supports were connected, something did not look quite right. Nonetheless I figured it just needed some straightening.

That is when I noticed the roof hub. All of the spines were extended outward from it, sure, but they were now – all of them – twisted to the right. The hub itself had rotated, but the legs had not. Now, they were all out of their grooves. Please note that this is not actually how you are supposed to assemble gazebos, so please do not take this chapter as proper instruction for assembling gazebos.

Yes, they still formed a spider branching out from the hub, but since the center hub itself was rotated, the tension wouldn't be there at the end of the legs to make sure the roof did not come off and flap in the wind, eventually landing somewhere in Brazil. Also, the top mini-canopy would not have enough tension to deflect the rain. It lay there, draped limply across the top as if to say "Aaron...why?"

When I realized my error – and what it would take to correct it – I slumped down onto the stepladder underneath the pinnacle and just gave a thousand yard stare off into the pasture, my hands in my pockets to deflect the cold. It was raining, and there was still snow outside, a bit slushy, but still there. Not ideal conditions. My jacket was a bit waterlogged and my hair rain-soaked.

I had been here before. I often think I am more able than I am when it comes to housework, yard work, work with tools, or anything more complicated than making toast. (Please do not chime in here. I *know* you butter it first.) In the end, I get frustrated and berate myself with the dependable, time-honored phrase:

"You can't do anything right." I do not know where that came from because neither my mom nor dad, nor any of my teachers had ever said that to me. But somewhere it took root.

Had I assembled the pillars with their supporting rails *first*, and had a complete bottom structure to simply lift the completed roof onto, I wouldn't have bowing…or twisting…or tension loss…or have to pee so badly since, because I had been sitting out there depressed for so long, single-celled paramecium had now evolved into fully-grown humans.

Shoulda looked at the freaking manual.

Was I going to give up? No. I eventually sighed, grabbed my hammer and pliers and started over on the roof. And I finished it. Is it perfect? Almost. Does it work now? Almost. Is the mutilated and jerry-rigged form factor a constant reminder that I should have done one thing? Entirely. What was the one thing?

Accept instruction.

Indeed, I could have saved myself a lot of frustration, double effort and cold toes, had I simply gone back into the garage and referenced the instruction manual.

Lesson? I still don't know everything. And I'm ok with that. Except that Taco Bell *IS* genuine Mexican food, and you cannot tell me otherwise.

So...are you green?

HERE'S ONE TO GROW ON:

"It's what you learn after you know it all that counts."

John Wooden

Drop That Beer And Get Off The Couch

THE BUSY LIFE OF A BUSY ENTREPENEUR BEE

"Man, if someone had told me what a voice talent also *needed to do to succeed..."*

Ever said that? Yeah, there's a lot. You're a Voice Talent, sure enough, and perhaps you've been told that you have a great voice and you should really do that. And in some magical ether, perhaps a parallel universe where everything is full of sunshine and rainbows, where things always work out in your favor 100% of the time, you'd have to do nothing else but voiceovers, and you'd be raking in trillions of dollars per day by just recording and sending.

But this is Planet Earth, and you actually have to do work here. *What?!?!?* *Perish the thought! No one said anything about WORK! I didn't sign up for this!*

Yeah. Work:

work
/wərk/
Learn to pronounce
noun
activity involving mental or physical effort done in order to achieve a purpose or result.
"he was tired after a day's work in the fields"
synonyms: labor, toil, exertion, effort, slog, drudgery, the sweat of one's brow; More
"they made sure the work was progressing smoothly" a task or tasks to be undertaken; something a person or thing has to do.
synonyms:
          tasks, jobs, duties, assignments, commissions, projects; chores
"haven't you got any work to do?"

Your work might not involve a lot of physical effort. But *man* does it require a lot of parallel work! It's been said that work stands for Weekly Overload Recreational Killer[82]. Ha! Ain't that the truth. You have a lot to do if you want to succeed as an entrepreneur. But is it really work? Is it mental or physical effort? Or is there part pleasure in there too?

HEART-POUNDING LABOR OF LOVE

I don't know about you, but when Sunday evening rolls around, and I'm lying there in bed with my restless legs flapping around so hard my toes are flicking the ceiling, I *cannot wait* to get back in the saddle for Monday morning.

I am no sloth. I'm not a beer-drinker, and although I love my Apple TV, I don't sit around with the remote in my hand. I make things happen. In both voiceovers and authoring, I have and am:

- networking and marketing on social media
- writing blogs
- writing articles
- Inspiring
- Encouraging
- sharing lessons
- attending local Chambers of Commerce meetings
- attending Meetups
- posting engaging content online
- teaching
- holding workshops
- encouraging
- providing business insight
- posting on Reddit
- doing free video consults
- running voiceover Meetups, and
- Making inspiring and entertaining marketing Posters, and posting them mainly on Instagram or Pinterest
- auditioning auditioning auditioning

My entire day is spent in front of my computer seeking out the next opportunity, the next client, the next entrepreneur colleague that needs help, making myself available, auditioning, connecting with, socializing, and generally just making sure that I'm somehow, in some way, always a rolling stone, gathering no moss, and moving, moving, moving. I was not made to sit still.

Is it a lot of upkeep? Yes. Is all of it necessary? In most cases, yes. Could I get by without it? Not a chance. It's not enough to have a website and sit (with beer in hand) in the wild hopes that someone will happen to flit along and land on my page and *maybe* request a quote or *maybe* listen to my reels. I must bring them to me. I *want* to bring them to me. It is my *passion* to bring them to me.

What about you? Do you feel the same restless urge, the same overwhelming excitement when Sunday night rolls around, knowing that the next week of chances and opportunities is right around the corner, waiting for you to succeed? If not, there's a fire that needs to be reignited somewhere, and you may have let something steal your thunder and reduce you to a smoldering wick. It's time to light the fire again, methinks. As Gandalf said once he freed Theoden from captivity to Saruman, *"Breathe the free air again, my friend."*

I cannot wait for Monday morning because, yes, it's work (labor)...but it's a labor of love for me, through and through, inside and out. The only point in the week where I'm bummed out is Friday afternoons, where it all comes to a halt and I'm forced to rest. Grrrrrr! Rest and untethering? Who needs it!? Let's light a fire again I say.

A BORN CAMPAIGNER

I am a born campaigner. What that means for me is that I have a strong desire to move toward something. Not sure where it ultimately came from, but I'm very goal-oriented, with a massive sense of instilled drive. Sitting still is good for rest, but I can't do that if it's between Monday and Friday, between 8am to 5pm. I *must* move.

When I did video production and videography, there was a voting contest that came around every fall and that's what I looked forward to all year long. I won that contest three years in a row through solid campaigning, through a fierce determination to win. There was very little else I thought about back then except how to get more votes. Does that ring true for you? I campaigned heavily to win the King 5 Best of Western Washington award. It's the hustle of campaigning that is what you will be doing 95% of the time in this industry. You're campaigning for them to elect *you* to serve them, and you must be shameless about doing so.

George Lucas said It. I've said it before, and I'll say it again: *Your focus determines your reality*. This phrase is *so* true. My focus is absolute success in voiceovers, because my heart's desire has become voiceovers. Over and above any other career I've ever tried out or hoped to achieve some measure of success in, voiceovers have far and wide eclipsed anything else that was even remotely satisfying, and nothing will ever touch it.

We're in campaign season now. All of these candidates are pushing toward a dream of the White House. They all have a singular focus, and they're all intent on one goal: being elected. They lie awake at night for the same reason I do: achieving their dream of success in the area of interest that is captivating them, desiring to settle for nothing less until that's accomplished.

THE DREAM CHASER

The Dream Chaser. No, not the space-plane by the Sierra-Nevada Corporation. I'm talking about me. I'm talking about you. I'm talking about us. And I'm sure, if you're a fellow voice talent, you've heard this phrase in at least *one* of your scripts to date, yes? I see it more and more: "we are the dream chasers."

Does the dream you're chasing consist of being able to put your feet up with a movie and a beer? Or does it consist of sending out that audition, being chosen, feeling a massive amount of elation, being paid a salary to do what you love to do, and then to be able to repeat that process *ad infinitum*? Does your dream revolve around desperate, addictive, stomach-churning hopes of achievement? How about passionately and repeatedly reaching out to potential clients all the live-long day?

Or does it revolve around being left alone to ponder your navel and snuggle up in your covers again while you drink in those reruns you already saw?

Abdul Salaam El Razzac, aka "Happy Man" in *Pretty Woman*, said it best:

"Welcome to Hollywood! What's your dream? Everybody comes here; this is Hollywood, land of dreams. Some dreams come true, some don't; but keep on dreamin' - this is Hollywood. Always time to dream, so keep on dreamin'."

I just love that!

I am a man of absolute unbridled *relief*. Why *relief*? Because for almost 28 years of employment, I did what somebody else wanted. I *did* crave that relief, and putting my feet up, because what I was doing wasn't mine. I yearned for deliverance: for something that would be compelling, delightful, inspiring, satisfying me on so many levels I can't even begin to express them all, fitting me like a glove. At age 43, I finally found it. After Dairy Queen, telemarketing, paper routes, office manager positions, administrative assistant positions, drywall support, front desk employment, and even *self*-employment (though providing different services)...*I finally found it*. I *finally* found what I had been looking for. Take *that*, U2.

Does your dream mean the world to you? Or do the remote and beer mean more?

It's Not You, It's Me

...BUT REALLY, IT'S YOU

Reconciliation is a long road. It starts with an offense and ends with an apology, or, at the very least, a lame half-ass offer to buy someone a beer. For this reason, I love being offended, because it means I will usually end up with an apology and a beer.

But that's just the rub: we *love* being offended these days. In this society, it's become the *de facto* response of so many to experience that kneejerk response: to ride that offense train all the way to Kingdom Come and back. It affords us the opportunity to play the victim, appealing for public sympathy with outraged Facebook complaint posts laden with ALL CAPS and lots of exclamation marks.

For me, I don't need sympathy. Just give me the alcohol. Sorry...was that last part not clear? Alcohol = forgiveness, always. Fill me up with alcohol, and we will be BFF's until Jesus returns. I trust He'll fill me in on which financial possessions I signed over to you in my drunken stupor.

On a personal note, I was recently offended. *What?!? No, Aaron, say it isn't so!* Indeed, 'tis the sad truth. I was going about my merry way of encouragement and posting things meant to inspire, and someone took offense at what I posted. THREE people, in fact! It was a crowded room of the bleeding wounded. And when I found out that they were offended – *wait for it* – I was offended.

It was a Glorious Offense-a-ganza, full of epic Grinch-like proportions, ladling out blobs of bitterness and irritation. They hurled gravy-like frustration over me, and I spouted frothy venom-like frustration back, well-concealed in clever silver-tongued etiquette and passive-aggressive polish. Sure, behind our forked tongues we meant well, but we really wanted to bite, because we were all offended. Am I exaggerating a bit? Sure. But the truth is that we all *chose* to be offended, meaning no offense to them. It truly is always a choice. Events themselves are inherently neutral: *we* are the ones who choose what meaning to assign to them, and whether or not to be offended. But lately, we choose to be so much more often than not. How did we get from there to here? How did we all become so easily offended? Were our spines removed in our sleep? Why do we as a civilization actively engage *Presume and React* mode instead of, as my wife encourages, "assume they're *for* you"? Why is someone's entire tenure of good behavior, integrity and solid principles immediately thrown out and discredited through what we choose to be offended by? One of the offended parties told me "I really believed better of you. MUCH."

Were her words surprising? Not really. Because, in the end, you can't please everyone, nor should you try. Ed Sheeran once said, "I can't tell you the key to success, but the key to failure is trying to please everyone."

It's not me…it's you. Actually, it's not you…it's me. But really…it's all of us.

At one point or another, we're all going to assume the worst, and then we'll:

- get bent out of shape
- be rubbed the wrong way
- become hot under the collar
- have our teeth set on edge
- get worn down, incensed
- get stuck in a paddy
- see red
- foam at the mouth
- turn blue in the face
- get hacked off, and
- have something stuck in our craw at some point.

The point herein is, let's take stock of **why** we're choosing to be offended.

SANTA'S CLAUSE

I'm sure if Santa followed suit, he'd make us all sign contracts loaded with enough indemnity clauses to make Johnny Cochran choke. He'd cover his velvet red fanny with clauses and protections to ensure that we couldn't sue him for wrongful delivery, damage to property, breaking and entering, stalking, insider trading, trespassing, invasion of privacy, and any other offended claim we could make under this red and green tinsel sun. Because that's the way of it – we're ready to sue at a moment's notice.

Just look at some of the lawsuits that ascended the court chain from 2010 to 2020, riding the coattails of precedent all the way up to nine sitting justices who decided their fate.[83] Some might argue that some of these were needed for societal change; others sue because they're opportunistic or emotional.[84] As *XInsurance* says, "Litigation can spring from your own mistakes, or the opportunism of a sue-happy society." There is sad psychology[85] behind this.

Look. 2020 sucked, and offended nearly everyone on the planet. Unless of course we're talking about Mr. and Mrs. Mouth-Click-Whistle-Snap-Click-Click-Whistle-Glottal-Stop-Click and their children Glottal-Click-Whistle, Whistle-Click-Glottal and Click-Glottal-Click, who live on that remote island in the bush and are interested in killing you with spears. Most everyone has been offended in one way or another by the coronavirus. Or murder hornets. Or Sean Connery dying. For us voice talent, it's that persistent neighbor always running his leaf-blower.

We:

- Hit send and then regret it
- Put that letter in the mail and then anxiously bite our nails wondering when the mailman will come so that we can run out and wave our arms wildly and shout "Stop! Stop!" and hope we were in time to retract that letter
- Fire off the angry talk, and once we see the expression of how it lands, backpedal with the ol' "Wait- wait- I didn't mean that."
- Post the angry note to our roommate for unwanted behavior, only to run and crumple it up as you hear them coming home up the stairs.

When did we forget to stop, take a deep breath, and just do it the Daniel Tiger way?

GIVE 'EM HELL FOR ME

Marc Broussard has an excellent song that just makes me smile. It goes as follows:

Give em hell for me...Dry your stupid eyes, you big baby
Just give em hell for me...Don't you ever take it too seriously

We are *so* easily offended, we humans. It's like the ol' SNL skit, "You Mock Me"[86] with John Malkovich. Go ahead, watch that now. You'll see what I mean. Only now we do it with lawsuits instead of harsh rebukes.

Merry Christmas. D'oh! Sorry about that. *Happy Hanukkah.* Oh, my bad! *Happy Holidays.* Too innocuous you say? My sincerest apologies!!! *Merry Christmahannakwanzikah.* After all, that's what we've become: praying we won't offend, walking on eggshells that we might; becoming so vanilla and innocuous to the point of neutrality and diluted inclusivity at all costs, until the potency of our original message is rinsed out.

As entrepreneurs, fortunately, we usually get to present a message that is not our own words: we're just the messenger, so don't shoot us. But in terms of community, we need to remember it's OK to feel a certain way that might be politically incorrect. We need to have our own ideas and perceptions heard, no matter how narrow-minded they might be. After all, Jesus didn't come to bring peace; He came "to bring a sword" (his own words). We can choose to be offended at a script. We can become jealous of another entrepreneur's success. We can misinterpret the message and kill the messenger. We're all messengers, us entrepreneurs. Let's not kill each other.

It's a foregone conclusion that someone out there is going to be offended that this chapter was not all sunshine and rainbows, gits and shiggles, as I usually strive for. But for this new year, resolve to not be so easily offended. Strengthen your spine. Go out and be strong, no matter what happens around you. Know yourself. Give 'em hell for me. Dry your stupid eyes, you big baby. Stand your ground. Hold the fort. Dig in that foxhole. Realize your inherent strength and fortitude. On the coattails of this "Season of Giving", give others the benefit of the doubt.

Did I intentionally set out to write a depressing and overlong chapter on the destructive power of bitterness? Yes, because it feeds my soul when I get to be a Debbie Downer. The truth is that in this world - and after 2020 in particular - it's sorely needed. I've been battling COVID-19 all year with comedy and lightheartedness: that's my calling. But I felt the need to end a serious year on a serious note and treat it soberly.

Buddha said, "Holding onto anger is like drinking poison and expecting the other person to die." Ease-of-offense will kill us. What I propose, going into this new year of a hopefully receding pandemic wave: let's choose to believe in each other. Drop the lawsuit-ready posture, eh? Let's assume that the other person is actually for us. Let's practice the golden rule and choose *trust* for once. As voice talent, we voice these kinds of scripts all the time from companies putting their best foot forward and declaring their super-ethical behavior through self-promotion: *"We're the brand you can trust."*

In the end, I apologized to those who took offense at what I posted, removing it and instead posting a watered-down version. But mostly I apologized because none of them drink beer. I know. I offered. Strangely, my beer looked and smelled like coffee, but who's counting?

HERE'S ONE TO GROW ON:

"Thick skin and a strong mind are essential if you want to survive in this world. Nobody can ever break you down if you don't let them."

- Unknown

A Most Unconventional Me

A HORSE OF A DIFFERENT COLOR

You know what I'm talking about. The exuberant green-coated door-warden of Emerald City says, with great gusto, "That's a horse of a different color!" And then, to their astonishment, within the walls of the great city there actually *is* a horse of a different color...and the colors continue to change!

Aaron Ryan has never been one to conform. I often feel like the Barack Obama of voiceovers, because I showed up one day and shot straight up. There were various individuals who were suspicious of me at first, though I won't name them here. Natural human tendency is to be suspect of *anything* that shows advancement or progress beyond the usual measure or pace. Ultimately, I've been working on voiceovers since 1993, in tandem with other projects. I just hadn't really explored doing them by themselves, as a service, until the fall of 2016. You could say I was "waiting in the wings." And then I burst out onto the stage like a glorious two-hundred-and-seventy-five-pound butterfly. (I'm planning on losing it...and this time, I'll keep it off).

I don't like to do things like everyone else. I come up with different branding ideas. I'm a creative and unconventional guy.

On the note of branding, let's zoom out a bit for a second and define that. Celia Siegel quotes Seth Godin's definitions. "Godin says a brand is 'the set of expectations, memories, stories, and relationships that, taken together, account for a consumer's decision to choose one product or service over another.' His definition of a personal brand is slightly different: 'a story, a set of emotions and expectations and a stand-in for how we think and feel about what you do."[87] What I love about branding is the symbolism behind it, and the representation of identity-drenched-in-meaning behind it. I'm a person, but I'm also a representation of something that people can identify with and gravitate towards. Why would they choose me for their voiceovers? Because they can relate. That's what branding does. People relate to it. I'm a brand.

But furthermore, I'm a try-er. I really, really like to try things at least once, and see how it fares. Where some will instantaneously write things off and poo-poo such ideas as not worth it, I have different bones and guts.

I like to at least try, and perhaps invest a little cash into it and risk. I like to see if it will take off. My risk tolerance isn't stratospherically high, mind you, so I do invest soundly and safely usually, but some risk is better than no risk at all, in my opinion.

I don't go with the flow in terms of conventional advertising. I like to make my own types of things. Some say don't tell people what you make in voiceovers. I say "bah humbug" to that. That's one of the main questions nearly everyone has getting into voiceovers: "Can this sustain me? If so, with how much per month?" "What's a reasonable expectation of producible income?" "Will this be enough to live on?"

All good questions to ask, and in my "VoiceOverdrive" livestream every Monday at 1pm Pacific Time on Instagram (@seattlevoiceoverartist), I transparently share what I made for the previous week, where I'm at for the month, and the year, how many auditions I did, where I got jobs from, who I'm marketing to, lessons learned, valuable tips, and more. All of this is an effort to show newbies and aspiring entrepreneurs that you really *can* do this. It really *is* possible to sustain a full-time career in voiceovers.

I hold regular workshops because I *love* teaching. Some might say, "didn't you just get here? What business do you have teaching?" All I can say is look at my numbers. Look at my success. And then, look at my personality. I love teaching, I'm gregarious, and I love to give.

Couple those three things with proven success, and you've got a teacher, no matter how long they've technically been on the scene. Longevity doesn't matter when someone is a proven success and has what it takes from the start. Track record is largely irrelevant if someone is naturally gifted and has a genuine desire to encourage.

DISCOVER YOUR GIFTINGS

I'm a naturally gifted guy. I don't say that with even the smallest shred of haughtiness. There are people who go to colleges and spend 4 years learning something. I have never earned an MBA or any kind of a degree. I attended a single quarter at Bellevue Community College. I don't have a college diploma. Everything that I've ever done has been primarily hands-on, naturally acquired, self-taught, and 100% learned by practical application as opposed to imparted to me through curriculum. I'm self-taught, and have natural giftings that I credit God with giving me. I'm very grateful. With creative tasks, for the most part I'm just able to get right in there. That's just how I was wired, and I didn't create myself: so, I can take no credit for it, nor boast about it. Look at the rookies who try out for something and they're obviously a natural at it. Some veterans have to work *very* hard to get at that rookie's level. I don't know why I'm the way that I am, but I'm very unconventional that way as well.

How else am I unconventional? Take auditions for example. I do on average about 200-250 auditions per week. Is that a lot? Oh yeah. Does it get me jobs? Oh yeah. Now, I treat every audition like the paid job, and I give it the attention that it deserves, I promise you.

I'm not just casting the widest possible net and hoping to strain out a minnow. I give them my all, but I *love* auditioning. I long to have as many chances as I can. The contrary is true: if you don't love auditioning, or if you start to develop contempt for those audition notices, you're a goner. Those are your chances to make money.

As far as success ratios, I don't tend to look at a booking ratio as proof that I'm succeeding, i.e., 1-in-20. No. After all, I said I was unconventional, right? As I've mentioned earlier, the way I look at it, I take the total amount of money I've made in voiceovers and divide it by the total number of auditions I've done. Essentially, it boils down to getting "paid" about $13 per audition. Would you step into your booth, read a few lines, process and fire off an audition for $13? Sure you would. It all adds up, and the unconventional side of me has me hustling. Not everyone will choose to look at it this way, but this strikes me as an appraisal to better fuel optimism. I deeply appreciate the hustle. I do hustle for the money that I make, because I enjoy the hustle. Some don't.

All that to say that I highly encourage you to find and make your *own* path. To discover your own giftings and really pursue them. If during the course of voiceover pursuits, you continually find that you are banging your head against a wall, whether that's marketing, technique, equipment, software, or proficiency in whatever else, give yourself a break.

Take a breather and refocus – or, perhaps, even look for something else. Yes, it's wonderful. For me and many others, it's a beautiful pursuit. You may discover something else in the meanwhile that is a beautiful pursuit that you yourself are naturally gifted in, and I myself am not. Earnestly seek to discover – and thus, begin to refine – your gifts, so that you can have a narrow, laser focus to do them well.

I love Ecclesiastes 9:10: *"Whatever your hand finds to do, do it with all your might."* Certainly try, and try, try, again if you don't at first succeed. But take whatever obstacles continue to stop you, and give them the honest assessment that they deserve. It would be a tragedy to throw thousands of dollars at something you were never meant to do in the first place.

Conversely, it would be a tragedy for you *not* to throw thousands of dollars at something that you were meant to do.

So, ask yourself: is voiceovers what you are meant to do? For the unconventional me, yes, most definitely, it is absolutely what I'm meant to do, and I know that deep within my bones. I finally found it. It truly is my calling, without a doubt, and it fits me like a glove. You must know it too, if you're going to be successful at it. If you "think it would be neat", well, that's just not the same. That sounds like pastime to me. That sounds like hobby to me. That sounds like a fling.

Flings don't last. They're one-night stands; they're short relationships; they're destined to end. For the unconventional me, voiceovers is forever; it's a long-term relationship, it's destined to go on even beyond retirement age because it has no end in sight for me. It is most definitely not a fling. It's a long-term investment I'm committed to.

YOU DO YOU BEST

Other signs of unconventionality? Hmm. I'm not legalistic about getting off work immediately at 5pm. I continually create new branded apparel to advertise. I have vinyl lettering on my car. I run an email spider (which I mentioned in a previous chapter "The Business of Voiceovers") to obtain valid email addresses to market to. Some people don't allow you to post your own voiceover work in their groups or Meetups. I don't believe in that. Some people are all about rules. I don't believe in that. At least, not legalism or tight-fistedness.

When walls close around people, they tend to be less creative. Call it being boxed in. When we as artists are boxed in, sure, maybe we spring into *prima donna* mode and demand our rightful place in The Arts, if you please – but ultimately it denies us our right to create, because things are being created for us, around us, and essentially preventing us from being us.

As artists, we need space to live and breathe and have our being. We need space to really get into our roles and our personas and execute the perfect delivery of the voiceover craft. We have an innate desire to have what we've created appreciated by others. To show them what we've done and say, "Look! See? Isn't this beautiful?" We need to be allowed to do that. Too many parameters can restrict the blood flow to our heart.

How can you be unconventional? How can you blaze a trail? How can you be original? After all, Kay Bess' main message, when she spoke as the keynote speaker for VO Atlanta 2019, was "be yourself." Be no one else but you. Only you can be you. Don't try to be someone else.

Marc Cashman says, "Everyone's voiceprint is unique, just like fingerprints. No two voices sound exactly alike."[88] Be your own voice. Oscar Wilde said "Be yourself; everyone else is already taken."

Go get 'em, you unconventional you.

Father Forgive Me, For I Have Spammed

GUILTY AS CHARGED

I'm Aaron Ryan. And I'm a spammer. ("Hi, Aaron…")

Well, I covered telemarketing, so it's only fitting that now we talk about everyone's favorite source of daily disgruntlement: the email spammer!

But first, let's zoom out and really examine Spam. What is Spam anyway? When we crack open a can of spam, we find meat substitute soaked in evil. So essentially, what these strangers from afar – especially everyone's favorite beloved Nigerian prince – are offering you, is a succulent entrée of Satanic beef replacement, which is about as delectable as a cup of warm spit.

I remember once eating Spam and experiencing that wonderfully distinct sensation of pre-vomit mixed with a pain I couldn't locate.

This is what the Can-Spam Act of 2003 was actually all about, because Spam actually comes in… you guessed it…a can. If anyone wanted us to actually read something they sent us, why in tarnation would they send us quasi-beef from the underworld? If they wanted us to actually read it, wouldn't it be more prudent to instead send us gold-soaked leaflets framed in gold bars covered in more gold, with gold filling? I'm all for receiving free leaflets, but even more when they're covered in lots of free gold.

Don't get me wrong…I'm flattered that so many people in Nigeria want to offer me:

- Viagra
- Belly fat pills, and
- a large, no-strings-attached inheritance all at the same time.

Oh that I should be so esteemed as to be doted on by complete strangers form faraway lands who somehow know that:

- I have erectile dysfunction
- I am utterly gargantuan, and
- There is not a penny to my name

…well that just makes me giddy all over!! So thank you, *NOREALLYIMEANITTHANKYOU*, Mr. "John Anderson" from Nigeria, who loved me enough to send me meat substitute soaked in evil. I appreciate it.

In the business world, we have our own share of spammers. Take Gareth Cole, or whatever name he's currently going by. Now this guy isn't just a spammer, he's also a *scammer*: a truly revolting combination. Here is a guy who routinely posts on Craigslist about an opportunity for his "new corporate client", and the job pays $1150, or $1350 or $Ridiculous-Amount-Too-Good-To-Be-True-But-I-Think-You're-A-Sucker-50, and you must record from his studio and pay a deposit. These guys hurl meat substitute soaked in evil that's also designed to defraud you!

You know, because meat substitute soaked in evil isn't bad enough.

HOW TO UN-SPAM-IFY

So here's my confession. While I'm no Gareth Cole, I could certainly be accused of being a spammer. It's not my aim to serve up revolting synthetic meat and induce vomiting. Were that the case, I would seat you at a table with a fork and a bib, before a nice plate of mangled animal carcass and a tall cool glass of Ipecac. But I do cherish the occasional opportunity to reach out to clients. How do I do that without spamming them, annoying them, or inciting my video-producer-slash-sorceress clients to hex my future grandchildren?

Easy. Make it about them. All marketing emails should really be All. About. Them.

We're all selfish narcissists who are only thinking of ourselves and haven't a care about anyone who isn't named "Me": a beautiful name that makes us swoon over ourselves because we're just so narcissistically swoonworthily swoonsome.

Without making all of my clients out to be Raging Self-Centered Egoists And Overly-Conceited Rabid Narcissists, there's a kernel of truth here. Flip the tables for a moment. When you get an email from scammers, why or why don't you open it? If you see Viagra in the subject line, do you instantly hit delete, or does it remind you – *oh, snap!* – that you need to order flowers for your wife and plan that hotel getaway? When you receive that email from that Nigerian prince with an inheritance, does it appeal to your better nature to help your fellow (scammer) man, or is its destiny the Recycle Bin with the other pseudo-beef from the nether regions?

Ultimately, we all need to be Ace Ventura: complimentary, fun to interact with, and most importantly, possessing awesome hair. Case in point, his "You smell ter-RIF-fic!" comment. Who wouldn't love to hear that? And who wouldn't think, "gee, what a nice guy, I think I'll whitelist this spammer?" Which is precisely why I form every marketing email like this:

Dear Soon-To-Be-My-Client,
You smell ter-RIF-fic!
This email is about YOU. YOU are everything. This email is NOT about Satanic beef substitute.
Benefits, benefits, benefits, blah blah blah, You smell Ter-RIF-fic!!
Sincerely,
Buy From Me
PS – I do voiceovers.
PPS – roses, right?
PPPS – permission to swoon granted.

You see? That's how I get all my clients.

Your mission, should you choose to accept it, O Worthy Spammer, is to make your spam messages so unrevoltingly winsome, that the whole world over will wantonly wish for your warm winsome welcome.

SPAM I AM

I'm a marketer. I have to be if I want to get business. So daily, I land in the inboxes of hundreds of people who are utterly thrilled to say "OK, who the hell is this guy." It's true! And it's exciting to sit here and anticipate the response on my end. I contact people the world over through LinkedIn, Twitter, Facebook, Reddit, Quora, and even Craigslist, when I'm done posting my scary personal ads. I reach out and connect with hundreds of people on a daily basis in an effort to sell my services.

Replies usually come back along the following lines:

- Where did you get my email address? -or-
- I am a vegetarian. -or-
- Did I give the slightest hint that I desired meat substitute soaked in evil?
- Stop now. -or-
- I will cut you if you email me again. -or-
- Refrain from emailing me or I'm contacting The People In Charge Of Stopping Spam -or-
- Why? Just...*why?* -or-
- The Restraining Order obviously wasn't enough. That does it. I'm calling Luigi to break your kneecaps. -or-
- Take me off of your, and ALL, lists, for the foreseeable future of all eternity. -or-
- You sound great! We'd love to have you on our roster! You're amazing!

It is this last one that is my mostest favoritest, of course. This is the person that you'll want to list in your will as your sole beneficiary, above any and all family members, because their niceness level and apparent genuine desire to always hear what you have to say has already reached a 100% batting average.

You see, for every 9 replies in the negative, I receive one whole favorable reply! It's delicious. Almost as delicious as Spam itself! It truly is a Remarkable Thing to land unanticipatedly in someone's inbox and shout, with an ear-splitting-grin whilst waving my hand wildly in utter joy, "Hi!" Thus, the replies I receive back usually run the gamut of emotions depending on whether that person has had lunch already and has a happy tummy, or if they're purchasing explosives and finding out where I live from the various online databases that so readily provide them to explosives-purchasing homicidal spam-recipient maniacs.

The point in all this is that it's OK to spam. Just do it sensibly, and know that for every 9 people that want to kill you, one lucky one might just bring you some business. Of course, the alternative exists that they're just being nice and will soon delete all traces of your existence: either by hitting delete, or by the explosives mentioned earlier. For your sake, I hope they bring you business and you both receive a happy ending instead of being blown to smithereens.

I'm a spammer, Spam I Am. Each day is a reach day. Every day I connect with people, offering my services to the world. Do they all need my services? Most definitely: they just don't know it yet. Do they all want my emails? Most definitely not. Thus the explosives that just arrived on my porch via Amazon Prime. Welp. At least they're not Satanic explosive replacements soaked in evil pseudo-beef juice.

Commence Spam!

TAKEAWAY & ACTION STEP

Direct emails can net you direct clients. Direct outreaches can award you direct relationships. Directly direct your direct attention to directing your directives directly.

There's nothing intrusive about a marketing email. You have an immeasurably invaluable service to offer – go forth boldly in that knowledge. Make those relationships today.

Accursed Red Badges And Pavlov's Dog

OUR CONDITIONED RESPONSIVENESS

I recently watched *The Social Dilemma* for a romantic date night with my wife. I assure you this is because *Transformers: Dark of the Moon* - the *ultimate* love movie - was out of rotation.

We'd wanted to for a while, but alas, were not yet members of the Netflix elite. Our entertainment diet usually consists of a strict regimen of Pixar, Disney+, Pixar, and time permitting, Pixar. We are after all parents to two children. "Children" is Latin for *Unsympathetically Over-demanding Juvenile Taskmasters Who Scream To Get Their Way And To Whom We Relent Because Please God Stop The Screaming.* So, on the occasional fortnight where they actually fall asleep before 2am and my wife and I can enjoy a good documentary, we have to have it all planned out ahead of time, or it's another steamy romantic night of not talking to each other and slipping into mutual oblivion, the popcorn bowl spilling out into our dog's ecstatic maw.

This time, we chose the hit documentary about social media addiction. We celebrated our blissful marriage by watching it while flicking through our respective Facebook news feeds and, again, not talking to each other. But, to keep the love alive, we made sure to throw the occasional "Wow, totally" at our spouse in response to some proffered revelation from the video. Then we returned to flicking.

As a man who has fingers, I found it fascinating that I too was an unwitting slave to all of these networks whose goal it is to watch my every move and plot my undoing through ritual bombardment of ads, ads, and more ads. I found, much to my chagrin, that my fingers were not in fact my own, but that they were rather unwittingly bound to flicking, scrolling, checking, refreshing, and clicking. I really had no choice in the matter – or so the documentary would have me believe.

Now I know what you're saying: *"I want a Schnauzer with my Weiner schnitzel."* And I would understand you: you're hungry, and Schnauzers are a delicacy. So, once you're back with a hot steaming plate to satisfy your innards, consider this alternate phrase that I suspect you may also be uttering: *"How can I possibly untether from my social media accounts and thus be trapped in 1937 forever?"* It's a conundrum, I grant you. The only greater conundrum than this conundrum is *why is conundrum such a fantastically intriguing conundrum of a word?*

Studies will reveal that I receive dopamine hits:

- Each time I realize there is a new red badge awaiting me from some app on the other side of my smartphone glass
- With every instance of every ping of every app
- Whenever someone likes, comments, shares, upvotes, friend requests, connects, or follows me.
- When my wife makes Macaroni with Aidell's sausage. #truestory

Believe me, that third one is uncontestable. I think I now have more followers on Instagram than Jesus had in his first year of ministry, and each new follower makes me giddy as they partake of my own Sermons on my own Mount.

Pardon me while I enjoy my dopamine hit.

I have returned.

It is true, and the phenomenon is real. Every time we're pinged with some new attention-sucking siren call, it's a pleasurable torment. If you are anything like me – *and let us pray that you are entirely not, because the world does not have the capacity for double this much awesome* – then you have, at least once, placed your phone on its charging cradle next to your bed at lights out…only to check it less than a minute later. Granted, you were probably bidding on that gold-plated Squatty Potty on eBay, and you wanted to make sure no one outbid you. Once more, I would understand you.

But if we're ever going to remain sane, is it possible to untether? And if a successful online career is tied to being active on social media – and it is – is it even realistic to expect that we take a break?

DOWN FOR THE COUNT

He was desperately trying to get my attention. I don't remember what for, but it was something probably along the lines of a Pteranodon who was carrying off Optimus Prime back to its babies to eat them, and that's when the UFO comes in and incinerates everything and turns it all into silly putty while Medusa looks on approvingly.

My 5-year-old has a very active imagination. He is incredibly creative with toys, and in his little mind, he stages all kinds of fantasy scenarios with an energy level that would rival those fuel rods in thermonuclear reactors. Geiger counters are acutely aware of him. It's frighteningly delightful, because you just never know when he will detonate. But detonate he would, at the unfortunate instance that I wasn't paying him enough attention.

You see, Brennan wants me to watch nearly everything he does. I try to communicate to him that my sophomore driving instructor Mr. Filbert always told me to keep my eyes on the road. But it's very hard resisting the gravitational pull of a 5-year-old yelling *"Watch! Watch, Dada, watch! Watch! Dada, WATCH!!!!"*

If I do not in fact watch, then my son detonates. If I *do* watch, then my entire car and all four of us detonate in a fiery collision. It is at this crossroads of conundrum *(hey! Great word!)* that I decide that my 5-year-old is expendable. I learned this while recently watching *Star Trek II* when Spock says to Kirk, *"the needs of the many outweigh the needs of the few...or the one."* A small tear rolls down my cheek as I send Brennan off to thermonuclear oblivion. But it's just then that I remember that I have Tree Top fruit snacks, which usually defuse any high-stress situation with him. Detonation averted.

But one time, I would not get away so easily. I was at home, scrolling through *whatever*, deeply engrossed in my hunt for *nothing*. Brennan had patiently lodged about 47 requests for me to watch, and for some reason was now growing impatient that I had not attended to him yet. (Brennan can be very unreasonable.)

Apparently *"Uh-huh, wow, that's neat, Bren!"* only works three times consecutively, and he wasn't having any of it. He said "NO, Dada. Watch *NOW*." And then he sighed heavily and continued firmly, *"5... 4... 3... 2... 1..."*

Being that I was skilled in reverse counting and frequently employed it on him, I knew where this was going. My preschooler just countdowned my ass.

Well, I realized my foolishness, and chuckled at his ingenuity. I paid him the attention that he deserved, and all was well again. Whatever it was – something about a Pteranodon and Optimus Prime I think – I now think back with regret about how immersed I was in my phone, caught up in the eternal time-suck that is Apple News... or email... or Facebook... or whatever, and how *not* caught up in my son I was. My precious 5-year-old who loves me and needs me and depends on me and makes me spend far too much money on Transformers and dinosaurs.

And when he was done with this eternally important spectacle with bearings on the entire cosmos, he returned to his normal routine, which consists of looking at me quizzically as if to say, "Are you still here?"

We so easily get sidelined by our interests, caught in a tractor beam of our phones and tablets. It's no conundrum *(What a great word!)* that our phones are all made so beautifully anymore: they call to us. They pine for attention, without even pining.

But there has to be something better, and I'm not even talking about going back to a can and string.

GIMME MY DOPAMINE I GOTTA HAVE MY DOPAMINE JUST NEED THE FIX MAN JUST GIMME MY DOPAMINE I NEED MY FIX

If you had been following my blog or books for a while, then I count you among the smartest people on earth. And you may have gobbled up my previous blog entitled "Stars, Listens & Likes, Oh My!" It's a darned good blog, if I do say so my darned self.

We crave validation. We crave affirmation. Likes, thumbs-up, stars, reviews, etc. It's the same dopamine hit. It's the conditioned response of Pavlov's dog. We know that if we receive any kind of:

- feedback on our audition, resume, interview, whatever
- response to our marketing email
- casting notice audition reply
- review from a previous job
- offers to work for an endless supply of Bottle Caps candy

…then we'll receive that dopamine hit there as well. Maybe it's just me on the Bottle Caps one.

We associate response with pleasure. And that pleasure, in the voiceover world, is borderline orgasmic. For myself, I receive a *huge* hit of dopamine when someone emails me indicating a desire to award me the job. It's amazingly satisfying. And so, when I send out an audition, any kind of response to that audition, is pleasure – even when it's them courteously informing me that they foolishly cast someone else. I hold no ill will! But I do have a son who owns a Pteranodon, so their time will come.

It's like an alternate reality: much like "reality TV." It's not really *reality*, I think we all know that. Rather, it's manufactured drama. Same with getting sucked into your phone. It's not reality. So, I propose a two-day fast from our phones. I propose no phones at the table. Get the Calm app and actually use it.

Is all this possible? It is. It is likely? No. But we all seriously need to untether. We need to get out and breathe and get some exercise. I know this last one is true because I *still* need to make sure my last will and testament is up-to-date before I attempt to bend over and put on my socks each morning. I need to get into better shape. I am not talking about a parallelogram. I'm talking about being utterly healthy. That includes being less addicted to my notifications.

But in the meantime, until I change my ways, keep those red badges a'comin'.

Now if you will excuse me, I must place a higher bid on eBay for that Squatty Potty, because seeing the face you make when you're outbid gives me a nice dopamine rush.

HERE'S ONE TO GROW ON:

"We are constantly trying to hold it all together. If you really want to see why you do things, then don't do them and see what happens."

Michael A Singer

May I Speak With The Person In Charge Of Purchasing?

THE TELEMARKETING GOLDEN YEARS

How did I get started in voiceovers? Sit back, pull up a mug of something light and refreshing, and let me regale you with a tale of old. Because I'm now old.

The year was 1993. Yours Truly was under the part-time employ of a telemarketing outfit in Bellevue Washington, where Yours Truly would contact business owners and summon all of Yours Truly's seductive powers to entice said business owners into parting with their hard-earned dollars to give to Yours Truly. After all, Yours Truly…was a telemarketer. Don't be mad. I was young: I needed the work. My available choices were telemarketing, Amway, or pole dancing. I was reluctant to try the second one, and the third one would scare away all women who are female and have eyes that see things. As a young man of healthy mating age, pole-dancing would effectively have been self-sabotage.

As a civilization, we like telemarketers about as much as a pool of throw-up. We much prefer *dinner* to throw-up, and even better is the ability to have dinner uninterrupted by telemarketers. Or throw-up. But back in the heyday of telemarketing - you know, when people still *answered* their phones - this was a thing. And a big thing, because it apparently worked enough times for one guy to start a firm in Bellevue and hire me, Yours Truly.
Although…when you think about it…when I was a wee small child, at no time did the words "When I grow up, I wanna be a telemarketer" emerge from my mouth. Still, I thought this would be a fun job. What the heck, it was better than a pool of throw up.

As I had brothers, I was actually already quite adept at harassing people. I knew if I put my time-honored techniques to work, I would be making lots of commission-based sales and be rich in no time. (Update: I am now one score years older. Second Update: I am not rich). I began cold-calling people and ultimately was very successful at harass- er, telemarketing. It still resounds to this day! Also, the restraining orders resound too.

DON'T CALL ME. JUST SHOOT ME.

My life and viewpoints have changed. Now, instead of having a telemarketer call me, I would rather puke coat hangers. (Man, there sure is a lot of vomit in this chapter!) Not that I answer my phone anyway, as I'm too busy playing Bejeweled or browsing through Important Things. But you know those times. The times when you're doing something like shopping on your mobile phone, and all of the sudden a call takes complete control over your life, like Regis Philbin.

Unfortunately, the "Answer" button just *happens* to be positioned *exactly* where the "Add to Cart" button was in your browser. Cursing and eye-rolling, you answer the phone sheepishly, and are entreated to what sounds like a middle-schooler being punished for misbehavior and sentenced to voice dull and mundane vacuum cleaner sales scripts for three hundred years.

And here's the rub – since the voice is adorable and cracks from puberty - *and* sounds suspiciously like Russell giving his Wilderness Explorer speech from *Up* – there's simply no break in the dreaded speech to interject a "not interested." The dreaded telemarketer has been stridently trained to ferociously ignore your pleadings for peace and quiet. In truth, your constant attempts at "Hello? *Hello??? HELLO?!?!?!"* to get their attention are about as successful as a healthy asparagus trying to capture my interest while I'm holding a drippy McQuadruple Half-Pounder Bacon Burger. It simply doesn't work.

I firmly believe that the only effective telemarketer agencies that still exist are required to now employ techniques that border on the bizarre. They're bizarre enough to leave you hanging in suspended animation after listening to the call or voice mail, wondering what you did to God for Him to allow you to be punished in such a manner.

Here's an example, and I am not making this up. Just yesterday I received a robocall from someone who stated from the beginning that "This may be a shot in the dark", and was offering to buy our home for cash. I promise you, Dear Reader, that I was doing *none* of the following:

selling our home: I do not wish to do so as my wife will cook me nothing but Top Ramen for six months as a consequence, nor posting *anywhere* that I'm desirous to sell, nor
contacting anyone anywhere at all henceforth about any sale of any house at any time ever in any way forthwith whithersoever pro forma concordantly vis a vis ergo motion in limine

Therefore, I can only assume that these people live in a mental ward and are allowed phones during their "outside time" so that they might harass the rest of us, causing us to ponder the meaning of "motion in limine." Seriously! Where do these whackjobs get off calling me with "shots in the dark" about me selling my home for cash? Do they think I'm that strapped for cash that I'd want to just up and sell my home? (Sidebar: I am.)

Personally, I do not enjoy telemarketing one bit. Therefore, nearly all of my marketing is done via email and social media. This stems purely from an equal lack of enjoyment when telemarketers decide to call *me*. I suppose that in the future I might, if the only alternative I am allowed is to be hanged, drawn and quartered, and then sprayed with acid and allowed to slowly disintegrate in the heat of summer while ants methodically chew off important parts of my body.

THE EMPIRE STRIKES BACK

Not that Empire. I'm talking about the empire of Americana. There came a point when Americana and culture finally said "Enough is enough!" and the collective psyche started to fight back. They threw their hands up and put their foot down, which told the world they had had enough! Oh and it also made for a funny dance visual.

Fast forward to now, and today you have services like donotcall.gov, which is telemarketer-poison. You have things like the fake-dating-phone number. You have pretend greetings put on by creative souls who like to mess with telemarketers as if it's a live person answering the phone with staged responses. It's deserved, because telemarketers are essentially still just below guppies in terms of societal rank.

So I don't cold-call. If you like to cold-call, God bless you. And I shall go on blessing you, while I am over here in the not-cold-calling-people-during-dinner section.

But here's how we get these people back. It's a revenge tactic, really. I fully understand that as a voiceover guy, nay, *business owner*, it behooves me to market to people, which may or may not include cold-calling. I'm fine with that, as long the cold-calling may or may not also include alcohol and may or may not include usage of the word "absquatulate." This will make the marketing much more enjoyable, and should result in an overall happier, although somewhat discombobulated, species.

I can imagine the watercooler chats they'll have about the voiceover guy who bothered them at dinner last night. *Oh but he was so funny!!* they'll say. *Yeah, he really was out of his gord!* they'll declare. *Hey, this might be a shot in the dark, but I'd like to buy your home!* they'll brazenly shout. At which point office security will be called and straightjackets will be applied.

The straightjackets will thus result in a drastically reduced workforce, which will thus result in less telemarketers, which will thus result in less people calling us during dinner, which will result in me selling my house less, which will result in less Top Ramen meals, which is really what this chapter is all about.

Hey, why are you absquatulating? Was it something I telemarketed?

Sincerely,
Yours Truly

How Not To Fly A Drone Into A Tree

WRITTEN BY A GUY WHO FLEW HIS DRONE INTO A TREE

So, I crashed my drone into a tree and stranded it there in the rain, because #skills.

And just like a "frame" *in medias res* movie that starts at the end and then flashes back to the beginning and explains the lead-up to the tragedy, I shall now take you down memory lane on an exquisite journey of intrepid adventure, aerial stunts, and a colossally epic amount of face palming. Prepare to:

- Read it through, and
- Engage SMH mode
- Stay tuned, because there's a valuable lesson here at the end.

BACK TO THE BEGINNING

Christmastime was great. I got some nice things. Though I much prefer to give, it is exceptionally awesome to receive the occasional freaking super awesome gift-o-rama. Not that I am overly specific or controlling as far as what I want, but that is what a vanity URL like www.buyAaronthisgiftnow.com leading directly to my Amazon Wish List is for, right? Admit it. You just clicked that link because you wish to purchase something for me. I respectfully accept.

This year, my wife spoiled me with a new, awesome drone.

When I opened up that package, I was immediately greeted by the glistening sight of a small *Pelican* case wanna-be. I knew instantly what it was! After all, I made the wish list. My hands trembled as I opened up the case protecting my mostest favoritest gift of all time.

A new, shiny Potensic drone.

I had never had a drone before. The closest thing I ever had to a drone was a hot dog I taped to another hot dog and then flung up into the air in a helicopter rotor fashion. I was successful at crashing that one too because I am told that synthetic tubes containing pork entrails are generally not suitable for aerial travel. Our Labrador Macy enjoyed these unsuccessful test-flights however, because, well, gravity.

But this was a drone, a *real* drone.

I flew it the day after Christmas, because I have two small children who are spoiled by grandparents that we firmly instruct *not* to spoil our children, and who acknowledge and respect our wishes by ignoring us and spoiling them. I do not think I am saying it correctly when I instruct them not to do this. Anyway, due to said spoiling it took me 24 hours to successfully wade through the mountains of Christmas wrap and already-broken presents just to get outside. (I forgot to tell you: our kids are small *and* reckless… bonus!)

The crisp winter pine air smelled fit for droning. So, I took it up, and it was beautiful. Epic. Serene. I piloted it all around our 3.88 acres and took some great snapshots and photos.

But something wasn't right. If you recall, I used to be a wedding videographer. Being such, I can tell good equipment from bad. And I already had a DJI Osmo camera that I used at weddings. In the back of my mind, a seed of envy for those DJI drones began to take root.

In less than 5 hours, I would manage to find my wife buried under that Christmas wrap, and after performing CPR, explain to her that, although she had purchased the correct item from my Wish List, I had in truth selected a substandard item, and was now setting my sights on an even greater prize: The DJI Mavic Air 2 bundle, complete with three 34-minute flight batteries, a carrying case, a micro-SD card, backup rotors, and a free manicure. I am kidding. The manicure was extra.

But still – this was the drone that eats other drones for breakfast. Remind me to schedule my next facial though.

It was time to upgrade.

SO HERE'S WHAT HAPPENED

Fast forward to Monday the 4th. I received my new drone a few days later, registered it with the FAA, polished it and flew it over and over again, amazing the neighbors, and that was me on the news that caused that high-altitude fiery helicopter crash "by some unknown drone operator. " I am sorry.

After a bit of a tough and stressful day, I went out to "unwind" a bit with Shaniqua. Oh! I forgot to tell you I gave her a name. Anyway, my unwinding regimen typically involves flying Shaniqua six feet above Macy, who repeatedly jumps and barks until she becomes hoarse and sounds like a smoker's voice box. I categorize Macy's activity under the column labeled "uproariously hilarious." Macy does not put this activity under any such column, as Shaniqua is not a hot dog, which is both confusing and upsetting to her. Also Macy does not categorize things. Also Macy is a dog. I believe it was the tears in my eyes from such side-splitting laughter which prevented me from seeing clearly, as I proceeded to give my poor canine a break, fly Shaniqua off into our pasture, send her into an unintentional nosedive, veer left…

…and promptly crash her 40' feet up in a pine tree.

Now, despite the promotional material that swore that Shaniqua comes with obstacle avoidance, she clearly decided to controvert all such marketing promises and lodge herself near some pinecones and birds' nests.

As you can imagine, I was a bit miffed. Shaniqua was my favorite Christmas present ever. But that Monday, Macy's canine justice was served, because now she was stuck in an evergreen tree on the corner of our property much higher than my ability to hurl my child at her to bring her down.

You see, God blessed me with a healthy dose of acrophobia along with only a 16' ladder and no periscoping tools of any kind. Along with this, I was reminded that the only thing I am *truly* skilled at is making macaroni, which does not help in extracting drones from trees.

So, my only recourse was to hurl other things up at Shaniqua in the mad hope that I might bump a branch and send her down into my arms while "Reunited" by Peaches & Herb played slowly in the background. However, me being me, the baseball bat that I threw up to nudge the drone became stuck, the storage tub lid that I threw up to nudge the bat became stuck, and I do not believe my mailman appreciated my grabbing him and launching him from our trampoline to get my storage lid. Now we needed to send in someone to get the mailman who went in to get the lid who went in to get the bat who went in to get the drone. I am confident my tree was laughing at me.

So now? It was time to call the EXPERTS.

But everyone I called flatly declined. I think one laughed uproariously and hung up. Fire department said no. This arborist said no. That arborist said no. Contractor friend said no. In fact, when he asked me how high up my drone was stuck in the tree, the only thing I was able to say was that I would probably need a drone to figure that out. That did not help us get any nearer our objective of rescuing poor Shaniqua, for now it was starting to rain. I still offered him some macaroni, however.

Enter Fire Station 35 in Lacey, who referred me to a cat rescue company. So, I called, down to my last hope that at least *someone* would be willing to rescue something that:

- was beyond the reach of my tippy-toes, and
- did not have whiskers

Welp, Tom came to the rescue! I wasn't expecting anyone until the following day, and was pretty sure that I was going to lose Shaniqua to rain damage. But Tom came over in pitch black at 6pm! He immediately suited up with what to my mind was 400 pounds of gear, straps, buckles, chains and other things that I am fairly certain are also used by the US military to extract confessions from Middle-Eastern detainees. He then proceeded to shimmy up the tree like a squirrel. His bushy tail, staccato "chee-chee" noises and mouth loaded with acorns only served as further proof of his *rodentia*.

I'm also fairly certain that I heard strains of the Indiana Jones theme playing in the background during all of this.

In the end, Tom rescued Shaniqua, and made me a very happy camper...albeit an incredulous one, because I was blown away grateful that a cat rescuer would come out at oh-dark-thirty to rescue something of mine that definitely purred but was not going to rip up anyone's couch. Tom is AMAZING. He is an expert in his craft, he was super safe, and now I can fly my beloved Shaniqua again. Thank you, Tom! What a guy. He said he'd be back in a week or so for the mailman, but that he doesn't do baseball bats or storage tub lids. I guess you can't have everything...where would you put it all?

For me, I dusted off Shaniqua, cleaned her up and did a test flight later that night. I avoided the pasture.

WHY IT MATTERS

Why does all of this matter, you ask? Because it's my aim to occupy your time reading my books while I sneak in and get those auditions you missed.

I jest. There's a deeper meaning here, as usual.

Peripheral blindness is a thing. If you don't believe me, try driving with two planks of wood nailed into each side of your head, and each plank sticking out at least a foot in front of you. I am joking. I just wanted to try out my new power of suggestion skills, and we all could use a good laugh after 2020.

A career in voiceovers, like flying a drone, requires a sense of presence. A sense of really understanding where we are, and navigating with care. There's a lot that can go wrong in a VO career:

- Auditioning or interviewing for the wrong jobs
- Selling yourself short
- Underbidding a colleague
- Overworking
- Choosing the wrong branding or logo
- Bragging

- Not balancing your work with physical fitness
- Avoiding coaching
- Producing your own demos
- Never giving back to your peers

This is an industry that requires that we maintain an understanding of where we are in the pecking order, where we're going, and avoiding obstacles that may hurt us and others.

It's critical that we take time to give an honest assessment of where we're heading, that we know the pitfalls and obstacles that will ensnare us, and that we take care to properly map our course beforehand. I think that's one to grow on, and I was reminded of that this past week.

If you don't believe me, just ask my mailman. Careful though, I think he has a bat.

HERE'S ONE TO GROW ON:

"Tell me what you pay attention to, and I will tell you who you are."

Jose Ortega y Gasset

Take Five

HEY! GET OFF MY YAWN!

Woke up tired and you have those auditions piling up? So? Take a break. Rest a while. There's a reason you feel this way. Your body is signaling for you to take a break, and it's ok. Say that with me. "It's ok to say a break." There. Sit, Ubu sit. Good dog.

I remember when I would play catch with a friend in the thick of summer in 1990 when I was a senior in high school. Suddenly, after playing for a while, I would grow lightheaded and crave an apple. An apple? Why an apple? I have no idea. That's just what my body was insisting that I have…and I can't explain why.

Medical News Today can.[89] For me, I just knew that I all of the sudden needed an apple, and I would be a bit faint and sweat a little bit until I had one. Low blood sugar, most likely.

It's *okay* to take a break. The industry of Voiceovers is so *reactive:* you're waiting for the next "big break" at any given minute, the next big "mortgage-paying job" at any given moment, and you want to jump on them. It's reactive. You get that beep, you drop what you're holding (hopefully not the baby), run upstairs, trip over something on the way (hopefully not the baby), and scream into your studio and start recording like a sweaty-toothed madman while you race to shoot something through the computer to them (hopefully not the baby). Then you pick up something comforting (hopefully the baby).

So, what if you don't do that audition for that $5k job right away? Have you been auditioning like crazy? You feel tired for a reason. Take that break. There will be other $5k auditions coming your way.

"Now, wait a minute, Aaron, I see what's happening here," you say. *"I know what you're up to. You just want me to forego auditioning on that job so you can audition for it and be awarded that job yourself!!!!"*

Yes. Precisely. Now go rest until you've regained your sanity and can evaluate people in a healthy manner again. I'll send you a commission check from your job that I won and you didn't, you weirdo.

MAY THE ODDS BE EVER IN YOUR FAVOR

The odds are in your favor that blessing will come around soon.

Any week can change just like that. I've had weeks where I haven't scored any jobs until Wednesday or Thursday. I've had weeks with 8 jobs and I've made $2500. I've had weeks with only *two* jobs and I've made $6000. Every week is different.

May the odds be ever in your favor. There are certain laws at work of sowing and reaping. Have you been auditioning like crazy? Some of those jobs will come around. You can take a breather and then dive in again. Everyone needs to come up for air once in a while, unless you're Cuvier's beaked whale, which apparently can hold its its breath for 67 minutes. I can't even do that if I'm inflated to the size of a blimp with raw unfettered oxygen. But even the beaked whale needs to replenish its oxygen supply.

KEEP UP THE HUSTLE

There's nothing wrong with hustling. The early bird catches the worm. The race goes to the swift. The hunter always gets its prey. Keep at it. Those moments of being awarded a job are also times to rest and back off. To drink deep in the wonder and awe of a job well done, of a pursuit in the sun, the satisfying victory of a race well run.

Keep at it, certainly.

This industry requires great, *great* perseverance. But doesn't anything? What does this industry require that another doesn't?

- Perseverance
- Tenacity
- Determination

- Goal-setting
- Goal-hitting
- Realistic expectations….and….wait for it….
- REST

Here's my acronym for rest. Real, Earnest, Satisfying Time-out. Take that break when you need to. The hustle demands it, because once you've hustled, you earn a break. Then, once you've recharged, only then can the hustle begin anew.

…BUT KNOW WHEN TO RELENT

In business, after nearly 13 years of self-employment, and near 27 in voiceovers, I cannot even tell you the sheer number of times I've been awaiting an answer on a particular job, or been hesitant to steal away because the next job inquiry could come in via email and I *had* to respond in the same lickety-split fashion that I usually did, or I would lose it and they would go to someone else, only to return home after deciding to take a much-needed break….and there was nothing to worry about. No emails had come in. Nothing demanded my attention while I was away.

Seriously! I was fretting being away. Several years ago I would go camping with my best friend and cousin, and it requires of me the single most difficult thing I can ever try to do: be untethered from a satellite signal. It is maddening. Who's texting me? Is everyone alright? What auditions await? Did my main client need something? Is the house ok? What marketing sources am I missing?

This cavalcade of questions just barrages me as I'm away…but eventually, I learn to rest. Returning from many of those camping excursions, the millisecond I was back in coverage range, I would quickly scroll through all of my notifications and find that there had been nothing to worry about, not one iota. Everything, and everyone, were just fine without me, thank you very much.

Chill out. Say it again with me. "It's ok to say a break." Do you believe it now? You must chill.

FAMILY FIRST

It's okay to take a break. Say that with me until you own it. "It's *okay* to take a break." There will be those frenetic awesomely busy days where you're running back and forth between your control room and the studio to record either auditions or paid jobs. Those days will come. They've come before, and they'll come again. But for now, sit down. Breathe and meditate.

Oh what richness awaits us when we step away from the mic and take off the cans. Our family awaits us to give and to receive…to bless and be blessed by. Take five.

One of my most favorite times of the day is the morning. Not because of all the auditions that await me – although that's exciting – but rather because I get to breathe. I get to sit down and have a devotional, pray, and meditate and breeeeeeeeeeeeathe. To prepare for a rigorous day.

In fact, I'm prompted all throughout the day to breathe by my Apple Watch. *Such* a helpful piece of equipment that really makes sure that I'm taking care of my body as my body is taking care of my finances. Breathing is key, and you can do that best when you take a moment to chill out and calm down.

Take that break with your family. Get away. Take a vacation, for crying out loud. You spend so much time sitting in a small room, or sitting at your computer editing your audio. Get away from it all and recharge your batteries. It's, healthy, it's right, it's good. And they need you.

Don't let *anyone* tell you that you can't slow down or stop. Stay away from the rat race. You need to recharge your batteries. Tell them "Hey! Get off my Yawn!" Take that Rest:

- Real
- Earnest
- Satisfying
- Time-out

Take it. You deserve a break today. Now go enjoy that McD's Quarter Pounder and hear your arteries hardening as you lie back and relax.

You Deserve A Break Today

PERISH THE THOUGHT!

I don't read a lot, as I prefer all things digital, and ultimately, it's far too many consonants and vowels for me, so I get tired.

I do however read scripts in exchange for money, and occasionally I will crack open a nice pop-up book with font 83 bold.

In any event, I don't remember ever reading *The Burly Man's Burly Guide to Being Burly*. Someone somewhere should write that, because a lot of us Y-chromosomers feel downright awkward about taking a load off and enjoying a well-earned break. It falls under the category of *Forbidden*. Like, the moment we do so, a giant flannel-sporting axe-wielding beer-guzzling Paul Bunyan-esque figure will loom large over us and hurl accusations of slothful behavior and slovenly living.

No. We must constantly be swinging axes and chewing tobacco and spitting and sweating and working under oily cars and constructing skyscrapers and sticking our burly chests out in a burly fashion while being burly. Otherwise, something must be wrong with us.

I know some people in my industry never sleep. My hat is off to them. I, however, require sleep to survive, or come 11:30pm I will quickly devolve from disheveled teddy bear, to Nazgul, to Satan incarnate. Ask my wife. You can find her out in the shed; she hides out there in terror until my kids give her the all-clear in the morning. This ogre needs his beauty sleep.

Why do I say all this as a lead-in?

- Because it's hard to actually intentionally take a break!
- Because it's hard to set everything aside, untether, and recharge, when all you want to do is accomplish.
- Because it's my book and not yours.

As for me, I'm a go-getter. I see it, I go get it. For whatever reason, it's deep in my programming, and in the programming of so many of my colleagues. It's inescapable, like haircuts or Shark Week. It's as predictable as death and taxes. Me trying to take a break is as difficult as a one-legged man in a butt-kicking contest.

But I must do it, or this flame will flame out, like an overtaxed dead shark who was overdue for a haircut and had only one leg.

PASS ME THE RECLINER, WILL YOU?

It was an ugly thing. Or so she said. My cousin's wife Sarah hated that recliner that her mother-in-law had brought into their house when she moved in to help take care of Sarah's newborn. It didn't go with anything, it wasn't exactly comfortable, and it made her itch. The chair. Not her mother-in-law.

To me, it's perfection. (The chair. Not her mother-in-law.) One man's trash is truly another man's treasure. One person's chucking-out is another person's cherishing-of. One somebody's garbage is another somebody's gratitude. One individual's – OK I think you get it now.

I love that thing. It's got the plush seat! It's got the flip out leg rest! It reclines! (Because it's a recliner; was that not clear?) It's amazingly comfortable, and because it comes in a shade of sand, it goes with our other furniture which are also shades of sand. What Sarah didn't want, I snatched up with great relish. I remember stuffing it into the back of my SUV and couldn't wait to bring it home and put it in our living room. I knew just where it would go, which is two feet in front of the TV, blocking out the light, and allowing those radio waves and invisible patterns of electricity and magnetism to be absorbed into my soul just like Mike Teavee from *Willy Wonka & The Chocolate Factory*.

I. Love. That. Chair. It's provided great guilt-free rest! If there's one thing I am willing to tear myself away from my work for, it's that chair. Or Bottle Caps candy. Or Bottle Caps candy IN that chair.

OR A RECLINER MADE OF BOTTLE CAPS!!

I digress.

If there was a point to be found in all of this, it's that rest…good, healthy, restorative rest…is so important in entrepreneurship, and it's important to break away to get it, even if Paul Bunyan has carved out plans to chop me.

So that's just what we did.

LTE > 3G > E > ANXIETY!

This past Saturday through Sunday, I dared to go camping where there was no signal at all. Not even smoke signals live there. Only bears and cougars and the Blair Witch. If you go there, you must prepare to be completely without signal of any kind, to look at your phone desperately as if to say "do something, damn you," and with a full willingness to be axe-murdered in the woods. Please note that through all of this, all your phone will do is show a clock that counts up to the time that you will be attacked by bears and cougars and the Blair Witch. Anything less than this, and you're just not rugged enough, and must be axe-murdered.

I remember driving down the dirt road and watching my precious five bars dwindle to a greyed-out underscore. I also believe my phone literally made a dying, gurgling gasp to underscore the gravity of the transition. For some reason I remember wondering if my will was in order. It's a truly unnerving thing, as I mentioned in a previous chapter: having no signal. But with internet out at *home*, at least we can run to the neighbors for help when chainsaw-wielding hockey-mask wearing hooligans show up. Camping offers little similar luxuries, save peeing in the woods.

Be that as it may, we took a break, and a much-needed one. We went with our church life group, and it was really, really nice. I'll admit it's challenging to take a preschooler and a toddler camping. The sheer amount of crap required to accommodate their every need weighs about the same as a grand piano holding a lead weight holding a small moon holding God. But! It turns out we had 0% signal, and yet we had 100% fun. I barely thought about checking my phone for email after the first hour, and instead prepared the roasting sticks for smores.

When we drove out the next day, we were rested and content. Yes, I did what we all did the moment my zero bars shot up to five and all those 3,491 notifications came rolling in: squeal with glee, plow into the car in front of me and send our luggage flying all the way to I-5. But after we had regathered it and toweled up all the spilled coffee, it got me thinking.

What would I have done had I been home instead? Probably make several trips to the studio to fulfill waiting auditions. Or marketing. Or networking somehow, constantly harkening to the siren call of the app badges on my iPhone. But to be Facebook-less, Twitter-less, Instagram-less, email-less, text-less and signal-less was actually…*less* stressful than I thought, and more rewarding.

Perhaps most importantly, I found that I could actually break away without experiencing a synapse misfire or a complete psychotic break.

Not that I'd do it again anytime soon. Are you kidding? There are bears and cougars and the Blair Witch out there. You'll find me right here in my sand-colored chair, tweeting on LTE, at least until 11:30pm which is when the screams begin.

TAKEAWAY & ACTION STEP

"The soul always knows what to do to heal itself. The challenge is to silence the mind." – Caroline Myss

Meditate. Quiet time. Rest. Rejuvenate. Unplug. Untether. What do these words mean to you? Are you trying to drown out some pain through business? If your output exceeds your input, then your upkeep will be your downfall. Take a break.

Please, Can You Please Say Thank You? Thank You

POLITENESS. IT IS SIMPLY TOO MUCH TO ASK.

I am a Businessman in the employ of Voiceovers, and as such I employ manners with my customers and colleagues. But there is a conundrum that continues to perplex me.

Correct me if I am wrong here, but I was taught by CocoMelon that "please" and "thank you" were all part of manners. Manners are when you say "please" and "thank you", which I have come to understand is the opposite of "Give me this now or I will kill you with a hammer."

I do not know when manners became suddenly *ex vogue*, but at one point or another, helping people has occasionally become somewhat like going absolutely bonkers and willfully volunteering to work with junior-highers, which no one should ever do due to Inescapable Side Effects:

- You will be consumed day and night with angst
- They simply do not grow older into reasoning, enjoyable human beings with whom you can share a beer which will currently land you in jail for doing so
- You are paid the sum of zero dollars forever
- You will develop pimples as a result of The Stress
- You will play "Iris" by the Goo Goo Dolls on a punishing loop
- You begin to understand that five side-effects are not enough, so this sentence is also here

As a widely-known voiceover mentor who gives of his time freely, I have helped many an aspiring entrepreneur. I count it my joy and my responsibility.

Occasionally, however, I happen upon the unthankful sap who faintly resembles a walking umbilical cord. They plug in, sap me dry, and when I cut the cord, they, and their gratitude, are nowhere to be found. They come back at random inconvenient intervals, posing intrusive questions and - I am not kidding - ***telling*** me to send them free things, with nary a "please" to boot. When I receive such requests, it warms my heart with that same comfy Antarctic chill I get when I am knocked out, my kidneys are removed against my will to be sold on the black market, and I am placed in an ice tub and then launched into deep space. Every time this happens, I miss Jeopardy, dammit.

As a result, I just do what comes naturally: *Ignore their email until they start saying please again.*

Passive aggressive? Sure. Satisfying? 100% enjoyably so.

It is also the same with some customers, who I want to kill with a hammer.

MIND YOUR PEATH'S AND PSSSSSS'S

I have written about this before.[90] When Brennan was a toddler and was learning to speak, he would say "peath" instead of *please*. It was adorable, and often made burly, unflappable lumberjacks pass out due to cuteness. We would periodically hold him up to random lumberjacks to test this.

Now that Asher is also learning to speak, his is a bit more whispery. Asher says "Pssssss", which the pediatrician tells us is a cross between:

- beckoning us to come to him,
- informing us he has just peed, and
- a signal that he is part serpent

But both of our boys understand completely that "please" and "thank you" are indispensable elements to receiving what they desire. They are grasping that these words are essential to receiving food, heat and love from us. Assuming they make it to teenagerhood, I am positive that they will discover that they no longer need to employ such pleasantries, and if my wife and I do NOT provide food, heat and love, we will be promptly sent to jail. At that point they will simply start demanding things from whatever court-appointed supervisor they are assigned to. Eventually we will have to share our jail cell with a growing count of court-appointed supervisors who have also stopped giving them things, and we will all sing campfire songs, talk to our hands, and plan to work with junior-highers.

Ultimately, that's the way society is headed. "Give me this now, or you receive a negative Yelp review." Extortion seems to now be required learning, and as one of my sons is part serpent, he needs alternative teaching to steer him away from this type of slithery behavior.

But for now, they are not teenagers, and they are doing well. Brennan, the ever-demanding prima donna actor-in-training (I simply do not know *where* he gets it!) will still sometimes slip into attention-seeking cries of "Hey! HEY! **_HEY!!!_**" before I angrily reach for the chainsaw. It is at this point that he realizes the need to shift gears and engage decorum, correcting that to a timid "Um…excuse me?" I then finally stop seeing red, and start handing him $20's.

And now you also know what to do should you ever need $20's from me.

THE CONTINUING EROSION OF MANNERS

How does this apply to our voiceover career? It applies because this is my book, and I am incapable of lying. *sound of wicked wife-laughter from a distant room* But the truth is -*sound of more wicked wife-laughter from a distant room* - that it applies because no one should *ever* work with junior-highers.

I am joking. That was unfair of me. They are human beings too; so, if we place these precious prepubescents in strategic positions throughout the summer camp along with the velociraptors, we will no longer encounter a dilemma of working with junior-highers.

As entrepreneurs, we are human beings who are to deal humanely with human beings. We are not unemotional cyborgs, and neither are our clients. It should be our aim to employ manners in all of our conversations with them. And it *should* be their aim as well. Doubtless, you will receive those last-minute requests from clients who fail to plan (and thus plan to fail), need everything *yesterday*, and then blame YOU for their shortcomings when you decline. Here I refer to an excellent blog by Paul Strikwerda on this subject.[91]

It irks me to no end to see clients take advantage of freelancers under the guise of "The Customer Is Always Right." I am sorry, but that is as true as anything that is utterly false, such as Wal-Mart saying, "Our customers are perfectly normal." Everyone knows Wal-Mart is filled with colorful characters who are anything but normal. Just the other day I saw a Wal-Mart customer wearing a halter-top around his knees, a saddle, a cape, and a battle thong. I am not kidding. The creature was shopping in the hosiery aisle with a stalk of lettuce in one hand and a Teen Beat in the other.

I do not think that was my point.

My point is that we live in an *anti*-social media world. Social media was designed for us to be social. And yet it has proven counterintuitive: driving our ubiquitous collective deep into our smartphones, seemingly oblivious to the stranger on our right who is mourning because a loved one has just died, sapping us of our ability to relate to each other properly.

Oh well. We have things we need to like and follow and subscribe to. I am sure they understand as hot lonely tears roll down their face.

I think we should try to be more social. Good social behavior necessitates using manners, and when people use manners, I have to use my chainsaw less frequently.

And as for our customers? Customers will always take advantage of us and expect things *yesterday*. It is up to us to take the abuse, deliver what they want and get paid, or get angry and insist that they buy a time machine to accommodate their yesterday needs more easily. What helps me personally when a customer is unreasonable and rude to me? I just pray quietly to myself, "May the fleas of a thousand camels infest your crotch, and may your arms be too short to scratch them." Then I pronounce Wiccan spells over them and all of their descendants. Especially their junior-highers.

See, when you are dead, you do not know you are dead. The pain is only felt by others. The same thing happens when you are irretrievably stupid. So please, use manners, and do not be stupid and cause pain. I should make bumper stickers.

And remember, *always* remember and never forget this: even if a client does not employ manners when dealing with you, always treat them with respect. It is never, *never* OK to kill them with a hammer.

Unless of course you are at junior-high summer camp and wearing a hockey mask you got from Wal-Mart. If so, go nuts…please.

HERE'S ONE TO GROW ON:

"Good manners will open doors that the best education cannot."

Clarence Thomas

Tell The Truth

APPEARANCES CAN BE DECEIVING

Frida Kahlo was a celebrated painter who told two lies about her life. She lied about the year of her birth telling people she was born in 1907, but the truth was she was born in 1910. She also lied about her father being a German Jew, which he was not. He actually came from a line of Lutherans.

President Bill Clinton was revealed to be a serial womanizer, with several women claiming to have had relations with him. The best known of these affairs is the Monica Lewinsky Scandal. Lewinsky denied having an affair with the President. Clinton also denied the allegations, famously saying, "I did not have sexual relations with that woman." But after a failed impeachment attempt, the whole story came out.

Professional cyclist Lance Armstrong was loved by the American public for his multiple Tour De France victories and his courageous battle against cancer. But in 2012, after years of denial by Armstrong, it was revealed that he was using performance-enhancing drugs during his Tour victories. Shortly thereafter, Armstrong was permanently banned from professional cycling.

In an effort to maintain her moneymaking image as America's Sexiest Virgin, Britney Spears went on for years telling the country that she had never had sex. Years later, after a nasty breakup Justin Timberlake exposed the lie for what it was and spoiled Britney's 'pristine' reputation.

While many call him "The Newton of Electricity," others call him "The First American." Whatever the nickname, we can all agree Benjamin Franklin was one of a kind. He was called a liar for experimenting on lightning with kite and key, because scientists proved that it's impossible. He was also a major troll; he would actually scare people by putting out fake news in a newspaper run by him

The four-time Italian Prime Minister and billionaire businessman Silvio Berlusconi was branded a "corrupt, sadistic liar" by those he once called friends, mocked by the media and villainized by his enemies. He lied about his affairs with models and escorts many times.

Watergate set the bar for a world leader telling lies when President Richard Nixon denied involvement in the snooping scandal, declaring, "I am not a crook," in a nationally televised press conference. . Two journalists Bob Woodward and Carl Bernstein from The Washington Post exposed the 'dirty tricks' of the Nixon administration.

Misa Bharti, the daughter of Lalu Prasad Yadav, posted a picture of herself standing on a podium at Harvard, claiming that she was invited to lecture the gathering on the Role of Youth. A Harvard spokesperson confirmed that she was never invited for a lecture in the first place.

Benedict Arnold whose name is synonymous with traitors everywhere, was an American general who betrayed both his country and the Oath of Allegiance he signed in May 1778 by defecting to the British just a year later. Despite having great success in battle against the British, Arnold constantly fought with fellow generals. The promise of a lot of money, land and pensions for himself and his family persuaded Arnold to turn his back on his newly formed country and become a British General making him the most notorious liar in history.[92]

What do all of these have in common?

Hiding behind a ruse.

Who are you in voiceovers? Are you the same person off-stage as you are on? When you sign on to social media, does a mask drop down over your face, only to be taken off the moment you sign off, so you can once again yell at your kids, belittle your wife, kick your dog and complain at your neighbors?

Are you who you say you are?

Granted, I'm certainly no saint. I'm a human being, flawed through and through, and in many ways I would never admit publicly. Only my wife knows them fully, and that's why I made her sign an NDA before marrying me. I am kidding. But the truth is that we're born that way: imperfect and in need of a Savior. Religion aside, however, doesn't human decency have a stake in your voiceover offerings?

Maybe the converse is true. Maybe you actually *are* a decent human being. And then when you flip the switch for social media, you become this aggressive unflinching titan, because you have something to prove. Are you actual…or are you just an act?

Social media fuels narcissism. It fuels selfies. It fuels addiction. But the worst is that it fuels image management. There's nothing worse than putting up a false front, only to live in fear that it could all come crumbling down, and you're exposed as a charlatan… a ruse… a liar… a *fraud*.

Man, I strive very hard to be exactly who I say I am. It's hard! It truly is hard to maintain an air of *have-it-all-together* and balance that with vulnerability and transparency. I realize I covered some of this in the chapter titled "Battle Scars", but ultimately, it bears repeating: are you who you say you are? Are you the genuine article? Whereas that chapter was about being vulnerable and transparent, letting your hair down as it were, this one is about making sure you're not putting your hair up too much. I deeply appreciate what Paul Strikwerda says on this: "If your product or service sucks, no marketing campaign – no matter how brilliant – is going to help you make millions, or even a decent living. Stinky flowers don't attract a lot of bees."[93] Be *real*.

If you are finding that your actor life is overtaking your humanity, there's a problem. In a previous book I talk about becoming a persona. This is very true. But personas do have humanity to back them up. The person behind the veneer *is* the person in front of it. They're what *make up* the persona. Conversely, there's the Jekyll-and-Hyde among us that simply don't know how to project themselves truthfully, and I find that very sad. Voiceovers are truly "theater of the mind", as James R. Alburger says[94]. Just don't get stuck in your own theater. It's OK to come out.

As entrepreneurs, we have a responsibility to tell the truth. We're storytellers, sure, but storytelling isn't always about fiction. Don't forget, we narrate biographical, documentary, and E-Learning too.

This has to do with instruction, authenticity, and truth. Are you telling the truth online about who you are offline? Or are you so wrapped up in a perfected image of you that the neglected *real* you is crumbling inside?

All important questions to ask yourself. I urge you to be very careful in what you put out there on social media. *I want to know the real you.*

Sometimes, the real you is buried in sadness.

BEAUTIFUL ACHES

He was born July 21, 1951 in Chicago. He died August 11, 2014, in Tiburon, California. He was known for manic stand-up routines and diverse film performances. We won an Academy award. His father was an executive for the Ford Motor Company, and his mother was a former fashion model. He learned to use humor to entertain classmates, and was a fan of comedian Jonathan Winters. When he was 16, his father retired, and the family moved to the San Francisco area. He studied political science at Claremont Men's College (now Claremont McKenna College), where he began taking courses in improvisation. He then attended the College of Marin to study acting but later received a scholarship to study at the Juilliard School in New York City. He eventually moved back to California, where he began appearing in comedy clubs in the early 1970s. By the mid-1970s he was guest starring on several television shows, including *The Richard Pryor Show* and *Laugh-In*. After guest appearances as the alien Mork on *Happy Days*, he was given his own show, *Mork & Mindy* (1978–82). The series offered him the opportunity to transfer the enthusiasm of his stand-up performances to the small screen and provided an outlet for his prolific improvisational talents. *Mork & Mindy* proved an immense success and was instrumental in launching his film career.[95]

I am of course talking about Robin Williams, the legendary comedian and persona who committed suicide in August 2014. As it turns out, he had been suffering from depression and anxiety. An examination of his brain tissue suggested he suffered from "diffuse Lewy body dementia."[96] His wife, Susan Schneider, said that in the period before his death, Williams had been sober, but was diagnosed with early stage Parkinson's disease, which was information he was "not yet ready to share publicly."[97] In an essay published in the journal *Neurology* two years after his death, Schneider revealed that the pathology of Lewy body disease in Williams was described by several doctors as among the worst pathologies they had seen. She described the early symptoms of his disease as beginning in October 2013. Williams's initial condition included a sudden and prolonged spike in fear and anxiety, stress and insomnia, which worsened in severity to include memory loss, paranoia, and delusions. According to Schneider, "Robin was losing his mind and he was aware of it ... He kept saying, 'I just want to reboot my brain.'"[98]

I feel tremendously bad for Robin Williams. His sudden passage shocked me as much as the next guy. *Any* time someone we revered dies by suicide, we're left wondering "What went wrong?" "What could we have done?" and "I wish I knew."

I cite Robin Williams here because the backstory is so important to the front. What goes on on the stage of your life can belie what's going on behind the scenes, and we need not get so lost in our persona that we avoid transparency and begin to cling to secrets wrapped in shame. It's my hope that the tangled knots of shame are unraveled, and you're allowed to, as Gandalf said to Théoden in *The Two Towers*, "Breathe the free air again."[99]

Franklin Delano Roosevelt is another story that comes to mind. His polio wrecked his body. His legs shriveled and he covered them up. He was determined not to fall in front of people. He ensured that his podiums were sturdy, and had them tested, so that they would support his weight as he leaned on them. At the Democratic National Convention in 1924, he refused to wave when he was giving speech, because he couldn't risk losing his grip on the speaker's stand. The sweat poured down his face, but he couldn't wipe it away. When speeches were over, he would slip back between the curtain and collapse into his waiting wheelchair.

For interviews, he would be seated at his desk, in place before the reporters arrived. From their side of the desk, his appearance was like that of any other politician or professional. In fact, he looked more impressive than most, because of the muscle he had added to his upper body. At his desk he could have been mistaken for a wrestler or a weightlifter. What the reporters did not see was that he was sitting in a special wheelchair, fitted with small wheels fashioned to fit under the desk.

Often, he spoke from the back seat of his open-topped touring car. A lap robe would cover his legs.

All this to keep up image management.

There have been times in my life where image management shameful secrets have ruined me. I've had to "come clean" with family and friends. All of it required a painful self-confrontation that many are unwilling to conduct. May the storyteller you are *offline* be infused with the same sweet vulnerability, authenticity and raw power that you project *online*.

Stories are important. The whole story has great value in providing context.

Let us in on your whole story. It's OK to do so.

HERE'S ONE TO GROW ON:

"If you tell the truth, you don't have to remember anything."

Mark Twain

Battle Scars

THE KNOW-IT-ALL

There's this illusion that people in show business really have it all together. It's called Image Management, and PR firms, managers and the talent themselves really try hard to keep that up, and to preserve all semblances of normalcy and upward mobility.

I'm here to crash through that. I'm often called a "rock star" and that I "have my sh$t together." Or that I'm "crushin'" or "killin'" it! I think we're all honestly at the same level, more than we know.

Did you know:

- I have plantar fasciitis with my left heel that makes it very difficult to walk sometimes, and that if I go for any kind of extended walk/run, I hurt and limp for days?
- Because I'm about 60 pounds overweight, I struggle with constant back pain?
- I'm exhausted after work?
- I have struggled with IBS since about 2005, and sometimes the pain has been so intense I've had to lay myself up and focus on my breathing, in order to recover?
- If I get really frustrated and stressed, I crave having a few smokes, because I had a regular smoking habit from 2000 to 2012?
- I'm noticing that I'm typing slower and making more mistakes with each passing day, and that I'm deeply frustrated with that, wondering if I'm developing arthritis?
- I am incredibly self-conscious and have been since I was young? (I know, shocker...)
- My twin brother is a transient and is unmotivated to do anything with his life?
- My older brother is a counselor and is incredibly abusive to our family?
- My wife and I have been cyber stalked?
- Sometimes I'll be reading my scripts and really struggle with my breathing, or say a word in the script that isn't

even there, and become supremely irritated, curse, and have to start over?
- I was born with a birthmark on my arm that I hate?
- I struggle with materialism and spending?
- Sometimes the bottoms of my feet itch so bad that I scratch them until I bleed?
- I overwork?
- I had a heart murmur?
- I've had two kidney stones so far?
- I am a candyholic?
- I usually struggle with the "never enough" syndrome, and am fiercely critical of projects I put together (voiceover or otherwise), like they should have been done better?

Perception isn't everything. We're all humans, and we're all fragile. For now, and through the future, as we struggle to come back together as a country, civilization and humanity, know that people don't quite have it as together as it might appear. Appearances can be deceiving. What we put out there on social media is NEVER the whole story. Let's look with insight into our fellow man's potential plights, and strive to get past the superficial supermarket exchange of "Hi there, how are you? Good. How are you? Good."

To quote one of my favorite books, *The Fellowship of the Ring:*

"All that is gold does not glitter,
Not all those who wander are lost;
The old that is strong does not wither,
Deep roots are not reached by the frost."

Here's to being open and honest and growing together.

What are your scars? What has scabbed over from conflict, overuse, mistreatment, accidents, misfortunate, birth defects, whatever? How can they be used to reach others? Voiceovers are, after all, a *ministry*. I am not getting all preachy with you or all Christian. The word *ministry* is not necessarily a Christian word. It's just a word, and it means reaching out and meeting a need. Got some lemons you can turn into lemonade?

Got an accident you can turn into an achievement?

Got a shame you can allow someone to help shoulder?

Got a bruise you need to let breathe?

Got a hurt that someone can help heal?

Bring 'em out into the open, I say. All of 'em. Shame flourishes in the dark. Perceived defects rob us of joy. And you have a lot to give.

Let's see those battle scars.

I'm no Superman. I love that Lazlo Bane song. I truly am not. I'm 60 pounds overweight and no matter what I do, I cannot seem to lose it. But being super is so much more than being in optimum physical shape.

Being super is, quite simply, about who you are as the sum total of your endurance quotient. How much can you take, and keep on going?

You're more super than you think, despite your scars.

HERE'S ONE TO GROW ON:

"Vulnerability: the willingness to show up and be seen with no guarantee of outcome."

Ourmindfullife.com

Every Day An Easter Egg Hunt

THE KIDS AND THE HUNTS

My preschooler is four. This is commonly known as the age where all parents everywhere try to sell their children, or to leave them behind at a truck stop "accidentally." But we're sticking it out because we love the little guy, and also because we got an extra $500 from the federal government in our stimulus.

And BOY does this boy love him some candy. If there is a sweet-tooth DNA gene that gets passed on from father to son, then he most certainly got it. We're in the process of finding a quarantine-friendly dentist to extract it however, as my candy tolerance has decreased, and I'd like my gene back, *thankyouverymuch*.

We all love candy. We all love searching for candy. We all love *finding* candy. Note that I said "we all love *finding* candy"; I did not however say "We all love it when our *spouses* find our own secret stash of candy." This is a different occurrence entirely and one that is designed to foster Feelings Of Animosity, along with, in some cases, Urges To Kill. Such an occurrence happened recently, and now I need an alternate wife who supports my candy cravings and will not steal from me. I may send this one to the same dentist to extract the candy gene from her as well.

We recently celebrated QuarantEaster (my candy-thieving wife and I) with our preschooler and infant. The infant doesn't know what candy is, or that it's incredibly delicious and fills the soul with utter bliss. His lack of both of these bits of knowledge fills me with immeasurable joy and reassurance that he won't be stealing my candy like his thieving mother, by the way: the scoundrel. But our preschooler could not be more excited.

This small sentient being apparently came pre-programmed to sniff out candy wherever it may lie, and can detect the presence of a Good & Plenty within a half mile. What I find fascinating is that there are so many Good & Plenty's that have fallen down into the recesses of our couch, yet he is unable to detect those, possibly because of the thick coat of cat fur that has protectively cocooned it over the years and blocks out any preschooler candy-detection telepathy.

Easter was fun. Despite being on quarantine, we had a nice Easter egg hunt in our very own backyard, which, with our preschooler at the helm, was completed in two seconds, all 21 eggs told. As my son pranced around in his adorable Easter outfit purchased by my beautiful thieving wife – who is skilled at stealing candy and not skilled at stealing Easter outfits (Walmart security released her early due to time already served) – I was reminded how every day, for us as marketers, is an Easter egg hunt.

Every day, truthfully, is full of candy to be found. Candy to be celebrated. Candy to be wrapped in a cocoon of cat hair to be preserved entirely for ourselves.

THE HUNT FOR RED...LICORICE

I think what attracts me to candy is the fact that it possesses the incredible, unquenchable ability to sustain my very life. Not even endless reruns of *Friends* can do that. There is something so immensely satisfying about finding candy and knowing that I have it.

There's eating candy, followed very closely only by dying and going to heaven, which is the same as eating candy. The only thing that comes remotely close to these two is sitting in my easy chair with my feet up and watching *Beaches*. God bless Bette and Barbara.

In the same way, when we find a client who is amenable to our marketing proposals, it's a rich thrill that provides a sugar rush - and the best part is that they're not even cocooned by cat hair, so they'll be able to honestly give us an unmuted listen.

I took social distancing literally. I do not like to mow, so I'm social-distancing from my mower.

But hidden out there in the tall green grass of the world – which is by now the height of Everest given that all Lawnmowing Men everywhere who have been on quarantine are also practicing lawnmower social distancing – are clients who are just waiting to be found. We search and search, we find one, and we crack open their plastic colorful shell and find them sweating in there for lack of oxygen, overjoyed that a large human has rescued them. It's a wonderful treat, and it's our preeminent goal: finding that candy each day.

That, and using "preeminent" in a sentence.

Now, to be clear, I do not eat my clients. It has always been my aim to provide quality voiceovers, not unswerving cannibalism. But when I do find a new client, I find that the rush of obtaining them is very akin to the rush I feel when I've found candy:

- I worked hard to find it (because I greatly wanted to)
- It's going to satisfy both of us inwardly (because of a deep sense of reward)
- I'm going to enjoy this (because of endorphins and hippocampus-related things and other sciency stuff)
- My clients are a sugary treat (because I needed a 4th bullet point to impress Google SEO enough to index me)

There's also the thought that goes through my head: "God help the poor wayward fools who dare try to wrest it away from me, whom I will righteously smash on with a grim Biblical fury the likes of which this cold world has never before witnessed and shall not witness again." Here I refer lovingly to my beautiful wife and children.

Whatever form candy takes, I will take said candy. Offer me a choice between a plate of candy or a healthy plate of quinoa, asparagus and organic steamed chicken, and in full maturity I will proceed to respectfully slap the chicken into the mouth of the dog, lovingly insert the asparagus into your ears so that you vaguely resemble a weathervane, and dutifully thrust quinoa so far up your nose that you'll lose all ability to correctly pronounce quinoa.

(Hint: it rhymes with: "pneumonoultramicroscopicsilicovolcanoconiosis"[100]).

EVERY DAY IS EASTER EGG HUNT DAY

For me, as an entrepreneur and a marketer, every single day I love the hunt. I've written about this before, comparing myself to a lioness. Now that I think about it, in another chapter of mine I'm a soccer mom. And in yet another, I wear makeup.

So while I do my nails, listen to Kenny G, take a bubble bath and work out my gender dysphoria, consider this:

- You can successfully market in the midst of a pandemic. All it takes is the right wording, a sensitivity to where people are at in their lives, and an offer of free toilet paper if they'll simply hear you out.
- You have only to continue looking. All this will require of you is a refined sense of commitment to stay in your home, a strong desire to provide food other than Top Ramen for your family, and a disdain for living under bridges due to being evicted.
- You can perfect your craft as you go, much like Elizabeth Taylor got better and better at getting married. I think we can all agree she nailed it after her 47th attempt.
- Clients are in need of your voiceover services. They're just *waiting* out there for you to call them and say "I bet you've been just *waiting* for me to call you." To prepare for what's next, I would take a moment to familiarize yourself with sailor-worthy profanity accompanied by a click and a dial tone. This is why I like email: I hate being reamed out by clicks and dial tones.

You see? There you have it. Every day, you're out there in that tall grass, finding those beautiful colored eggs, opening them up and finding wonderful oxygen-starved clients in there who will do just about anything - *anything* - including casting you for multi-thousand-dollar paying roles with residuals as long as you promise to please not seal up the egg again.

It's empirical, I've tried it, and I have eighteen reliable clients that I keep wrapped in cat-hair, sealed up in plastic eggs in a colorful wicker basket in my office to prove it.

So happy Easter Egg hunting, every day!

Sincerely,

A Man-Woman-Soccer-Mom-Lioness-Makeup-Wearing-Guy, and his Candy-Thieving Wife

TAKEAWAY & ACTION STEP

"A hunt based only on the trophies taken falls far short of what the ultimate goal should be." - Fred Bear

Marketing is an acquired art and not everyone loves it. Not everyone is cut out for it. Are you? How can you expand your comfort zone in order to try new modes of marketing, to explore new worlds and new civilizations, and to boldly go where no man has gone before? Explore a new marketing arena this week and try marketing to ten people.

Pinocchios

I CANNOT TELL A LIE

The Proof is in the Pudding.

This section is about pudding, because it is pudding, and that is enough. I am confident that pudding was invented by Jesus Himself, and that there will be pudding in heaven. I have yet to record a voiceover script about pudding, but all good things come to those who eat their weight in pudding. I have now said pudding seven times.

But fear not: I almost always have a point. My point this time is this: I do not like disclaimers placed on my pudding, cereal, or *anything*.

"Some settling may have occurred."
"Contents may have settled."
"Package sold by weight, not volume."

I recently opened my pudding cup, only to see less than the maximum. I am sorry, but I paid for the *maximum* product made by Jesus Himself. I did not *want* two-thirds of Jesus, nor did I *pay* for two-thirds of Jesus. False advertising! The pudding; not Jesus.

Packaging should not be visually misleading as to the quantity contained, and this "slack fill" problem is becoming an epidemic. There is truly nothing worse than opening a package – *any package* - only to find that it is only filled 66% full of whatever goodness I expected 100% of. Cereal boxes are another example. The inner plastic bag reaches to only 2/3 of the top of the box, and – *even worse* - the bag itself is filled only 2/3 full.

HOW ON EARTH DO PEOPLE GET AWAY WITH SUCH SHENANIGANS?!?!?

I am calm now.

Finally, to add insult to injury, I recently received my new container of Spark from Advocare. My canister was…you guessed it…2/3 full.

Because of all of this, I am therefore going to propose that that is no longer called *settling*, and instead called *robbery*. Examples:

"Some robbery may have occurred."
"Contents may have robbed you."
"Package sold by robbery, not non-robbery."

To apply this in practical situations, I will be handing out 2/3 of any further $20 bills to the cashier who is taking 66% of my order before I walk 2/3 of the way out of the store and am 2/3 arrested by 66% of the store security.

It is the same with traffic. Just this past weekend we were heading north to pick up my mother from the airport, who had flown in from Tucson to see her grandchildren. My wife and I, who are known as The Taxi Drivers Who Exist To Simply Transport Her And Get Out Of The Way Of Her View Of Her Grandchildren, dutifully drove to pick her up from SeaTac. From the moment we entered I-5 northbound, we were sitting in bumper-to-bumper traffic for, if my memory is correct, four hundred and thirty-nine miles north. It is at this point that I would like to ebulliently thank the makers of Veggie Tales for helping to keep the small creatures in the back of my van passive.

When we got to the end of the traffic jam, it just sort of… dissolved. No cataclysm; no fiery wreck, no travesty. What was the reason for the traffic jam then??? No smoking asteroid embedded into what was left of the highway, with cars snaking their way carefully around it on either side. I was honestly disappointed at this anticlimactic conclusion. I had half-expected to see the blackened fiery charred husk of an overturned car, and a grisly wreck spanning the width of the highway, because then that would make sense of our delay.

I am sure it is just me, but if you are going to delay me in stop-and-go traffic for a whole hour, then I feel I am entitled to see dismembered humans staggering clumsily through smoke and fiery misery, like the zombies in Thriller. As the zombies are now 2/3 alive, this jives perfectly with my new life approach.

Stupid pudding cups.

LIFE IS PAIN, HIGHNESS

I am now going to refer to the source of all goodness. It has been around for ages, and is filled with truth, light, music, and beauty. Here I am not referring to Jerry Springer. The source of all goodness is not even The Bible.

It is *The Princess Bride*, a movie that has been around since a long time ago before movies became about superheroes. A phrase was uttered in that movie that still resonates today. It is a powerful phrase. I am not referring to "Where's the Beef?" I am talking about what Wesley said to Buttercup: *"Life IS pain, Highness. Anyone who says differently is selling something."*

Wesley was right. I have experienced pain through, particularly, *deception,* and I am not OK with it. Aside from pudding and traffic, here are some examples of when I have been deceived:

- **Fad Diets.** I was told that certain pills might be effective for me because the problem is that obesity runs in my family. They did not actually work, however, because the actual problem is that *nobody* runs in my family.
- **Meat.** Some people have expressed to me that eating meat is murder. Fine. It is murder. Delicious, flame-broiled murder. Stop ruining my dinner.
- **Thin Mints.** A Pennsylvania man is suing Smart Water for not making him smart, and so I too would like to formally announce my lawsuit against Thin Mints.
- **Pac-Man.** There has been a lot of talk lately about today's video games causing young people to respond to stress negatively with aggression and acts of violence. Popular games from MY childhood taught kids to deal with stress a different way, by constantly running from their problems and binge eating. See "Thin Mints" above.
- **Defensive Driving.** I was told to practice defensive driving, and was led to believe others were taught the same. Highway behavior, however, appalls me; and I do not enjoy having to be nice to someone I would really like to just throw a brick at.

- **The Return of the King Movie.** I was told movies have a single ending.
- **Cats. Also Kittens, which are Evil soaked in Cute.**
- **Exercise Instructors.** They assign me pointless activity that is not nearly as enjoyable as simply laying down. I did do a push-up today, after all. OK fine. The truth is that I fell down, but I *did* have to use my arms to get back up, so…close enough. Now I need chocolate.
- **Casinos.** All of them, especially the ones that never paid me anything.
- **All Doctors Everywhere.** I cite a recent conversation with my doctor:
- Doctor: "You have this disease"
- Me: "oh no"
- Doctor: "But you can cure it with a healthy diet and exercise."
- Me: "OH NO"
- **Revenge.** I was told that revenge is a dish that is best served cold. However, people also say that revenge is sweet. So, basically, revenge is ice cream.
- **Siri.** I will never forget desperately trying to make the 1st generation Siri do my bidding. I desperately tried to painstakingly and slowly enunciate the phrase, "Find - the - nearest - bowling - alley." I assumed speaking louder and slower would help. Siri replied with, "I'm sorry, I don't understand 'find the newest burrowing owl leave me.'" And, well, pretty much anything else Siri says.
- **Weather Forecast Apps.** Because never.

All I wanted was 100% of my pudding. Stupid pudding cups. The truth is that life *IS* pain. You cannot solve everything with something, so do not resort to lying and deceiving. Unless you are a politician of course. Then they pay you to do it.

SO HOW DO BUSINESSPEOPLE UN-DECEIVE?

Why the latest rant by Aaron Ryan? I will tell you, because you deserve to know. Also because if I do not write another book, you will forget me. But mostly the first thing.

In voiceovers, you have only one responsibility. Well, actually, *three* responsibilities wrapped up in one. They are:

- Deliver an impeccable performance
- Deliver stellar audio quality
- Deliver utter commitment to customer service

All of these are part of your responsibility to truly *deliver* for your customers. That is, after all, what they are paying you to do. So, I ask you now, are you committed to 2/3 of an impeccable performance? 66% stellar audio quality? An "almost" commitment to customer service?

I run voiceovers as my primary business. I treat it like a business, and I treat it professionally. I treat my customers professionally, and I do that 100%. Any less, and I risk losing a repeat client. I risk a bad review. I risk them not paying on time. I risk them telling a partner not to work with me. So, it is in my best interest not to deceive them. To *under*-promise, and to *over*-deliver. Not the other way around. James R. Alburger explains, "Voiceover is part of 'show business.' It carries with it the potential for all the celebrity and excitement of being a star...the larger part of that phrase is 'business.' Most entrepreneurs are truly creative individuals for whom the details of business are the last thing they want to do. But mastering the business side of voiceover is critical to achieving any level of success. You must be willing to become proficient in both performing *and* business skills *(italics mine)* if you are to become competitive and considered to be a professional."[101]

Do you do any of the following:

- overpromise and underdeliver?
- say you can have it done in under an hour and you get it back to them tomorrow?
- lie about the quality of your hardware, software, or who your previous clientele have been?
- maintain an image of having it all together, when really you are falling apart inside? Essentially, are you an imposter?

- Or worse, are you a coach who is promising students repeat voiceover bookings once they pay $2400 and sign on your dotted line?

If you do any of the above, then you are a Pinocchio, and Jesus would like to speak to you. This way, please.

As James R. Alburger says, "Be aware that no workshop coach or demo producer can guarantee your demo will be heard by an agent or talent buyer, or even that you will be accepted for voiceover representation or work. No matter what they tell you, you are the only person who will determine your success in this business. Do not rely on someone else to do it for you."[102] Or promise you!

Deception is not always so obvious, is it? For example, King Théoden in *The Two Towers* trusted an advisor named Wormtongue. **Wormtongue**. It was right there in his name. But our names do not have to be *Wormtongue* or *Slick McSalesGuy* in order to deceive our customers.

Lord help us see clearly, and neither deceive nor be deceived.

Lord help us to be truthful in advertising, and in all of our voiceover ways.

And Lord, above all else, thank you for making pudding.

Please also let there be no more traffic.

HERE'S ONE TO GROW ON:

"Anyone who doesn't take truth seriously in small matters cannot be trusted in large ones either."

Albert Einstein

There Can Be Miracles... When You Believe

HOUSTON AND CAREY HAD IT RIGHT

In 1998's *The Prince of Egypt*, a wonderful song was delivered by two pop divas. No, not Ethel Merman and Jessica Rabbit. The *other* two divas: Whitney Houston and Mariah Carey. I'm talking about the theme song, "There can be Miracles."

Wow, what a matchup! They were a team...er...sort of. Two divas duking it out with all their vocal gymnastics and sending us a beautiful message about the possibility of miracles, even in the midst of a giant scratch-your-eyes-out-listen-to-me-do-audio-acrobatics-right-over-you-cat-fight to prove who sings better. And then if I remember correctly, Mariah Carey launched into an octave that only dogs on Pluto can hear, glass shattered, ears bled, and it was all over. Whitney's "One Moment in Time" turned into "I Have Nothing", and then we all bade her farewell with "I Will Always Love You." Ah well. Not all miracles end happily.

But there truly can be miracles when you believe. I recently did an Instagram video on this: about the power of belief. Every time we set foot in the studio, we had better be armed with the utmost of belief in our abilities; otherwise it's time to give it all up and apply for a position as "Masky, The COVID-19 Clown" for birthday parties and bachelor stripper cakes everywhere.

We're actors – we have the ability within us! But sometimes it's the belief that evades us. As much as we might hate to admit it, we lose sight of such things sometimes, and they do evade us.

Let me give you an example. For our household, what evades my wife and I is sleep. We have a nice California King sized bed that our preschooler has somehow figured out how to slither into, undetected, in the middle of the night, and proceed to stretch out all his limbs to the point where my wife and I are shoved off of the bed and smushed into opposite corners of the room. I am not kidding. I don't know how he does it, but he does it. Look at him, lying there peacefully while we slowly slide down the walls in our own ooze, reaching in vain for the Ambien.

Belief evades us. This chapter is here to help you get it back, and to soar high, high in the sky once again – just like Mariah Carey's paint-sniffing dog-friendly Pluto-notes.

FLY HIGH AND PROUD

"Don't Cry Out Loud" by Melissa Manchester. Another song, and a wonderful Top-40 hit that encourages us to suppress our emotions, and entirely renounce grieving, you sad sap of a wuss. In the same vein as the truly horrifying song "Smile" (Charlie Chaplin), it's one of those feel-good songs that tells you to shut the #@$& up and stop your blubbering. Yay! More please. Add in the creepy 1978 music video with depressing fluffy clowns, and you've got yourself all the makings of becoming a certified whack-job.

But oh the enchanting melody! Thank you, Dr. Melissa! What powerful delivery. And such invaluable advice that is sure to help me learn to be an expressive human being and truly be vulnerable with other carbon-based lifeforms. I'll put that nice poppycock hootenanny in my pipe and smoke it.

But, to her credit, a few lines later, we have the anthemic exhortation to "Fly high and proud." What ministry! What positive urging! What tremendous encouragement to spread your wings and sail on the headwinds of life! If only we could have such belief as we head into another round of auditions, preparing to produce a read the likes of which this world has never seen. We're going to knock 'em dead, I say; not just somewhat sleepy. Take it from some pros: "Sometimes all it takes is a button on the end of your audition – an extra comment, a punch line, a laugh, or a chuckle – to get your read moved to the top of the list."[103] Those producers and casting directors will flat out weep upon receipt of our audition: they will wail and mourn because of the sheer goodness that has been foisted upon them, begging for mercy from the onslaught of perfectionist gravy that we ladle over them. That's when we'll hit 'em with Mariah's thirteenth octave until they finally relent and promise to cast us for every single voiceover until Jesus returns.

Lately, I've been struggling a bit with belief, as sometimes the auditions can seem like monotony. I just did one. Or I've already done thirty. Or I hit a dry spell today. Or I'm tired, have a hangnail, and the stay-at-home neighbors won't stop blaring Juice Newton, which was something I truly didn't know you could blare.

But do let's talk about one more song, because this chapter is all about music and singing and joy and hope and light streaming down through hallelujah choruses. Oh and creepy clowns.

I humbly present Gavin DeGraw. He of the "I Don't Wanna Be" fame has a beautiful song called *Belief*. Here are the lyrics for you:

Belief makes things real...Makes things feel, feel alright
Belief makes things true...Things like you, you and I
Tonight, you arrested my mind...When you came to my defense
With a knife in the shape of your mouth...In the form of your body, with the wrath of a god
Oh, you stood by me, belief
Belief builds from scratch...Doesn't have to relax, it doesn't need space
Long live the queen and I'll be the king...In the color of grace
Oh, tonight, you arrested my mind...When you came to my defense
With a knife in the shape of your mouth...In the form of your body, with the wrath of a god
Oh, you stood by me, belief
I'm gonna yell it from the rooftops..I'll wear a sign on my chest
That's the least I can do, it's the least I can do...

Thank you, Gavin, for imparting lyrics that deal with Belief.

BELIEVING IS SEEING

What do we need to believe in?

- Belief that we'll be okay and not have to sell everything to make ends meet?
- Belief that we'll be provided enough funds to survive?
- Belief that that every job will be awarded us?
- Belief that there is more to life than worry?

- Belief that our nation will vote the correct man into office every four years?
- Belief that whatever we set our minds to, we can accomplish?
- Belief that we can read every script with passion and…well…belief???

Oh, with a knife in the shape of your mouth…in the form of your body, with the wrath of a god…

Oh you stood by me, Belief.

Just for contrast, let's look at some *incorrect* beliefs:

- I will be awarded every single job
- I can mix a gallon of bleach and a gallon of soap in my washing machine, let it run and disinfect my entire house in 40 minutes
- If you hit your head really hard, you might have a Caucasian
- A pandemic is not enough, God. So please add in some Murder Hornets, you know, to spice things up a bit.
- I sound exactly like the perfection that is Sam Elliott and Morgan Freeman and James Earl Jones wrapped up in one beautiful mammal
- If I'm dissatisfied with my chocolate fudgesicle, I can simply slather a cup of BEHR Ultra Premium White on it, and *voila!* I humbly present vanilla.
- If Christopher Reeve and Henry Cavill can do it, why can't I? *jumps from ledge, does NOT fly, curses R Kelly all the way down*
- Those little tiny "bump indents" on your steering wheel are in Braille so that blind drivers have no trouble finding the horn to alert other drivers when necessary. #themoreyouknow
- I have worked hard. Therefore, I am entitled to enter that bank vault unescorted.
- If there is a thermonuclear war, you should move to Ni'ihau, because what are the odds that they'll be able to hit that tiny island?
- Any side of the highway will do; whichever side gets me to my destination faster wins

- Every producer will cast me every time
- If you take four pregnancy tests and they all come out positive, you're having four babies, dangit, so you better get ready

Now that you know that those are just plain silly beliefs, lets revisit the real ones.

There are laws. And there are helpful tips and guidelines for those suffering from a Wee Bout of The Stupids. Ultimately, belief is grounded in reality. It is a reality that we can in fact succeed within physical limitations. It is a reality that we can do what we set our minds to as long as it's safe and productive and we're not plummeting from buildings while singing "I believe I can fly." It's a reality that there are laws to keep us alive. Belief grounded in reality moves us forward and helps us *live*.

Belief moves at the very leading perimeter of reality, and pulls us along. Belief makes things real. Believing is seeing. There CAN be miracles…when we believe. I pray we stand in belief that everything we need will be provided for us, and that we'll all be OK.

As it pertains to winning jobs and being successful in business, whatever your trade is, I pray you stand in the unassailable belief that you have everything it takes to get under those words, lift them off the page, and bring them to life. Because you do.

Breathe. Know. Step up in faith and deliver valiantly. You *can* do this. Paul Strikwerda writes, "If you think you're too small to have an impact, you've never had a cricket in your sound booth."[104] And Yuri Lowenthal and Tara Platt write, "Sometimes you get pages and pages of script; sometimes it's a single word on a piece of paper. But whatever you have, make sure you explore it to its fullest so that you can best do that thing you love: act! So now you're not only a detective, but a miner too, excavating the page for little gems of knowledge."[105]

I couldn't agree more.

Even dogs on Pluto know this.

To quote Phil Morris, Actor:

"The world of VO is an incredibly creative one where I've worked with the most talented actors I've ever been around. All of them have their own unique abilities and sounds. The best ones have never left their 'child-like' honesty, and are able to go into the most amazing vocal areas. I think that as long as you never grow up, have some acting ability and a healthy, passionate interest in your fantasy life, VO can be one of the most satisfying experiences you can have in this crazy business, and I have made life-long friends as a result."[106]

Believe that it's the best business. Believe you're a little crazy. Believe that you have a child-like honesty.

Believe.

TAKEAWAY & ACTION STEP

Belief makes things real.

What can you start to believe into existence? What attitudes about yourself do you need to change in order to "claim" your future self? Are you your own roadblock? How can you get out of your own way?

A Long, Long Time Ago, Thinking Was Invented

OPEN YOUR MIND TO ME, QUAID

You know him! You love him! Let me start over.

You only just know him and do not even wish to! That squishy little belly mutant protruding out of some dude's tummy in Paul Verhoeven's 1990's smash hit, *Total Recall*. I remember seeing that hernia-like Muppet protrude from Marshall Bell's abdomen, and I experienced a pain I could not locate. I have truthfully never been more afraid of a psychic, a Muppet or a psychic Muppet.

Now, I know what you are thinking. Whenever you think about the past, it just brings back so many memories. There, there. I hear you, and I understand. Every time I think about the *future*, my brain melts, and all I can manage to vocalize is "nougat." I do not know why this is. I thought we were sharing.

I recently heard a joke. An elderly lady named Betty had a bad memory. Betty lamented to her elderly friend Marcia, *"My memory is so bad!"* Marcia responded sympathetically, *"Oh no! How bad is it?"* To which Betty responded, *"How bad is what?"*

The past does bring back many memories. But it was in the past that the most glorious thing happened. You see, a long, long time ago, Thinking was invented, and Planet Earth would never be the same again. It is this glorious gift that enables us to do calculus and not fall down. Also, that helps us to withstand the evil thing that is called schoolchildren practicing the violin. Also, episodes of The View.

Apparently, the human species would have gone on mindlessly staggering around like slow pinball zombies had God not intervened and said, and I quote, "Knock it off, stupids." And it was at that precise moment, that the gracious gift of thought, rationale and reason were generously imparted to all humans everywhere, except those who drive on roads.

True, some things are not thinking issues - you do not have to think about them:

The Wall Street journal recently had an article entitled "Should You Really Shower Every Day?"[107] I am sorry but this is not a question. No reasoning human born with a nose will want me to be asking myself such a poppycock question, as it is in the planet's best interest that I always wash off my yesterday.
Injecting yourself with bleach. I do not need to expound on this.
Not jumping into the path of a combine. Violators who do this usually miss lunch.
In the event that you and a friend should encounter a bear, make sure that you always carry packets of seasoning with you in order to sprinkle over your friend as you run, making them delectable while you get away. Also make sure you can run faster because right about now your friend will start pursuing you too.
Never eat spaghetti with crushed Oreos in it, because, ew.

These are all obvious to members of the human race who possess a cerebellum.

IF I ONLY HAD A BRAIN

Some people clearly do not think about what they say, think, or do. All one needs to do is to turn on the news. To illustrate my point, I have compiled several instances where people have clearly not been thinking. These are actual and true (which means actual) stories. They make me questionably proud to me part of the same species as these people. Enjoy.

- Pilot to Maintenance Worker on maintenance report: "Left inside main tire almost needs replacement." Maintenance Worker to Pilot: "Almost replaced inside main tire."
- A Los Angeles man who later said he was "tired of walking," stole a steamroller and led police on a 5-mph chase until an officer *stepped* aboard and brought the vehicle to a stop.

- One more Pilot to arguably the same Maintenance worker: "Number 3 engine missing." Maintenance Worker to Pilot: "Engine found on right wing after brief search."
- The Chico, California, City Council enacted a ban on nuclear weapons, setting a $500 fine for anyone detonating one within city limits. I am confused.
- Another Pilot to arguably the same Maintenance worker: "Something loose in cockpit." Maintenance Worker to Pilot: "Something tightened in cockpit."
- Swedish business consultant Ulf af Trolle labored 13 years on a book about Swedish economic solutions. He took the 250-page manuscript to be copied, only to have it reduced to 50,000 strips of paper in seconds when a worker confused the copier with the shredder.
- When two service station attendants in Ionia, Michigan, refused to hand over the cash to an intoxicated robber, the man threatened to call the police. They still refused, so the robber called the police and was arrested.
- And yet another Pilot to arguably the same Maintenance worker: "Evidence of leak on right main landing gear." Maintenance Worker to Pilot: "Evidence removed."
- A man in Johannesburg, South Africa, shot his 49-year-old friend in the face, seriously wounding him, while the two practiced shooting beer cans off each other's head.
- As illustrated in the previous chapter, a man is suing Smart Water for not making him smart. As such I would also like to join the growing ranks of those formally announcing their lawsuits against Thin Mints.

Raise your hand if you are proud to be a fellow human.

THE THINK BONE'S CONNECTED TO THE...SUCCESS BONE

So how does this apply to entrepreneurs, you ask. I am assuming you just asked.

As the proverb goes, "As a man thinketh, so he is." *Always* think about what you are going to say, do and even think.

What you *SAY* clearly matters:

- Clearly, I preach truth here, because you are an entrepreneur.
- Your voice has the power to make people think. Use it wisely.
- Clearly, what you say does matter. So, say correct things. Your clients are watching you.
- By the way there is no such word as irregardless, which actually means "with full regard to." Stop that, irregardless of whether or not you think it is right or not, regardless.

What you *DO* clearly matters:

- Clearly, you have a reputation to uphold in voiceovers, and people are watching you.
- Do not think that you should skip coaching, rent that overpriced studio space or spend a fortune on expensive VO hardware without solid education.
- Also please stop posting foodies and politics. No one likes spaghetti with Oreos, and we all voted for the other guy.
- Clearly, what you do does matter.
- Oh - and never hang up when you are on hold, because your call will have been answered in the order it was received, and you were next. Your call is very important to them!

What you *THINK* clearly matters:

- What do you think about yourself, and others?
- Are you beating yourself up because you're not as good as Ms. So & So Voiceover Gal?
- Are you punishing yourself because you did not get that VO job you longed for?
- Do you persist in telling yourself you do not have what it takes?
- Are you trying to do calculus but keep falling down? Stop. No one uses calculus anyway - the last known usage was in 1836 in the recipe for Play-Doh, which is apparently evil.[108]

- Think about your goals.
- Think about what you want your future in voiceovers to be like.
- Think about each script and how you should deliver it.
- Clearly, what you think matters, so use your head. In business, in life, in all of it...use your head.

As a man thinketh, so he is. Straight outta Proverbs 23:7.

The point here with all these - and *please never, ever* forget this all-encompassing truth - is that I overuse the word "clearly".

At least, I think so.

HERE'S ONE TO GROW ON:

"Think with your head, not your pride."

Unknown

When Life Gives You Murder Hornets

YOU MAKE MURDER HORNET LEMONADE

Because a Global Coronavirus Pandemic just wasn't enough, we're in the thick of it now.

A teacher missed her classroom so much that she knitted all of her students[109], which is another way of saying, "I went nutso." Now, I don't mean knitted them together against their wills, mind you, or she'd be in the Big House, which I'm told is NOT where you want to be during a pandemic. But isn't that sweet? It just goes to show you how connected we really long to be with each other. It's beautiful, in a creepy, imprisoning sort of way. Not to brag, but I've been an expert at avoiding people since well before the pandemic started, so maybe the Big House will suit me. I'll let you know what felony I've settled on. If there are no further chapters after this one, you'll know I was successful.

In other news, it's come to my attention that John Travolta was hospitalized for suspected COVID-19, but doctors now confirm that it was only Saturday Night Fever, and they assure everyone that he is Staying Alive.

Seriously though, those little nuggets aside, I've been thinking a lot about coronavirus lately, because we're in the middle of planning for a move, and there is a lot on my mind. Is this the best time. Will we be moving into a coronavirus-infected home. Why do these questions end in periods.

It's been such a time of hysteria. We've been cleaning a lot lately in preparing for our move, and it's amazing how much I find myself touching my face to wipe off sweat. It's crazy, really. After all the stupid things I've done in my life, if I die because I touched my face, I'm going to be annoyed. So I've chosen a full-body mask that should be here by 2022. It's nice because it doubles as a mask (protection from the virus) AND a blanket, which is protection from being cold. Now if it could only protect me from receiving bills from creditors. I'd buy *all* the shares of *that* stock.

It's a crazy time. We now have a chance to save the world by lying around and watching TV. Let's not screw this one up. We need to hold together. Knit us together, oh Knitter Teacher. Because in the midst of all of this, something greater is bearing down on us. Do you hear it? There's a faint buzz of an approaching danger. It's about 1.5" long in some cases.

You know what I'm talking about. The Murder Hornet.

BUZZ BUZZ STING STING

I don't think we really had enough to worry about with a global pandemic that has killed over a million people. Thanks, Nature. Glad you spiced things up a bit by throwing in Murder Hornets, which apparently have a penchant for decapitation. Because of that I would assume that they originated from within the ranks of ISIS, but alas, *Vespa mandarinia* come from Asia, ranging from Japan and Russian down to Thailand and Myanmar. They're pesky little creatures, and I think that while they obviously prefer honeybees, they would develop a taste for Aaron Ryan's succulent flesh in no time flat, I'm sure. So I wasn't going outside before, and I'm not going outside now. Because they're out there. They're watching. And waiting. And you're not even safe in the Big House. *Scratches "Do Felony" off of to-do list for now*

So if we're not safe from pandemics, and we're not safe from Murder Hornets, then what can we do?

What's to be done? I think I just might have the answer.

ADAPT AND OVERCOME. OH, AND DRINK UP.

When life gives you Murder Hornets, you make Murder Hornet Lemonade. It's true. You always have to take the evil, the frustration, the sadness, the trauma, the difficulty, the negative, and turn it on its head. That's really how life works, right? I also think that no one has in fact to date *made* Murder Hornet Lemonade, which is entirely the purpose of this chapter: to provide you a delicious recipe for overcoming. With that, let's begin.

Step 1: Find and retrieve 7200 Murder Hornets and catch them. Somehow.

Step 2: Obtain a collection device of some kind. Note: This should have been Step 1.

Step 3: Lather yourself with a Sting-prevention material of your choosing, such as an ointment, a jelly, or the former members of The Police who didn't like him and are expendable.

Step 4: Ensure that your voiceover booth is fully sealed should the Murder Hornets get loose and try to find you in there. You should be safe in there until you run out of oxygen, at which point you will need to reorganize all of these Steps, with the new Step 1 being "Pray unceasingly."

Step 5: Once all Murder Hornets have been caught in your Collection Device, pronounce incantations and spells over them which contain the phrase "Expecto patronum." This will of course have no bearing on the Murder Hornets' behavior, but will of course drive prepubescent Harry Potter-loving girls absolutely wild with a hornet-like fervor. Collect them as well before they sting you too.

Step 6: Insert Collection Device into Even Larger Collection Device Holder That Squishes, so that Even Larger Collection Device Holder That Squishes does a squishy operation that, well, squishes said Murder Hornets into a fine putty.

Step 7: Retrieve the extracted juices of the squished Murder Hornets from the Murder Hornet Juice Catching Reservoir, which goes into the Murder Hornet Juice Catching Reservoir Dispenser Thingy.

Step 8: Add a dash of salt, a pinch of lime and five gallons of Tang to season.

Step 9: Drink.

Step 10: Perish, because Murder Hornets, as everyone knows, are highly toxic.

Step 11 (should you survive Step 10): Rinse and repeat until all Murder Hornets have been turned into Murder Hornet Lemonade.

Bonus Step 12: Return to the production of your voiceovers, and stop dilly-dallying.

Bonus Step 13: Look up the meaning of dilly-dallying.

What? What's that you say? Oh, you're welcome – my pleasure. Of course! You're very welcome. What's that? No, no, I don't require any remuneration. It's my good pleasure to assist you with your survival! I'll be back with tips on surviving Assassination Sharks, Slay Sheep, Kill Frogs, Slaughter Beetles and Eradication Hummingbirds in the next issue.

TAKEAWAY & ACTION STEP

Turn lemons into lemonade.

Do you mistake adversity for inconvenience? Do you view a momentary setback as an insurmountable problem or an insignificant pebble? What blows have you been dealt in your life, and how can they work out for your good? List five "setbacks" in your life that ended up working out for your benefit after all.

The 10 Commandments Of A Successful Businessperson

LISTENETH TO THE WORDS THAT COMETH OUT OF MY MOUTHETH

OK, OK, I know this one goes right to the Bible, and that's a touchy and uncomfortable subject for some people. *Insert eye-rolling and face-palming here.* I guess the only place left to go to make you SUPER uncomfortable is…Jesus! Oh no! Sound the anti-religion claxons! Bring out the dogs! Bay, dogs, bay! Raise the shields! Not Jesus! Take evasive action!

Now that you've squirmed a bit, you're ready to endure. Read on.

I. THOU SHALT PRAY, TRUST & INTEND TO GET JOBS

Step one. It's all about a mindset. If you go into your studio simply hoping that you might maybe possibly on the off-chance kind of *happen* to get a voiceover job, you'll never get a voiceover job. If you go into it praying, trusting in God (or whatever Higher Power you wish to), praying and asking for blessing, and moreover, with full intention of being the recipient of the awarded job, your odds go up significantly. Do you know that book, "As a man thinketh, so is he"[110]? Yeah. That. It's a mind game, for sure.

You want to go in confidently, boldly, knowing that you do have what it takes to earn this job…to be awarded this voiceover… to be asked to represent this brand. There's nothing like a scared wet fish to frighten off a client and make them click "next audition."

It's up to you to go in boldly in prayer, faith, trust and intention, resolute on doing the very best you can and trusting that God will do the rest, and work you into the ears, minds and hearts of the decision makers. It's not up to you – all you can do is give your best. The rest is not up to you. Let God sort 'em out.

II. THOU SHALT REMEMBER THAT IT IS NOT ABOUT REJECTION, IT'S ABOUT SELECTION

Did you think you were going to get that job? Did someone beat you out of it? Get 4 stars and you *still* didn't get it? So? It's about "selection, not rejection," per Paul Kirby. They didn't reject you or offer any commentary on the quality of your craft or the readiness of your talent; they simply selected another talent. The sooner you can wrap your head around this, the better off you'll be. You didn't get rejected. Another got selected. Another didn't get rejected. You simply got selected. Round and round we go.

III. THOU SHALT MARKET TO AT LEAST 50 PEOPLE PER DAY

I suggest marketing to at least 50 people per day. Up the ante a bit, eh? Get yourself out there. The more you cast your net, the more your chances of landing a job. How long does it take to fire off an email? Use the same text, but personalize it. How long does it take to reach out to several LinkedIn clients? Use the same text, but personalize it. Copy-paste-personalize-send. How long does that take?

Let's revisit the marketing percentage of your entrepreneurial pursuit. If you treat your voiceover career like a business and work 8 to 5, that's 9 hours (without a lunch). 90% of your 9 hours is 8.1 hours. You have 8.1 hours to market each day! Whether that's cold calling, emailing, connecting, whatever, make sure you're casting out your reel. You should always have something coming down the pipeline. And the ROI for your marketing may not pay off by tomorrow. Or next Tuesday. Or next year. It may pay off, as he says, between the 5th and 12th contact. But you're sowing seeds that will eventually come around, even if you *never* hear back from that particular client – who just happened to refer you to the one guy who referred you to their sister who referred you to the marketing guy whose brother does E-Learning, who booked you for a massive E-Learning job, and you just never found out about the connection.

IV. THOU SHALT REMEMBER THAT THY FOCUS DETERMINES THY REALITY

George Lucas said this one. Stop and wrap your head around *that* for a minute. The creator of Jar Jar Binks penned this line. *Whoa.* Figure out for yourself what that means. What is your focus? What are you so obsessed with today that is going to determine your reality? Think about Michael Phelps. Michael Jackson. Pablo Picasso. Michael Jordan. Blaise Pascal. People who had natural abilities and honed them, honed them, honed them until they were tired...and then honed them again. Over and over and over...until they became the best that they could be, and in fact, the best there ever was. These people sacrificed free time, social activity, and more, through constant refinement and focus on honing their craft, to ensure that their focus became their reality.

What's your focus?

V. THOU SHALT ASK THYSELF DEEPLY, "WANTEST THOU THIS?"

Have you done this yet? Have you sat down and really, really, really *yearned*? Have you finally found the love of your career life, after long searching and sleepless nights? Did you leave a full-time job for this?

Did you step out in faith? How long has it been since you really cried into your pillow, wanting so badly for this to work? Was it a passing fancy? Or was it your life's compulsion, your utter motivation, your happiness and pleasure...and is it still? If so, what's got you frozen in concrete? Are you at an impasse? Why?

Can you take some time to figure out again, perhaps find your reset button, and see where you go from here? If you don't *really* want this, then find out the reasons why. What happened? What stole your thunder? Who cut in on you and kept you from running the race?

If you don't want it so badly you can feel it in your *teeth*, then something's wrong.

VI. THOU SHALT VIEW EXPENSES AS INVESTMENTS

Do you view things you purchase as expenses, or as investments? An expense is an "Oh well, I have to buy this, so I guess I will, because I have no other choice." An investment says "This is going to take me to the moon. I *must* have it for the long run if I'm to succeed." Expenses are short-term irritations. Investments are long-term seed-sowings. Every single thing you spend for your voiceover career is an investment. That new mic. That new software. That advertising. That workshop. That coaching. *All* of it is an investment. All of this ramp-up towards success is going to take money and capital, no doubt about it. Nothing in life worth succeeding at comes free. In 2 Samuel 24:24, King Araunah says "No, I insist on paying you for it. I will not sacrifice to the Lord my God burnt offerings that cost me nothing." He viewed it as an investment, not an expense. He saw it as a long-term necessity, not a short-term irritation.

Believe me, I *know* it takes a bit of cash to start up a voiceover career. But when you compare that to an accredited cosmetology school program, for example, which will usually cost anywhere from $5k to $15k, or to attend a top beauty school, which costs anywhere from $10k to $20k, only to see them make $20 per haircut, isn't up to $5k in voiceover startup costs a cool drink of water by comparison?

VII. THOU SHALT ALWAYS STAY IN LEARNING MODE

Kenneth Blanchard said, "When you stop learning, you stop growing."[111] So true. You stagnate. Your muscles atrophy. You grow fat and bloated. Ok maybe it's not that bad. But really: keep moving. That includes your brain. Stay engaged with teachers and teaching subjects. Make it your life's aim to always better yourself. Got a coach, or had a coach? Get one again. Attended some workshops a few years ago? Book some more.

Networked in a Meetup with some other voiceover peeps? Get back out there and mingle. Joined an online vocal workout through Facebook and think they're beneath you? Squat down and get back in there again. I'm always amazed at the kernels of truth that come out of revisiting something. When I stop learning, I die a little from the pride that comes from thinking I know it all. And that's not where I want to be, nor should I. Nor should you. A rolling stone gathers no moss, they say. Unless you've got an endless supply of Moss-B-Gone, roll ye onward, valiant stone!

VIII. THOU SHALT AUDITION AUDITION AUDITION – FOR IT IS A NUMBERS GAME.

Meet Jack. Jack got into voiceovers. Jack signed up for a P2P and did 20 voiceover auditions that first day. Jack was happy because he knew he was going to book all those jobs! Jack didn't book any of those jobs: they all selected someone else. Jack instantly grew disenchanted because he wasn't grounded in realistic expectations, and he left the P2P and now works at Burger King, where his expectations of flipping burgers successfully every day are easily met.

Not the case with you. Audition. Keep trying. Keep pushing forward. Keep attempting to secure a role. Look at each one as an opportunity to grow and perfect your craft. View each audition as yet another way to get yourself out in front of people, potential audiences, new contacts who will pass your name along. Approach each audition with the knowledge that you can actually be the one awarded that project, because you do have what it takes. Gain momentum from the auditions you did before this one.

Above all, keep at it. Rome wasn't built in a day.

IX. THOU SHALT BE THYSELF

Contact Kay Bess for absolute clarification on this one. She's wonderful. It was her keynote from VO Atlanta 2019. Unless you're yourself when you audition or record your narration, you're not being true to you. No one is looking for a copy of another. Sure, there are endless "Say it like Sam Elliott" auditions out there. But ultimately, don't be a copy of a copy of a copy. Be you. The voiceover world needs more you-nique voices such as…you. Celia Siegel says "Branding allows you to tell your story in a way that is entertaining, concise and specific. The trick is to focus in on exactly what that story is and then emphasize important aspects of that story that your ideal customer will find interesting."[112] All of this is in an effort to tell no one else's story but *yours*, which is truly unique.

X. THOU SHALT ALWAYS BE GRATEFUL

Now, I'm not God (thank *God*). I didn't write anything in stone, nor did I issue any instructions or edicts or laws for man to follow. But I am enormously grateful to the one who did. My perspective hinges on the presence of a loving God who wants the best for me, wants me to have what my family and I need (and sometimes, even what we want; they're different by the way: wants and needs), and cares for me. And even if you don't believe in God, it's time for you to sit up and confidently state that there is some order out there in the universe that revolves around certain laws.

One such law is sowing and reaping. Sow gratitude, reap provision.

An attitude of gratitude will take you farther than you ever thought you could go. It'll provide you a sound bedrock knowing that everything that comes your way is a gift and blessing. What do my wife and I teach our son to say when he receives a gift? "Thank you." It's adorable when he does so. But he's starting to do it automatically.

Where did we as adults lose this reactionary phrase, this reaction of acknowledgment that we were given something that perhaps we didn't deserve…or at the very least, didn't expect?

Any time I'm awarded a job, I am *instantly* elated. And immediately following that, I'm *instantly* resounding gratitude. The first thing out of my mouth is "Thank you Lord." It is by the grace of God that I've been given what I've been given, and I'm extraordinarily grateful for everything that I've been given.

Now, does this imply that he who isn't grateful won't get anything or experience any success? Not at all. I just don't want to be that guy, ever. I want Someone, Somewhere, to know that I am extraordinarily grateful for this gift. I want that gratitude to come around full circle and bring in more blessings. Again, round and round we go.

SUMMARY

Does this chapter really need a summary? I don't think so. It's up to you to believe what you want and to proceed how you wish. For me, these have worked for me and I wanted to share them with you as foundational pillars that work in my own voiceover journey, and help me to proceed in an attitude of focus, success, gratitude, and passion. Not all that works for me will work for you. I just hope these ten will. And I don't think it's too far-fetched to say that the universe revolves around gratitude.

Be thou blessed as thou obeyest these commandments as thou wilt!

Politics, Politics, Politics

IT'S UNAVOIDABLE

Oh no. Another dreary chapter loaded with exactly zero funnies. But such is the case: this is a necessary one. If you're venturing into the wide world of voiceovers or authoring or any other form of business, that's one thing. If however you dare to aspire to greatness, well now that's a whole new ball o' wax, son. This chapter is to prepare you for what may come, and it's only fair that I do so. A view only through rose-colored stained-glass windows is unfair both to you and everyone else out there, because that's just not how the world works. It's about balance.

To quote Wesley to Buttercup in *The Princess Bride*, "Life *is* pain, highness…anyone who says differently is selling something."

It's true, the voiceover community at large is brimming with optimism, team-spirit, affirmation and encouragement. There are people in there that just love to give. I'm one of them. In his book *Step Up To The Mic*, Rodney Saulsberry says "some of you are not the most social people in the world. You tend to shy away from people, you don't attend industry functions, and you pride yourselves on being reclusive individuals. Well, that's ok in some occupations, but it's a big mistake in the voice-over community. Bonding with your peers is of paramount importance if you want to hear about the latest projects that need talent like yours…you will be constantly blessed with topics about trends, events, and other matters crucial to the advancement of your career."[113] There are coaches who simply aren't very much in it for the dollar; they're in it because they simply *love* coaching, and they want you to succeed out of a genuine belief that when you succeed, they succeed. It's a vicarious victory, to be sure, but they just love doing it because seeing raw talent blossom into paid jobs is an amazing thing we all get to behold. The voiceover community, like lots of communities out there, contain a lot of people like this. In regards to coaching, perhaps John Wooden said it best: "A good coach can change a game…a great coach can change a life."

Unfortunately, it also contains people who do not have your best interests at heart, and some other elements that are deeply protective of their own wins, their own reputation, their own product, and their own success.

They may be team-players on occasion or for the purposes of acclaim or the limelight, but when it comes right down to it in direct conversation, and you've stripped away all the marketing-speak and taglines of award-winning this or don't-settle-for-anything-less that, they're not very team-oriented.

They might be part of the "old guard", "the establishment", or "the regarded elite." Whatever label you want to slap on them, it doesn't guarantee them unassailable status, nor do they hold the franchise on what's best…for the industry, or you for that matter.

Saulsberry puts it this way: "These are people who claim to be your friend – but they are silently hoping for your demise. They don't want you to get the voice-over job you have always coveted. They give you advice they know is wrong and meant to make you fail."[114] Yikes. I don't want those people in my orbit.

WHY THE SOUR NOTE?

Now, this chapter does not exist to sour you, to point fingers, or to assign blame. It exists merely to reveal that, though everything may appear glistening and untarnished, all that glitters is not gold. You should still be wary.

Unfortunately, I've run afoul of a few people along my journey in both voiceovers *and* authoring. Some of them are just plain toxic. Some are the "up and comers" who think they know everything after a few months in business, who think they should dive right into coaching everyone because they've already got this thing all figured out. They charge $45/hour to simply give bad advice. They are tragic conveyer belts of misinformation. They're the kind who survive off of one P2P and think they're making bank. Yet they are part of the problem of the continual rate erosion in the VO industry. They're toxic because they can't… don't… *won't* listen to those who have gone before.

And there are others who are toxic as well. Some are jealous. Some are the "old guard" of voiceovers and business. They distrust anyone who doesn't do it their way, and you simply can't do right by them. Some of these people think they know it all, and they walk a little too high and mighty for me. If I choose to use a particular P2P, and they don't like that one, they can rain down fire and brimstone like nobody's business. And they'll sour your good name in the process, and extinguish your fire right quick. It was such an occurrence that happened very early on in my budding voiceover career, and I learned quickly that there are those who simply operate a different way, and if you choose a path that they personally find unviable for them (probably because they never gave it the attention that it deserved and thus they'll berate it due to it not working for them…because *they* didn't work it) then they'll attack you.

Others you'll recognize by many of their offerings, which many times contain their own name. Whether that's for branding purposes or not, I don't know. I deeply suspect that it's because they put an inordinate amount of stock into their own selling power, and unless the product is in fact *them*, it won't sell. Anyone can sell a product containing the word "voiceovers."

Still others run groups on Facebook and elsewhere and are obsessed with rules, and constantly highlighting them. Their group is their One Ring, and they're obsessed with protecting it and keeping it close. They don't – and won't – let you post your perfectly valuable offering there, as there's a sense of encroaching on their turf, and they don't like that, *o no My Precious*, not one bit.

And yet there still exists an even sadder demographic within the VO population: those who will distrust you because of your very success. They're threatened by you, they're jealous of you, and they don't want you to succeed. They'll talk about you behind your back, and subtly undermine you whenever and wherever they can. I once had a run-in with an individual who runs a very prominent Facebook group, and I was not admitted because he told me that I had stolen his ideas and was repurposing them as my own. Sure. I've been doing voiceovers off and on since 1993, and have run my own business since 2003. I've learned from countless sources both inside and outside the VO industry in terms of marketing, advertising, strategy, running a sound business, organization, goal-setting, and more. Ecclesiastes tells us that "there is nothing new under the sun". Yet this individual thought he had the franchise on marketing tactics: some of which I learned from him, and a billion others I did not. When he heard that I had recently presented material that sure sounded a lot like his, he attacked. I was never given the chance to rectify things with him, though I asked for a phone call on a few occasions. It's a true shame, because he's a fellow Christian, and as a Christian, it's astonishing how I take my worst wounds from them. Oh well. I pray it works out.

HERE'S WHAT YOU DO

What's the point in all of this? The point, my friend, is that people are human beings, subject to every emotion there is out there: happiness AND sadness; excitement AND skepticism; rejoicing AND jealousy. They can do as Robert the Bruce's leprous father did in *Braveheart:*

"You will embrace this rebellion. Support it from our lands in the north. I will gain English favor by opposing it from our lands in the south."

They'll put on one face and celebrate with you in public, but in private conversations, the politics will take over, and they'll hold private conversations with like-minded miscreants, and tear you down. It's the very nature of the beast in sales. I got my start in voiceovers through a telemarketing agency way back in the early 90's at an outfit in Seattle. One of the top salespeople there, Dennis, was not a team player at all, though in team meetings he would root for the team of course, while eyes were upon him. He was on Cloud 9 when he was selling...but boy oh boy, if *you* were selling and he was *not*, you were no longer friends. That team spirit eroded before my very eyes one day when he scowled at me after I was having a superbly successful day. Thanks Dennis.

It's not all sunshine and roses. You have to walk softly and carry an armored tank division. You need to be innocent as doves...but also wise as serpents. There will be many who will be supportive of your rise, even if it's meteoric...and there will be a few who oppose it. Should you rise to the status of "teacher" or "coach" (more on that later), you may find rather painfully that there is an established clique in voiceovers, a group of untouchables as it were, that are firmly cemented as The Ones From Whom We Learn, and it's an impenetrable wall guarding The Untouchables.

It's been very hard for me to break through that, because my love language is giving and I desperately *want* to give back. But some people just don't allow you to give, because it doesn't quite fit within their parameters of how they see giving. And, once again...there's the clique. If you're in, you're in; but if you're out...

Rodney Saulsberry encourages giving in the strongest sense, citing the origin of giving: "When you serve others, you almost always reap the rewards. In many ways, it is wrong to hoard your good fortune because, if you really think about it, someone directed you to your winnings. Someone intentionally or unwittingly paid it forward to you. And so, it is your spiritual and positive duty to help someone less fortunate than you."[115]

I also really, *really* love what Yuri and Tara say about this in *Voice-Over Voice Actor*: "Networking should never be about what you can *get* from others. Treat them as you would your friends, and be friendly and personable. You just may be someone they will want to befriend and (who knows?) maybe work with one day."[116] Networking is sowing into others as they sow into you.

When I was coming to prominence in voiceovers there was a voiceover guy who for the purposes of anonymity I'll name Merle. Now, I've never studied Merle's teaching, and I've never wanted to. I've never approached any of the students he coached, or purchased any of his training programs. But I do remember one post on Facebook where someone labeled him as a "serial purveyor of bad advice". In retrospect, I can't help but feel like he was pushed out, because he's no longer providing voiceovers.

So here's my counsel when you butt up against politics.

People are people. They always will be. They're loaded bags of individual history, and they all have their own formative journeys of opinions and learning that molded and shaped who they are today. Use your giftings where you can, as much as you can, but don't push hard to try and get into any pre-established cliques. You'll know when you've arrived, because you'll start getting invited to share at events. You'll be asked for your opinion. Aspiring entrepreneurs will seek you out for proper training. You'll be asked your opinion on hardware, software, coaches, conferences, other entrepreneurs, technique, locations, marketing, advertising, business operation, booth building, acoustic materials, plug-ins, and much more.

But don't be too eager. Don't be obsessed with followers and likes and mentions, and look wistfully (read: jealously?) at those who have followers numbering in the thousands, to your puny dozens. It didn't happen for them overnight either. It all takes precious sweet time to get there.

Don't get bent out of shape if you're handcuffed in your giving, or if you earnestly have a genuine skill in teaching, and are restricted from doing so. If you feel on the outside looking in, and all you want to do is to offer what you've learned in true humility and gratitude, but are faced with prerequisites and probationary periods. With some, you simply have to earn your stripes. Give it time. The stripes will come.

Your journey to the inner circle doesn't fit inside a microwave; the only thing that accommodates it is a crock pot, cooked nice and slow.

You'll know when you've arrived. In the meanwhile, nose to the grindstone. Work hard, love what you do, keep at it, and just produce. People will see those results, if you're so inclined to share them on social media. Those who will rally around you and lift you up will do so. Those who are inclined to judge and sling mud will do so out of the cowardly dark corners of the internet.

Hold your head high and march forward proudly. Sing it just like Matthew Wilder did:

Ain't nothin' gonna break-a my stride
Nobody gonna slow me down, oh no
I got to keep on movin'
Ain't nothin' gonna break-a my stride
I'm running and I won't touch ground
Oh no, I got to keep on movin'

You got this. You may run into occasional politics. Don't let 'em get you down. Rise above and know who you truly are. I rose above in the spring of 2023 and actually left the online voiceover community because it had clearly grown toxic. Someone I deeply respect in voiceovers, and a known leader, eventually did the same as well. Sometimes, familiarity breeds contempt, and perhaps the door swings both ways on that. The counsel I can offer you is that if you are seeking to cut ties and break away, know that the grass *can actually be greener on the other side.* It was for me. I broke from the community and never experienced a greater creative boon than that year. I produced three music albums, resurrected several old ones and reprinted them, toured musically, and then dove headlong into writing and producing fictional novels, as well as publishing a book of poetry, and this book as well. I would not have done that had I still been stuck in the rat rate of the voiceover community, which, for me, had become more political than a community.

When that happens, it's okay to say goodbye and move on. Sometimes, it's the healthiest thing you can do. And I daresay I'm far healthier now that I've made that break. Was I scared to do it? Yes. Am I better for it?

A resounding yes. Remember that phrase again, shared with me by agent Liz Atherton: "someone's endorsement of you – or lack thereof – has very little to do with your trajectory."

TAKEAWAY & ACTION STEP

"I can't tell you the key to success, but the key to failure is trying to please everyone." – Ed Sheeran

You can't please everyone. Who in your life are you (perhaps desperately) seeking affirmation from? Who do you feel is silently judging you? Resolve to be yourself anyway. Determine to lace up your bootstraps and soldier on despite perceived disapproval.

Organization: Your BFF

SPRAY ON SOME CLUTTER-BE-GONE

Back to reality for a second.

In any entrepreneurial pursuit, you'll need to get your ducks in a row once and for all. It's amazing how many people I see, as I go through this life, who are incredibly disorganized.

I'm very polite and respectful when I say this, but my wife is an *absolutely certifiable freaking disaster of epic proportions.* I love her, and I find her very sexy and cute and adorable and lovely. But she's an absolute mess at organization. The funny thing, and this is what is so amazing about her, is that she has the memory of a steel trap. I swear she is part elephant, though that praise is "hardly complimentary" as Wesley would put it to Buttercup. She never forgets. She is incredible at remembering even the most finite minutiae from a person's life that she's met only *once* in a crowded and loud diner. She's absolutely amazing that way. I remember scanning the menu deciding what to eat. She scanned the person deciding what to love. I am crazy about her for many qualities, and this one is at the top.

All that to say that while she never forgets about you, she's one hundred percent ridiculous about keeping things in order. I mean it. It makes me want to harm small animals. Towels strewn around the floor. Books and papers over there; the pens and bookmarks for them way over *there*.

Her: *Where did I leave my phone again?*
Me: *Honey, just use your Apple Watch to ping your phone and you can find it that way.*
Her: *Oh yeah!*
Pause.
Her: *Where did I leave my Apple Watch?*

I swear the woman needs to have every possession lo-jacked. But somehow, she remembers where everything is ultimately, whereas I will be the one resorting to the technology.

I routinely use the Voice Memo app on my phone to commit important thing to *its* memory, so that *it* doesn't forget them, because if I keep those important things in my own mind, I will most assuredly forget them. I make great use of Microsoft Outlook for all of my notes, contacts, calendar appointments, etc., so that I have complete organization over all of my life's affairs. My Windows Explorer file structure is impeccable. There are subfolders aplenty. All of the things – well, ok, *almost* all of the things – on my desk are at right angles. I can tell when something isn't right with the organization in my life. I feel off, and I need to get back to normal again.

How you choose to organize your billing, calendars, client folders, communication, auditions, marketing materials, and all of that, is ultimately up to you. But organize it, for goodness' sake. It's something that needs to be done, without question. One of the reasons I book so much is because I've streamlined my workflow. I'm not opening up Reaper and wondering which channel my plugins are enabled on. No: because I have templates that are ready-set-go. I have countless resources at my disposal that enable me to be productive. Here's just a few, and these will differ somewhat from Mac to PC, but there are of course comparable workarounds:

- Microsoft Outlook, for email/calendar/contacts/reminders
- Windows Explorer, for organization of client files
- A naming structure for auditions and files
- iPhone
- Keyboard shortcuts so that I don't have to type the same thing over and over again
- PhraseExpress on my PC that enables keyboard shortcuts there as well
- Microsoft Access database that acts as part CRM, part accounting software. This is something I designed myself, and is compatible with Microsoft Access in the Office Suite. Check it out at www.supervoiceover.com/firstvoicedata
- Voice Memo recorder
- Dictation on my phone
- Two different browsers to separate business from personal social media

- Passwords document
- Marketing folders and subfolders
- Zoho CRM online for mass marketing emails
- Demo Folders
- Video production folders for training materials that I create
- Assets for my authored blogs
- Assets for my authored books

There are many more, but these are some. This list is nowhere near exhaustive. The tools you choose to adopt for your own organization are entirely meant to shave time off of your day, so that you stop hunting and start finding.

Thibaut Meurisse, in his excellent book *Success Is Inevitable* (which I narrated!) talks about organization and about it becoming muscle memory. Check this out: "Deliberate practice and repetition creates a mental representation of patterns of information held in long-term memory. These patterns contain various elements - facts, images, rules, muscle memories or relationships - organized in a coherent way. Deliberate practice leads to the creation of effective mental representations which, in turn, enhance performances. For instance, mental representation allows taxi drivers to find their routes in complex cities and enables chess masters to play blindfolded."[117]

Once you develop a system of organization that houses everything important to you in a coherent layout, you'll be able to function in muscle memory. Free from clutter. Free from distraction. Free from insanity.

Organization is truly your BFF in business…and in many other facets of life. The sooner you get yourself organized, the less on-the-spot searching you'll need to do when it comes to it. The more ready you'll be to audition. The less consternation you'll cause yourself when you can't find something.

Finally, here's a tip. Get a great computer with lots of space and room to grow. This is an area where you can't scrimp and save. I love what John Malkovich's character says to a table of businessman in *In The Line of Fire:* "Your average American businessman... looks at a product, a marketing scheme, what have you...and he sees the length and width of it. The Japanese see the depth, the long-term effect. We look at the next fiscal quarter. The Japanese look at the next quarter of a century."

Don't be short-sighted and get something just because it's on sale or at a discount. If it doesn't have what you need *long-term*, you simply don't buy it. You need to look long-term. I don't delete files. I have all of them forever: all of my auditions, all of my produced client audio. Why would I delete that? Why would I delete communications in Microsoft Outlook that I might for whatever reason need ten years down the line?

Get something that accommodates your future, not just your now. Challenge yourself to spend a bit more to get what will take care of your needs for not just the next fiscal quarter, but the next quarter of a century.

Do yourself – and your clients – a favor, and get organized.

TAKEAWAY & ACTION STEP

"Disorganization can scarcely fail to result in efficiency."
- Dwight D. Eisenhower

Do you have a system where you know precisely where things are in the middle of your heap? Can you find what you need at a moment's notice? What in your life needs to be categorized, alphabetized, organized? Take stock of your current picture and set aside some time to clean up.

I Hate Burpees

SOME THINGS SIMPLY SHOULD NOT BE

I'd like to preface this chapter by stating emphatically, in no uncertain terms, that exercise (see definition: *cruel and unusual punishment*) is of the devil (see definition: *exercise*). I mean, let's be honest. There is no way the human body should have to tolerate such rigor in the name of the almighty beach bod. I have certainly never read in my *Human Being Instruction Manual* anything that mandated that I engage in any activities that make me lose bodily fluids faster than I gain them. I've read it, and it's just not there, so please. *Please.* I beg you: let me keep my flabby gut and saggy man-breasts.

Exercise falls into the same category as Yanni music. It's arguably unnecessary, you're bound to be let down, and, when played at a slower tempo, it may just stop your heart. Programs like "Insanity" are named that way for good measure. I believe P90X stands for *Probably 90 Minutes Left Until You Expire.* And Taebo means *Little Kicking Bird Who Eat Rice and Stay Thin Which Impossible Because Reason.*

But there is one activity that jolted back into my memory recently, which I must address. It's a topic of constant scorn and ridicule, because it's an activity that transforms the average human into one of those flailing inflatable tube men.

I'm talking about the shameful and indefatigably evil procedure known as the Burpee, and I would like to submit that it should only be for those in active-duty military because they are trained to be voluntarily abused.

My brothers and sisters, this activity simply should not exist. I was graced with an endoskeleton and a spine, which I am told are not supposed to bend like noodles. Perhaps I am different from other humans in that capacity. Mine are not capable of transforming into jelly at the whim of some barely accredited fitness instructor for the viewing pleasure of teenagers who come prepackaged with DNA that facilitates expert mockery.

Also, maybe it's just me, but any word that contains a suffix or prefix with the word "burp" in it is very funny to me. This is because I am apparently still 13. Burps are funny as early as age 4, and I can prove this to you by injecting Coca-Cola into my 4-year-old and then loaning him to you for an hour.

But whereas a burp may be inherently funny, the word "Burpee" tends to sap all of the happiness right out of me, especially when demanded by someone who is about as thin as a wafer, which is a thinness that I fear I shall never be unless I take a nap in front of a moving steamroller. I remember one instance where my fitness instructor told me to get some Burpees in, and she was alarmed to see that I had disappeared entirely, only to reappear in a few moments with a thick slushy ice drink. It is not my fault that she said Slurpee: my hearing appointment wasn't until the next day.

FIT AS A FAT FIDDLE

Why am I talking about this? Because we, as entrepreneurs, need exercise. We are very sedentary, because Entrepreneurs ultimately come from the same Latin origin of *Homeo Slothimus Collapsicus Dontcareicus*, which is where I believe the rest of all humanity hails from.

We don't want to do all that working out and sweating and needlessly perfecting ourselves, when our easy chair is *right there*, we've *already* got our triple-Eggnog-with-marshmallow-and-seventeen-Splendas-mocha, and we're wearing our Lycra spandex that highlights everything that is supposed to stay concealed to hide our oh-dear-God-put-that-away-my-eyes!-kill-it-before-it-spreads hideousness, spread out on the couch for Judge Judy reruns.

We're sitting and editing audio all day, and with each keystroke or mouse movement to edit those .wav files, waves of fat are developing in our underbelly.

And to compound things, a whole new year is here: full of resolutions that we will swear by on January 1st and will change our lives all the way through January 2nd, at which point a national forum will be held to abolish the politically-incorrect word, "resolution." They will in fact be resolved to remove it. (See what I did there?) But we must do our part to remove our fat, before it grows Violet-Beauregarde-style into a big round mess of near-bursting magnitude.

For me as a voice talent, I need air to breathe. Air comes from healthy lungs. Healthy lungs are positioned in close proximity to the stomach. If the stomach is bulging, healthy lungs cannot expand properly, depriving us of the ability to inhale air so that we can get up and grab our remote and chocolate and beer. My friends, you see how urgent and dire our need is. We **must** have our remote and chocolate and beer in order to survive. This is why my wife and I deliberately bore children, who we named Servant 1 and Servant 2. They are superb at fetching remotes and chocolate and beers.

So! Let's get physical. Thanks Olivia! Let me hear your body talk.

TRIMMING THE FAT

First things first, before we figure out how to make ourselves thin and healthy again, I must offer a warning. Be sure and steer clear of old people, as well as the elderly, who are old people dipped in malice. The reason for this is because they will tell you the truth about your physical fitness or lack thereof, whether you requested any such thing of them. For example:

Aaron: "don't I look good in this outfit?"
Old person: "why, no, no you don't. You should begin exercising at once so that you can start losing those 4,392 extra pounds of whale blubber."
Aaron: "I see. And may I ask why you just go on living and living with no end in sight?"

Or an alternate example:

Aaron: "What time is it?
Old person: "Oh my! Heavens to Betsy. It looks like you've gained even more weight than the last time I saw you!"
Aaron: "I see. Here. Drink this keg of Metamucil."

I mentioned such exchanges in a previous excerpt[118].

We need confidence to exercise, to commit to goals, to ensure that we're going to balance this sedentary career with lots and lots of exercise. In the pandemic world in which we're currently embroiled, we must get out and get some fresh air. *Breathe in, breathe out…*

Or…at least that's what the paramedic tells me when he finds me collapsed in a crumpled heap on the side of the road after having attempted a Burpee during my morning run, er, walk.

Now get out there and do some good collapsing! Entrepreneurs need air to read scripts! Go get some good air! And if you'd like to skip the exercising process altogether, they also have special supplemental oxygen tanks you can steal from old people.

Here's to great fitness with no burpees and more Slurpees!

HERE'S ONE TO GROW ON:

"Exercise should be regarded as a tribute to the heart."

Gene Tunney

The Biggest Myth In The Universe

IT'S AN ABSOLUTE F'ING MYTH

No, I'm not talking about Sasquatch. Nor am I talking about the Loch Ness Monster. I'm not talking about Comcast's delightful and exemplary (this one is a *super* myth) customer service. I'm not even talking about Santa Claus. Whoops, made a few people cry there. **pat pat, yes honey, Santa Claus is real, there there**

I'm going to expose something in this chapter that is a hard and fast, outright *myth*. Something that every single one of us, at least at one point, wanted desperately but have never had, and never can have, in any way, shape or form.

My life view and foundational guiding principles stem from an understanding that God is ultimately in control, and when I attempt to see this crazy, fallen, skewed and outlandish world through His eyes, I begin to understand more clearly.

A RECENT LESSON

If you read or had subscribed to my blog (ended in 2023), you'll know that we recently had a baby. All 6 pounds and 8 ounces of Baby Asher have rocked our world, and really impacted our lives, inside and out, through and through.

Our baby boy was born on Wednesday, June 12th at 10:21pm. His due date wasn't for another 10 days. Why did he come early? One word. Pitocin. Look it up. Ever got your coat caught in the doors of a moving vehicle? Did you have fun trying to keep up? Did you smile and sigh contentedly as you enjoyed the ride? Or did you scream your head off, begging for mercy, yelling, shouting, pleading for relief as you were stuck in that dang door and dragged well past your desire to be dragged, and well into fear? Yeah. That's what Pitocin does. You're just along for the ride, and you have to keep up, and you can do little else but try…oh and of course scream.

I already shared about our birth experience. It was not what we wanted. Then our baby boy decided to lose close to 10% of his weight (it's normal for babies to lose some weight after birth). Not what we wanted. He then decided to have nursing and latch problems. Not what my wife wanted. We would have totally liked for it to be absolutely perfect in every way, seamless, easy, enjoyable. It was none of those things, at all, in the slightest...not even close.

SO, WHAT'S THIS ALL ABOUT?

What's the myth, Aaron?

I'll just say it.

Control. That's the myth. To quote a longtime *pastor* friend of mine, Bill, "it's an absolute f'ing myth." (He actually said "f'ing", abbreviated....not the real one).

Us having control is an absolute and outright myth...and it's a lie. We never had it. We never will have it. Just like Ellie says to John Hammond in Jurassic Park: "You never had control: that's the illusion!" John Hammond was still under the impression he was pulling the strings. He was deceived.

Myth stands for:

Moves
You
To
Hallucinate

Seriously. Let's be real. There are known myths in this world, some of which I outlined above. Some you can't even see. Not because they're myths, but because they are principles that you cling to, and you proceed with an expectation that something is going to happen exactly your way, how you desire, according to your own worldview, interests and hopes. You hallucinate and expect that things will be a certain way… but you're living under an illusion that you had control, which you never did. It's that simple.

Nothing you expect is guaranteed to come true. Your dreams are most often doomed to failure and disappointment.

There. Have a nice day.

WHAT ON EARTH DOES THIS EVEN HAVE TO DO WITH VOICEOVERS?

It's simple. And I'll use plain speech this time rather than taking a while to get to it. In voiceovers, as in all other things in life, you have absolutely zero control. None whatsoever. Zero. Zilch. Diddly. Bupkus. Nada. Niente.

Think of it this way:

- When you get a speeding ticket, you have no control. You have to pay that fine.
- When you drop that glass on the floor and it shatters, you have no control. You must sweep and mop it up.
- When the price of gas goes up, you have no control. You must pay the new rate.
- When someone you love dies, you have no control. You must mourn, bargain, plead, be angry, then accept it and move on.
- When you're sentenced in court to do time, you have no control. You must serve your sentence.
- When your baby is born prematurely, you have no control. You must deal with it.
- When your preferred candidate isn't elected president, you have no control. You must persevere.
- When you receive that diagnosis, you have no control. You must decide to live through it, with it, or past it.
- When your car breaks down, you have no control. You must fix it.

These are just nine examples of the trillions that are out there. Here's where the rubber meets the road as a businessperson:

- When you didn't get that audition, it's because you have no control. You must suck it up and try again.

- When the role you were promised was then given to someone else, it's because you have no control. You must swallow your pride and keep auditioning.
- When your client doesn't pay their bill on time, it's because you have no control. You must respectfully follow up and be patient.
- When your client wants you to do the read one more time, and you've already provided him seventeen reads in a directed session, it's because you have no control. You must indulge them. As Marc Cashman says, "Always be unfailingly polite, and if the situation calls for it, joke a bit – you can usually tell whether or not the person at the other end has a sense of humor."[119] Remember, for that session, they own you. Sure, we all like to be supervised about as much as we like dental visits. But the client is paying for this service and they want it a certain way. It's your job to be friendly and to give it to them in a pleasant, engaged way, because *they* have all the control in the session.
- When you are marketing like crazy and things just aren't happening, it's because you have no control. You must continue to push forward and build for your future.

Don't spend all your hours looking back and wondering, or worse, resenting. Get back into gear, get up off the floor, mop up your tears, invert your frown, and move on.

Sure, you can drive by the speed limit, be more careful with your glasses, shop elsewhere for gas, take care of your loved ones, don't commit a crime, nurture your body for an optimum delivery, encourage all your friends and family to vote for the president that you want, change your lifestyle and eating habits upon receiving that diagnosis, and try to take better care of your car. This last one is actually the one that pertains to all of them: *taking care of*. You can try your very best to take the very best care you can of everything. But things break, *people* break, and they are bound to break, because all things eventually break.

When I step into my studio, each and every time, I say to myself "I've already been awarded these jobs." There's an intention there, sure enough. But what I also pray, each and every morning in my devotional, is "Lord, please turn these auditions into jobs." Does he do so each time? No, just like God does not necessarily love the Seahawks.

My best intentions will never trounce lack of control. They never will. They are limited to intention. Control is all-encompassing, and is *outside my control*. The *only* one in control, whoever was and who ever could be, is God Himself, because He's sovereign. So, the best I can do is trust and hope.

FLIPPING IT ON ITS HEAD

So since we can't have control, what's the opposite of control? What *can* we have? What *can* we do?

- Hope
- Trust
- Intend
- Pray

Hope that all will be well. Trust that your life and times are in God's hands. Intend to do your very best with whatever resources or people are in question, and then do it. Pray for blessing.

That's all you can do. That...really is...all you can do. The rest is left to God and blessing, or if you don't believe in God, then it's left to chance, and to a numbers game.

Janine and I hoped that Asher would continue to gain weight. He's doing much better now. We trust that his life and times are in God's hands. We intend to do the very best in taking care of him that we can. We pray for blessing. But the control over his life is not up to us. We can raise him the very best that we can, and he can be an absolute juggernaut of a man, handsome, powerful, influential, gracious, and confident.

- And then he can be hit by a bus and it is all over.
- And then he can purchase that one doomed plane ticket.
- And then he can die from cancer, or from murder, or from choking on the weirdest things.

Control is not up to me. It's not up to my wife. It's not up to you.

As an entrepreneur, I can flip control on its head by hoping, trusting, intending and praying. That's all I can do. That's all I can *ever* do in this lifetime. I can keep auditioning in hope, trust, intent, and prayer, knowing that I'm doing my very best and giving it my all. What I do not want to do is to get stuck in the rut of manipulating clients into hiring me....circling back again and again over that one job I should have had....revisiting and nursing old wounds from jobs that passed me by...hating that I've invested into something and I'm not seeing returns. All of that leads to the genesis of grudges and resentment and bitterness....and ultimately, failure.

On the subject of prayer, I can't stress it highly enough. My wife and I are unabashedly Christians. We thoroughly believe in the power of prayer, because we've seen the manifested results of doing so in our lives, and that includes bounty in voiceover jobs. Prayer is a link between you and your Higher Power, whoever that is for you. For us, that's God, the creator of the universe, who knows me well and knows what I need, loves me and wants to provide for me. Prayer puts me on a wavelength of gratitude, knowing that in my own skin I can only do so much; but when I send that request for provision upwards, I know He can do so much *more*. Prayer is critical for me in the success of my voiceover pursuits. It also keeps me in check knowing that it really is not, nor has it ever been, all about *me*.

I've talked about prayer already in this book. It's important. And control is a myth. It's true.

There are moments where I very likely should have died. In 1991 I dove off a rock with a friend in Mazatlan, out into the ocean, on a bet for 20,000 pesos, which back then was *six dollars*. You know, on a dare, to swim out where sharks and jellyfish swim. Upon my returning to the rock, a big wave came in and swept me off the rock and slammed me up against a smaller rock, scraping me all up and filling the water around me with blood, sounding the shark dinner-bell. And then, upon being rescued by someone with a life ring after treading water for about six minutes, on my way back up the rock I stepped on a sea urchin, and had my foot impaled by 30 tiny spines.

Another time, back in Washington, there was a big storm in the mid 90s. I was driving back from visiting a friend in Lynnwood, and my brother and I were in my little Honda CRX. We were in the midst of a tremendously gusty storm. After turning south off of 148th in Lynnwood onto Highway 99, I began to hear noises on the roof of my car like the pelting of small objects, and scrapes like tree branches.

I looked up, looked around, eyes wide open. It was then that I looked in my rearview mirror and literally ten feet behind me, in the place I had just been, a giant tree crashed down onto Highway 99. Those tree twigs and pinecones, and that giant trunk of a tree were meant for me. All I could say, repeated two hundred and forty-six times while looking at my brother in astonishment, was "oh...my...Lord...wow."

And then...there were the kidney stones. I don't even want to talk about those. Let's just say I could see the face of Jesus through the fog...thought I was surely "on my way out."

In the words of Michael W. Smith's song, *Everybody Free:* "It's only in surrender that our freedom comes." My dad once told me "Many years ago I had to decide to just release you three boys to the Lord; otherwise I'd go crazy." He's not crazy. He's *free*. Am I? Are you?

Give up control. Live free. Try, *sure*: don't *ever* stop trying. But allow yourself to know that Someone Else is in charge, and He has great big hands and abilities beyond the farthest reaches of your imaginings. He can provide for you in ways that you never could for yourself. It's called Hope. It's called Trust. It's called Faith.

I wouldn't call it "casting it out there into the universe" or even *The Secret*[120], but I've always believed that I'm going to make it. I have the utmost confidence that I'm going to be provided for. "I can see clearly now, the rain is gone." It's a weird intangible thing to explain, but if you proceed in belief and faith that you'll be provided for, nothing can stop you from seeing it realized. I *expect* provision. I *expect* greatness. When it doesn't happen, I'm a bit confused.

But it does. So, I'm not. *smile* I'm truly a blessed man whose focus has become his reality, all due to an unshakeable faith that he will be provided for, things will work out, bills will get paid, we *will* keep the house, the car *won't* be seized, and "all's well as ends better" like The Gaffer says in in *The Return of the King*.[121]

After church today there will be a nice potluck in the fellowship hall. See you there.

Maybe Depeche Mode Had It Right All Along

ENJOY THE SILENCE

A farmer I am not, nor do I pretend to be one. Do not call me a farmer. Straw hats would look about as good on me as a Michael Bolton song would look in any playlist of mine. It just does not belong, and I wish to delete the @#^$ out of it.

However, I now own a pasture. Owning a pasture, according to the Universal Pasture Owners Guide Edition 17 means, in some respects, that I have become a farmer, although this was never my intention, let me assure you, but it was my intent to use a lot of commas, in this sentence, particularly.

If you look at the sheer number of technological devices hemming me in on all sides, I am about as "City Boy" as they come. Apple knows this. The 18 Apple devices that we own assure Tim Cook on a daily basis that I am his willing and enslaved Apple Sheep for life. Baaaaa.

Ultimately, we moved to our new house for peace and quiet. And to get away. And because of Covid-19. And because we were paying too much. But mainly for peace and quiet. And to have a pasture.

I just never thought that having a pasture would bring so much serenity. We now live on 3.88 acres of complete serenity, minus the occasional thermonuclear practice runs by the local joint Air Force / Army base which sends my dB meter momentarily skyward. I have written about this before in my previous book, which you should now buy. Truly, living close to a military base keeps one on one's toes, and the occasional shellacking is a delightful reminder that my toes have not yet been blown off. Sidebar: Please take time today to appreciate your toes. I often feel that people are not grateful enough for their toes....but I'm sure you feel the same.

You see…often times in life, we do not know where we are. We are confused. We all turn into men (unless we are already men; in which case we just turn into weirder men), reluctant to ask for directions at the gas station. It is during these times that we need to sit down and just *breathe:* to take in the air and feel the stillness around us. For myself, I do this in my pasture. I sit in the grass and breathe. I relax. I enjoy the feel of nothing but wind and birds, and the slight tickle of that fire ant crawling up my leg that is about to meet its Maker.

My pasture is where I find Shangri-la. My pasture is where I find my peace. My pasture is where I find fire ants.

Maybe I am a farmer after all.

STOP TRYING TO FIGURE EVERYTHING OUT AND JUST BREATHE FOR CRYING OUT LOUD WHAT IS WRONG WITH YOU KIDS TODAY WITH YOUR LOUD MUSIC I JUST DO NOT GET IT AND MY ANGER AT YOU OVER THIS HAS TURNED THIS INTO THE LONGEST SECTION HEADER EVER

I sat there in my pasture and felt the pulse of my Apple Watch (see *enslavement* above) buzz against my wrist, signifying the arrival of an audition notice. I did not care, because I was there to untether and regroup. And kill fire ants by slapping them with a girlish shriek (see *weirder men,* above).

I have been a business owner since 2003. In that time, I have taken exactly eight vacations, not counting my honeymoon, which I am told is a requirement for you to be on once you have gotten married, or you risk your new spouse experiencing what is commonly known as homicidal tendencies. So, I painstakingly rescheduled all of my sitting around time to ensure that I would be there with her. However, counting the other eight vacations, that is only *nine vacations in 18 years!* The skinny of this overdrawn explanation is that I have not untethered and gotten away nearly enough. This is exactly why we planned a 2-week trip to Hawaii this coming July, for which I am both:

- as excited as an 11-year-old girl and

- confused as to why I switch genders and drop 36 years when excited

Sure, I have previously taken weekend camping excursions and such. On one occasion I was sleeping on logs and driftwood on the precipice of the Pacific Ocean, because my cousin and I had a daring appetite for danger, as well as no girlfriends to live for. I will never know why we did this. Bears roam the woods and also driftwood and also places by the ocean. Why we would combine all three of these factors into one dangerous place – *and sleep there, defenseless* – is beyond me. I was actually brandishing a toothpick, however.

The point? I think we as a species try far too hard to figure everything out instead of just relinquishing and relaxing. In all of my profound wisdom, let me help you untether. There are things which you will never understand, so it is best to let go and unwind. Here is the complete list of things you will never understand:

- Women
- Why there are interstate highways in Hawaii.
- People who listen to Michael Bolton (see *not ever going to be on my playlist* above).
- Men.
- The fact that *sour* cream has an expiration date. I do not need to explain this.
- All drivers on all roads everywhere always.
- Why you get a penny for your thoughts, but you have to put your two cents in. Someone is making a penny.
- The color of "flesh": It is not orange. It is not cream. It is not gold. We simply do not know what color flesh is, so we call it flesh, because we are original and inventive like that. Just the other day, I did not know what a device was called in my inherited tool-shop, so I called it Thing Which I Do Not Know The Name Of. I assume this also works for my children when they are bothering me. If they exhibit an unknown behavior I find annoying, it is called That Which Is Done By The Small Human That Boils My Blood. (Note: this label covers most of their behavior categories.)
- The correct way to mount toilet paper rolls on a dispenser.

- Why people ask me, "Can I ask you a question?" which is not a fair question, because they have already imposed.
- If lawyers are disbarred and clergymen defrocked, why can't electricians be delighted, musicians denoted, cowboys deranged, models deposed, tree surgeons debarked and dry cleaners depressed?
- Why lemonade has imitation flavoring, but furniture polish contains real lemon juice.
- Evolution. If man evolved from monkeys and apes, then someone please tell me why there are still monkeys and apes.
- Why I turn the radio down when I'm driving looking for an address.
- The word "Depeche."

SO...WHAT KIND OF MODE IS DEPECHE?

All I ever wanted
All I ever needed
Is here in my arms
Words are very unnecessary
They can only do harm

These are brilliant lyrics, and as entrepreneurs, it would behoove us to pay attention to them. When Martin Gore of Depeche Mode wrote this song, *yes:* he was talking about a relationship where he preferred silence. I personally believe it was because his girlfriend was talking during a WWII nature documentary which, for all men, is grounds for separation. However you slice it, his words ring true. "Depeche" means "hurry" in French - but maybe they knew that, and this song was their self-realization that they needed to slow down.

We spend all day talking. We spend all day listening to ourselves talking. We spend all day editing our own talking and listening to voices. Some might say we're schizophrenics-in-the-making. I say: we all need to untether once in a while.

Do you ever just pull the plug? Do you ever just venture outside for a walk and clear your head? All that marketing… that recording… that script perfecting… that analyzing… that headphone-editing… all of it… *just put it out to pasture.*

To me, relaxing out in our pasture is the perfect antidote to days where I bust my hump in marketing, contracts, auditions, networking, teaching, and paid jobs. Sometimes, it can get to be all too much. It's why I play relaxing Ocean Starfield[122] in the background of my office all day.

For me, I say "Depeche" means *hurry…to your place of Shangri-la.* Get there quick, and enjoy it. For me, that's relaxing in my pasture for a while, watching the green blades of glass blow back and forth noiselessly. I'll gladly lie in deafening silence and feel my chest rise and fall while I do nothing else. I'll unquestioningly hear my heartbeat in dull, calm thumps as I recharge my batteries before diving back into the world of technology. And if technology *does* creep into my head while out there, it will only be ruminations on the very best tech to completely annihilate fire ants.

Thanks for the reminder, Depeche Mode. Let us all enjoy the silence. After all, I am done speaking for the day, and words are very unnecessary: they can only do harm.

HERE'S ONE TO GROW ON:

"Sometimes the most productive thing you can do is to relax."

Mark Black

Psssst! Hey, Sellout! Yeah, You! Over Here!

THE FINE PRINT

Paul Strikwerda says, "People who only compete on price...are making a huge mistake. By doing so, they are devaluing what they have to offer, even before the client has had a chance to respond. As soon as you start competing on price, you treat your valuable service or product as a dime-a-dozen commodity."[123] He goes on later to say "Do you want your service to be known for being the cheapest on the market, or for high quality? Competing on price is a losing battle."[124]

It is time to toe the line, fellow entrepreneurs. More so than ever before. The continued erosion of the industry pay-scale is harming all of us to the point of near-irreparability. Low-ballers abound. Clients present contracts with "unlimited use in perpetuity throughout the known universe in all forms of media with unlimited cut-downs", and naïve, ecstatic tenderfeet swallow these contracts without question: hook, line and sinker.

"It is not uncommon for clients booking through Internet audition sites to offer a fee that, at first glance, may appear reasonable, but upon closer examination is little more than minimum wage for a considerable amount of specialized work." (That's from James R. Alburger again[125].) *Do. Not. Empower. These. People.* Help them see the light. Don't sell out. Stand your ground and know you are worthy of market rates.

Do not cater to these "clients that expect a gourmet meal at a fast-food price and at drive-through speed."[126] *You are worth more than that.* You don't have to be part of the erosion of industry rates just because you want to feed your kids or need something on your resumé. You are better than that. I and countless others implore you.

Sites like Fiverr capitalize on naïveté, and offer patently offensive rip-off bargain-basement pricing for national spots that they profit off of. Arguably, they are making the full amount, and paying us a pittance. Oh, to be a fly on the wall while they are doing their books.

I cannot count the number of times where I have traversed this particular course as detailed below:

- Receive casting notice
- Observe terms and stated usage
- Submit my audition and my bid commensurate with stated usage
- Receive confirmation that client wants to book me
- Gather information from client to create contract
- Generate contract with clauses that reflect usage stated in the casting notice
- Send to client
- Receive word back from client that either:
- The usage on my contract needs to be adjusted to reflect "unlimited in perpetuity", or
- I am required to sign *their* contract which states some poppycock hootenanny such as the following: "Artist acknowledges that client and their respective affiliated entities shall have the complete and unencumbered right, throughout the world in perpetuity, and in all languages, to distribute, record, reproduce, broadcast, transmit, license, sublicense, publish, sell, distribute, perform and use for any purpose, in any manner and by any means and formats and in all media, all or any results of Artist's services hereunder including any associated cutdowns or new versions, and to market, promote, exhibit and otherwise exploit all rights in and to the Recordings in perpetuity solely for Company's use, with no further obligation or compensation to Artist." In other words, they want to pay me a *specific limited amount* for an *unspecific and unlimited usage*. In the words of Dana Carvey doing former President George Bush Sr, "Nah gah dah."
- I inform the client that the casting notice stated very *specific* usage, therefore, I quoted a price commensurate with that specific usage, and were I to grant (by signing their contract) their *requested* usage, my price would have been much, much higher
- We dicker back and forth

- Client finally informs me that unless I can sign their contract or modify my own to agree to their expected usage, they cannot use me.
- I bid them a fond farewell.

I sleep better.

This has happened several times in my career. It is a freaking crying shame, a freaking irritation, and a freaking waste of my freaking time.

Let me tell you why.

TOW THE LINE

There are individuals among us who call themselves entrepreneurs - and are nothing of the kind. They will take any and every job that comes their way, in complete desperation, offering up what they call "quality services" to receive a few coffee bucks in exchange, simultaneously licking the fingers of their captors. They do not care to read the fine print or truly understand what agreeing to such terms (as I showed an example of above) would do to them or our industry.

These people are the cause of the rate erosion. They are DH's: and I do not mean Designated Hitters. They are Destructive Hobbyists: they do not care about their fellow man. They are in this entirely for themselves, and in the name of "it all adds up" and "I'll take what I can get", they lap up everything that comes down the pike: regardless of morality, ethics, or team-spirit; to say nothing of the extent to which their voiceovers may be used improperly.

Like a dog, they are undiscerning, indiscriminate, and need to be collared.

In short, they are *sellouts*.

Doubtless this chapter is going to ruffle some feathers, and the "live and let live" refrain will sound angrily. Nonetheless, I urge you, on behalf of [nearly] the entire ethical voiceover community out there, to *toe the line*.

Know your worth.

Visit and adopt the GVAA Rate Guide[127] or the GFTB Rate Guide.[128]

Develop a spine. Stand up for your rights and your rates! Do *not* sell out! I fully realize that some clients can be hard-nosed and run you through a garlic press in order to get you to comply. I realize that $500 might be a hefty paycheck for a job. But it is not – and in fact is an *insult* – if the *real* wages for that job are $10,000. Can $500 go far? Sure. Can $10,000 go much further and ensure that you can sleep at night knowing that you towed the line?

I once lost a job for $2400 because of a similar situation. Basically, the client wanted to use my voice, unpaid, over and over again, with no residuals or royalties...*or respect*. It just simply does not work that way. Am I upset that I lost out on $2400? Sure. Am I upset, however, that this client wasted my time? Yes. Do not dangle rotten carrots in front of me: I *know* they are rotten, and I am not blind.

It is so very important to have a contract in place. Will it cost you some jobs in cases where their feet are held to the fire? Most definitely. But again, we come down to it: you deserve to be paid market rates and you deserve to be paid for wherever and however long your voice is used. If a client has chosen you, that means they like you. If it is a high-dollar contract, even better. But both of those do not mean that you should throw the usage factor out the window. Yes, I could have used $2400. But I would honestly much rather have a client who appreciates the value of my voice, and is not prepared to take me for granted and steal from me, unpoliced. That is what is most important to me. That is what having a contract in place is all about. That is what having self-respect is all about.

In truth, I do not know how some "entrepreneurs" sleep at night. If you are in contract negotiations with a direct client, and feel you are being forced to relinquish all rights to your voiceover, *do not cave*. I have also had experiences where I stood my ground, and I reached Step 12 above...*at which point the client came back and* ***they*** *caved. They* relented. They took off their poker face, buckled under the pressure and decided to pay me what I am worth.

The fight is worth it. *Please*, I beg you: know your worth, and toe the line.

As voiceovers become further commoditized, our service value goes down, and the further our blessed occupation gets pushed onto the cheap shelf right next to destructive services like Speechelo,[129] Descript,[130] Vocal ID[131] and other wretched AI voice synthesis producers. We deserve better than that. We *are* better than that.

I am going to quote what Chris Mezzolesta said in his May 10th 2021 joint interview with fellow voice talent on Voquent.[132] This article is about Fiverr, but his thoughts are spot on:

*I can't imagine why anyone would want to align themselves with something that will telegraph either **cheap** or **amateur**, thus tagging themselves and their 'brand' with these attributes. 99% of my "competition" on Fiverr will be selling voice-over services for the price of a hamburger or maybe a #6 combo. Those hiring do so based on price and not quality. Most seem unaware of what a professional benchmark or standard even is. My years of experience in the business and investment into my skills and my pro home recording studio are incompatible with charging $20-$40 —or whatever— for a TV commercial. Even those who might read this comment and think, "Oh, this dinosaur doesn't get it at all, I charge $125 with the add-ons!". Which is still far below what the work is worth (based upon both SAG-AFTRA rates and surveys like the GVAA Rate Guide). Just because there is a new or disruptive way to do something does not mean it is better. And the anecdotal "But it works for me! It's none of your business how I do my business!" is also invalid. These are side-hustles, paid hobbies, not legitimate businesses if they harm others in the meantime, and that is what is happening. A voice-over recording has rights inherent in it that only convey to another party with the creator's permission (the talent). The Internet generation of voice talent has primarily not worked the legacy style of a union-only talent agency, physically go to a studio to record, etc. The mechanics of the trade are lost in the otherwise ease of PayPal & online casting and the rise of the 'digital branding agency' and the fall of the traditional 'advertising creative director'. Beyond the obvious and frequent abuse of these rights by taking a local radio spot and transforming it into a national TV spot. There is now also ambiguity around web usage, e.g. paid vs non-paid media and its* relation to broadcast rates. A talent can leave tens of thousands on the table just by booking through an online casting site that has snuck an automatic transfer of rights into their TOC. Whilst this is patently unethical, it is also harmful to talents – these rights are all we have, particularly in the non-union world. Protecting these rights is crucial. Saying NO to situations like a release of all rights, usage in perpetuity, or one fee for multiple "cuts, lifts, edits, revisions, etc." is difficult for the individual talent. We need talent agents and casting directors to step up and help protect our interests by pushing back when auditions are circulated. Lately, I've seen an increasing amount of capitulation by my agents, whom I love dearly, to the clients demanding these terms. We need them to be the first ones to say NO before auditions get to us so that we can better decide on the viability of an audition's terms. The client will only receive a voice-over at a fair rate for the amount of usage requested and the number of actual spots requested. We want to work WITH clients NOT against, but as equal partners at a fair rate for our work. Then, of course, there is a conflict of interest. It is a talent's business to know about conflicts and their ramifications so that voicing a campaign for one product does not put them out of the running for any other products in that category. Offering a buyout in perpetuity means you can never work for the brand's competitors that have your voice in their campaign for the length of time they run it. The fast path to the low-end VO business omits this and probably about every other crucial piece of information needed to run a good voice-over business. When the craft of voice-over is lowered in status to just another 'gig' on a 'platform', essentially becoming "McVoices", it hurts the industry as a whole.

Don't be a sellout. Be like Chris.

THE PROBLEM, OR THE SOLUTION?

I am not one for stern rebukes. We will *never* say "shame on you" to either of our sons, for any reason whatsoever. Guilt is about what you did; shame is about *who you are*. So, I do not want to pronounce that over anyone. But I will say that a stern rebuke is in order for those who continue to undermine the industry and do damage to these established market rates by selling out and undercutting everyone else.

There is one particular spring chicken voice actor out there that I detest; I won't name him by name, but he is blogging absolute toxic untruths and promoting the sellout agenda., whilst flying the flag of Voices.com in the process.

Update: three months later, he was nowhere to be found and his website was released back into the public domain. See?

We are all faced with a choice to make in our voiceover pursuits. Well, to be frank, not "a" choice *per se*, but with *many* choices. In fact, it is the exact same choice, over and over again, repeated throughout the day, and the week, and the month, and the year...with every single audition we submit.

Do we profess to care about preserving our industry and our fellow entrepreneurs, only to lowball and underbid on online marketplaces? Do we breathe fidelity and team-spirit out of one side of our mouth, whilst out of the other side of our mouth pledging to do whatever it takes —even compromise— to put bread on our own table?

Do we have spine, or are we sellouts? Will be part of the problem, or the solution?

Believe me, *I get it*. We all want to make money and provide. I am reminded of the scene in *The Abyss*, where Ed Harris' character "Bud", is trying to stand up to the powers that be floating up there on the surface, while his deep-sea oil rig is having unfair demands placed on them. The corporate powers on the surface of the ocean are "requesting" for them to go retrieve and disarm a nuclear missile from a sunken submarine.

The crew is all for it, but Bud declines, at which point one of the crew says, *"This is a paycheck, man!"* However, Bud vehemently states that "When it comes to the safety of these people, there's me and then there's God, understand?" He is adamantly opposed to the mission that they are being enlisted in due to its inherent dangers. But the crew protests because, it is a paying job.

I am also reminded of the crew of the *NSEA Protector* in *Galaxy Quest*, when discouraged by the behavior of their castmate, Jason Nesbitt (Tim Allen). They refused to take another job playing the same old stale "Star Trek" characters, but upon sitting in silence in a van together, they all have the same epiphany: we actually *need* this job. They end up caving and accepting.

Both situations come at a cost. For the first, it came at the cost of safety. For the second, it came at the cost of their standards. Both parties wanted the job though, no matter what it took. *I understand that!* I really do. However, the more you cow-tow to the continuing erosion that is our collective pay scale:

- the less professional you become
- the more selfish you reveal yourself to be, and
- the more you harm *all of us* by resorting to the gig economy mindset.

Your voice is not worth just a gig; your voice is worth **gold**.

For my own career, there have been weeks of plenty, and there have been weeks of want. There have been feasts, and there have been bare cupboards for Mother Hubbard.

I completely get the desperation that faces us in accepting jobs no matter the usage or what they will do with it. I get it! But I will tell you this: there have been times that I have rejected a high-paying job because of the inherent ensuing usage violations, and almost immediately on the coattails of that I was awarded other jobs that *did* honor me and my worth.

Audentes Fortuna adiuvat. May fortune favor the "foolish."

Tow that line, and see what goodwill comes back around to you in so doing. These rates were established for a market standard, and you are entitled to them, no matter the length of your tenure in voiceovers. Do not *ever* think that inexperience...or desire to just have *something* on your resume...or length of tenure...or equipment quality...or who you coached with, void your merit of market rates. None of these factors do.

As I have said before, the rates are the rates are the rates. Do not ever accept less unless *you* make that call for a good cause, with a clear conscience. And do not let *anyone* run away with your voice. Have a contract in place that ensures that your voice...your product...*you*...are protected.

We are all counting on us to toe the line.

HERE'S ONE TO GROW ON:

"It's called basic human decency, and I deserve no credit for doing what every man should."

Courtney Milan

I'll Give *You* Free Work!

WITH A SIDE OF SHAME AND A MEDIUM GUILTSHAKE

Free Work. I like to do it as much as I like having my eye poked out with a searing hot firebrand. It's not that I'm uncharitable or a hardened cynic, don't care or don't have time, it's just that I don't want to.

Especially in the case of pickups, when it's been a really long time since I recorded the original content, I've received payment, and we've both gone on our merry way since then. When the client comes back and asks for just a few teency weency pickups for free, I truly get a pain I can't locate.

More to the point, it's particularly irritating when any client also happens to throw in "We have very little budget for this" which are of course the most favorite words any contractor can ever hear. My favorite clients are the ones that can't pay me anything at all - but I'm sure you feel the same. They humbly request my holiest charity mindset. Little do they know that I've flipped that switch to "off" and ripped out the wall cabling long ago.

With a cringe and a specially perfected eye-roll, the first response that I'm inclined to provide is, "Why yes, I'd be more than happy to have you take advantage of me – thanks!" Their exuberant reply is sure to include:

- "Great! We knew you'd see reason"
- "Here's the script. There might be a few changes" which means the same thing as "Here's the script. There will be an incredible amount of burdensome changes that will require you to record and then re-record and then re-re-re-re-record everything all over again. Thank you once again for your holiest charity mindset."
- "You are doing the right thing" which means the same thing as "You will never escape my clutches and I have hereunto obtained you as my servant for all eternity. Please drive this awl through your earlobe."

- Next, I receive their copy, which is of course riddled with typos and pronunciations of names or nouns that could be pronounced no less than exactly thirty-six different ways. And, of course, there's the end tags that they want to be able to cover multiple markets, and would like me to record for free. *What's that, Aaron? Those cost extra? You mean you want to receive revenue for the professional work that you do? Bwwaaah-hahahahaha-hahahaha!!*

So how do I make it easier for myself?

The point in all this is that clients who undervalue you, or approach you with a predetermined limited budget based on their own valuation of your services, are not the types of clients you want, and you would be better served to pour hot molten lava over their telephones and weld plate steel over their mouths in order to prevent such requests from coming your way again. A rather violent and police-inviting solution? Perhaps. But at least you won't have to roll your eyes anymore.

Again, in his marvelous and required-reading book *"Making Money in your PJ's"*, Paul Strikwerda is quoted as saying that there are clients that "expect a gourmet meal at a fast-food price and at drive-through speed." Such clients irritate me. I highly recommend you purchase Paul's book. Right after you purchase mine of course.

I recently had to deal with such a client who has, for each of the three times they've approached me, explained in detail how they don't have much of a budget for this, times are tough, their children were just abducted by ravens, the mob found them yet again, and they are currently calling me with their voiceover requests while falling down an endless mine-shaft. (I had wondered what that sound of rushing wind was.) In any event, their pathetic pleas did not reach my heart, which has now been reinforced with cement and impenetrable guilt-proof ray-shielding. My response was "I do have my minimum session fee, and good luck with your mine shaft."

In the end, they paid my minimum session fee, and I think there was a trampoline at the bottom of the mine shaft, so it turned out well for both of us.

But seriously - what can we do to handle those pick-ups and make it worth our while? Here's how I do it, and this is the irrefutable way, so prepare to be world-rocked:

- Make sure to save the original files and settings from the first recordings
- Have a contract in place that specifies that if the word count is under a certain percentage (say, 1%?) of the original script, it's free. If it's over 50%, then it's 50% of the original script charge. If it's over 75%, then I change my legal name to Rumpelstiltskin and your child is mine. I can promise you that I don't get Imposter Syndrome, and your child *shall* be mine. *Insert maniacal laugh trailing off into an unguessable distance here*

And those clients who want you to work out of the kindness of your heart? Prepare to be world-rocked again:

- Explain to them that your voice is like a pilot of an airplane. That your voice is in fact the pilot who takes their message somewhere. That ultimately, they are entrusting their very message to you, and your services are immeasurably valuable in order to reach their target audience. It's your voice that is representing their brand, and you've been doing this for years, so you have earned the right to charge professional fees. At some point in your explanation, discover that they have hung up.
- When the client decides to brandish their "I can just go to Fiverr, but we'd rather use you" sword, carefully articulate that the client can indeed go to Fiverr, which is essentially the same place as Wal-Mart, where you find bargain basement pricing, unprofessional hobbyists, and nut-jobs who wear fish-net kilts and say things like "Does this mask make me look fat?" I was just in Wal-Mart recently, and I am not kidding: someone actually said this.
- For that one wonderful client who springs the non-profit argument, that they don't in fact have a budget for these sorts of things and that they are currently being eaten by giant salamanders so can I please just provide free voiceover services, get ready. Say the following, in this exact order: "Sir, A rough estimate of annual nonprofit sector marketing spending puts it at $6 billion[133]. You

aren't fooling anyone. Nonprofits are spending[134] an average of 4 cents on digital advertising for every $1 raised online last year and almost 70 percent of those advertising budgets were devoted to lead generation and new donor acquisition. So, good sir, I DO think you have a budget for these sorts of things, and I resent the fact that you are overinflating this "help a good cause" approach and in so doing attempting to get me to lower my rates so that you can keep your four cents. Good day to you, you cotton-headed ninny-muggin! Get 'em, salamander, get 'em!" Please note however that calling clients names generally ensures that you will not receive a voiceover job from them.

In the end, there will always be those people out there who want something of high value for free. Rather than be taken advantage of myself, I just encourage them to become a burglar.

TAKEAWAY & ACTION STEP

Anything of value comes at a price.

Unless you enjoy having your price whittled down and then being taken advantage of, make sure that you understand who you are. Don't sell out. Your services come at a cost. You know it, and they know it. Research rate guides and know how valuable you are.

Mentorship: Just Do It

YOUR FIRST (AND ONLY?) INVESTMENT

Coaching is the very first expense everyone in their right mind should always suggest to anyone who seeks to get into the voiceover industry – or ANY industry for that matter. You MUST have a mentor, plain and simple. It's the very first and perhaps the only thing you'll need.

Why the very first? Because it will pre-date any other expenses in your voiceover world by allowing you to have a sound evaluation and see where you go from there, before you spend a lot of money on hardware, software, resources, conferences, workshops, plugins, memberships, etc.

Why the very last? Well, because it potentially will *spare* you from spending any money at *all* on hardware, software, resources, conferences, workshops, plugins, memberships, etc., when you really don't have what it takes to be an entrepreneur in the first place.

Is that mean? No. Is it grounded and helpful in order to spare you certain harsh realities so that the dismal scene of you sitting in front of a mound of an unusable waste of expensive equipment doesn't become an even more harsh reality? As unpleasant as that reality might be (that you shouldn't be an entrepreneur), wouldn't you rather learn it now, rather than having spent a fortune on setting yourself up on a failing endeavor and eventually looking back in dismay?

Ultimately, coaching entails great, fun, enjoyable one-on-one sessions, so don't get me wrong. They talk about all the ins and outs of the voiceover business, what you should do, what they recommend, what they've learned, etc. They give advice. And, also, they give you an evaluation of your style based on a few reads that you do. All of that is in an effort to gauge your performance ability, your business acumen, your networking savvy, your social media prowess, etc.

It's all meant to tell you the truth: either to pre-screen you and then screen you out, or to pre-qualify you and give you a blessing of the wind at your back. Coaching is essential for you starting out.

WHY IS COACHING NECESSARY?

In any worthy pursuit, you want to, or at least you should, lean on those who've gone before. Learn from them. Adopt their habits. Practice their approaches. Learn from them and, in essence, reproduce what they do. The business model of replication applies here.[135] It is of the utmost importance that you learn from those who have gone before.

My coach, Scott Burns, is a wonderful man. He is *incredibly* generous. He totally modeled for me the importance of giving back to the voiceover community, and I can't thank him enough. He is astute, hilarious, encouraging, and an incredible cheerleader. But he also told it to me straight and didn't pull any punches. He advised me on what equipment to get, what direction to take, pratfalls to avoid, and techniques to master, as any good coach should. He is well-regarded and vetted in the voiceover community, which is something else you'll really want. The unfortunate byproduct of any endeavor is that there are those who go through the system and think that they know it all. They end up becoming predatorial in their aim to coach…and it ends up being all about the money for them. And sadly, there are two victims in such a tragedy: the mentee *and* the mentor. The mentee gets led astray; the mentor gets blacklisted. Neither are desirable outcomes. Therefore, you really do have to screen your coaches well, because there are "coaches", and then there are *coaches*.

Which one is the "coach"? Well, the coach can come in a few forms, but one of the worst is the well-intentioned coach who simply thinks that they're supposed to be a coach, but is ill-equipped to really answer questions thoroughly (or correctly), knows just enough to make them dangerous, and is not prepared to fully engage with their mentee. These "coaches" end up being basically just advice givers, and not all of that advice is good.

I once talked with an individual who wanted to get into coaching. I heard from three individuals who sent demo files to this individual requesting that they review them. They never received replies. Additionally, this individual's experience did not include specifically voiceovers; it was from a radio DJ background. And yet they felt they could coach voiceovers, even though they were just entering the field. Meaning no disrespect, but you can't coach what you don't know...and isn't it courteous to respond to people who send you demos to review, when that's exactly what you promised them that you'd do? A coach will coach even before they're paid for coaching. It's in their *blood* to help. It's not because of wanting to make more money. It stems from a genuine desire to teach and see the growth in *others*, not their pocketbook. It's their *calling* and their great delight to help people.

The advice-giving coach will fall dreadfully short on several counts, and you'll know fairly soon that you're not in good hands if you land with one of them. As Paul Strikwerda says, "Advice from friends, family, and other nitwits, no matter how well intended and pleasing to the ear, is probably the worst advice you can get."[136] Word.

It's been said that those who can't do voiceovers, teach voiceovers, and those who can't teach...teach *shop*. As Jeff Goldblum's character in Jurassic Park says, "*Your people were so preoccupied with whether or not they could that they didn't stop to think if they should.*" Lots of people think they can coach, but they never stopped to think if they *should*, nor did they ask anyone else if they thought that they should either.

Which one is the *coach*? Ah. The coach's coach. The one all coaches can relate to. The one who really truly believes in their client. A good coach will have a sound teaching structure and/or curriculum in place. They'll be invested in you! They'll check in with you between sessions. They'll have great scripts you can practice with. You can feel their energy in the sessions themselves, and the genuine desire that they have for you to succeed. And in many cases, they are prepared to walk you through demo production and produce a high-caliber audio demo for you. I am not a coach nor do I produce demos, though I do have the hardware, software and experience. What I would rather do is refer colleagues to Scott, who *does* coach and *does* produce demos. I know they're in very capable hands from that point forward.

For *any* entrepreneur, coaching is critical for your success. Like any entrepreneurial pursuit, there is a *lot* to learn. There's a lot to digest! Here are some things you'll learn in coaching:

- Technique
- Auditioning
- Contracting
- Rates
- Invoicing
- Running a voiceover business
- Marketing
- Warm-ups
- Cool-downs
- Recording environment
- Recording hardware and software

There truly is a lot to coach for anyone who is interested. While I don't coach, I do counsel on running a voiceover business. The cold hard truth is that you can get into voiceovers as a hobby and make a little bit of side money, or you can get into it as a business and make a six-figure income. I don't know about you, but I've made my choice, and it has five zeroes after it.

But it isn't just about running a business. You can come into a lot of money and sink it into buying all the right equipment, the right hardware, the right software, the right conferences, the right associations, the right memberships, blah blah blah. But in reality, you are absolutely talentless when it comes to voiceovers. Wouldn't it be prudent, before you start shelling out your thousands, to learn how to rake in millions through a voice that has been refined, that can impact people, that can communicate and connect and motivate and move, and has proven experience having gone before you? One that can show you how to truly lift words off the page and breathe life into them?

A coach will provide training to enable you to marry those two all-important T's: *technical* and *technique*. You can deliver a script with all the power in the world, but unfortunately, you're using a cheap Sharp mic and Audacity with no plugins, and your breaths haven't been removed and your plosives are all over the place and your ss's are too sharp and your mouth is clicking wildly. Or, you can have the most refined studio environment with the most expensive mic and hardware this world has ever seen, and your audio quality sounds fabulous! – but your technique sucks, and you don't connect. To quote Paul Strikwerda once more: "A good coach does more than teach an old dog new tricks. Rather than create a clone, a good coach taps into your unique potential and draws things out of you that you never even knew were there."[137]

You really do want to marry those two T's and ensure that both of them are top of the line, if you want to stand a chance in getting your audition through to a decision maker. A coach can give you the tools to deliver those scripts well, and help you with hardware recommendations and plugin settings to make sure your sound quality doesn't get in the way of your performance.

Coaches. Are. Essential. Get coaching first, then demos made, then website, and then start marketing and auditioning. Don't hit the ground running naked. Get clothed with skill, covered in quality, and equipped with tools.

Do I still have a coach? Yes. It's Scott. Do I still need a coach? Yes, I do! Even after all this time, yes, I do. Coaching is critical to refresh, to revisit the fundamentals, to retrain, to *de*-train (meaning, to remove assumptions and routine delivery that has gotten rusty), and to refocus. Marc Cashman mentioned an article he read where the author was talking about the difference between teaching and coaching, where in teaching "there is the presumption that, after a certain point, the student no longer needs instruction. You graduate. You're done."[138] Not so with coaching! Coaching goes on. Coaching can be revisited. Coaching is necessary to refine you and make your blade sharp again.

Don't have a coach? Get a coach. Every good student needs a good teacher. I will never stop recommending Scott Burns. Contact him today at scott@bookscottburns.com.

In my best commercial copy sounding voice: "You'll be glad you did."

In Search Of

ALWAYS SEARCHING

"The answer is out there, Neo. It's looking for you. And it will find you, if you want it to."

These words were spoken to Neo by Trinity in the 1999 movie, *The Matrix*. Neo was searching, apparently night after night, for Morpheus. Trinity came to him amidst that search.

Did you know, as of April of 2021, Google now processes over 40,000 search queries every second on average which translates to over 3.5 billion searches per day and 1.2 trillion searches per year worldwide? The chart below shows the number of searches per year throughout Google's history:

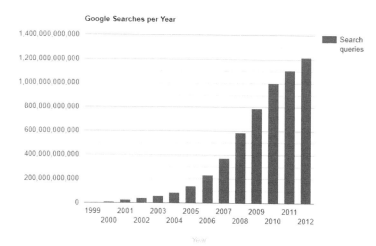

139

In 2020, the top 10 searches were:

- Coronavirus
- Election results
- Kobe Bryant

- Zoom
- IPL
- India vs New Zealand
- Coronavirus update
- Coronavirus symptoms
- Joe Biden
- Google Classroom[140]
- Why is Aaron Ryan so incredible? Ha! I am joking. I made that last one up.

People are truly searching every day for everything. The answer is out there, Neo.

Your clients are searching for voiceover talent. They're searching for ways to improve or augment their business. To streamline their marketing. To cut down on overhead. To better reach their target audience. To network and refine. To eliminate wasteful spending and better manage resources.

People are searching for meaning and answers. You may use Google to research political news, status of the stock market, information on upcoming movies, ways to eliminate mold, best local auto repair shops, find the best streaming service, check reviews on a company, look for a treatment for inflammation, ask about daylight savings dates, inquire about sports scores, etc.

But Google is so much more than that. They can be one your greatest sources for new clients.

What answers are you searching for in voiceovers? Did you know that you can truly use Google to improve your business? Here are some things that you may not have already known:

- Did you know that you can use a tool like *SearchTempest*[141] to scour all of Craigslist for voiceover jobs or gigs?
- Did you know you can search, from your clients' *clients'* perspective, "I need an explainer video made"? That is what some of your clients' clients will be searching for. That will take them to someone who produces Explainer Videos. And searching as your clients' clients do, will take *you* to *your clients*.

- Did you know you can search for E-Learning directories and find producers who produce content for you to narrate?
- Did you know you can create a Google Local page and create a listing for your business that allows Google to "see you" and index you, and in so doing, local clients can find a local entrepreneurs that way?
- Did you know you can use an E-Mail Spider such as *E-Mail Extractor 6* to crawl such directories in order to pull down viable e-mail contacts to harvest and market to?
- Don't want to pay for ads on Google? Did you know you can place organic ads on places like Craigslist and Yelp (I personally despise Yelp, so choose wisely on this one), Bing Places, Pinterest, Instagram, Twitter and more, Locanto, Geebo, OLX, Oodle, and more, which Google can index? Check out this site for an exhaustive list of where people can search Google to find your VO business.[142]
- Did you know that Craigslist and Angie's List, two leading providers of paid listings for contractors, have posts that Google will index, so you can search there and pull up a broad range of people who can help you with your VO business, such as marketing specialists, branding experts, CPAs, and more?

Get to know Google better. Yes, you can get a ton of business by referral and the good word of a trusted colleague in a Facebook group. But those answers take time and conversation. Not to say they're not worth it: they are! You may just be able to find your answers, and your clients, quicker – through Google.

Happy searching. The answer is out there, Neo.

HERE'S ONE TO GROW ON:

"They call us dreamers, but we're the ones who don't sleep."

Emma Rose

Quitcher Whinin'

CRYBABY

Don't use social media to complain and lash out with all caps and multiple exclamation marks. Donald Trump does (or did) that. Are you Donald Trump?

I see it all the time. People with expectations invest into something and they get *super* stoked about it…only to crash and burn when it doesn't meet their expectations, shake their fist at the wind, and go on massive tirades online with multiple exclamation marks and ALL CAPS to prove how disappointed and incensed they are. On the one hand, I get it. I do understand let-downs and regrets. But why is the de facto response to jump on Facebook and scream at the world?

Do we really feel like we're rallying people to our cause by screaming and flailing our arms like a madman?

Are we that insecure that we need people to side with us in our grief, so it's important that we employ five exclamation marks and all caps after everything we say, just to underscore our fury?

Is there a better way?

A SOLUTIONS MINDSET

Those with a Solutions Mindset can overcome anything. They may experience momentary setbacks like the rest of us, but they overcome. They push on. They find ways through the maze. They take the Kobiyashi Maru approach – the "I don't believe in the no-win scenario", like Captain James T. Kirk once said.

Confession time. I was once in an Anger Management course. Don't judge me or it'll just tick me off. (See how much I've grown?) One of the core teachings from that course is that all events are inherently neutral. What tilts them either to positive or negative is the emotion we assign to said event.

If we can assign objectivity to any given event, then that event is a *neutral* event to us. Our response then is conditioned on the neutrality of the event, and we get less bent out of shape that way.

CRYBABY

Finally, here's the most important point of this. As a trusted storyteller, you have a great responsibility. Not just to carry the message, but to carry the brand. You're a brand ambassador! Does a brand ambassador post all-caps tirades about that undesirable political candidate, on the same social media channels as their business? Does a brand ambassador use profanity and vulgarity? Does a brand ambassador project an air of defeatism and woe-is-me when their studio fails, their equipment fails, their project fails, their bank account fails, their life fails?

No. A brand ambassador needs to develop a Solutions Mindset.

Those with Solutions Mindsets don't freak out and tell the whole world how miserable their situation is in order to garner support for their cause, in a desperate attempt to encircle themselves with huggers and reassurers. They aren't stopped dead in their tracks with mascara dripping down their cheeks in rabid wretchedness. They solemnly assess, they painstakingly arrange, and they responsibly restart. It's like ants in a hive: the moment you kick over an ant hive, they will immediately start to rebuild. Like the comedian Brian Regan says, you would think at least one of them would stop and look up at you and scream *"Oh MAN! I can't believe it!! LOOK AT THIS!!!"* No. They rebuild.

Your clients are watching what you post as well. On the one hand, they may just mute you. On the other, they may decide to drop you from their roster. We've all heard stories of employees fired for their conduct on social media, or in life. Do you want to be that guy or that gal?

Negativity repels. Positivity attracts. There is absolutely nothing wrong with having a devil's mindset or looking at things with a fair degree of skepticism: after all, it's the cynics that keep us from turning into lemmings. What *you* don't want to become is the cynic who derides everyone else for trying. Who is consumed by jealousy. Who is seething with envy.

Who cannot seem to embrace any setbacks as learning opportunities or chances at growth.

Don't be that guy or that gal.

Quitcher whinin'.

HERE'S ONE TO GROW ON:

"When you can't find the sunshine, BE the sunshine."

Unknown

You'll Never Get A 100% Job From A 50% Attempt

HEDGING YOUR BETS

I'm going to use a voiceover audition as an example for this chapter, but this chapter pertains, for example, to when you submit a resume, when you interview, when you contact someone to connect with them, when you try out for *any* position you want to achieve.

When we audition, do we count on actually being cast in that role? When we interview, do we count on being hired? Is it something that we really want? Or are we cavalier, just rapid firing out multiple auditions so that we'll *maybe* get something here or there, hedging our bets as it were, so that it will kind of work out for us one way or another? Casting a super wide net to reel in at least one minnow? Paul Strikwerda offers the following: "If your custom demo (audition) sounds too rushed, you won't be considered. If you take too much time to perfect every second, you'll miss the boat."[143] It's about balance.

I recently had a conversation with a colleague and they were telling me that they don't ever really give their "all" during an audition; they save it for the actual read. I had to scoff at their logic, for obvious reasons. I literally made a scoff sound, which sounds something like a cross between a gag and a profound urge to pee.

Huh? Saving it for the actual read? *Mon ami*, you'll never get to the actual read without giving it your all to get there.

You can't get a 100% job from a 50% audition.

THE PRODUCER'S CHAIR

Let's look at it from the Producer's perspective for a moment. You know they're developing audition fatigue as they go through the onslaught of submitted auditions. You know they're losing the will to live as they *next-next-next* their way through scores of them. Is it reasonable to assume that you, appearing in their lineup with your half-baked and noncommittal audition, are going to make the slightest impression on their casting choice?

They say there's a lead line. Michael Bell says the following:

One thing I've learned is that your VO audition must capture the casting director's attention in the first 10 seconds or they will not listen to the rest. They simply don't have time.[144]

And he's right. If you don't, you're a goner. Literally, you're dead in the water, and the producer will never even remember your name. You'll never even get to the "Money Line" (as Bill DeWees calls it)[145] before you're shot down.

But how about this. How about if you, with all of your muster and luster and bluster, can take that audition, supercharge it, and make such an impression that they have no choice but to remember you?

Your goal is to knock 'em dead. Not to knock 'em somewhat sleepy.

IT'S ALL OR NUTTIN'

Armageddon. Lord of the Rings. Mission Impossible. Raiders of the Lost Ark. Empire Strikes Back. Cujo. Close Encounters of the Third Kind. Taken. Tootsie. Aliens. Meet the Parents. E.T. Finding Nemo. Star Wars. Blair Witch Project. It's a Wonderful Life. The Goonies.

Name *any* movie, and you'll recognize that there's a plot. A goal. A mission. The protagonist(s) in any movie has a mission that they must accomplish, and they must go on a journey of self-discovery in order to get there. They must change and grow and learn. And they're committed to their goal(s) and their mission(s).

Just because you're not in the movie yet, should your audition be with any less feeling? It's Sam saying, "No, Mr. Frodo. But I can carry you! Come on!" And then Sam slings Frodo over his shoulder and carries him the rest of the way up Mount Doom.

Half-baked food doesn't taste very good. And half-assed attempts don't resonate with anyone. If your goal is to get in, why would you be content with just quietly knocking at the front door?

There's so much more to say on this – but is there? Is it really necessary? It's simple. There's no getting around it. You can't *almost* your way into a role. You can't *kind of* do it. You *intend* your way into a role. Otherwise, you intend your way into frustration.

I HAVE A LOT TO GIVE. SO, HERE'S A TINY LITTLE BIT

Every role, every time, in every way requires everything you've got. You've paid that membership to that P2P. You've contacted that client and swore that you could do something marvelous. So, live up to your investment and promise.

Chew on these examples:

- Baseball's heavy hitters don't swing for the infield, hoping to lazy-lob one.
- Football interceptors don't race across the field, planning to stop in the midfield.
- Basketball players don't charge down the court, wanting to just stand under the hoop.
- Politicians don't run for the presidency just so they can increase their Twitter followers.
- Top chefs don't strive to make the best Top Ramen.
- Tourists don't go to Rome and hope to avoid the Coliseum.
- Fishermen don't cast their line out, wishing for minnows.
- The Beatles didn't take their music to America, desiring to play only in garages and talent shows.

Entrepreneurs don't hope to do a mildly acceptable job. Is it risky to give your all and put yourself out there? Sure. But the cold truth? You have more to risk by not risking.

It's called giving your all. It's called going the distance. They call it 100%. There's no such thing as conserving your energy in voiceovers. The audition maketh the job. Go forth therefore, and give thou in all thy fullness! *disengages King James mode*

Focusing While Working At Home

If you are determined to make it in any field, you have to be prepared to say NO to distractions and keep your eye on the prize." – Paul Strikwerda[146]

WHAT'S TO BE DONE?

Close the door to your office.

Turn off your phone notifications.

Untether.

Detach.

Remember what your end goal is.

You're welcome.

Your Makeup

I TAKE MY MAKEUP WITH ME EVERYWHERE I GO

Do you wear makeup? What type do you prefer? Do you like mascara? Eyeliner? Lipstick? Rouge? Foundation? Blush? I apparently have raided my wife's makeup carousel.

As an entrepreneur, I *love* my makeup. It helps me feel confident! I wear it because I am ready to take on the world when I wear it. When I wear makeup, I feel equipped and valuable and a person of worth. I especially like that cucumbery stuff. I feel saucy.

Why do you wear makeup? Do you wear it because otherwise you fear people tossing out phrases from Wesley in the Princess Bride ("you warthog-faced buffoon", "Dear God, what is that *thing*")?

Or do you wear it because you're supremely confident in how it makes you feel?

HOW MAKEUP HELPS ME

What does makeup do for you? Does it:

- Make you feel pretty?
- Equip you with confidence?
- Help you be social?
- Impart abilities you didn't have before?
- Allow yourself to be more than you were before?
- Help you really let loose in the studio and be that *saucy* individual you've always wanted to be but were too shy to be in front of people?

As an entrepreneur, I could not survive without my makeup. I really must have it...day in and day out.

My makeup is absolutely *critical* to who I am as an entrepreneur.

WHAT'S MY MAKEUP?

I think by now you've discovered that we're not talking about prettying up your face. That would be too easy.

Actually, we're talking about what makes you, *you*, and me, *me*.

As an entrepreneur, I can look back at my entire life and see skills and tendencies and behaviors and formative experiences that have led me to where I am, and *who* I am, today. They've brought me to today, with a whole host of knowledge and skills and insight and perception and readiness to be who I am, and to be successful at what I want to do.

Since I was a child, I thought a certain way, I handled things a certain way, I behaved a certain way. Through the myriad jobs that I've worked at in my years, including *fourteen* of them from 2003 to 2007, I kid you not - they've helped me assemble a cache of skills and abilities to be successful at voiceovers.

I see administration and management from the associated jobs that I've had in management. I see creativity in when I was a professional singer. I see continuous laughter and comedy from my youth.

I see leadership and guiding people from the teaching roles I've held. I see marketing prowess from the various marketing jobs that I've held.

All of this goes into a melting pot that is called Aaron Ryan, Seattle Voiceover Artist / Voice Actor / Voice Talent / Author, or whatever it is that you choose to call me. I choose to call myself a professional male Voiceover Artist & Author - and with that moniker comes a lot of history.

A lot of background went into who I am today, and I can confidently assert that I was made, nay, *destined*, to be a successful voiceover artist and author. I can see the:

- administration and management I've learned – equipping me to run a business soundly

- creativity from my singing and artistic days - equipping me to design my logo and imagery, my business branding, my letterhead, and my marketing materials
- laughter and comedy - funneling into many of the performances I've done, and equipping me with inspiration in the posters, memes, infographics and blogs I create
- leadership and guiding people - equipping me to teach and hold workshops, encourage and provide voiceover video consults
- marketing prowess - equipping me to reach out to customers and engage in self-promotion to provide work for myself

All of this comes from confidence in past traits and learned behaviors. All of this comes from formative experiences, learned behaviors, studies, traits, applied practices, and everything that goes into making me, *me*. All of this comes from my *makeup*, which I wear proudly.

WHAT'S YOUR VOICEOVER MAKEUP?

What went into you? What makes you unique and allows you to be successful? Can you look back on various jobs that you've held, and recognize and pinpoint formative elements that are assisting in your success today? How about the opposite? Anything holding you back, based on what you've learned, been taught, or experienced?

You can have new wiring...you can have new makeup. It could be that many of those negative formative elements can actually be flipped on their heads and you can - albeit perhaps with some determined effort - focus in on the inherent positives within them.

Maybe adversity taught you resilience. Maybe hardship taught you to push through. Maybe depression and isolation are currently teaching you that it's actually ok to lean on others, and that there is such a thing as a safe place to land, as my poetic, wordsmith (as well as sexy, beautiful, wonderful, fantastic) wife likes to say.

There are myriad voiceover communities on Facebook and elsewhere that would just love to reach out to you and offer you support in your race to be free.

Today is the day to recognize your makeup and wear it proudly.

I'm Aaron Ryan, and I approve this message. And my makeup.

Living The Dream

PINCHING MYSELF

I wake up every day at 5am. Wait - no, I don't. I have an infant. So, let me restart. I wake up every day at 2:20, 2:55, 4:20, 4:25, and then again at 2pm because I no longer care about anything.

Kidding. I usually wake up promptly at 5am and get started with my day, if my infant and preschooler allow me to, that is. I wake up looking like I slept with a coat hanger in my mouth because *I can't believe I get to do this and get paid.* Voiceovers truly are the good life.

I've had weeks where I've slaved and slaved away and done 150 auditions and come away with $700 in jobs. I've had weeks where I've done literally nothing and come away with a $5000 job. I've done work for 7 minutes – seven minutes, mind you – and been paid $4000. It's absolutely amazing. I've been signed by agents, I've influenced and helped many, I've taught, I've listened, I've learned, I've encouraged, I've grown. As an artist, it's the best thing in the world to grow and develop. It's amazing what one can learn when one is still receptive. Ray Kroc of McDonald's fame once said "When you're green, you're growing. When you're ripe, you rot." *Que profunde!*

I truly am living the dream as an entrepreneur. I pinch myself when I wake up. I have to face the reality that I'll probably never retire because it's such "easy" work…but then again…would I want to? No. I think I'd like to be buried in my studio when it's my time. That would be fitting.

FIND WHAT YOU LOVE TO DO

The old adage is true, "Find what you love to do, and you'll never 'work' a day in your life." I so love that quote with all my heart. It's been key to me with voiceovers. I've never worked harder, and it's not even work. It truly isn't! When you're doing your passion, it doesn't feel like work. It feels enjoyable, rewarding, intrinsically satisfying, fundamentally fulfilling in a profound sort of wake-up-happy sort of way. Your blood pressure benefits. Your body benefits. There's a spring in your step. I think I'll probably live longer because of it. (But then do bury me in the studio, please, when it's time.)

I have to say this in all sincerity. I came from a place of some deep darkness. A place of dreadful despair, indeed. What is that place? I'll tell you. It's called "filming weddings." See? Horrible. That was a place where once upon a time I was flourishing, once upon a time it was my passion and I loved it, and I was making good money. But ultimately, it's a place that is full of emotional narcissism and stratospheric levels of immaturity. I was trapped in this career, and I didn't see a way out.

So, I threw it all away.

It was easy, really, because voiceovers were now paying our bills and providing for us. It was a hallelujah moment when I booked my last wedding. When we filmed our last wedding. When we packaged up and mailed our last wedding DVD's. When we said goodbye to the domain names and camera kits. I didn't need weddings anymore, because I didn't need the headaches anymore. In fact, scientists have now concluded empirically that wedding videography businesses and headaches are actually the same thing.

All along, while I was doing wedding videography, I was doing voiceovers. I just never thought of providing them as a service unto themselves until 2016. And since that time, I've thought of *nothing else* for my career. I'm so tremendously grateful – which is a theme I'm sure by now you've noticed is incredibly prevalent in this book: gratitude – for what voiceovers have brought to my life, my confidence, and our bottom line. It's had an immeasurable impact on our financial success and my creative joy. It's been what I've dreamed of. It's all I want to do from this point until I'm room temperature. I don't actually see myself retiring because it's a career that is so fulfilling to do, and I have everything I need to do it well. Until the AI voices take over, I'll be here, fighting the good fight.

Bill DeWees pens "You can't think of it as messing around behind a microphone just to see what happens."[147] So the question you have to ask yourself: do you want to do this? Do you *really* want to do this? Not try it out, but do it? As Yoda said, "No. Try not. *Do*, or do not. There is no try." Many people are told "Hey, you've got a great voice, you should do radio" and they figure, well, this must be it. So, they choose to "test out the waters" on voiceovers. (Believe it or not, to my recollection I've never *once* been told that). They try it, and then they un-try it. They don't realize that it's not about your voice at all. It's about how committed you are. Taking my cue again from Paul Strikwerda, here's a great excerpt from his book:

"Take it from me. It's not about the voice. Having a nice voice certainly helps but it's such a small piece of a big puzzle. Owning a Steinway does not make you a pianist. It's what you do with it that matters. Being able to play a few notes doesn't make you a musician. Only a few musicians will ever make it to Carnegie Hall. Once you're ready for Carnegie Hall, you still have to beat out the competition."[148]

It is most certainly *not* about having a good voice. That's just the tool that you use. You run a business with your mind.

Talk is cheap. Work is valuable. Are you ready to do the work?

Goonies Never Say Die

WOMP-WOMP-WOMP

We all know that sinking feeling. Ever play Super Mario Bros? Pac-Man? Space Invaders? Frogger? Other games from the 80's because I have no idea what the cool games are now? Seriously, it's the truth. I am no longer familiar with what falls under the "cool" column. Once, ages past, when puppies were the oldest animals, I was sure of myself, and the word "cool" conjured up all kinds of things that were universally acceptable. Now, the only universally acceptable thing I can conjure up is The Goonies. Oh snap – that's from the 80's too.

Speaking of the 80's. Wave hair. Gotcha pants. Tie-dyes. Lionel Richie's "All Night Long." The trifecta of The Material Girl, Michael Jackson, and Prince-who-eventually-became-the-symbol-that-no-one-could-pronounce-so-we-all-just-said-whatever-and-still-called-him-Prince. The *original* Battlestar Galactica. The *original* "V" Miniseries. The *original Beaches.* The *original* Poltergeist. The *original* Pet Sematary. E.T. All the games mentioned above. "New" Coke, which was essentially Old Coke soaked in desperation. And of course, the *original* Transformers. (All hail Megatron.) Remember when life was good? I do. The only super concerning thing then was engaging in full thermonuclear war with Mikhail Gorbachev's forehead birthmark. For the record, I think we could've taken It.

But we all know the pain. To quote Linkin Park's song *In The End* (hey, I jumped back to the future! Thanks Marty McFly!):

"I tried so hard, and got so far, but in the end, it doesn't even matter…"

We've all played those games and gotten up to Level 238 where we were set to face off against the Sinister, Not Nice, Fire-Breathing Ooga-Booga-Dragonlord, and we bit the dust. We could only bury our face in our hands and weep bitterly as the wind was sucked right out of us. We were crushed – if only for a moment – because then we saw it, as but a glimpse through our fingers.

Light streamed down from the heavens as we realized with blessed hope that God saw fit to grace that blessed Atari controller with that magical button that would stop time…hold us mesmerized…breathe blessed life into our wills again…and start us back at one, restore our energy meter to full, allow us to respawn in a new place, and begin the quest anew.

What was it, you ask?

THAT BLESSED RESET BUTTON

Goonies never say Die.

Sean Astin became galaxially (it's a word) famous (so is that) after uttering those four words in Steven Spielberg's classic. The way I see it, there are two truths in that phrase:

Goonies never say Die, meaning they just don't say it because Death is not an option…meaning they're alive and well and among us today. Which would make sense, except that Aaron Brolin played Brand in Goonies, and then he played Thanos in Avengers. But Thanos clearly died, having been reduced to ash, which means Brand must have too because they're both the same person, so ultimately a Goonie truly can die. Or, *Goonies never say Die,* meaning they're not allowed to, because once upon a time, waaaaaaaaaaay back in the early years, one of the original members of the early species of Homo Goonicus Sapienus dared to utter the word "Die" amongst his clan while chanting naked with sticks, and was cast out, because that's clearly an English word and they were only allowed to speak in grunts and wheezes back then. They even took his naked chanting stick! Jerks.

Either way, death is not an option, or at the very least, it's not to be spoken. So how does this apply to entrepreneurs?

Well…

Gimme a minute… I'll think of something… *pause*

Aha! I have it! *Entrepreneurs never say Die!*

Phew. Dodged a bullet there, which could of course make me di-uh....perish. (Phew! Dodged another one).

Even when you're down and out and no auditions are coming in, and no agents are signing you, and no jobs are being awarded you, you, valiant knight, can reset. You just have to mount back up on that flying ostrich, and *Joust* your way back into total Voiceover world domination! It's always a matter of just-keep-playing. As long as you have enough quarters, that is.

The Goonies represent the best of adventure, youth, tenacity, and belief. When I was a boy, my dad affectionately used to call me "Goona." I don't know why, because he made up a lot of strange and bizarre coinages that only increased in weirdness as I began my slow march into adolescence. But I can't shake the inescapable feeling that he was really, all along, unbeknownst to me, intentionally mispronouncing it. He was really calling me a *Goonie,* and pronouncing adventure blessings over me. The alternative being that he is of course certifiably insane; but then again, to all adolescents, all dads are.

ENTREPRENEURS NEVER SAY THE D WORD

You're an Entrepreneur. You're made of stern stuff, do you know that? You've willingly, intentionally, deliberately chosen a career fraught with risk of failure. People bounce in and out of this industry all the time, over with and burnt out quicker than Britney Spears & Jason Alexander's marriage.

A lesser person would choose to play basketball for a career. Or be a doctor. Or run for president (I'm not implying anything with that one). But nooooooooooo....you went and chose something that is destined to kill you. To make you di-...um....perish. What is that career?

Voiceovers!

It's a career that will destroy your hope, pillage your confidence, lay waste to your ambitions, steal your thunder, ransack your dreams, annihilate your goals, pummel your confidence, besiege your best-laid-plans, thrash your desires, slaughter your objectives, assassinate your aspirations, pull the carpet out from underneath you, leave you frustrated and kick you out of an airplane bereft of anything remotely resembling a parachute. It's a vocation that can starve you for work, famish you for provision, and deprive you of income.

Great Choice!!!

You have chosen wisely, O Stern-Stuff Warrior.

After all, who wants to play basketball when you can get elbowed in the face just going in for a lay-up? Who wants to perform heart surgery when you can sew the patient up and forget that you left the scalpel inside them and then be presented with a lovely malpractice suit? Who wants to run for president when no one likes you no matter what you do, and your approval ratings sink lower than a thimble doing the limbo under a rug? Actually, who wants to run for president *period*. Yeeshk.

No. You, in all your wisdom, have opted to pursue a career where you may in fact di-....um...keel over from being overcome with....absolute *pleasure*. Pleasure in:

- Being awarded jobs
- Auditioning and perfecting your craft
- Becoming a brand ambassador for a company or product
- Networking and connecting
- Achieving something wonderful
- Accumulating direct clients
- Being intentionally *chosen*
- Performing great pieces of literature or copy

Let's face it. You're an Entrepreneur. So, you, by extension, are a Goonie.

PERPETUAL SURVIVAL

Goonies never say Die. You, my friend, are a Goonie. You're an Adventurer. A cave-traveler. A ship-rider. A treasure-collector. A gold-hunter. A world explorer. A buccaneer. A swashbuckler. A trailblazer. You get to escape Mama Fratelli and her henchmen! You're lucky enough to meet Sloth! You are bestowed the rich privilege of cavorting with that fantastic adolescent inventor, Data. You – *yes, You!* – get to be a Voiceover Goonie and go on the adventure of a lifetime! Rich and bountiful treasure and loot await!

You're in for perpetual survival. And there are tools innumerable available to you online should you boldly and courageously choose to be a voiceover or author goonie. Reddit forums. YouTube videos, Blogs. Voiceover and author communities online. Facebook, LinkedIn, Reddit groups and forums for ANY trade out there imaginable. Meetup groups. Coaching. SO many resources.

It's an adventure for sure, and to help you along your way, you, just like Mikey, have a supporting cast of characters ready to help you along your way and ensure that you survive:

- Mouth
- Data
- Stef
- Brand (although he eventually becomes Thanos, so watch your back)
- Sloth
- Andy, and of course, your journey wouldn't be complete without…
- CHUNK!!!!

The di-…uh….lot has been cast. And you've been chosen! Fare thee well, my brave Voiceover Goonie! Go with good fortune, and may the wind be at your back! Good fortune awaits you!

Oh, snap. My Pac-Man just di-…uh…perished. Can you spare a quarter? I'll do the Truffle Shuffle if I have to.

Oh What A Rat You Are

"EVERYWHERE I WENT, I WAS RUNNING!"

Remember Forrest Gump? Boy, could that boy run. His wonderful quote to Jen-nay: *"And after that? Everywhere I went...I was runnnnning..."* Such great memories! Tom Hanks' finest.

Anytime I look at Forrest Gump and that slim, healthy physique, it's like looking in a freaking mirror. The mirror of course being one of those circus fun-house mirrors that is comically warped to the point of utter shameless deceit, sending me on my way in ignorant bliss with the top button on my pants popped out from the cotton candy, elephant ears, ice cream, double-cheeseburger, fries and soda.

But when I think of Forrest Gump and that gripping montage of running scenes from his namesake movie, it's immeasurably inspiring. He ran so far and so long, at one point reaching the Santa Monica Yacht Harbor: I love it when he pauses, thinks, turns around, thinks, and resumes running in the opposite direction. And then, finally, after 3 years, 2 months, 14 days and 16 hours, he was done. He had accomplished his mission of running. He was full-bearded, skinny, and he had amassed a following and inspired a nation with memes and more.

He was done.

Forrest Gump inspires me every morning. I get up, yawn and stretch, and with a smile look out and see the bright sunrise; I know my time has come. I slap on my running shorts, throw on the Apple watch, don the headband, lace up my running shoes, and run downstairs to the couch to watch reruns of *Snapped*. (It concerns me when my wife watches it with me and takes notes).

Kicking back in my couch, I think, "Man, what a workout." *grabs beer*

Forrest Gump I am not. But I sure do like to run, and I sure enjoy the race.

YOU'RE IN A RAT RACE – DEAL WITH IT

Voiceovers are a rat race. Like any entrepreneurial pursuit, it's all about keeping something coming down the pipeline. It's running to get to the next client, hopefully before the other entrepreneur does. Sure, we extend a great deal of congratulations and genuine joy when another artist receives a voiceover job, perhaps one that we ourselves were auditioning for, but secretly, we yearned for that one too. So, as we firmly grip the hand of the backstabber-I-mean-colleague who stole-I-mean-rightfully acquired the job that we wanted, we can't help but exude contempt-I-mean-joy for them as we plot their demise -er- celebrate their success. It's a rat race, and you and I are rats. Nice whiskers.

It's really not as bad as I make it out to be. I do imagine the "I'm so *happy* for you" scene in Dumb & Dumber where Jim Carrey firmly grips the hand of Mary Swanson's husband with a sinister begrudging grip, refusing to relinquish his bitter, icy clutch. But that's not us as Entrepreneurs.

Instead, we rejoice in the accomplishments of our colleagues, and we celebrate when those we've taught, helped, trained, or simply encouraged, rise to the level of Voiceover Accomplisher. We're truly, innately thrilled for them, you know, in the same way that a black market kidney victim is genuinely thrilled for their unintended recipient, or…how a bear is thrilled for another bear that snatches that giant salmon jumping out of the river in mating season. Ya know…*thrilled*.

Honestly however, as long as it's not the same job that I wanted, I'll celebrate your joy and do nothing to subvert you of course. If it *is* the same job I wanted, I may harbor, well, a *wee* bit of frustration – temporarily – and start calling up hitmen, but that's just so that I can engage in a little fantastical retribution. I'm not *really* going to do anything, and I'm not mad at you. Really. I swear. You look peaceful when I watch you sleep by the way.

In this great thing called voiceovers, boy is it ever a Forrest Gump bum-rush to get clients, to put bread on the table. Each day I do the following:

- Send 50 Advertising Emails
- Connect with at least 20 target contacts on LinkedIn
- Follow at least 10 video producers or VO's on Twitter
- Send at least 20 Instagram emails to target contacts
- Eat five pieces of taffy
- Send at least 20 emails to E-Learning developers
- Send at least 20 emails to Realtors
- Contact at least 10 YouTube Producers
- Contact at least 10 Vimeo Producers
- Envision what else I can bring to the VO community
- Yodel
- Contact at least 100 leads a day
- Watch the Morning Show
- Shower, time permitting

The yodeling is necessary, I assure you. The taffy is most assuredly not.

It's a Rat Race. Every. Single. Day. Do I love being a rat? Yes. Do I love racing? Yes. Do I love being a Rat in a Race every single day? Most assuredly. Each morning I wake up and I can't wait to check things off of my daily goals sheet. It's my intention to race to the finish line strong, fast, and determined, and to finish each day well, without complaining and without whining.

So, the question for you is, are you ready to enter the Rat Race?

TIPS ON SURVIVING A RAT RACE

The Rat Race can be difficult. It can be brutal. If you're ready, I salute you. But to therefore help you successfully navigate and in fact survive the Race, I've constructed the following helpful Rat Race Rules list for you to implement:

- Prepare for the Rat Race by having clear, defined, attainable and reasonable daily goals
- Do not eat your fellow Rat

- Droppings are to be offloaded OFF-track so that subsequent Rat Racers do not slip and fall in your entrails
- Focus on making each day extraordinarily productive
- In the event you are depressed in the race, no Rat shall be allowed to commit Hari Kari. Violators who do this shall miss lunch.
- No Rat shall at any time be allowed to use the slur "rat" on another rat as an epithet. This rule has been created so that I might be able to finally use the word "epithet" in a sentence.
- As a Rat, your primary objective is to run the race. Run it well, and you get fresh cheese. Run it poorly, and your cheese will be stale and will be stuck in Accounts Receivable for 60 days.
- No cheesily cutting in front, and no frontal cutting of the cheese.
- Running the race does not at any time insinuate that you will in fact *finish* the race. Many do not. Your tenacity will determine how well you run; your perseverance will determine how long you run, and your commitment will determine if you finish the race. Therefore, have tenacity, perseverance, and commitment. All three of these are essential ingredients – and they are multisyllabic words that will assist you in games like Balderdash.
- All Rats race. We don't not want all rats to not stop stopping to not race. Does that clear it up? Anyone seen sitting on the sidelines shall be fed to The Unemployment Cat without mercy.

Abide by these 10 Rat Race Rules, and you'll do just fine. The race doesn't belong to the swift, by the way; it belongs to the sturdy. It belongs to Forrest Gump. It belongs to those who seek to run a marathon, not a sprint. But every day, you can win the war by winning little battles…which all consist of running the race well and Forrest Gumping your way toward your goals.

So, rise up as One Nation of Voiceover Warriors, O Mighty Rat Racers One and All! Steel yourselves! Get ready to nibble your way through your goals, swish your tails, and go through the mouse wheel with your little legs pumping hard, your whiskers flaring, and your little black eyes bent on world domination!

"Run that race! Run that race!" is what I'll chant from my couch with my beer during *Snapped,* because such pursuits in life can make you tired! And speaking of life: it's kinda like a box of beers. You never know what you gonna get, Jen-nay.

Listen To Oscar

YOU DO YOU

"Be yourself; everyone is already taken." Oscar Wilde uttered that golden phrase, and it's become a mantra of mine.

In a world of clones, copy-cats and carbon copies, the more you can stand out, the better. We all have unique identities, branding, personality, personas, behaviors, and *modus operandi*. There is no one quite like us on this planet. God made each one of us absolutely unique – and though we may share similar characteristics, no two of us are the same. Even cookie cutter cookies are slightly different.

There's no one who does you quite like you.

In the voiceover industry, as with any industry, one of our main challenges is to stand out from the herd…to be different, and to be recognized and chosen *because* we're different. After all, it's that little signature nuance, affectation, or emphasis we put into any given audition that makes the listener's ears perk up and say "Hmm…that was unique." I love what Yuri Lowenthal and Tara Platt say in their incredible book, *Voice Over Voice Actor:* "Sometimes all it takes is a button on the end of your audition – an extra comment, a punch line, a laugh, or a chuckle – to get your read moved to the top of the list."[149] I agree! Something – *anything* – to make your read that much more unique.

But it goes far beyond that. How we live our very lives is a huge factor in how successful we are as entrepreneurs. So let me ask you a few questions.

- Are you profane in any of your posts? Do you post content that some might find objectionable, such as religious, political, hate-based, or otherwise questionable content?
- Are you posting the same nonsense over and over again, such as foodies, diluting the message of your social media channel?

- Do you withhold support from your VO brothers and sisters when you know there is a need?
- Do you shun gatherings and networking opportunities?
- Are you a boaster, a braggart or a showoff?

I've always felt that who you are on stage should be the same as who you are behind closed doors. We performers should live in a glass house, and be the same. It's what helps customers, colleagues, mentees and others to know that they can rely on us. That we are who we say we are.

In an earlier chapter I talked about Robin Williams. It's an absolute tragedy that the public persona that some performers are required to put on prohibits them from letting their hair down and taking off the makeup. Society and fandom don't let them, and that's tragic. And it comes with tragic consequences sometimes, as seen with Robin Williams.

May this never be the case with us as entrepreneurs!

Be who you say you are. Be you. Everyone else is already taken.

This also applies to not trying to be someone else. In all of the free video consults I provide – usually 10 a week – I invariably connect with someone who thinks they're on the air 24-7. Immediately upon greeting me they sound as if they're recording a show, and I find myself instantly wishing that 20 minutes would somehow feel like 5 minutes. I want it to be over.

I want the *real*, not the *put-on*.

Over the years I've spoken to so many people who have bounced in and out of voiceovers simply because a sense of their own identity was never impressed upon them. A sense of responsibility to be true to themselves…was never acknowledged or owned.

To succeed in voiceovers – or *any* industry as a freelancer – you must be acutely aware of who you are, what your giftings are, and what you are capable of. You have entered an industry where to stand any chance of actually succeeding, you must be set apart from the herd.

In truth, you must be "holy". *Holy* literally means "set apart." It means separate from. It's why God is separate from sin. Now, I'm not going to preach at you, so unclench. I use this term because far too often in the clamor for more jobs, we're resorting to "cool voices".

I can't begin to tell you how many times people come to me and say, "Yeah I was told that I have a cool voice and should get into voiceovers." I'll say it again. *So? So what?* Why should you or I or anyone care about how cool your voice sounds? It's the person behind the voice that is cast, not the voice itself.

Mel Blanc could do amazing voices, yes. Don LaFontaine was the king of movie trailers and was called upon to voice them because he sounded cool. These are exceptions. The overwhelming majority of voices today that are cast come from scripts calling for "conversational", "friendly", "natural", "guy next door" and "everyman."

"Now, Aaron," you say, "wait a minute: if they're asking for an 'everyman' voice, doesn't that mean that they want someone who sounds like everyone else?"

No. It does not mean that in the slightest. What they are requesting is someone who sounds human...*not put on.* Natural...*not an announcer.* Everyman...*not "the" man.*

You can only be you if you're acutely aware of who you truly are. If you're constantly striving to be someone else, or to sound like someone else, or to do everything someone else does, then you're not you. Yes, you can emulate other talent's approaches to success, and there is no shortage of courses available to teach you to do just that. But know this...You'll never make your own mark if you're always living in the shadows of someone else's.

Unless your casting notice specifically says "We're looking for a Tom Skerritt soundalike," they're *not.* Don't cater to the already's. Make your own sound, your own mark, your own stamp, your own persona, your own approach, your own life.

No one wants carbon copies or cookie-cutter. If they did, we'd all sound the same and it would be pointless to have many of us.

Your identity are a super responsibility, and it's your responsibility to be super. Super means "above."

It's kind of like being "holy."

Be a holy businessperson. One that stands apart; that is unique; that is completely isolated in their own identity and persona. I've often taught that in *branding*, it behooves you to shed the person and become the persona. Always be human in whatever you do, but start to think of yourself as a persona: unique, memorable, amazing in every individual way, and 100% yourself.

Be yourself. Everyone else is already taken. Thank Oscar for that one.

HERE'S ONE TO GROW ON:

"Your time is limited, so don't waste it living someone else's life."

Steve Jobs

More Cheese With Your Whine?

AHH, COMPLAINING...MUSIC TO MY EARS

Woe to the Woe Is Me-ers. Gotta love it. Don't you? The whining. The ineffable charm of a complainer. The moans! The irritating and life-sucking drain of a nitpicker flailing in misery! *Waaaaah waaaaaaah waaaaaaaaaaaaaaaaah.* Ahhhh! Music to my ears, and makes life worth living!

I love complainers. Almost as much as I love getting sucker punched in the face by a random passerby, and then doused with acid. It gives me the proverbial warm fuzzies, puts a skip in my step, and kinda makes me feel like Julie Andrews: *The Hills are alive - with the sound of whining...ah-ah-ah-ah....*

There's nothing quite like listening to someone drone on and on (and on and on and on)....and on (and on)....about how equipment costs this much and membership costs that much and software costs this much and training costs that much and on and on.....and on. (And on.) Complainers. Whiners. Woe-is-me'ers.

I *love* the chapter "There's no Crying in Voiceovers" from Paul Strikwerda's excellent book, *"Making Money in your PJ's: Freelancing for voice-overs and other solopreneurs"*. The man doesn't pull any punches and is sock-you-in-the-face brutally honest with you. It's required reading.

Stop your whining, people. Such people are "Glum" from Gulliver's Travels, saying "It'll never work! We're doomed!" They bring balance to the planet and a song to my heart in the same way as having my femur bone cracked in half. Those individuals whose lofty ambitions exceed their ability to fulfill said ambitions. Those poor unfortunate souls whose determination is crushed into a bloody pulp by the weight of reality.

They're "Sadness" from Inside Out:

Sadness: "Wait, Joy - you could get lost in there!"
Joy: "Think Positive!"

Sadness: "OK. I'm **positive** you will get lost in there!"

But could it be…is it even conceivable…that one can change one's perspective, reframe one's outlook, and reset one's viewpoint to look through the lens of possibility instead of despair?

The answer is yes, you sad, whimpering bonehead.

SISTER HAZEL SAID IT BEST

Remember that song by Sister Hazel called "Change Your Mind"?

If you want to be somebody else,
If you're tired of fighting battles with yourself
If you want to be somebody else
Change your mind…change your mind

I love no-BS songs like that. I love when the truth isn't sugar-coated and we honestly tell it how it is. Oh – and also, I love lyrics that make me shout "Fine!" and tramp off to my room to slam the door and cry over my toys in utter isolation while the world misunderstands me.

Ever seen the "No Whining" button or sign? Too often, many individuals look at a mountain they want to climb, and they dream big: that pinnacle becomes the object of their desire, the focus of their ambition. And then, they arrive at Big 5, grab all their rappelling gear, ropes, helmet, harness, crampons, pulley, etc., put it in their cart and amble on up to the cash register with all the optimism of an unflappable one-legged man entering a butt-kicking contest. Mr. *I Think I Can* receives the total…and here comes the waterworks. *Whaddayamean it's gonna cost that much? But what about my dreeeeeeeeeeeeeeeaaams???? Waaaaaaaaaaaaaaaaah! Waaaaaaaaaaaaaaahhhh!!! Waaaaaaaaaaaaaaaaaaaaaaaaaaaaaaaaaaaahhh!!!*

Sigh.

Yes, Captain Long Term Focus, your dreams take investment too. *Change your mind.*

There's a *wonderful* author who has written on this subject before, about the difference between expenses and investments. His name is Aaron Ryan, and oh boy is he wonderful. Oh – and did I mention that he's wonderful? Seriously, Full of Wonder. Check out his magical, wonderful blog at www.itsthevoicesinmyhead.com. He's wonderful.

If you wanna be somebody else, if you're tired of fighting battles with yourself, if you wanna be somebody else, change your mind. Narcissus[150] didn't want to be anyone else: he was comfortable admiring himself until he died of thirst. If only. If he had just changed his mind and decided that he needed to invest in some water. If only. Don't be Narcissus. Be an Investor.

I can't tell you how frustrated I get with people who use software and service and all things that are free, because they're free. That does *not* mean that they're the best. I can't count the number of times I've said "there's a *reason* it's free." Usually, when something is free, it sucks. Its life will be short-lived, it's not as good as the rest, it has no resale value, it's underperforming, it's subpar, etc. You don't use something just because it's free. You *invest* into something that will genuinely serve you. I get it – there are lots of expenses and you need to start economically. But you don't have to *stay* economical. Eventually, you'll need to demonstrate belief through investment.

Remember, *good is always the worst enemy of best.*

I can't tell you how irritated I get with people who want to do voiceovers but scowl that there are in fact some startup funds needed to, ahem, *invest* into your business. It's a business. It takes time to grow. Just like planting a fruit tree, you need to invest in shovels. Seed. Water. Buckets. Fertilizer. There are investment requirements to any startup.

As far as I know, there is no career that pays you to sit on your couch with your feet up, drinking beer and watching TV all day. If there were, everyone would be doing it! Except for me. I'll take an Appletini, because I'm a CAW, which stands for Certified Alcohol Wussy. But this raises an interesting scenario, so let's talk about this one for a moment, shall we? What investment are you making into your couch-drinking beer-glutton profession? Isn't it costing you money for beer, TV service, furniture, and utility bills for water and heat because please for the love of God get up and take a bath? Doesn't it require you to invest into your profession in the same way that any other profession has a cost?

Let's zoom out a bit and look at this even more:

- Doctors aren't just issued a license and then hop into an O.R. and start cutting up patients, unless of course they're Hannibal Lecter.
- Lawyers don't just take a bar exam without studying, and start representing clients
- Pilots aren't just whisked into a 747 and then start flying people intercontinentally
- Basketball players don't just stride out onto a court for the first time ever and pull a Michael Jordan flying dunk
- Astronauts don't just waltz into the Space Shuttle and go sauntering off to the moon.
- Voiceover Artists don't just suddenly score a national TV campaign with 60-year residuals

Dreams take investment. They require drive *and* commitment. They require you to change your mind. And I'm not talking by a lobotomist, hypnotist, or any other -ist. Not even Kuato from *Total Recall* can get into your mind enough to change it. I'm talking about real, attitude, perspective and willingness change... that all starts in your mind. Like Morpheus said to Neo: "Free. Your. Mind."

MIND IF I ASK WHAT'S THE MATTER WITH YOUR MATTER OVER MIND?

When you let your hopes get squashed by the fact that you'll have to put out before you can reap in, that's pitiful. When you whine and complain that something you deeply desire has a cost, that's pathetic. At that point, I'm sure even Jesus is saying "Come to me, all ye who labor and are heavy laden...uh...yeah, uh...except you in the third row, ya nitwit. Tone it down, will ya? I'm trying to walk on water and you're really bringing me down." Even Philippians 2:14 says "Do everything without complaining or arguing."

What's the matter with the matter? Is it a matter of mind over matter, or a matter of matter over mind? Does it even matter what the matter is? My philosophy has always been one of "just do it", or at the very least, "just try it." When I was faced with the prospect of coughing up another $400 annual membership fee to another pay-to-play voiceover marketplace, my thoughts didn't really consist of "Oh well, I *hope* I even make this money back."

It was so much more one of *intention*.

It was "I intend to make my money back." The people who whine and grovel over such a fee make me want to slice my ears off, bronze them, mount them, and then present them to the whiner so that they might install them in their home somewhere in Grovel Central in order for them to have something they can perpetually whine to and has no choice but to listen. Because I certainly don't want to. Granted, I won't ever hear anything ever again....but I'll be lying back with my hands behind my blood-soaked head, grinning and bleeding profusely out of my ears in complete silence, devoid of whining. *Ahhhhh....*

When I was faced with purchasing the Sennheiser MKH416 microphone for $1000, I didn't throw myself onto the floor and pound my fists and cry out "The price isn't fair! Why? Whyyyyy? Whhyyyyyyy?!?!" It was something I needed, and I deemed the stated price to be reflective of the quality of investment I was making. It was a no brainer. Also, in a bit of a materialistic way, I saw that as the price level to strive for. Why pay $200 when I can play with the big boys and have *their* mic, the top of the line?

Seriously, folks! It's called an *investment*. Does an investment carry risk? Yes. Any one of them does. But it's a reasonable risk. Let's zoom out again. If you were to purchase an annual membership at $395 a year, that averages out to $1.08 a day. *One dollar and eight cents a day.* Certainly, you spend more than that on other things per day. I think the primary issue is you might just not have that money on hand *at this very moment.* You could charge it, as I did, and then be preoccupied about paying off your credit card, but if you've received coaching and you're diligently auditioning, you'd doubtless have that $395 paid off after a month or two with the jobs that you'd be awarded. Or you could simply wait and save until you have the money. You could also rob a bank, but I fear the subsequent challenges you'll face would be greater than having no money so don't do that please.

The point I'm trying to encourage is let's swap whining for genuine Belief. It's less irritating, more palatable, less eye-roll inducing, and Jesus won't hate you: bonus! Stop whining. I mean it. Cut it out. Believe in yourself, and as they say, "Let God sort 'em out." Sometimes you just have to go in with some piss and vinegar, rockin' the Sister Hazel. Otherwise I'll need to sucker-punch you in the face. Cool?

You Can't Do Everything

THEY'RE ALL THE SAME, RIGHT?

Be excellent at a FEW things, not mediocre at a lot of them.

Ever been told you have a "face for radio"? This is a kind way of someone telling you that your face is hurting their eyes. It's another way to politely say "Please stop hurting me visually." I have never once been told this, because I only hang around blind people. It helps with my confidence level. In all sincerity, I've never once been told "Hey, you've got a great voice! You should do voiceovers!" Not once. Never. I hear that other people have been told that. No one has ever manufactured such a sentence and aimed it at me. So, there are three possibilities that come from this:

- I'm in the wrong field
- I'm in the right field, it's just that no one around me speaks English
- I'm in a completely different field in a completely different ballpark on a completely different planet where it's just me and grass, and grass doesn't say anything except "please sir, may I have some water?"

So, I'm going to go with 4) I'm good enough, I'm smart enough, and doggonit, people like me, final answer.

JACK OF ALL TRADES, MASTER OF NONE

You know those people. The "Jacks of All Trades, Masters of None." The ones that think that they're just great at everything. The ones that want to do voiceovers because they're a singer. Or sing because they do podcasting. Or do radio because they're a voice talent. Or zipline because they eat Cheerios. One thing doesn't have anything to do with the other, like Ben Affleck and acting.

You can be good at a few things, but that doesn't mean that you're great at everything. Nor does it mean that you're automatically an expert at one craft just because it uses a microphone just like that other craft does, which is about as truthful as "I load luggage into an airplane so I therefore must be able to pilot one." The frenetic and panicked look on your passengers' faces should validate this truth, as will their screams of terror coming from the cabin behind you. Please be a nice pilot and bring the plane back; it doesn't belong to you, nor do those people. Jack Bauer and CTU will be along in a moment.

I meet a lot of people who want to get into voiceovers because they have been on the air. I'm also friended on Facebook by a ton of people who, after a cursory look at their profiles, are clearly radio DJ's, post cat videos, believe in leprechauns, snap foodies and post those annoying "if you agree with me repost this and send it to eighty trillion of your closest friends or this planet will explode in five seconds no its true you must believe me on this lives are in peril where are you going get that straightjacket off of me" posts. Also, they believe in the Kardashians. I maintain no such belief.

So, with that, I kindly hit the "delete request" button and fill out the restraining order paperwork.

The "I can do everything" people are nice people deep down, I'm sure. They are friendly, capable people who just want to try their hand at something new; believe me, I get it. But a Crossover SUV is still an SUV. If it really wants to be a sedan, then it needs to learn how to become a Sedan, which is a different type of vehicle entirely.

When someone tries to do *everything*, they usually fail at *something*, unfortunately. Take me for example. I believe with every fiber of my being and the fire of a thousand suns that I can do voiceovers *and* put up a curtain rod. However, one of those things is bound to fail. Putting it in checkbook context, I make money with voiceovers. Paul Strikwerda adds, "Either outsource what you can't handle, or get up to speed as fast as you can."[151] Since I know in my heart that I will *never* get up to speed on house projects, I'll gladly outsource it to someone who won't blow up my home.

When I try to install a curtain rod, I then have to expend money to hire a Fixer to fix the fix that I fixed and actually put up the curtain rod above the window and not accidentally install it into the backyard, which is what I have done. At the point where your normal man would be finished, that's when I've lost the will to live, and I decide to live in a tent instead. Therefore, I choose voiceovers, because A) we keep more money and B) my wife isn't forced to stay on the second floor for privacy reasons because there are already successfully installed curtain rods up there. *Curse you, Make-It-Look-So-Easy-DIY Home Depot videos.*

For example, it's been rumored that it's possible for men to change their own oil in their car. While this may be possible for men, I, a man, seem to not be able to do this. Each time I try, it ultimately results in tears and a disaster of Biblical proportions, and then I have to buy a new car because that one just doesn't want its oil changed by me. Cars generally don't seem to want to allow me to do things most men can do. For instance, I remain very unable to look like Matthew McConaughey driving a Lincoln while at the same time being Aaron Ryan driving a Honda Odyssey. My Odyssey doesn't want me to do that, and it continues to pull over to the side of the highway when I try. Exorcisms don't help: they just make my minivan angrier and people look at us funny.

So, don't you see? All things are *not* possible to those who believe.

I THINK I CAN I THINK I CAN WE KNOW YOU CAN'T

Being able to talk into a microphone does not a good voiceover artist make. I realize that in so saying, you might now like me about as much as giving birth with your femur bone cracked in half. If you are unable to understand the comparison, then I suggest giving birth with your femur bone cracked in half. Then you'll know.

Overconfidence is a big thing, just like Shark Week. It's inescapable, it's terrifying, and it dominates the programming for a while, until we come to our senses and need to take a break from all those sharks and go get some shark-fin soup. (Dangit!) In the same light, remember The Little Engine That Could? It's a great story. The big train thought that it could do it all by itself. But ultimately, the big train required a tow from a little think-I-can train to get it over the mountain. Both needed willpower, and they both needed to *believe*. But the object lesson I'm making here is that one train did one job, and the other did another job, and they each needed different skills to successfully make it over the mountain.

Let's get something straight. I'm tolerant and accepting of other people's choices and their desire to be who they think they are.

I know this is going to offend some people, but here goes.

The other day, this podcaster I was talking to wanted to be a voiceover artist. We were on a voiceover video consult, and from the beginning of our conversation I could hear Michael Bolton in the background blaring loudly. We had a nice chat, and then he told me he was gay. His boyfriend came into the screen, and I could see them kissing. I can tolerate a lot, but there was something new to all of this for me. They kept on kissing, and they just wouldn't stop. Now, like I said, I'm tolerant, so I politely reaffirmed who he was and who he wanted to be. It's all good. But then they went even further and they started complimenting my hair and my eyes and my voice. I had had enough. I shouted at them. I couldn't believe I was shouting! But I told it to them straight: "Dude! If you're a gay podcaster, be a gay podcaster! If you want to be a gay voiceover artist, be a gay voiceover artist!" And here's where I let him have it. "But you've been playing Michael Bolton since the beginning of our conversation, and you're *still* playing Michael Bolton!!!!"

I hate Michael Bolton.

Integrity: It's All You've Got

NO TWO WAYS ABOUT IT.

I'm going to use one of my chapters to gripe. Ultimately, it's not directed at anyone in particular…except to say that it *is* in fact directed at every single person in my life who has not kept their word, and all those who don't keep their word.

The way you run your business is going to be a reflection of how you run your life. Are you a person who keeps their word? Or are you a person who overpromises and underdelivers? Are you one of those people that never show up on time, or always come up with some sort of colossal earth-shaking reason why you just can't make it today? Do you coincidentally "get sick" each and every time one of your supposedly beloved friends throws a birthday party for their child?

If you are going to be a success in the voiceover business – nay, in *life* – then you had better start adopting integrity *yesterday*. If people can depend on you as far as they can throw you, then what good is your word? You are a fair-weather friend. You are someone who simply can't be trusted to deliver. Your theme song would be the opposite of *Friends:*

I won't be there for you
(When the rain starts to pour)
I won't be there for you
(Just like I wasn't there before)
I won't be there for you
('Though you're there for me too)

Is that truly the kind of businessman you want to be? If you offer under one hour turnaround time in print and digital media, you darn well better deliver that, because that's what your clients will be expecting. If you say you're going to redo files, you darn well better do that because your clients have timelines. If you say you're going to send a client a quote, you darn well better do that in a timely fashion, or they just might go somewhere else.

My friend Paul cites an example in his book, *"Making Money in your PJ's"*:

I read on your website's Contract page that you'll get back to me within 24 hours. I sent you a message three days ago and I have yet to hear from you. What other promises aren't you going to keep? My project has a strict deadline. If you can't meet your own, how can I be sure you'll meet mine?"[152]

Ouch. Right on point.

You are a businessowner. But you are not the *only* businessowner. There are tons more like you. What makes you think clients will hang their hat and hold their breath for your reply? If you can't deliver expediently, what incentive is there for the client to wait for you? You're entering a very reactive industry loaded with time-sensitive clients with time-sensitive projects.

On the flip side, what about your colleagues? Did you say you'd review someone's demo? Did you? Or is it sitting in your inbox from two weeks ago? Did you say you'd make that voiceover Meetup, but keep stalling and offering lame excuses?

Are you a man/woman of your word…or *not???*

Here's the definition of Integrity:

in·teg·ri·ty
/inˈtegrədē/

- noun
- noun: integrity
- the quality of being honest and having strong moral principles; moral uprightness, i.e., "he is known to be a man of integrity"
- the state of being whole and undivided, i.e., "upholding territorial integrity and national sovereignty"
- the condition of being unified, unimpaired, or sound in construction, i.e., "the structural integrity of the novel"

What do you think happens when I continually invite someone in my life to an event, and almost every time, something catastrophic happened in their home, where everyone "got the flu and we've done nothing but puke all weekend LOL. There's puke everywhere!" Such embellishment might be tolerated and believed once; but believe me, I've had people in my life – and so have you – that this is their default go-to, their *modus operandi*. They commit in the heat of the moment out of a sense of excited allegiance and wanting to make you feel good, only to set you up for the inevitable letdown and the epic Biblical explanation of colossal craziness in their home. It's the people who RSVP right away to your Evite, only to cancel with hours to spare before the big party, or just simply not show up at all.

I have a question for you. Do you do that to your clients? If so, you won't last. People who do this don't last. As Joey in Friends said, "Sooner or later they just....stop lastin.'"

Your clients screen sometimes *hundreds* of people for their beautifully-scripted voiceover. They want the best person for the job. The best person doesn't just have the best voice and know how to read their script the best. The best person *is* the best – at everything. Communication, timeliness, broadcast-readiness, punctuality, professionalism, the list goes on. They want and deserve someone who not only promises them all of this, but actually delivers. And the one who delivers...is the one who gets hired again...and again...and again. That's why I promise "no hassle" and "projects done right the first time around" for all of my clients. They don't want hassle; they want to rely on me!

Are you a hassle? Are you lying through your teeth just to get a job, knowing full well that you have other obligations to meet, or think you'll do just fine "skating by" once hired? Clients don't like skaters. They like deliverers.

I didn't have this chapter in the original version of this book. It was a last-minute addition. Integrity is all I have. My word truly is all I've got. If people can't rely on my word, then *another* word will spread like wildfire: word of my lack of integrity. That will cost me everything in the end.

I talked about manners earlier. "Please" and "Thank You" and "Sorry" go a *long* way. They save you. They mend fences. They usher you in. They get you where you need to go. Along with manners and being a gentleman/woman is integrity. You need all of these in order to be someone people can rely on.

Tightrope walker Charles Blondin's greatest fame came on September 14, 1860, when he became the first person to cross a tightrope stretched 1,100 feet (over a quarter of a mile) across the mighty Niagara Falls. People from both Canada and America came from miles away to see this great feat.

He walked across, 160 feet above the falls, several times... each time with a different daring feat - once in a sack, on stilts, on a bicycle, in the dark, and blindfolded. One time he even carried a stove and cooked an omelet in the middle of the rope!

A large crowd gathered and the buzz of excitement ran along both sides of the river bank. The crowd *ooooh'd* and *aaaaah'd* as Blondin carefully walked across - one dangerous step after another - pushing a wheelbarrow holding a sack of potatoes.

Then at one point, he asked for the participation of a volunteer. Upon reaching the other side, the crowd's applause was louder than the roar of the falls!

Blondin suddenly stopped and addressed his audience: "Do you believe I can carry a person across in this wheelbarrow?"

The crowd enthusiastically yelled, "Yes! You are the greatest tightrope walker in the world. We believe!"

"Okay," said Blondin, "Who wants to get into the wheelbarrow?"[153]

Can you be Charles Blondin? Are your customers willing to ride in your wheelbarrow?

Weddings Suck

GONE ARE THE DAYS

There was a time in my life where weddings where my main breadwinner. How fun was it to celebrate someone's union and get paid at the same time? And the food was occasionally truly awesome. Especially delightful was when the main guests were provided Lobster and Dom Perignon, and we vendors were provided a kid's table and served cold ham sandwiches, water, and a dried-up orange wedge, far away from the guests in another zip code. Now that's love. I wrote about some of this in my blog, entitled "Why I threw away $460,000" (chapter included in this book) wherein I detailed why I intentionally set fire to my wedding videography career. Serving as a wedding vendor is akin to being waterboarded for a consecutive forty-eight-hundred years, or forced to listen to the doo-doo-doo's of *Baby Shark* on a punishing loop. The enjoyment level of being a wedding vendor is akin to the enjoyment level of being crucified.

With that in mind, I swiftly (OK, OK: eleven years after I started) left wedding videography for the greener pastures of voiceovers. Do I regret it one bit?

Not one bit. And here's why. Voiceovers Rule, and Weddings suck.

Allow me to expound on this declaration to preempt any kind of Biblical rage on the part of any category of -zilla out there (there are many). The worst is the dog-zilla who doubles as the Ringbearer and is all uppity because no she-dogs were invited to get down and boogie with.

A MEANS TO AN END

Sure enough, weddings provide a great bounty of work, no matter what vendor type you choose: whether that's videography, officiating, photography, catering, DJ'ing, floral, or bringing along your drunken, belligerent uncle. Or the grandpa whose pants always fall down while dancing. It's pure magic. It's truly a lucrative line of work, and you can profit off of these giddy days of happiness and celebration. No matter what economic downturns or pandemics we face, people will *always* get marry and be married, and thus, for a stretch, I chose to be very merry while Harry and Mary were getting married by Scary Larry.

But there's a flip side, and, dare I say, a dark side, to all this mirth. I call it the Me Trap. It's the inevitable deep plunge into abhorrent and rampant narcissism that makes the day all about the bride and groom, and I don't need to justify my position with the countless available stories of terrorism conducted by brides who charge their guests admission, brides who insist on a wedding gift from their bridesmaids, or brides who intentionally fatten up their bridesmaids in the name of vanity and flattering photographs. I am not making this up. These are all true stories.

Basically, it's the brides. That much is clear. All brides are inherently evil and, prior to their nuptials, should all be sent traipsing off into the Amazon by themselves on a three-week Hunger Games-like trek whilst completely naked, armed only with a toothpick and slathered with lamb juice. That'll teach 'em humility.

In over 460 weddings, there was always some kind of conflict, if even on a superficial level. This wasn't right, or that wasn't perfect, or why were those people invited, and where is the weed? Nothing was ever quite right, and ultimately, you could cut the palpable tension with a knife. Me, with my affable and disarming personality, did my absolute best to connect with clients who were on some level, prior to the wedding day, human. On the wedding day itself however, most clients bore a stark resemblance to the Wampa from Empire Strikes Back, ready to hang you upside down in a freezing cave and scarf down your Tauntaun if provoked. And that is why I *always* bring a lightsaber to my weddings.

It wasn't all bad, but *pause* ...well, actually, yes it was. "Hindsight is 20:20" they say, and now that I can look back and see through the fog, it's clear to me that I was embroiled in a vocation where the will to live slowly ebbs away in the fiery crucible of pleasing unpleasable clients. Even while attending weddings of people I actually love (there are four), I find myself praying that it would rain, so that the couple would receive the painfully unambiguous realization that it truly is NOT all about them. Plus that gets us inside and to the cocktails much faster.

So, if you're sitting at a crossroads, unsure of which direction to take in life, to assist you with the choice of whether to pursue either wedding videography or voiceovers, I offer you a comprehensive Q&A to amplify your reasoning prowess, and help you make an Informed Decision.

Q: Should I get into wedding videography?
A: Yes, if you have a letter from your doctor stating that you should engage in pursuits that jeopardize your life and could cause you to pee your pants from cold fear.

Q: Are voiceovers actually better than wedding videography?
A: Yes, in much the same sense that living in Heaven is actually better than burning in hell.

Q: I received a request to help a good friend film their client's wedding. Should I help?
A: This is a trick question. A good friend would never jeopardize your life for such low pay.

Q: It sounds like one can make a lot of money doing wedding videography. Wouldn't that be motivation enough to do it?
A: Yes, if you enjoy the pleasurable sensation of being crucified.

Q: Would you ever do wedding videography again?
A: *Bwahahahahahahahahahaha!!!!!!! BWAHAHAHAHAHAHA AHAH AHAHAHAH HAHAHAHAHAHAHAHAHA!!!!!!!* *deep inhale* *BWAHAHAHAHAHAHAHA AHAHA HAHAH HAHAHA HAHAHA HA HAHAHAHAHAHAAHA!!!!!!!*

FACING VOICEOVER OBSOLESCENCE

I hope that helps. Were I to ever return to slavery, uh, I mean wedding videography, it would have to only come as the result of Artificial Intelligence taking over all sectors of society and running me out of voiceovers entirely. As a means to an end, yes, it was financially lucrative. However, making $300 for 3 minutes of work on an Explainer Video will always beat, hands down, serving a wedding client for an indeterminate amount of time, and having delightfully cumbersome and unreasonable demands placed upon me, such as:

- "Do this extra thing for me at no charge, or I go straight to Yelp!"
- "Give me the Silver package amenities at the Economy Pig Slop package pricing, or I go straight to Yelp!"
- "Worship me all day long! Be at my beck and call! For I am Satan! Worship me!!!"
- "Pay you for your wedding videography services???" *wicked cackle of incredulity* "Never! You shall pay ME for the privilege of serving ME, I say! Me! Me! **ME!!!!!**"
- "Yelp Yelp Yelp, yelp-yelp-yelp Yelp!"
- "Did I mention I'm a self-centered narcissist who knows everyone on Yelp and has the power to destroy your business unless you Photoshop my non-ideal body down to the ideal thinness of a sliver?"
- "Yelp Yelp Yelp, yelp-yelp-yelp Yelp!"

I think I've chosen aright. My wedding videography career is over, and I sleep more soundly now. It's gone (more fist pumping), and with it a legacy of indentured servitude to clients who disagree when you insist that you're a human being and have certain rights to be treated fairly. Oh I enjoyed it on Wedding #1. But much later, after a long while, by Wedding #2 I realized that I had essentially traded enjoyment for handcuffs, and was rushing toward the cliff like a lemming to his doom. From that point on it was a careful balancing act of desperately trying to please every single client with every fiber of my being, and learning to smack myself in the brain with an oar.

So no, *thank you,* I don't think I would ever go back to wedding videography even if voiceovers became obsolete and you paid me a gajillion dollars. I'm comfortable with my healthy level of contempt now. I would instead probably elect to be hired by a sadist, and be subjected to daily waterboarding, set to Baby Shark Music.

What the heck, it beats traipsing through the Amazon covered in lamb juice.

Don't Be A Jackass

HUMANS LIKE HUMANS

I've said it before in other books and blogs of mine. I'll say it again. Humans like Humans. No one likes someone who appears inhuman and is unattainable.

The Voiceover world is not immune from celebritizing, nor is it immune from celebrities. There are those among us who carry with them an air of arrogance, and unaffable untouchability. They carry their noses a bit too high, and they're convinced they're God's gift to the earth. We should count our lucky stars that they should find it in their goodness to descend and dwell with the rest of us mortals.

These are the types of people who are always ready to flaunt their wealth, highlight their multiple cars and their multiple houses and their multiple multiples of multiples. They present an air of elevation that many voice artists find distasteful, while they hover above us with a bit of a sneer.

No one likes those, so don't be one.

HUMANS LIKE SUPERHUMANS

"But, *Aaron*" you say, "what about *Superman?* Superman hovers above us and is an immortal; are we to dislike and distrust him too?"

The short answer? Superman was also Clark Kent: goofy, affable, attainable, relatable. He was someone who we could connect with and, though his alter ego was beyond the scope of mortal man, he willingly put on this disguise to connect with us. Some could say the same of Jesus.

When I think of Voiceover Superhumans, I think of Scott Burns. For those people who are tremendously successful in voiceovers and choose to give back to the community, they are a *huge* asset.

They contribute to the common man, because they know their roots, and are all too willing to invest in those who are as they once were. It is this characteristic that distinguishes the SuperMan from the SuperSnob. Perhaps it's a bit of Robin Hood: robbing the rich to give to the poor. The hero of the people. Zorro. Nelson Mandela. And ordinary everyday heroes like the ones listed at this link.[154]

I once saw a friend post on Facebook:

I'm a badass. I'm a badass. I'm a badass.
I'm a badass. I'm a badass. I'm a badass.
Sometimes I cry. I'm a badass.

I like and appreciate this stance, because of the vulnerability therein. *Yes*, as voiceover artists, some of us attain a bit of a celebrity status. But it's in the letting-our-hair-down, and the transparency, the touching-earth moves that we make, where our cape stops flapping in the wind, hanging limply behind us, and we let people see us up close, warts, pimples, graying hairs, crow's feet, sagging skin and all. *Everyone* looks beautiful framed against the sun. I'd rather sit on this log with you in the greying twilight, unafraid and real.

The message here? Simple. If you're famous, don't flaunt your fame. If you're a celebrity, don't carry yourself too mightily. If you're a star, don't blind others with your light. Carry it humbly.

We all know you're human anyway. You're not fooling anyone.

We all remember Scooby Doo. At the end of each episode, after the main antagonist gets unmasked, they always offer a similar refrain: "And I would have succeeded too, if it hadn't been for your meddling kids!" It was someone being someone else, to hurt other people. It's Dr. Jekyll intentionally drinking the serum so he could gallivant around as Mr. Hyde, and feel the power of the alter ego.

Do you remember *Invasion of the Body Snatchers*? A truly creepy movie that for whatever reason, I was able to see when I was a child. I'll never forget the dog with the human face on it. *shudder*

The point being, sometimes people get taken over by a superiority complex and delusions of grandeur. They project themselves as bigger than they are. They flaunt their wealth and their accomplishments and fly in the face of humility. Don't be that person; you make yourself unattainable, and frankly, a jackass. We're all on a level playing field here, and we can all build each other up. The question then becomes, do you even want to?

Make no mistake. If you are successful in voiceovers, good for you. I salute you, and I genuinely share your joy. Just keep humble about it. Share your successes, but always thank God for it. Always share in humility with the sole purpose of encouraging and inspiring others to know that *they can join you on the stage.*

HERE'S ONE TO GROW ON:

"Every jerk has a silver lining. They come with lessons to teach. One of 'em: Be nothing like this jerk."

Karen Salmansohn

With Great Power Comes Great Responsibility

HINDSIGHT AND FORESIGHT

When I was a little boy, I wanted to be a policeman. And then I wanted to be a fireman. And then I wanted to be Batman. And finally, I decided on Superman. But then I wanted to be a singer. And I think I also wanted to be a doctor. In short, I wanted to be someone who could swoop in and respond to emergencies in a melodic way, saving people's lives with a grapple gun.

When we're little, we don't really know what we want to be, but we look at those tall figures towering over us, especially the ones who seem to be defying logic (or gravity) in some heroic way, and we seek to emulate them, and we seek to adopt a similar mission for us. It's called "idealizing." Sometimes it's even called "idolizing."

However you slice it, rewind 40 years and ask me if I wanted to be a voice actor, and I may have responded, "Do I at least get to wear a cape?"

In my humble opinion, voice actors are some of the most underrated citizens of this planet. We are indispensable. We will not be so easily replaced by AI and will not go quietly into the night. We can't. It's not in our makeup to not be heroic. True, there are some of "us" out there that treat voiceovers as a passing fancy, and some that masquerade as heroic, yet piggyback on the profit of others as they seek to teach. There are corrosive elements within any community, and there are charlatans that know nothing other than profiting off of you rather than off of hard work.

But the true voiceover superhero is someone who wears plainclothes, who humbly seeks to produce something that will be quietly moving. Thought-provoking. Stirring to action. Uplifting. Compelling. That's our job as entrepreneurs. Our job is to move.

To make people think. To motivate them. To encourage. To get them to do what our client wants.

And sure – it's the client that writes the script, and we just voice it. But is that all it is?

In *Star Trek: The Motion Picture*, the character V'ger asks "Is this all that I am? Is there nothing more?"

Many people suffering from imposter syndrome experience something similar and may voice a similar refrain. I do understand it, believe me. In many of my past vocations, I've suffered from it, and I daresay many people have sat at their desks across our great planet, holding a thousand-yard stare and wondering "Is this it?" We are trained to grow up and "become something"…but what if we arrive after all those years of forward momentum, education, expense, striving, etc., and we realize with horror that it wasn't what we expected?

OUR GREAT RESPONSIBILITY

The true voice talent will stare down the barrel of a gun knowing full well the great weight that we carry as voice talent, and willing to do absolutely everything required of them to ensure that their career flourishes, and their dream thrives. The same is true for any career we have.

"To whom much is given, much is required." – Luke 12:48

"With great power comes great responsibility." – Uncle Ben, Spider-Man

"Responsibility is accepting that you are the cause and the solution of the matter." - Anonymous

"The price of greatness is responsibility." – Winston Churchill

I am sorry (and I'm really not), but this is not a career that anyone can approach flippantly or cavalierly. It doesn't work that way. This career and this pursuit are rarely ever chosen at age 7, much less idealized or idolized. Sure, it might be glamorous to impressionable minds, but not all of those minds are cut out for this endeavor, and saturation shows us that.

Are you the cause and solution of the matter? Did you bring yourself to voiceovers intentionally? Do you intend to make every single voiceover you deliver stellar? Do you strive to please every single customer and ensure that their script is brought to life in such a rich way that they come back to you, because they can trust you? That's the mark of someone who understands the great responsibility we carry. It's not just speaking into a microphone.

"I was told I have a good voice, so I'm doing voiceovers."

Is that you? Or are you more like this:

"Voiceovers are my mission, and my highest calling. I seek to lift those words off of the page and breathe life into them. And I aim to honor every single client's long, hard, efforts to painstakingly write something wonderful."

James R. Alburger says, "All acting is based on initial choices and adjustments are made to those choices as a performance develops. As you work with a piece of copy, you will be making lots of decisions and choices about dozens of aspects of the story that can affect your performance. It is important to commit to these choices in order to be consistent throughout the recording session."[155]

Choices. Performance. Decisions. Commitment. All of that takes talent.

Regardless of what you wanted to be when you grew up, you're here now. You're a voice talent. But what does that word, *talent*, really mean?

tal·ent
/ˈtalənt/

noun
1.
natural aptitude or skill.
"he possesses more talent than any other player"

Are you really talented? Do you understand the great responsibility that comes with that natural aptitude or skill? You've been given a gift, before you were born, in your very makeup. A gift that somehow, in whatever way it worked out, enables you to read a script so compellingly that your audience actually believes you believe it.

Alburger says, "Suspension of disbelief in voiceover is essential for creating a sense of believability. The audience must believe you, and for that to happen, *you* must believe in what you are saying."[156] Will you honor that talent? Will you respect it? Will you seek to refine it?

Will you use it for good?

NO CAPES

In *The Incredibles,* Edna Mode reproached Bob Parr with the following admonition:

"NO CAPES!"

Bob was obsessed about remaining a superhero, and needed a new outfit. Edna was his designer. As his ideas for his new appearance began to take shape, he envisioned colors and patterns…and capes. Well, Edna rejected that outright, and proceeded to cite a number of examples of superheroes that came to an untimely end because of their capes. *Thunderhead. Stratogale. Meta-Man. Dynaguy. Splashdown.*

NO CAPES!

The truth is this: *real heroes don't wear capes.* These are Policeman. Firemen. Teachers. Volunteers.

Entrepreneurs.

What?

Yes, Entrepreneurs. You're a capeless hero! You have great power. And with great power comes great responsibility. Know that. You have great talent and natural aptitude or skill. Your delivery is your superpower. Your ability to produce great voiceovers makes you rise above the rest of the mortals. The fact that you get paid for it is secondary.

As Daws Butler says, "I want you to understand the words. I want you to taste the words. I want you to love the words. Because the words are important. But they're only words. You leave them on the paper, and you take the thoughts and put them into your mind and then you as an actor recreate them, as if the thoughts had suddenly occurred to you."[157]

Understand the words.

I may not have grown up to become any of the things I envisioned, but I don't care. I'll wager many adults don't care that their childhood career fantasies didn't come true.

And then there are some whose dreams did come true: the astronaut who, as a child, lay on the ground and stared wistfully up at the stars and said, "One day." The Sea Shepherd whale warrior who was a sensitive child and cried when he saw a mouse in a trap, struggling painfully to get free. The London Symphony orchestra flautist who in their youth would listen and listen and listen again to symphonies, figuring out the progression of notes. The hairstylist who loved to playfully create dreadlocks and ponytails and other stylizations on their friends' craniums.

But for most, they've accepted where they are and are content. What I love about where I'm at and what I do is that it isn't in the slightest what I envisioned for myself as a child, but I am more than content. I unintentionally landed on a very heroic profession, and so, in many respects, I *did* end up becoming a policeman. A fireman. Batman.

Superman.

Looking back, are you where you want to be? Do you understand the great power you have in you, and the great responsibility it carries? In *whatever* vocation you are in, you have tremendous responsibility to represent it well. For me, that's voiceovers and authoring.

Will you answer the call?

HERE'S ONE TO GROW ON:

"Every privilege comes with a responsibility. If you don't take the responsibility, you will lose the privilege."

Sadhguru

I Simply Can't Not Fly

BLOOD TYPE: B+

Let's end on a note of sincerity.

Let's talk about me for a second.

I suppose it's my blood type. I'm B+ after all. Which, I'm sure you can tell, is code for "be positive." One might say I was born this way, so that's how and whom I have to be. I have an unquenchable positivity, and when the chips do get down, I usually (after reading the manual), find a way to get back up again. "It is this inner spirit that allows [me] to succeed on a day-to-day basis. What [I] show to others on the exterior is manufactured by [my] inner spirit."[158] Truth!

Lest I be misconstrued here, I'm not talking about voiceovers. I'm not talking about the actual craft. No. I'm talking about everything that surrounds the craft of voiceovers, or *whatever* your craft is:

- Encouraging
- Providing free consults
- Writing blogs
- Authoring books
- Providing training
- Facilitating workshops
- Providing interviews
- Affirming others in social circles

There's a reason, and it's because swirling around this little thing called business is a massive amount of energy. Positive energy. B+ Energy. That's what I have inside of me, and that's why I do what I do.

You could attribute a lot of what I do to a profound welling over of immense gratitude, and you'd be right to do so. When you've been freed from something, it's all you can do to not talk about it. I've been freed from a vocation that was bleeding me dry, and sapping all of my vocational happiness. I've not been ambiguous at all as to what that was. It became madness. It became doldrums. It became monotony. It became a prison.

I have been freed from wedding videography, and what I get to do now is to share in the delight of a craft that on so many levels, is incredibly, intrinsically satisfying. It's not a pastime or a diversion; not a fad nor a leisurely pursuit. Rather, it's something that I can look back upon and see incredible accomplishment, heart-filled networking, solid friendships and partnerships, and massive reward heaped on me from above as I walked in it faithfully.

As I invested into my career and took financial risks, reputational risks, marketing risks…*all kinds of risks*…it has all proven to be a leap of faith. That's what I want to encourage you to take. Take that leap.

It's Indiana Jones stepping off the chasm-side onto the invisible catwalk.

It's Atreju daring to pass the Sphinxes.

It's Captain Kirk and crew courageously endeavoring to slingshot around the sun in the hopes of bringing a whale forward in time to save humanity.

Might it not work? Perhaps. But at least you tried. At least you stepped. At least you dared. At least you endeavored.

'TWAS NOT TO BE

Let me share with you a sad episode in our lives.

When my wife and I decided to move in April of 2020, we did so with much fear and trepidation, knowing the current state of things. There was a pandemic ravaging our planet, plain and simple. However, it was a buyer's market, and we had steadily grown disenchanted with where we were living. I, in particular, was longing for a less expensive change. We were paying far too much for far too little in the cramped cul-de-sac where we were. Property taxes were rising. We didn't really know hardly anyone in our neighborhood. The neighbors across the street always polluted our street with far too many cars…far too loud music…and far too annoying little yipping dog that would not shut up.

Aside from that, we didn't really feel all that connected to our home church, and now that we were on lockdown due to the coronavirus, Brennan was out of school and not able to have any physical interaction with other kids. Even the playset down the street was off limits.

So we decided to go find our *own* playset.

We began our search, and it didn't take us long to settle on a home that was absolutely, in ever sense, the *dream home*. It was built in 2009 and cost $734k, but that was not out of reach. It had 3600 square feet, a playset, bullnose corners (I wanted those!), 4 acres, 5 bedrooms, and an office, and a great room, and a formal dining room, and a huge laundry, and an exercise room, and a playroom. It was unbelievable! It had vaulted ceilings, and was naturally bright. It came with a firepit, trampoline, walking trails, gated community, hot tub, and even an elegant doghouse for our dog. It was simply too good to be true! We *ached* for this house: finally, something that would allow our little boys to grow up with lots of room to breathe and run and have their being. A safe place where they could ride their bikes and not get clobbered as they rode carefree down a row of driveways and potentially fatal accidents. No: this house was the one for us, and by a mile over any others that we had looked at. No: this was the one. I could not pull myself away from the Zillow listing and just adoring the photos.

We drove down and checked it out and were smitten. We had our agent go down with us next, and that day we made a full-price offer.

It was accepted! The sellers accepted our offer! We were elated. We got preapproved for lending, and we were off to the races. There was just one thing, and that was that the owners were government employees and so the sale was actually going to go through a mortgage relocation company, and *they* were ultimately responsible for making the final decision on who to sell to.

So, we waited. Patiently. Impatiently.

Less than 2 days after making our offer, the word came back: we could not do a contingent offer, and our current home would literally have to be pending – not pending inspection, mind you, but pending *sale* – and unless it was, our offer would not be considered. To compound matters, there was another full-price offer on the table, and they were being considered as well.

We were crushed – but only for a moment. Was this house slipping away from us? I felt in my heart that this was absolutely where God wanted us to be. How could it slip away? It was not possible! And I was not going to let it.

After panicking for a few brief moments, I knew what needed to be done and what was being asked of me. I sprang into action and began to race through the house, packing nearly everything I could into the garage as we began to stage our house and get it ready for sale. We were going to get that house. I cleaned, I scrubbed, I grabbed boxes and the garage began to fill up. We were going to get that house. I worked around the clock and decided to forego auditions in order to do what was necessary. We were going to get that house. In about two days, we had all the excess crap in our house all stuffed down into the garage, our realtor was out getting comps, and we arranged for the photographer to come take pictures of our home so that we could create a listing. We were going to get that house.

Then our realtor called us the next day. The sellers had accepted the other offer.

I remember being paralyzed. Stunned. Frozen. We were not going to get that house. Our dream house, the one God had chosen for us, the one we fell in love with, would not be ours after all, and we wept. It was beyond frustrating, and I simply didn't understand. I had busted my ass over two days, sweat like a pig, and ran madly to and fro in order to get our house prepared to sell. Little did I know how unrealistic it was at the time that we would be able to accomplish that before someone else snatched up our dream home. There's so much work that goes into selling a home. And we hadn't had a single interested buyer walk through ours yet. Heck, it wasn't going to even be on the market for another week.

We were not going to get that house.

As dismayed as I was, my wife and I begrudgingly stayed the course. We could not tear ourselves emotionally away from our dream home, but what we could do was to try and find a suitable replacement: something that would have enough similarities so as not to be a compromise. It was going to be emotionally taxing and draining, but we were up to it.

Why do I tell this story? Because twice throughout this process, I vaulted into action in pursuit of a dream. I would chase that dream until I was lying face down in a ditch and had nothing left to give. At the start, did I know that dream wouldn't ultimately be fulfilled? No. Was I conscious that there existed the possibility that all of my efforts would prove unfruitful? Yes. Did I do it anyway?

Yes.

This was our dream, my dream, and, as always, I gave it my all. I'm not sorry that that particular dream didn't become reality, because I gave the chase my absolute all.

And the good news? We found and got our dream home, and we lived happily ever after.

WHAT'S YOUR DNA?

I have in my blood a deep desire to dare, to risk, and to try. I'm *incredibly* driven. So much so that I forget to rest sometimes. I'm nearly *always* thinking about *something* business or dream-relatred in my cranium. I'm so grateful for the positivity that has been fostered in me from a young age, and I sincerely want to thank my parents here for instilling in me a great sense of organization, orderliness, creativity, participation in drama and other activities, and loads of affirmation. I am who I am today because of them. Just like I want my own boys to grow up and be who they are because of me: confident, affirmed, stalwart, positive, and most of all, knowing that they are thoroughly loved.

I do what I do because I am who I am. And I love what I do, and love who I am and get to be in voiceovers. I wrote in my previous book, "Voiceovers: A Super Business · A Super Life" about *makeup*. I have makeup that makes up who I am. Here's an excerpt from that book:

As a businessman, I can look back at my entire life and see skills and tendencies and behaviors and formative experiences that have led me to where I am, and *who* I am, today. They've brought me to today, with a whole host of knowledge and skills and insight and perception and readiness to be who I am, and to be successful at what I want to do.

Since I was a child, I thought a certain way, I handled things a certain way, I behaved a certain way. Through the myriad jobs that I've worked at in my years, including *fourteen* of them from 2003 to 2007 – I kid you not - they've helped me assemble a cache of skills and abilities to be successful at voiceovers.

I see administration and management from the associated jobs that I've had in management. I see creativity in when I was a professional singer. I see continuous laughter and comedy from my youth.

I see leadership and guiding people from the teaching roles I've held. I see marketing prowess from the various marketing jobs that I've held.

All of this goes into a melting pot that is Aaron Alex: Singer / Voiceover Artist / Author / Poet / Musician / Producer Guy, or whatever it is that you choose to call me. I choose to call myself a professional male Voiceover Artist & Author - and with that moniker comes a lot of history.

A lot of background went into who I am today, and I can confidently assert that I was made, nay, *destined*, to be a successful voiceover artist and author.[159]

What kind of blood do you have? What's in you that's inherently fitting for voiceovers? What makeup do you possess that enables you to be thoroughly committed to pursuing your dreams?

I want to share with you a quick story. It's about identity. My B+ identity, my *be positive* identity, carries me through the toughest of times, and enables me to survive *and* thrive. I want the same for you. Business, even a voiceover business, is not easy. It takes rolling with some heavy punches, suffering some setbacks, and staying in it for the long haul. When you know who you are through all of that, nothing can stop you. But you must know who you are.

"I believe I can fly" was a hit because people can identify with it. Everyone *wants* to fly. But not everyone *commits* to flying.

= = =

One day, a chicken farmer found an eagle's egg that had fallen from its nest. The farmer put the egg in his chicken coop with his chickens to keep it from perishing.

Soon the egg hatched and the young eagle grew up with the chickens believing that he too was a chicken. He was awkward and funny-looking to the other chickens, as he tried to be the best chicken he could be, but he began to think that something was wrong with him.

Since the chickens could only fly for short distances, the young eagle-who-thought-he-was-a-chicken believed that he could only fly for a short distance. He thought that was what he was supposed to do. So that was all that he thought he could do... and that was all he was able to do.

He lived like a chicken. He scratched the earth for worms and insects. He clucked and cackled. And he would thrash his wings and fly a few feet into the air.

One day, the eagle-who-thought-he-was-a-chicken happened to look up at the sky. High overhead, soaring majestically and effortlessly was an eagle!

"What's that?!" cried the young eagle-who-thought-he-was-a-chicken in awe. "It's magnificent! So much power and grace! It's beautiful!"

"That's an eagle, the king of the birds," they said. "He belongs to the sky. We belong to the earth, we are chickens."

Days later, the old eagle was flying over the barnyard and noticed the young eagle running around with the chickens. He swooped down and landed in front of the young eagle.

"What are you doing?" asked the older eagle.
"What do you mean?" answered the young eagle-who-thought-he-was-a-chicken.

"What are you doing running around with these chickens?"

"I am a chicken and these are my brothers and sisters."

"No, you're not! You're an eagle. You belong in the sky soaring high above this barnyard." Said the older eagle.

"No, I'm not! I am a chicken... I can't fly."

"You can't fly because you've never tried... you're an eagle, just like me."

"Even if what you say is true, I've lived my whole life like a chicken, I'm not an eagle anymore."

"It's the heart of an eagle that matters, not the way he lived... Come with me."

The young eagle-who-thought-he-was-a-chicken took a look at his friends now hiding from the eagle. "Don't listen to him!" they shouted, "don't go with him, it's a trick,"

But deep inside the heart of the eagle-who-thought-he-was-a-chicken, a faint voice told him what he needed to do... maybe he really was an eagle! He took another look around the barnyard. Then he turned to the older eagle.

The older eagle instructed him to get onto his back. Moments later, they reached a cliff. They stood next to each other on the edge of the cliff looking down at the mountains in the distance. Without a second of hesitation, the old an eagle jumped off the edge, spread his wings and soared upward toward the heavens.

The young eagle watched the older eagle with a sense of awe.

The eagle flew back to the cliff to his young friend. "Now it's your turn," said the older eagle.

The young eagle looked down from the cliff and trembled. He'd never flown before. Maybe he would die. Maybe he should go back home.

"Don't look down," the older eagle said, "Look up at the sky. Aim towards the sun and spreading your wings."

The young eagle lifted his sight upward, spread his wings, and with a little push from the older eagle, he leaped off the edge... and he flew!

From that day forward the young eagle no longer thought he was a chicken, he no longer lived like a chicken... he now knew he was an eagle.[160]

= = =

Are you destined to be an eagle of voiceovers? I'm an eagle, and I know it. I don't hang with the chickens. I soar, and I streak through the sky at breakneck speed sometimes. Other times I'm in my roost with my chicks. But mostly, I'm soaring...because that's what I was made to do.

TAKEAWAY & ACTION STEP

"Be you. Everyone else is already taken." – Oscar Wilde

Lest it cost you everything, you must know yourself, and find out who you are, and what you were made for. Spend some time journaling what makes you **you**, and why you are the way you are. Then, see how those qualities fit within the confines of voiceovers – or whatever endeavor you pursue.

From Darkness To Dawn

IT'S BEEN A LONG TIME COMING

Alright! Enough with the funnies and the instruction. I'd like to close out my book with a pensive, reflective chapter, because this part of the story means the world to me. I get to tell you a fable. Grab your bottle and your blankie and get ready, because boys and girls, this is as real as it gets.

It's been about 27 years. But has it, really? Ultimately, I've done voiceovers for a really, really long time. I mean, a *really* long time. I've done them since 1993…but I have done them in a more concentrated sense since 2007. And then, I went full-time with them in 2016. Have I ever looked back? Yes. *But only to see how far I've come.*

And when I talk about far, I'm not talking about length. I'm talking about experientially. Existentially. It's not about chronology. It's about therapy.

Let me take you on a journey. I'm fixin' to get all psychological on ya'll.

A GREGARIOUS SOUL

What does gregarious mean to you? To me, it means boisterous, self-assured, fun-loving, dramatic, open-handed, exuberant, and pursuing joy. Ultimately, that's who I've always been as a person, even when the chips were down. I've *always* wanted to see the positive, to pursue hope even when there wasn't even a sliver of it to be found. I still wanted to pursue it.

Has my life ever ebbed to the low, low depths of despair? The answer of course is yes, otherwise, this chapter would most certainly suck. I mean it when I say that there have been times in my life where I've been despondent to the point of suicidal ideation, especially during my teenage years. I've flirted with moving past this flesh and this mind and this bondage, to be free of it all. But what then? Would that really be the end? Would that be true freedom? Or would it really have been just trading bondage for bondage, forever slave to the knowledge that I had been beaten? I think the answer is clear. I would have taken the easy way out and robbed my future self of countless victories. I don't write any of this to shame or put down anyone who has committed suicide: I have a few friends in my life that have been deeply impacted by suicide and I am thus deeply respectful of it. There is *always* more to the story than meets the eye. And I too have been on the periphery of it, during periods of angst in my life.

Gregariousness can have its costs. It is sometimes attributed to people like Robin Williams…and we know, tragically, what happened. All seems well on the outside, but on the inside, he was crumbling. Ultimately, I know now who I am, but there was a time in my teenage years where I didn't, and I sought relief.

Sometimes I sought relief through acting…through drama…through performance. I could easily slip on a role and hide…perform my way through the pain. So, I think I can relate all too well to the performers of yesteryear - and today – that are struggling with such loneliness. I wanted to work through it, desperately… the self-consciousness, the self-loathing, the feelings of inadequacy, etc. But I found that I just went stir-crazy inside myself, and the only real way I could cope was to perform. To put on a happy face.

Do you know the song "Smile" by Charlie Chaplin? *I hate that song.* I truly hate it, with every fiber of my being and the fire of a thousand suns. I hate it. It's a pretentious and hollow song. It avoids dealing with the real. I love when Wesley says to Buttercup in The Princess Bride, "Life *is* pain, highness – anyone who says differently is selling something." I *love* that quote. It's not about pretending that all is well, when all is in fact not well at all.

RETREAT

I conquered. I stayed alive. I moseyed on through life, joyfully, working through my pain, relying on others, living, breathing, conquering, learning. We all do. I achieved, I pursued, I attained, I grew. And always, *always*, as sunset follows sunrise, there are challenges that bring us back down into the depths and test our metal. I too have had my share. Here's where I'm going to get painfully vulnerable, to the extent that I can.

My wife and I went through an excruciating ordeal in 2013 that lasted several years, and to this day, still does not have real closure. At times, it nearly tore us apart. We were haunted by extreme difficulty – I won't say what it was because it was deeply personal and private to us as a couple. The pain has talons, and though it has abated, we remember it well, with tears and sighs. It cost us peace…it robbed us of sanctity, it harmed our sense of well-being. We lost trust in people, we became skeptical, we yearned for justice.

In the crucible of fire, testing and pain, after two long years, in 2015 we finally found some form of relief. We found intervention by someone who helped us. I realize I'm being intentionally vague and ambiguous, but there's a reason for the nebulous details, and it's deeply personal. The someone helped us, and slowly we began to heal.

But then, not six months later, *The Pain* was back. It came in different forms of attack, and, this time, sadly, we retreated. The honest truth is that there were people in my life, that literally wanted to silence me.

So, this gregarious soul, along with his wife, went into hiding. We retreated from public view and, really, from the world, for a while, as we closed ranks and dealt with what was harming us…as we tried to heal. It was:

an excruciating time, as we were constantly on defense, and trying to mitigate pain that we could not control.
a time of loneliness…and sadly, it was right around when our first child was born. What should have been a time of great rejoicing became a time of stress, endless tears and frustrations one after another, and pinning our hopes on eventual deliverance. We lived in the shadows, with curtains drawn and in hiding. We were really hurting, my wife and I. In the midst of singing lullabies to our son, we were crying from *The Pain*.
a time of hard growth
a time of questioning God

And through that entire time, my gregarious soul was being erased, as its light was being extinguished in the dark. I weep as I write this, because I *remember*. We walled ourselves off from social contact as we tried to deal with what was harming us from within.

I think every human being has a game-set-match, however, no matter with how much emphasis they pound their fist and say "I can't do it." Eventually, something snaps and they decide enough is enough. That point finally came for me in late 2016, and I truly had had enough. I was tired of living in the dark. I was not being true to myself. We were depriving ourselves of the world, and more importantly, depriving the world of us. I threw open the shades. We let the light stream in. I'm reminded of Gandalf bringing Theoden back to life: "Breathe the free air again, my friend." It truly was necessary, and we desperately needed it.

I was time for a new dawn. I would not be silenced.

A BUSINESSMAN REBORN

Also, right around that time, a dear friend of mine, Paul, had encouraged me to go into voiceovers full time. I had done it for years as part of video production services, and it had its roots, as I've said, back in 1993; but I never thought of pursuing it as a service unto itself until then. I decided it was time. We needed to make more money at the time anyway, since my wife was now a stay-at-home mommy. So, I was really earnestly looking for something to pad the pocketbook – and the answer was right under my nose all along.

Seemingly coincidentally, I was asked to be a Sunday morning host at our church. Clarifying the role for me, my pastor told me that I would be welcoming our church into the sanctuary with announcements, jokes, humor, whatever, to really energize the crowd. I didn't have a pair of pom-poms, nor was I the *"Rah rah, here we go"* type that he sought, but there desperately was a need, and I thought this might just further help me get out of the dark cloud that we'd been living under. After all, earlier, my Pastor had told me that "it's not in your nature to run." Those words were life-giving and affirming, and I needed them.

So, I bravely stepped forward. I began hosting, and quickly became the church's favorite Sunday morning host in a rotation of four people. I started doing it more frequently, and I genuinely began to look at it as a veritable *ministry*: it was my rich calling to welcome people into worship, to cheer on the body of Christ, and to stir them to praise. I loved that time. It was genuinely freeing. It helped me to open up, to be more...*gregarious*. To re-develop my confidence and to reclaim my calling to put myself out there for people. It was tremendously liberating to take on that mantle of ministry each week, and to usher God's people into worship. Coupling that with entertaining them, it was one of the greatest times of awakening in my life.

Concurrently, my voiceover business had taken off. Being non-union, it was easy for me to start off with some pay-to-play online marketplaces. I truly enjoyed getting on there and auditioning all the time. I loved – and still do to this day, with all my heart – being *chosen*. It is the way I measure my success for that week: How many times have I been chosen. My pastor once said, "to be unchosen is a terrible thing." The opposite is resoundingly true. To be chosen, is a wonderful thing. And with voiceovers, I get chosen a lot. I had the skill all along, nurtured back in 1993 and constantly developed over the years, then perfected in self-employment since 2007.

LET THE LION RUN FREE

I can't tell you what voiceovers truly mean to me. It is simply impossible to sum it up in words. It is the perfect business for me, because it couples all of my management skills, my administrative skills, my business acumen, my marketing prowess, my humor, my vocal delivery skills, my teaching abilities, and my love for performing, all wrapped up in a beautiful bow. It has truly become the most satisfying endeavor I've ever pursued...save my marriage and my family. It allows me to be *free*. It allows me to perform, to entertain, to represent and speak for someone, to bring words to life, to network, to encourage and affirm, to uplift, and to be the person I was created to be.

I have been self-employed since 2007, but that wasn't always in voiceovers. Nevertheless, it was always mine. No one could take it away from me. But now, with voiceovers, it's something that I would fight tooth and nail, to the death, were anyone to try and wrest control away from me. It's my very heartbeat, my joy, my delight.

Every morning this entrepreneur gets up and has a devotional and prays to the Lord. I pray for Him to have His way in my life. As it pertains to voiceovers, I pray that He would bless me indeed, that He would turn these auditions into jobs, that He would allow me to connect with the ears, minds and hearts of my listeners. That is truly what I pray. I want to honor God with my business, and I want Him to bless it.

Voiceovers aren't for everyone, to be sure. You can have a great voice and, frankly, suck at marketing and business operation. Or, you can be an excellent businessperson raking in the dough, but not be able to sound like you're not reading. You must be both:

As a voice actor, part of your success comes from reading without actually sounding like you're reading. I have to genuinely believe that *you* genuinely believe in what you're telling me. Voice actors, are after all, storytellers.

As a marketing & businessperson, *all* of your success comes from treating it like a business and not a hobby. A hobby brings you bowling money. A business pays your mortgage. Bill DeWees says, "Voice over is an unlimited career now. If you can talk and tell a story that conveys a message, you can produce voice overs. If you can learn to market yourself, you can have a successful career producing your voice overs."[161]

I am both. And for that, I'm extraordinarily grateful. In a previous chapter I talked about "makeup" – and as they say, *hindsight is 20/20*. I can look back at my life, and the painful experiences I've had, and see how I was always, *always* destined to be a voiceover artist and author entrepreneur. I was made for this. These are truly my callings. I've pursued other endeavors, yes, but nothing even a tenth as fulfilling as these. I know who I am. And I know who I was made to be, and what I was made for.

So, you see? Voiceovers were exactly what I needed, and they were right under my nose all along. They were the craft, the art form, the pursuit, the delight, and the end goal I had always needed to allow me to emerge into the light again. I yearned for something to crack me open and say "come out, it's safe." I found it.

I'll remind you of a key adage again: *"Find what you love to do, and you'll never work a day in your life."* I *love* what I do. I *love* writing books. I love teaching. I love performing. I love sharing and encouraging. I love it. I Love it. I LOVE it. More than anything I've ever done, I love it. And I'm so very grateful. It has, as I've mentioned, actually liberated me from other lines of work that have been, or have become, far less meaningful: lines of work that were once my passion...but never to the same extent.

This is my story.

This is my testimony of what voiceovers mean to me, and why they mean so much. They have enabled me to breathe the free air again. They've enabled me to breathe deeply and delight in what I do. This is me, emerging from the darkness, and springing into the dawn with purpose and clarity of vision. I am alive.

You are alive too. And you are utterly privileged to be able to use the very thing that God used to speak the world into existence: the power of the voice. You use it to inspire, to motivate, to compel, to encourage, etc. It's utterly and fantastically *astonishing* to me that I get to do what I get to do every day, and to use my God-given gift to encourage others. I thank God for the power of my voice, and what I get to do with it. I thank Him daily.

Thank you so much for reading this. I finished the preliminary writing of this book in 2019, on the eve, the cusp of 2020: a year of vision...a year of clarity. I pray that's what you get for your voiceover business: vision and clarity. Remember what Terri Apple said: "Having a great voice isn't enough. Learning what to do with it is the key to a long and lucrative career."[162]

I hope and pray this book has been greatly illuminating, inspiring, and empowering for you as a budding or established entrepreneur. I've been there, said that. Go there and say that too. Bill DeWees talks about his success frequently throughout his book, *How to Start and build a Six Figure Voice Over Business*: "I am not dreaming about being a big star, or getting well-known. I don't care about Academy Awards or any other awards, for that matter.

I care about making as much money as possible in my voice over business and I do whatever it takes to make it happen."[163]

I love this quote because it speaks to my own desire to hustle. I have an innate sense of hustle and *drive* that cannot be extinguished easily, save by staying up late because of my two boys and desperately craving sleep the following day. I am *pulled* back into my studio to get work done. It is my pleasure, my joy, and I love what I do. That drives me to succeed, and I couldn't care less if I ever won any kind of award for best male whatever. I love to work hard, and I love to give of my knowledge of how I do so. I hope you have received just a smidge of that through this book.

I want to be a tremendous part of your success. That's why I wrote this book: to pay homage to those who have been a great part of my success and to edify them, but also to encourage you that you too can continue the legacy of success and far exceed what I and so many others have been able to accomplish in this business called voiceovers.

May all your dreams come true in this endeavor, and may God bless you, fellow superhero. See you in the skies. You are an anomaly. A superhero. You have giftings in you that can propel you skyward. But it's all about balance. It's all about being YOU. So be willing to stick your neck out and stand out from the crowd. That's what the world needs: really unique people who are really super.

Oh! And if you want the secret to my success, it's Gloria Jean's Butter Toffee Coffee with Hazelnut creamer and six mini-marshmallows. Every single day, without fail. Drink this, and you too will become a superhero anomaly.

Just make sure you steer clear of Michael Bolton along the way.

About The Author

Aaron Ryan lives in Washington with his wife and two sons, along with Macy the dog, Winston the cat, and Merry & Pippin, the finches.

He is the author of the "Dissonance" quadrilogy, the sci-fi thriller "Forecast", several business books on voiceovers penned under his former stage name "Josh Alexander", as well as a previous fictional novel, "The Omega Room."

When he was in second grade, he was tasked with writing a creative assignment: a fictional book. And thus, "The Electric Boy" was born: a simple novella full of intrigue, fantasy, and 7-year-old wits that electrified Aaron's desire to write. From that point forward, Aaron evolved into a creative soul that desired to create.

He enjoys the arts, media, music, performing, poetry, and being a daddy. In his lifetime he has been an author, voiceover artist, wedding videographer, stage performer, musician, producer, rock/pop artist, executive assistant, service manager, paperboy, CSR, poet, tech support, worship leader, and more. The diversity of his life experiences gives him a unique approach to business, life, ministry, faith, and entertainment.

Aaron's favorite author by far is J.R.R. Tolkien, but he also enjoys Suzanne Collins, James S.A. Corey, Marie Lu, Madeleine L'Engle, C.S. Lewis, and Stephen King.

Aaron has always had a passion for storytelling.

Visit and subscribe to Aaron through his website (www.authoraaronryan.com) and blog:

Subscribe to Author Aaron Ryan

Recommended Reading

I highly recommend the following reading materials for your voiceover pursuit and career!

Making Money in your PJ's: Freelancing for Voice Actors and other Solopreneurs
Paul Strikwerda

The E-Myth
Michael Gerber

The Mastery Series
Thibaut Meurisse

How To Win Friends and Influence People
Dale Carnegie

Bibliography

[1] thoughtcatalog.com/ryan-holiday/2016/03/dont-say-maybe-if-you-want-to-say-no/
[2] *Master Your Success*, by Thibaut Meurisse, pp 68-69
[3] *Step Up To The Mic*, Rodney Saulsberry, 2007, page 47
[4] www.inc.com/marcel-schwantes/warren-buffett-says-4-choices-in-life-separate-doers-from-dreamers.html
[5] www.foxnews.com/lifestyle/bride-arrested-photographer-pay-wedding
[6] www.dailydot.com/irl/yelp-wedding-reviews/
[7] en.wikipedia.org/wiki/Lee_Harvey_Oswald
[8] *The Lord of the Rings Volume I: The Fellowship of the Ring,* Chapter II: *The Shadow of the Past*, J.R.R. Tolkien
[9] *Empathy* by Alanis Morissette from the *Havoc & Bright Lights* Album, 2012
[10] *Making Money in your PJ's: Freelancing for voice-overs and other solopreneurs* by Paul Strikwerda, 2014 edition, page 325
[11] http://www.projectcoyote.org/endkillingcontests/
[12] https://6abc.com/5686481/
[13] *Voice Over Man*, by Peter Dickson, 2020, page 20
[14] *Success is Inevitable*, by Thibaut Meurisse, © 2019, p 57
[15] *Voice-Over Voice Actor:* 2018, Yuri Lowenthal & Tara Platt, page 170
[16] *Step Up To The Mic*, Rodney Saulsberry, 2007, page 104
[17] *How to Start and Build a Six Figure Voice Over Business* by Bill DeWees, 2013 edition, page 30
[18] *Making Money in your PJ's: Freelancing for voice-overs and other solopreneurs* by Paul Strikwerda, 2014 edition, page 396
[19] www.youtube.com/watch?v=HaZ7TJloups
[20] *Making Money in your PJ's: Freelancing for voice-overs and other solopreneurs* by Paul Strikwerda, 2014 edition, page 377
[21] en.wikipedia.org/wiki/List_of_films_considered_the_worst#The_Avengers_(1998)
[22] thatguywiththeglasses.fandom.com/wiki/When_Are_Critics_Wrong%3F
[23] www.bookscottburns.com
[24] www.jmcvoiceover.com/2018/12/12/updates-from-voice123-regarding-the-new-site/
[25] www.beautyschools.com/the-cost-of-beauty-school/
[26] www.amazon.com/Upgrade-Yourself-Strategies-Transform-Mindset-ebook/dp/B079VN6HK9
[27] *Making Money in your PJ's: Freelancing for voice-overs and other solopreneurs* by Paul Strikwerda, 2014 edition, page 404
[28] ibid, page 84
[29] *How to Start and Build a Six Figure Voice Over Business* by Bill DeWees, 2013 edition, page 26
[30] *Voiceover Achiever: Brand Your VO Career. Change Your Life* by Celia Siegel, 2018 edition, page 4
[31] *The Voiceover Startup Guide: How to Land Your First VO Job* by Chris Agos, page 64
[32] *There's Money Where Your Mouth Is* by Elaine Clark, Fourth Edition, page 276
[33] *How to Start and Build a Six Figure Voice Over Business* by Bill DeWees, 2013 edition, page 90
[34] *Making Money in your PJ's: Freelancing for voice-overs and other solopreneurs* by Paul Strikwerda, 2014 edition, page 166
[35] ibid, page 180
[36] ibid, page 317
[37] www.seotribunal.com/
[38] www.huffingtonpost.com/ian-mills/5-reasons-you-absolutely-_b_5122485.html
[39] *Voiceover Achiever: Brand Your VO Career. Change Your Life* by Celia Siegel, 2018 edition, page 68

[40] www.amazon.com/Billion-Dollar-Bully-Davide-Cerretini/dp/B07QV5RQTZ
[41] *How to Win Friends and Influence People,* Dale Carnegie
[42] *Making Money in your PJ's: Freelancing for voice-overs and other solopreneurs* by Paul Strikwerda, 2014 edition, page 177
[43] www.searchtempest.com
[44] *Voiceover Achiever: Brand Your VO Career. Change Your Life* by Celia Siegel, 2018 edition, page 112
[45] *How to Win Friends and Influence People,* by Dale Carnegie.
[46] *Making Money in your PJ's: Freelancing for voice-overs and other solopreneurs* by Paul Strikwerda, 2014 edition, page 167
[47] personalexcellence.co/blog/big-rocks/
[48] www.fatherly.com/health-science/pitocin-induction-safe/
[49] www.healthychildren.org/English/ages-stages/prenatal/delivery-beyond/Pages/Dads-Can-Get-Postpartum-Depression-Too.aspx
[50] supervoiceover.com/we-have-your-toilet-paper-and-if-you-ever-want-to-see-it-again/
[51] cnbc.com/2020/03/11/heres-why-people-are-panic-buying-and-stockpiling-toilet-paper.html
[52] reddit.com/r/legaladvice/comments/3lxw2o/copyright_image_100000_payable_to_firm/
[53] heitnerlegal.com/2020/12/07/what-to-do-if-you-receive-a-higbee-associates-copyright-demand-letter/
[54] fairuse.stanford.edu/overview/fair-use/what-is-fair-use/
[55] nethervoice.com/the-copyright-trolls-are-coming-after-you/
[56] reddit.com/search/?q=picrights
[57] quora.com/I-reposted-a-news-photo-on-my-website%E2%80%99s-blog-A-company-picrights-com-is-demanding-money-instead-of-simply-issuing-a-cease-and-desist-order-is-this-extortion-and-or-even-legal
[58] extortionletterinfo.com/forum/getty-images-letter-forum/picrights-com/
[59] *Voice-Over Voice Actor:* 2018, Yuri Lowenthal & Tara Platt, page 51
[60] *Making Money in your PJ's: Freelancing for voice-overs and other solopreneurs* by Paul Strikwerda, 2014 edition, page 325
[61] *Voice-Over Voice Actor:* 2018, Yuri Lowenthal & Tara Platt, page 185
[62] *Batman Begins* movie, quote from Bruce Wayne to Alfred the Butler
[63] *Voice-Over Voice Actor*, 2018, Yuri Lowenthal & Tara Platt, page 166
[64] makingmoneyinyourpjs.com/
[65] www.youtube.com/watch?v=BC2ZwdQjtCs
[66] en.wikipedia.org/wiki/Glienicke_Bridge
[67] www.geekwire.com/2019/zillow-2-0-era-begins-real-estate-giant-posts-454m-revenue-first-quarter-since-major-business-shift/
[68] www.quotes.net/mquote/133355
[69] *Making Money in your PJ's: Freelancing for voice-overs and other solopreneurs* by Paul Strikwerda, 2014 edition, page 23
[70] www.americanexpress.com/en-us/business/trends-and-insights/articles/7-ways-to-promote-your-business-online-for-free/
[71] *Voiceover Achiever: Brand Your VO Career. Change Your Life* by Celia Siegel, 2018 edition, page 108
[72] www.quicksprout.com/social-media-for-small-business/
[73] www-users.cs.york.ac.uk/susan/joke/essay.htm
[74] www.foresthillretirement.org/stress-reducing-hobbies/
[75] *There's Money Where Your Mouth Is* by Elaine Clark, Fourth Edition, page 290
[76] www.voicezam.com/
[77] Matthew 18:23-35, NIV
[78] *Thank U* by Alanis Morissette from *Supposed Former Infatuation Junkie* Album, 1998
[79] www.huffpost.com/entry/how-to-have-an-attitude-of-gratitude_b_8644102
[80] thedailybeast.com/trump-im-like-really-smart-a-very-stable-genius
[81] nytimes.com/2021/02/19/us/florida-women-vaccines.html?smid=tw-nytimes&smtyp=cur&fbclid=IwAR2Viq1UhuQ5x45mudcRGet0X4aNpwOgzeiGpF5n-NbiJnCI9aYoLVNx5M0
[82] www.abbreviations.com/term/2070380

[83] vox.com/2019/12/26/21024188/nine-supreme-court-citizens-united-obamacare-muslim-ban-religion
[84] xinsurance.com/blog/three-reasons-people-sue/
[85] lawyersweekly.com.au/sme-law/18830-why-do-people-sue-each-other
[86] youtu.be/B81U7Vunhuc
[87] *Voiceover Achiever: Brand Your VO Career. Change Your Life* by Celia Siegel, 2018 edition, page 32
[88] *V-Oh!: Tips, Tricks, Tools & Techniques to Start and Sustain Your Voiceover Career* by Marc Cashman, page 85
[89] www.medicalnewstoday.com/articles/318441.php
[90] supervoiceover.com/welcome-to-voiceover-manners-101/
[91] nethervoice.com/my-worst-client-ever/
[92] indiatimes.com/culture/11-of-the-most-notorious-successful-liars-throughout-history-339350.html
[93] *Making Money in your PJ's: Freelancing for voice-overs and other solopreneurs* by Paul Strikwerda, 2014 edition, page 164
[94] *The Art of Voice Acting*, James R. Alburger, 2019 Edition 6, page 15
[95] britannica.com/biography/Robin-Williams
[96] "Robin Williams coroner's report finds no illegal drugs or alcohol in system". *New York Daily News*. Archived from the original on November 9, 2014. Retrieved November 11, 2014.
[97] "Robin Williams 'had Parkinson's'". *BBC News*. August 14, 2014. Archived from the original on August 14, 2014. Retrieved August 14, 2014.
[98] Schneider Williams, Susan (September 27, 2016). "The terrorist inside my husband's brain" (PDF). *Neurology*. 87 (13): 1308–1311 doi: 10.1212/ WNL.0000000000003162. PMID 27672165. Archived (PDF) from the original on July 22, 2020. Retrieved July 23, 2020.
[99] *The Lord of the Rings: One Volume Edition*. J.R.R. Tolkien, 1994, page 504
[100] en.wiktionary.org/wiki/pneumonoultramicroscopicsilicovolcanoconiosis
[101] *The Art of Voice Acting*, James R. Alburger, 2019 Edition 6, page 17
[102] ibid, page 13
[103] *Voice-Over Voice Actor:* 2018, Yuri Lowenthal & Tara Platt, page 88
[104] Nethervoice.com Blog
[105] *Voice-Over Voice Actor:* 2018, Yuri Lowenthal & Tara Platt, page 80
[106] *Voice-Over Voice Actor*, 2018, Yuri Lowenthal & Tara Platt, page 2
[107] wsj.com/articles/do-you-need-to-shower-every-day-11608564443
[108] onehotmessalaska.blogspot.com/2015/06/play-doh-is-satans-modeling-compound.html#:~:text=Play%20Doh%2D%2Da%20colorful,Ruler%20of%20All%20Demons%20Himself.
[109] www.nhnieuws.nl/nieuws/264969/juf-ingeborg-breit-23-poppetjes-die-op-haar-kleuters-lijken-ik-mis-ze-zo
[110] www.amazon.com/As-Man-Thinketh-Complete-Original/dp/1523643536
[111] quotefancy.com/quote/1096618/Kenneth-H-Blanchard-When-you-stop-learning-you-stop-growing
[112] *Voiceover Achiever: Brand Your VO Career. Change Your Life* by Celia Siegel, 2018 edition, page 43
[113] *Step Up To The Mic,* Rodney Saulsberry, 2007, page 71
[114] *Step Up To The Mic,* Rodney Saulsberry, 2007, page 62
[115] *Step Up To The Mic,* Rodney Saulsberry, 2007, page 79
[116] *Voice-Over Voice Actor:* 2018, Yuri Lowenthal & Tara Platt, page 217
[117] *Success is Inevitable*, by Thibaut Meurisse, © 2019, p 82
[118] supervoiceover.com/im-a-voice-talent-but-im-no-superman/
[119] *V-Oh!: Tips, Tricks, Tools & Techniques to Start and Sustain Your Voiceover Career* by Marc Cashman, page 112
[120] https://en.wikipedia.org/wiki/The_Secret_(book)#Synopsis
[121] *The Return of the King*, New Line Cinema Edition, page 329
[122] music.apple.com/us/artist/ocean-starfield/1272801429
[123] *Making Money in your PJ's: Freelancing for voice-overs and other solopreneurs* by Paul Strikwerda, 2014 edition, page 308

[124] ibid, page 316
[125] *The Art of Voice Acting*, James R. Alburger, 2019 Edition 6, page 375
[126] *Making Money in your PJ's: Freelancing for Voice-overs and other Solopreneurs* by Paul Strikwerda, 2014 edition, page 325
[127] globalvoiceacademy.com/gvaa-rate-guide-2/
[128] rates.gravyforthebrain.com/
[129] speecheloofficial.com/
[130] descript.com/overdub
[131] vocalid.ai/
[132] voquent.com/is-fiverr-good-for-voice-over-talent-five-voices-speak-out/
[133] hbr.org/2009/05/why-nonprofits-should-spend-mo
[134] www.thenonprofittimes.com/npt_articles/1-digital-donors-cost-charities-4%C2%A2/
[135] www.sciencedirect.com/science/article/abs/pii/S0024630110000361
[136] *Making Money in your PJ's: Freelancing for voice-overs and other solopreneurs* by Paul Strikwerda, 2014 edition, page 8
[137] ibid, page 46
[138] *V-Oh!: Tips, Tricks, Tools & Techniques to Start and Sustain Your Voiceover Career* by Marc Cashman, page 148
[139] internetlivestats.com/google-search-statistics/
[140] weforum.org/agenda/2020/12/google-most-popular-search-2020/
[141] searchtempest.com
[a]cting
your-website/
[143] *Making Money in your PJ's: Freelancing for voice-overs and other solopreneurs* by Paul Strikwerda, 2014 edition, page 63
[144] www.backstage.com/magazine/article/essentials-every-vo-audition-9190/
[145] *How to Start and Build a Six Figure Voice Over Business* by Bill DeWees, 2013 edition, page 47
[146] *Making Money in your PJ's: Freelancing for voice-overs and other solopreneurs* by Paul Strikwerda, 2014 edition, page 50
[147] *How to Start and Build a Six Figure Voice Over Business* by Bill DeWees, 2013 edition, page 32
[148] *Making Money in your PJ's: Freelancing for voice-overs and other solopreneurs* by Paul Strikwerda, 2014 edition, page 22
[149] *Voice-Over Voice Actor:* 2018, Yuri Lowenthal & Tara Platt, page 88
[150] www.psychologytoday.com/us/blog/hide-and-seek/201803/who-was-narcissus#targetText=Narcissus%20grew%20ever%20more%20thirsty,bright%20face%20and%20bowed%20neck.
[151] *Making Money in your PJ's: Freelancing for voice-overs and other solopreneurs* by Paul Strikwerda, 2014 edition, page 88
[152] *Making Money in your PJ's: Freelancing for voice-overs and other solopreneurs* by Paul Strikwerda, 2014 edition, page 235
[153] www.inspire21.com/stories/faithstories/CharlesBlondin
[154] aarp.org/home-family/friends-family/info-2018/hero-within.html
[155] *The Art of Voice Acting*, James R. Alburger, 2019 Edition 6, page 83
[156] ibid, page 104
[157] www.pinterest.com/pin/565061084475488533/
[158] *Step Up To The Mic*, Rodney Saulsberry, 2007, page 29
[159] *Voiceovers: A Super Business · A Super Life*, Aaron Ryan, 2020, page 232
[160] http://www.discoveryourlimitlesspotential.com/ready-soar-eagle.html
[161] *How to Start and Build a Six Figure Voice Over Business* by Bill DeWees, 2013 edition, page 8
[162] *Making Money in Voice-Overs,* Terri Apple, Lone Eagle Publishing Company (1999)
[163] *How to Start and Build a Six Figure Voice Over Business* by Bill DeWees, 2013 edition, page 105

Made in the USA
Middletown, DE
23 June 2024